A New Chapter?

A Carpenter and Philly Novel

(Seventh and Last in a Series)

Ken Behar

A New Chapter?
(Seventh and Last in a Series)

978-1-7366824-0-1 (paperback)
978-1-7366824-1-8 (eBook)

Library of Congress Control Number: 2021916390

Published by: Ken Behar
Lexington, Massachusetts

Cover design © by Angela Valenti.

To the Yogis

Bailee
Coleen
Genevieve
Jordan
Karen C.
Karen R.
Laurel
Leeann
Lizzie
Mick
Sanil
Tony

Also by the author:

Ghosts Can Only Go Straight
(Turn of the Century Tales)

Not Too Shabby
(Barrister Tales from Ed's Breakfast Emporium)

HOOPS

Carpenter and Philly Novels:
Turn The Page
No Right Answers
Coin Flips
Full Circles
All
Lines in the Sand
A New Chapter?

Contents

January

Philly's Spinning Playlist

"Lose Yourself"

Eminem

1

A Businessman
A Law School Dean
A Lawyer

Philomena Sullivan couldn't remember the last time she and Carpenter had together interviewed a prospective client in person. Watching Henry Frazier sitting across from them in the conference room shared by their Boston Milk Street law office, Philly realized that Skype interviews of prospective clients were inadequate because she missed out on Carpenter's reactions.

"How do you know Clyde Atkins?" Carpenter asked, mentioning last year's client who had recommended them to Frazier.

"We belong to the same gym. Over the years, we've ended up on adjacent elliptical machines and gotten to talking. I don't think I've seen Clyde outside of the gym, but I think of him as a friend."

Frazier was a big guy, over six feet tall, and thick-set. He struck Philly as someone who would have to log long hours at a gym to keep his weight under control. She surreptitiously checked her watch. Her kids were at home and she wanted this meeting focused so she could rescue her babysitter as soon as possible. "Mr. Atkins said you were involved in a family business dispute," she offered, to curtail pleasantries.

"My father promised to step aside and let me run the family business. He's gone back on that promise and that leaves me screwed. I turned down a lucrative job offer based on his promise. At my age, I won't see another offer like that come along."

"What kind of business are we talking about?" Philly asked.

"High end stationery. It's called Elite Scripts."

"Hasn't Internet use put a huge dent in a business like that?" Philly followed up.

"For a lot of businesses, yes. But that hasn't happened for us. Fortunately, people still use paper in serious business matters and for important social functions.

And some people still use personal stationery. We create custom designs and people are willing to pay for them."

"Why isn't your father honoring the deal he promised?" Carpenter asked.

"He says it's not the right time for him to step down. I think that's pretty lame, but that's what he's come up with. Yet he bumped up my salary so I'm making what I would have made if I took over."

"Is your father paid what you're paid?" Philly asked.

"No. When he increased my pay, he reduced his own pay to what I had been making. But contrary to our deal, he continues to make management decisions and won't transfer stock in the business so that I hold the majority of shares."

"Do you expect your father to deny he made a deal with you?" Carpenter questioned.

Frazier opened a narrow maroon canvas briefcase, removed two pieces of paper, and passed them across the conference room table. "He sent me an e-mail confirming what we had agreed on, so I don't think a denial is going to work."

The e-mail was dated a little over three years ago.

> *"I'm glad that's settled and behind us. You'll take over the business in three years. We'll work something out with the stock so you own a majority of the shares. I can't tell you how relieved I am that the business will continue in the family."*

Apparently it was sent from an office e-mail account, and Philly noted the father's titles, President and CEO, below the message. She cast a sideways glance at Carpenter. He was staring at Frazier, probably not seeing the potential new client because his jaw muscles were working which meant that he was totally absorbed in sorting out Frazier's problem.

Carpenter appeared to emerge from a trance. "Did you confront your father with this e-mail?" he asked.

Frazier nodded. "I actually felt sorry for him. He said the timing was all wrong and he couldn't turn the company over to me just now. He apologized to me, said I had to trust him. But when he refused to be specific about what was going on, I started to feel less sorry for him."

"Do you have access to the company's financial information?" Carpenter asked.

"I get the company's monthly, quarterly and yearly financial reports."

"If you hire us, you'll need to get us those reports," Carpenter said. "Also, you're probably going to want someone to look at the numbers behind the reports."

"Why?" Frazier asked, looking perplexed.

"Because my guess is that your father's change of mind has something to do with money."

"Are you suggesting that my father is stealing?"

"I'm not suggesting anything. Based on the limited information you've shared with us, I'm making an educated guess that money is behind your father's change of mind."

"He increased my pay," Frazier noted, as if trying to rationalize that nothing was amiss with the family business.

Carpenter shrugged. "Yes, but he lowered his own. Maybe he's trying to buy some time by keeping you happy."

"I'm not happy," Frazier groused. "I'm here for God's sake!"

"Good point," Carpenter said. "Our mission, if you hire us, is to get you to a happy place. But just so we're clear, that's not going to happen until we do some digging and find out what your father isn't telling you."

Philly thought Carpenter was headed in the right direction. He believed that money or sex was what motivated most people to do something stupid, and sex seemed to have nothing to do with Frazier's situation.

Frazier sighed and looked like a happy place was not a destination he expected to reach in his lifetime. "If I hire you, what's it going to cost? I don't have the kind of money to throw around that Clyde has."

Philly began to relax. Frazier was going to hire them. Carpenter would deliver the spiel she had heard countless times before.

"Litigation is the big variable," Carpenter explained. "If you need to go to court, representation could get expensive. That said, you may get lucky. If you produce a lawyer who demands that you see the company's books and records, your father will receive the message that you're serious and might decide to avoid litigation and level with you. I'd estimate that initial legal and investigatory work will be about two thousand but will run much more if we have to go to court. I'd recommend we send a letter to your father on our letterhead demanding to see the company's books and records and demanding that he honor the deal he confirmed in the e-mail you showed us. If he stonewalls, you may have no choice but to go to court."

"I haven't gotten lucky yet," Frazier said, his frown in place. "But what the hell! You're hired."

"Excellent, Carpenter said. "I'll send you an engagement letter by the end of the day. We'll require a two-thousand-dollar retainer."

Frazier stood up and gathered his overcoat, looking somber. 'It never failed,' Philly thought. A client's forking over money drove home the point that there would be an outflow of cash before things got better. And for Frazier, when it came to cash and control of the family business, things might not get better than his recently increased pay.

"What's your take?" Carpenter asked when he returned to the conference room after showing Frazier out.

"I'm leaning in your direction that money is at the root of this situation."

"I'm thinking we get Lily Tompkins to take a look at the financial reports Frazier sends us."

"Now there's a name I haven't heard for a long while," Philly responded with a broad grin. "That should be fun." It had been years since they had used Carpenter's friend on a case. Lily was a tax lawyer and a CPA. The accountant was a brash, frumpy looking woman with a sharp tongue. She had a way of needling Carpenter that Philly's sadistic side enjoyed.

"What do you make of the father's change of heart?" Carpenter asked next.

"The e-mail struck me as sincere," Philly replied. "The thought I had was maybe the family business is now in the crapper and the father didn't want Frazier to know."

Carpenter nodded. "Yes, or maybe it's not just a business slump. Here's a sobering thought. Right now, Frazier doesn't know about anything illegal or shady going on. If we find out that not everything's kosher, Frazier will have knowledge of wrongdoing and won't be able to ignore it."

Philly stood up and struggled into her ski parka. "Do you have to find a silver lining in everything?" she deadpanned and then changed the subject. "I wonder how our partners are making out?"

The other half of Carpenter, Sullivan, Jeffries & Boyle were currently at the Sloane-Webster School of Law, and Rachel Boyle was thinking that not all law school deans are created equal. Last year she and Simon Jeffries had represented their own alma mater, Spenser New England School of Law, where Dean Stanley Stockman's office had been posh with lawyer-client meetings held in plush chairs surrounding a modern conference table in a section of the office set away from Stockman's desk. In contrast, the office of Janet Martin, dean of the Sloan-Webster School of Law, was a functional, no frills space. There was no separate conference area, and Rachel and Simon had taken two plain visitors' chairs in front of Martin's cluttered desk. Sloan-Webster and Spenser may have been on a par in terms of rank and reputation among Boston area law schools—each was in a tier of law schools below Boston University School of Law, Boston College Law School, Suffolk University School of Law and Northeastern University School of Law—but if deans' offices were any indication, Rachel suspected that Sloan-Webster was on a less solid financial footing than Spenser.

"Dean Stockman speaks very highly of you," Martin offered as an icebreaker. She struck Rachel as too young to hold a dean's position. Martin was trim, had an engaging smile, and showed no obvious anxiety over the fact that the institution she ran had been hit with a major lawsuit similar to the one filed against Spenser last year.

"Dean Stockman should speak highly of us," Simon said. "We did an excellent job for Spenser."

Rachel wanted to press a rewind button. They'd agreed that Simon would lead this meeting, but would the dean be put off by Simon blatantly tooting their firm's horn?

"Which is why you're sitting here," Martin said, not put off by Simon's boldness.

A knock on the dean's door was followed by the flustered entry of a short, slender man with thinning gray hair and black glasses who immediately apologized for being late. "I got lost," he confessed, embarrassed.

"Don't worry about it," Martin said reassuringly. "It's only your first day on the job." She turned to Rachel and Simon. "Meet our new Assistant Dean of Students, Ralph Cray. Pull up a chair, Ralph."

"What happened to Norah Warren?" Simon inquired.

"She's no longer with us," Martin said. "Do you know her?"

"We know of her," Simon explained. "Before we start the main discussion on why we're meeting with you, Rachel and I need to say a few things. We want to be up front with you from the outset."

Dean Martin appeared both curious and somewhat taken aback, perhaps wondering why the matters Simon was about to discuss weren't brought to light before this meeting. But Rachel and Simon had wanted the meeting and were convinced that the best approach was to get their feet in the door and discuss potential complicating factors face-to-face.

"We know of Assistant Dean Warren," Simon continued, "because we are familiar with a lawsuit brought against Sloan-Webster by a student, Noreen Clark, who was falsely accused of plagiarism by former Assistant Dean Norah Warren."

"I'm listening," Martin said in a clipped tone.

"As you know, Ms. Clark was represented by Meredith Sweeney, and she prevailed. Although Meredith isn't formally a member of our law firm, she was working out of our office at the time of the Noreen Clark case, and all four of the partners in our firm were involved in discussions of that case. We want you to know that. And if Sloan-Webster hires us for the present case, we would want to use Meredith to help with discovery and to review documents. We need to know whether that would be agreeable."

Martin mulled over Simon's information without expression. "Aren't you glad you came on board?" she directed to Cray.

"I'm not really following this," the new assistant dean said defensively.

"Which is totally understandable," Martin said. "I wasn't trying to put you on the spot."

Martin closed her eyes and sat perfectly still. It seemed to Rachel that the dean had stopped breathing.

"Everything said at this meeting is confidential, right?" Martin asked, opening her eyes.

"Right," Simon confirmed.

"And confidentiality applies whether we hire your firm or not?"

"Correct."

"Nothing discussed about the Clark case is to be relayed to Ms. Sweeney. Agreed?"

"Yes," Simon acknowledged.

"I was largely responsible for Ms. Warren's leaving Sloan-Webster," Martin said. "In my opinion, she didn't acquit herself well in the Clark situation and her handling of the matter cost Sloan-Webster a fair bit of money. Clark received a substantial settlement from the law school. As far as Ms. Sweeney assisting you in the case against Sloan-Webster, I personally have no objection. But you should know that the Board of Directors will have the final say on choosing the law firm that will represent us, and I will fully inform them about your disclosures."

For the first time, it occurred to Rachel that their firm might not be chosen to represent Sloan-Webster. A conservative Board of Directors might not want to get involved with a law firm that had a history that was, perhaps, contrary to the law school's interests. On the plus side, however, that same law firm had successfully defended a suit similar to the one now filed against Sloan-Webster. They would have to wait and see.

"I don't see any reason why I shouldn't fill you in on the suit that's been filed against us since anything I say will remain confidential." Martin paused as if to give anyone a chance to disagree with her view of confidentiality. No one did.

Cray produced one of those bound notebooks with a hard, black and white cover and a ballpoint pen. Rachel felt a bit sorry for the new hire, who would soon realize the depths of the mess he had stepped into.

"Three fairly recent graduates of Sloan-Webster are the plaintiffs in the lawsuit against us," Martin began. "The plaintiffs graduated in the classes of 2009, 2010, and 2011. Each graduated in the top half of his or her class. Each has tried unsuccessfully to land a law-related job."

As Cray began writing furiously, Rachel jotted down a few notes of her own. Christopher Blaisedell, the lawyer representing the plaintiffs, plainly had learned from his mistakes in the lawsuit he had filed against Spenser School of Law. This time around, Blaisedell must have screened his plaintiffs carefully. In the Spenser case only one plaintiff had graduated in the top half of her class.

"What is the law school alleged to have done?" Simon prompted.

"First, we're accused of having a useless, non-functioning placement office. Second, we're taken to task for not advising applicants during the admission process that they are not likely to find a legal position if they graduate. This is claimed to be a misrepresentation because it's an important fact to be considered by someone seeking admission before paying out more than one hundred twenty thousand dollars in tuition payments over three years. The court complaint pretty much accuses us of being in it solely for the money." Martin paused. "Oh yes, how could I forget? Third, the law school is accused of providing misleading information in its promotional materials. For example, the plaintiffs focus on a paragraph in a promotional brochure which boasts that the legal education students receive at Sloan-Webster is excellent because our faculty is topnotch and on a par with the faculties of other area law schools. The plaintiffs claim that statement is false and that the faculty at Sloan-Webster is inferior to the faculties at competing law schools."

Blaisedell had made similar claims in the suit he had brought against Spenser. But this time around, Rachel suspected that he would be better able to back up his allegations.

"Let's take those claims one at a time," Simon requested. "What's the story with the placement office?"

"We have one," Martin said, "but it doesn't do much. I have two administrative assistants. One of them, Jane Snelling, works part time on placement. When job openings come to her attention, she posts them on a placement bulletin board. She tries to answer students' questions. That's about it."

"What do the law school's promotional materials say about the placement office?" Rachel asked.

"Very little," Martin responded. "It's not something we've played up. Essentially, one of the brochures states that the placement office is available to try to answer job placement questions. That statement is true and appears on the placement office link on our website."

"Does any brochure describe the percentage of graduates who find law-related jobs?" Rachel followed up.

"No."

Cray looked nonplussed by the dean's disclosures. Rachel wondered how thoroughly he had investigated Sloan-Webster before accepting his new position.

"Does Ms. Snelling have any training in placement or any kind of placement experience?" Simon asked.

"Nothing formal," the dean replied.

"Let's turn to the plaintiffs' claim that applicants for admission should have been told about the unlikelihood of finding a job on graduation," Rachel said. "You noted that the law school doesn't mention the percentage of graduates who land legal jobs. What does the law school say about graduates finding legal work?"

Martin sighed audibly. "As I mentioned, we don't provide any statistics about graduates landing legal jobs. In fact, we don't maintain such statistics."

"Do you send out questionnaires to recent graduates to find out what they're up to?" Rachel asked, remembering that Spenser had engaged in that practice.

"No," Martin replied.

"Has anyone at the law school been asked about Sloan-Webster's track record on getting graduates jobs?" Rachel followed up.

"Nobody's raised that question with me," Martin said. "Jane Snelling might have been asked that question."

Rachel was struck by how little effort Sloan-Webster had made when it came to finding jobs for graduates. Spenser, in contrast, had made an effort to locate legal jobs for graduates, and had staffed its placement office with a full-time employee. Blaisedell had claimed that Spenser's placement efforts were deficient; when it came to Sloan-Webster, he would claim they were nonexistent. But nonexistent placement efforts did not necessarily mean that Sloan-Webster had committed a legal wrong. If Sloan-Webster made no effort to find jobs for graduates and didn't lie about that fact, the law school could claim that it told the truth and never misrepresented anything.

"You said that Sloan-Webster claimed its faculty was on a par with the faculties of other law schools," Simon touched on the third claim against the law school that Martin had mentioned. "What was the basis for saying that?"

"The statement appeared in promotional materials before my arrival at the law school. I couldn't tell you what the statement was based on when it made its way into a promotional brochure. Until this lawsuit, I never really focused on the statement. I would say that the statement reflects the judgment of our administration that our faculty is comparable to the faculties at other law schools. Since I've been the dean, we only hire the most qualified applicant for a vacant faculty position."

"Do you have any superstars on your faculty in any area?" Rachel asked.

"I wouldn't claim that anyone on our faculty is a superstar," Martin said grudgingly, "but I would say that the members of our faculty are competent and good at their jobs."

"How is your faculty ranked?" Rachel asked. From the Spenser litigation, she knew that law schools were ranked by an independent body and that one of the factors considered was the law school's faculty.

"Sloan-Webster has a low national ranking," Martin owned up. "In the three years I've been here, its ranking has inched up slightly each year. We remain below Spenser. I know you're both Spenser grads but I'm going to tell you that one of my current goals is to surpass Spenser when it comes to national ranking. Our faculty was evaluated lower than the faculties of our competitors. We also got comparatively low marks in such areas as physical plant, students' college grades and college rank, and graduation rate."

Cray wrote down these observations without enthusiasm. Rachel had heard all she wanted to hear at this initial meeting. "We appreciate all this information," she said. "Is there anything you wish to ask us?"

"Naturally, I'm curious what you think of our chances," Martin said. "After all, you've been through this with Spenser."

"We need to think about what you've told us," Simon said, and Rachel noted Martin's displeased look. Plainly the dean was looking for a more informative response. Rachel didn't want to displace Simon as the leader of this meeting, but she also wanted to land the new client.

"I'm sure you understand," Rachel said, "that even though we've been through this before with Spenser, we are not free to divulge anything that went on in that case." She paused and vowed to remain silent until Martin acknowledged this constraint.

"I understand," Martin said. "Confidentiality."

"Exactly. Generally, in a case like this, the plaintiffs will be looking for untrue or misleading statements on behalf of the law school. So, for example, if a promotional statement touted a highly experienced and active placement office when a placement office was inexperienced and did nothing proactive, those facts would not be helpful to the law school. That doesn't appear to be the case here."

"But the placement office doesn't appear to have done anything," Cray responded.

"Yes, that's true," Rachel conceded. "But the law school has not promised that its placement office would do anything except, as I understand it, try to address students' questions."

Cray looked unconvinced by her reasoning, but since Simon didn't appear to mind that she had now taken the lead at this meeting, Rachel decided to soldier on.

"As to the claim that the law school should have warned applicants about not finding a job after graduation, the law school simply didn't maintain that kind of information. Here again, the law school appears not to have issued any false or misleading statement about finding a law-related job."

Cray continued to look troubled. Martin's expression was a cipher.

"I am concerned about the promotional statement relating to Sloan-Webster's faculty," Rachel continued. "We would need to understand more about the law school rankings you told us about to determine whether this claim might be successful against the law school."

Nobody said anything for a long moment.

"This is pretty discouraging," Cray broke the silence.

Rachel kept her peace and was now convinced that Simon would do the same.

"I'll be getting back to you after sharing our discussion with the Board of Directors," Martin said rising. "And Ralph, I don't mean to be piling things on your plate on your first day on the job, but my current thinking is that you're going to be the point man with any law firm we hire."

Cray appeared downcast at that prospect.

"I want fresh eyes to view this case as it develops," Martin explained, "and the freshest eyes belong to you." She stood up, clearly ending the meeting, and turned to Simon and Rachel. "Thank you for coming. I'll get back to you as promptly as I can."

Walking back to their own office, Rachel smiled at the way Simon had bundled up to ward off the cold. Downtown Boston was windy and raw in January, and

Simon was so skinny he probably needed all the insulation he could get. Still, it was comical that with a heavy black coat that reached his ankles and a long, bright red scarf wound double around his neck with the tails reaching down to his knees he had pretty much doubled in size. Rachel, on the other hand, had opened the top two buttons of her coat. She disliked wind but had come to enjoy clear, cold days and nights, a development she attributed to her boyfriend. She and Josh were still getting used to living together but she had taken up running with him, and whether they began or ended the day with a run, she had discovered the exercise kept her energized. “I hope you didn’t mind me letting Martin know what I thought about Blaisedell’s legal claims,” Rachel said.

Simon shook his head. “It was weird,” he said. “All of a sudden I lost patience with the meeting and wanted to leave. When we defended Spenser, I was charged up because it was our alma mater. But for some reason, I couldn’t get energized this morning.”

“We need this case,” Rachel pointed out. “It could take the financial pressure off for the start of the year.”

“I know,” Simon said ruefully.

“It’s going to be a tougher case than Spenser,” Rachel observed. “Especially if we have to work with Cray, who knows nothing about the school.”

“Cray! Now there’s a guy who’s wondering if he made the right career move.”

“I thought you handled the Meredith factor well,” Rachel said.

“There was only one approach, the direct approach. Speaking of Meredith, I wonder how she’s doing.”

Noreen Clark was giddy. ‘And why shouldn’t she be?’ Meredith thought. Clark had been wrongly accused of plagiarism while she was a student at Sloane-Webster and had lost a new job because of it. Meredith had successfully sued the law school, and this was a day of celebration. After taxes, Clark had put over $170,000 in her pocket from the Sloan-Webster settlement. The legal job she had lost was now hers again, and she would be starting work in two weeks. And this morning they were in the enviable position of discussing a promising additional legal action against the law student who had knowingly made the false accusation. Clark had insisted on treating for lunch in an upscale Boston restaurant whose high prices forecast small, exquisitely arranged portions. Clark looked relaxed and happy. She had just recounted getting back together with her former boyfriend who had provided helpful testimony in her lawsuit. Meredith foresaw a leisurely lunch. Her former client was sitting upright, confident and poised. Clark's previously long black hair had been cut short, a change that emphasized her blue eyes and high cheek bones. And her outfit, obviously new, flattered her height, which was at least an inch or two beyond Meredith's own five-eleven. "You know what's funny?" Clark asked, and then didn't wait for an answer. "If Caryn Wheelwright hadn't lied about what we said to each other, I never would have gotten all that money from Sloan-Webster. Maybe I shouldn't be suing her. Maybe I should be thanking her."

When Meredith first met Clark at the office of a Boston headhunter firm, the woman had been a sobbing, distraught train wreck. "Just remember what she put you through."

"I know. But it's now like one of those unpleasant things that with the passage of time seems less horrible than it was."

"Are you saying you no longer want to sue Wheelwright?"

"I guess not," Clark said without enthusiasm. "Wheelwright was a bitch and a liar. Still… "

'How quickly we forget,' Meredith thought. If her current boyfriend Flash hadn't been a computer whiz able to document that Noreen hadn't plagiarized anything, Noreen might still be wondering whether she would ever land a legal job. "Wheelwright knew exactly what she was doing when she set you up for that plagiarism charge. She was willing to ruin you without a second thought."

Clark sighed in the face of Meredith's pointed observation. "What if Wheelwright has no money?" she asked.

"Wheelwright has money," Meredith responded, wondering whether Clark was looking for reasons not to sue. "She's currently working for a law firm and being paid a salary. She may want to settle with you quickly to avoid having your lawsuit receive any publicity. Do you think the law firm that hired her is going to look kindly on what she did? If she lied about a fellow student to get ahead, what would they imagine she'd do to a professional colleague?"

The waiter approached deferentially, and Clark immediately ordered a glass of wine. Meredith chose iced tea deciding that she would need her wits about her during this luncheon.

"Okay, go ahead," Clark said. "I suppose you're going to have me sign another contingency fee agreement."

"I am," Meredith confirmed. "I'll get one off to you before the end of the day."

"Enough about business," Clark said, noticeably perking up. "Tell me what you're up to. Have you got a job yet?"

"Nothing permanent," Meredith said. "I hope I can keep freelancing for the firm that helped me out on your case last year. Simon and Rachel are both good, and so are the other two partners."

"You look good," Clark observed.

"Thanks." Meredith felt good. Flash was improving her attitude and disposition. But Clark didn't have to know that. "That headhunter firm where we met never worked out," she said. "But we both seem to have landed on our feet."

"I'd say so," Clark concurred. "And in my case, I owe it all to you."

Carpenter sat at his desk grateful for some alone time. Meredith had been the last to leave the office, bubbling over with relief and enthusiasm that Noreen Clark had promptly turned around an engagement letter. They had avoided the subject of whether she would continue to work in his office in the event Sloan-Webster declined to hire Carpenter, Sullivan, Jeffries & Boyle.

Carpenter considered the firm's caseload. It was several days after the firm's one-year anniversary and the Frazier case was their only billable hour matter. Therefore, there was a lot riding on the decision of Sloan-Webster to select their firm as counsel. Ideally, the law school would hire their firm and agree that Meredith could help with the case.

"Christ," Carpenter muttered under his breath. Another year was unfolding and, as was the situation at the start of last year, his firm needed a major infusion of new business.

2

This afternoon at Philly's three-story house in Brighton, The School of Sarah was in full swing. Philly and her family shared the house with another family and an older, single woman who provided much of the childcare for the two couples. To ease the burden of taking care of three little kids, Sarah Ferguson had come up with the idea of obtaining afternoon help from teenagers who wanted to learn how to babysit. For no charge, she would teach a student how to deal with little ones and would present the youngster with a certificate listing what the student had learned. Currently helping to police the three small children were June, Sarah's first student, and Cassie, a newcomer. The noise in the living room was deafening. Were she to retreat to her second-floor office, Philly doubted she would escape the din. Not for the first time Philly was grateful for her living arrangements. For the most part, she could work from home, retreating to her second-floor home office. When work permitted, she could easily join the others.

Sarah was holding Daniel and manning Philly's boom box. She had arranged a game of musical chairs with three dining room chairs and four participants. Each time she stopped the music, Daisy and Rosalind shrieked with excitement as they scrambled to find a vacant chair. When Daisy found an empty chair she could, with effort, climb onto the seat. Rosalind's walking was still hit-or-miss and she often tripped when searching out a free chair. Also, Rosalind had to be content with holding any free chair; climbing to claim a seat was beyond her. June was definitely caught up in the frenzy. June was a natural with the little kids; once you got by her piercings and punk hairdo you could see that her matter-of-fact approach to little ones won them over. Cassie, decidedly un-punk, seemed tentative, less spontaneous, probably wondering what she had signed on for.

Before Philly headed for her upstairs office, she savored the scene. Daisy, at two and a half, had picked up the game instantly. Rosalind was now close to twenty months old and determined, one way or another, to try to do whatever Daisy could do. Daniel, beginning his fifth month, was eyeing the goings on with a serious, focused expression. He reminded Philly of how Daisy had always liked to be held upright so she could observe her surroundings.

Philly abandoned the chaos in the living room, mounted the stairs, and settled in behind her desk. Waiting for the connection to the server in their Boston office to kick in, she realized that Carpenter was in the air, headed for the Caribbean. Their partnership didn't have a formal structure—no one was technically "in charge." But Carpenter, with his depth of experience, was clearly the de facto leader. In his absence, Philly supposed, she was next in line. He had left contact information for the hotel he was staying at, but Philly was damned if she was going to interrupt his vacation.

The case they had met about earlier in the week was falling into place. Henry Frazier had signed off on the letter to be sent to his father, and Philly made final edits before printing the document. Donald Frazier would be given one week to respond to his son's demands for financial information and to cede control of the family business. She suspected that Donald's first approach would be to contact Henry directly to explore whether the two of them could work things out without lawyers. She had tried to inoculate Henry against taking his father up on such an overture but doubted she'd been successful.

Without telling Henry but with Carpenter's concurrence, Philly had bought two hours of time from the private investigators she and Carpenter used. Barney Freedman and Herb McCauley, former City of Cambridge Police Department detectives, had been charged with providing as much information as could be obtained in two hours about Elite Scripts. Her own search of the Secretary of State's public documents had turned up little. Donald Frazier held each of the corporation's officer positions. Donald and Henry were the corporation's two directors, but Donald, as the corporation's majority stockholder, could eliminate Henry from a director position instantly.

Philly was startled when her office phone rang. She didn't recognize the caller ID number. "Philly Sullivan."

"It's Rainy. How the hell are you?"

"Rainy!" Philly was genuinely pleased to hear the voice of her former lover. She had been the one to break things off, but she knew Rainy cared for her. He'd been there for her during one of the bleakest times in her life, after Philip's death, and spearheaded a group effort to get her to join AA. And she genuinely liked him even though, as a couple, things had never worked out. "This is a surprise. How are you and Monica and the baby?"

"We are all good, very good. This fatherhood stuff takes a little getting used to but I'm getting the hang of it."

"Great! To what do I owe the pleasure of this call?"

"I gave your name to someone who needs a lawyer. It's a teacher thing."

"Are *you* involved?" Philly asked. Rainy taught social studies in a Boston middle school.

"No. This happened at another school. It's weird as shit. Just when you think you've heard and seen everything, something comes along to set you straight. You ever hear of the Parker Hill Elementary School?"

"No."

"It's mostly made up of African-American kids but there's a fair number of Hispanic kids. Let's just say the two groups don't get along. There was a playground fight between a bunch of fifth grade African-American and Hispanic boys. It's not clear to me how the fight started and if you get involved, you might never get an answer. Anyway, the principal—who is Black—must have felt the Hispanic kids were at fault because he punished them. During lunch, he made the Hispanic kids eat on the floor off of those paper liners that get put on lunch trays. He wouldn't let them use the trays or the chairs and tables where the Black kids got to eat their lunches."

Philly bristled at the Hispanic kids' humiliation.

"It was ugly," Rainy continued. "The Black kids were making fun of the Hispanic kids eating on the floor and some of the Hispanic kids were crying."

"Are the Hispanic kids going to sue the principal and the school system?" Philly asked.

"I'm sure they will," Rainy answered, "but that's not what I'm calling about. One of the fifth-grade teachers is a friend of mine. She had broken up the fight and later on told the Hispanic kids to get off the floor and eat at tables. She also told the Hispanic kids to tell their parents what had happened. The principal found out about that and fired her."

"What's with this principal? He sounds like an asshole."

"Yeah, he does, and he probably is. Anyway, my friend, Sasha Barton, wants to sue the principal and the school system. I gave her your name."

"Is she Hispanic?" Philly asked.

"No, she's Black. The principal gave her some shit about undermining his authority. But Sasha saw those kids eating on the floor and it really got to her."

"What about the teachers' union?" Philly asked.

"The union will file a grievance that will go nowhere, and the union gets to approve who represents Sasha because they'll be paying for her suit. But the union may be conflicted. It's a very racist environment at that school and a lot of African Americans who are active in the union think the Hispanic kids got what they deserved, and Sasha should have butted out."

"How did things get so bad?" Philly wondered aloud.

"You'll have to ask Sasha if she calls you. It's up to you, but this might be one you want to stay away from. The racism behind this is ugly."

"Yet you gave this Sasha my name."

"I did. I figured you'd make your own decision. And anyway, if the racism doesn't put you off, maybe Sasha will."

"Why, what's her problem?"

"If she calls you and you meet with her, you can form your own opinion. I'd like to be a fly on the wall if the two of you get together, but that's not going to happen. She's a single mom and a piece of work. Let's just say she's very strong-willed. Know anybody like that?"

"What aren't you telling me?"

"Nothing I can think of. You know what I know."

"Do you have time to look at something?" Josh asked, setting a document near Rachel's seat at the small kitchen table in their apartment.

Rachel looked up. She'd been wasting her time making lists for a case they hadn't been hired to take on, jotting down possible defenses and discovery requests relating to each claim against Sloan-Webster School of Law, free-associating, recording every stray thought that popped into her head because, as Carpenter liked to say, there is no such thing as a dumb idea.

"What's this?" she asked, glancing at the document.

"A business plan."

Josh eased onto the chair across from her. Since moving in together they had become more... domesticated, although that wasn't quite the word Rachel was searching for. For some reason she couldn't explain, Rachel missed the frantic juggling of schedules and the high volume of text messages that had driven her crazy before they landed in their new apartment.

"What?" Josh asked.

"What do you mean what?"

"You've got that look."

"What look?"

"The one you get when a cloud passes over your sunny disposition."

Rachel wished she was less transparent. Apparently, every emotion that touched her could be deciphered from her expression. She knew a couple needed to communicate, but wasn't it also a maxim that a couple didn't have to share everything? 'You couldn't win,' Rachel thought, so she opted to come clean.

"Do you ever miss the craziness of our lives when we weren't living together?"

Josh smiled at her question, and Rachel felt that flutter in her gut whenever Josh's happiness spilled over. He was still the long-haired, health-food-loving, jock she had fallen for. Here it was January and he still had the remnants of his summer tan.

"I miss it and I don't miss it. I like it that we've slowed down. I like this," Josh added with a sweeping gesture that took in their small one-bedroom apartment. "I like going running with you. I like waking up with you next to me. And in case I haven't told you recently, I'm in love with you."

"We don't seem to be having sex as much as before we moved in together," Rachel pointed out.

"There's nothing to stop us from picking up the pace."

"You know what I mean."

"Yeah, I do. But I wouldn't change anything. Now, pretend you're my lawyer and look at this."

Rachel began to read. Josh and three other sports instructors proposed to tutor athletes, critique their performances, and provide in-person and video feed back. The working name for the company was Pro Team Solutions. There was even a budget projection for launching the venture.

"Wow! Where did this come from?"

"These guys and I have known each other a long time. We stay in touch and we got to talking about this in e-mails. I'd be the tennis and golf guy. My friends would cover baseball, soccer, basketball, and swimming. There are other groups out there doing this, but we think we can make a go of it."

"Did all of you come up with this business plan?"

"It was mostly me."

"What if one of you produced more revenue than the other three?" Rachel asked, hoping she wasn't throwing cold water on the project."

"We actually thought of that. We need to come up with a formula that rewards a person who is producing more cash than the rest of us. By the way, I'm hoping the big cash producer is me."

"Then why not do this alone?"

As Josh considered her question, Rachel was again struck by his deliberateness and the unselfconscious way he took his time before speaking.

"I guess it just feels right going in with a bunch of guys I know and like. We're hoping we can refer people to each other and really build a business."

Rachel took her time rereading the business plan. It was hard to focus as a lawyer where Josh was involved. But after her second review, she concluded that the four friends had thought of nearly everything. "This looks pretty good. Are you guys planning to borrow the money for start-up costs?"

"No. We've each got some cash we're willing to put in. But we are going to need a lawyer to set up the company. Know a good lawyer who's willing to charge us little or nothing?"

"I might. Let me think about it while you get more specific about picking up the pace."

When Frank Stevens stayed over at Simon's apartment the living space shrank. Frank was a big guy who took up a lot of space. It was still a bit of a mystery to

Simon how he—small, lightweight, and nine years Frank's senior—had acquired a tall, muscled, football player of a boyfriend. But Simon realized that feeling cramped also had to do with his liking to be alone. Did this mean that he wasn't cut out for a long-term relationship? He remembered thinking last year that he could turn out to be one of those gay guys who never had kids in his life because he let work consume him until the parenting option was no longer viable. Was he going to latch on to liking solitude as a reason to find fault with the only relationship that had ever meant anything to him?

Frank was watching a college football all-star game with the TV at high volume. He claimed this was a big game and for all Simon knew it was. Legal notepad in hand, Simon was seated next to Frank on the secondhand couch that faced the TV set, although sports in general, and football in particular, held no interest for him. He thought of retreating to the bedroom for privacy but felt guilty for even entertaining the idea—after all, how often was Frank on a break from college and in town? But with Frank cheering loudly for one team—Simon wasn't clear which one—it was impossible to concentrate on setting down his thoughts on the Sloan-Webster case that might come their way. If he and Rachel were hired, the case would be a more difficult battle than last year's Spenser litigation. Still, there had to be a line of attack that would make defending Sloan-Webster less daunting. No such game changing gambit had yet made its way to Simon's yellow legal pad; the top page was blank and, as long as the football game continued, was likely to remain so.

Frank rose during the next commercial break and returned from the kitchen with a beer. "Don't you ever stop?" he asked as he resumed his seat.

"Hardly ever," Simon owned up. Typically, he was preoccupied by the case of the moment, but now he had sunk to the level of obsessing over a case he wasn't currently hired to pursue.

"That's not a good thing," Frank said. "I could teach you a bit about football if you like."

Simon would have preferred to eat glass but held that thought. "I'd just as soon take a rain check," he replied diplomatically.

"I want you to do me a favor," Frank said.

"Do I get to hear the favor first?"

"No. It's nothing outrageous. I promise. And I want you to promise to humor me and do what I ask."

Simon set down his legal pad. "Okay."

"I want you to imagine yourself not thinking about work all the time."

"I think I can do that," Simon said, regarding the request as more modest than he had expected.

"I'm not finished. And then I want you to actually live for a week as the person you've imagined who doesn't think about work all the time."

"That sounds easier said than done."

"This is important," Frank said. "I worry about you. You don't seem to have outside interests. I know you don't like football and other sports, but sports are a big thing in my life. What do you have that's comparable?"

Simon came up with nothing.

"Will you do it?" Frank pressed.

"Sure."

"Starting now, right?"

"Okay." Simon grinned at Frank. "For starters, which team are you rooting for?"

3

This time Sloan-Webster's dean had arranged their meeting in a small conference room. The dean was again accompanied by Ralph Cray, who looked even less acclimated to his job than he had on his first day at work. Rachel figured that they wouldn't have been summoned for an audience if they weren't going to be hired, but Simon had voiced an opposing view. "I think she wants to tell us the bad news face-to-face," he had said on the walk to the law school.

For one of the few times since Rachel had known him, Simon looked distracted as he fidgeted in his chair. Missing was his usual, inscrutable expression.

"I won't keep you in suspense," Martin began the meeting. "The Board of Directors voted to hire you. You should know that it was not a unanimous vote. In fact, it was a very close vote. The matters that you disclosed to us led to some lively debate. My sense is that your experience with a similar case was responsible for the final vote coming out as it did." Martin paused. "And the fact that your fees are reasonable in comparison to your competitors didn't hurt your cause."

This engagement was a coup for their firm, so Rachel was surprised that Simon continued to look ill at ease.

"There's a lot riding on this case for us," Martin continued. "Should the law school lose the litigation and be publicly humiliated in the process, the institution may have a difficult time recovering."

'Talk about piling on the pressure,' Rachel mused.

"What are the next steps?" Martin asked.

Simon glanced her way and Rachel realized that she'd be carrying the ball at this meeting. "There are two main tasks in the immediate future: answering the complaint and responding to discovery. We'll prepare the answer, and you can take it as a given that we will ask for an extension to do so. It's simply not feasible to do the preparatory work to file the answer within the required twenty days following the law school being served with the complaint. A fair amount of that twenty days has evaporated due to holidays and the time taken to select legal counsel."

"Won't asking for an extension of time be viewed as a sign of weakness?" Cray asked.

"Perhaps," Rachel said. "But it doesn't really matter. We need to do some investigatory work to be truthful and complete in responding to the plaintiffs' allegations."

"Why can't you move to dismiss the case?" Cray followed up.

"That's an option," Rachel acknowledged. "But based on the information that came to light at our first meeting, I don't believe that a motion to dismiss will be successful."

Cray frowned, apparently not liking her answer. Rachel decided to give the assistant dean another unappealing alternative to think about. "If you're worried about the plaintiffs perceiving the law school as weak, you need to think about what happens if the law school files a motion to dismiss and the motion is denied. If that occurs, the plaintiffs will be emboldened and think they have the law school on the run."

Cray appeared to dislike her second scenario as little as her first. Rachel sensed trouble brewing with Cray in place as the liaison to the law school's outside counsel.

"Let's move on to the second task. The law school has also been served with discovery requests seeking voluminous information. We will also seek extensions of the time to respond to those requests. We can tell you from the Spenser case that responding to discovery requests will be very time consuming and costly. But the time simply has to be spent going through all documents."

"That reminds me," Martin interjected. "You're free to use Ms. Sweeney as you see fit."

"Excellent," Rachel said as she wondered why this news failed to lift Simon's spirits. "Is it possible to dedicate a secure room for documents?" she inquired.

"Ralph and I will consider that request. It makes sense, but we have some logistical issues to address."

"Thank you. We'll be sending you an engagement letter and if you have any questions about it, please call one of us before signing." Rachel paused and studied the two administrators. Probably neither fully understood what was required to deal with the initial matters she had described. "One more thing," Rachel said, deciding to go with her instincts. "I want you to think about what would constitute a victory for Sloan-Webster, short of getting the plaintiffs' case thrown out."

That got Simon's attention. He was giving her the fisheye, but Rachel didn't care. If he had taken charge of this meeting, she probably would never have made her request.

"I don't see how anything but getting the case thrown out could be viewed as a victory," Cray said.

"Just think about the issue," Rachel said. "We'll revisit it the next time the four of us meet."

Cray gave a dismissive shoulder shrug. Martin showed no reaction to her request. "Mr. Cray," Rachel addressed the assistant dean. "Would you please take charge of assembling the documents that the plaintiffs have requested. When you have a fair number of documents in hand, give us a call and we'll begin our review. I'd recommend that your secretary keep a list or index of the documents you assemble."

Cray didn't look pleased with the assignment, but Rachel flashed him her sweet smile and thanked him. When the dean rose, she knew the meeting was over.

"Where were you off to during that meeting?" Rachel challenged Simon as they began the walk back to their office. The wind was hitting them head on and Simon's scarf whipped around his neck as he lowered his head and trudged forward. "Do you think law is the only thing in my life?" he asked.

"What kind of question is that?"

"It's a question that was posed to me."

"I'm sure you have other interests."

"Name one."

Rachel thought about her partner and came up empty. "It's not as if we hang out," she said.

"See!" Simon said with an element of triumph. "You can't think of anything."

"I don't really know you outside of work."

"We've worked together for years and you don't really know me? That speaks volumes."

"What brought this on?" Rachel inquired.

"It came up in a discussion Frank and I had before he went back to Wesleyan."

Rachel let that revelation sink in. Simon cared for Frank; that fact was obvious when she observed them together. They seemed to have come to terms with the nine-year age difference between them. But Simon had never showed any interest in Frank's passion—sports—and perhaps the couple was wrestling with the fact that they had little in common. "What kinds of things do you do when you're together?" she asked.

"Not much, when you come down to it. With Frank in college in Connecticut, we try to make up for lost time when we're together if you know what I mean. But besides eating out there's not a lot that we do together."

"What does Frank like?"

"Sports. Sports. And did I mention sports?"

"Sports, huh. Sounds a lot like you."

"Very funny."

Rachel thought about how she and Josh spent free time. He had gotten her on a physical fitness kick which she was enjoying. Beginning in the spring they'd make time to play the sports he taught—tennis and golf. She liked the theater and Josh willingly went along whenever she proposed seeing a play. Going to a live rock concert was a rarity that probably qualified for their walk on the wild side, but if there was a group performing that they liked, they sometimes attended.

"If it wasn't for that golf case we had two years ago, I would never have met Josh," Rachel observed. "Like you, I'm not into sports but I love playing golf with Josh and he's giving me tennis lessons. I like doing things with him because they're, well, with him, and I've made a conscious effort to try things he likes."

"What's your point?"

"My point is that I tried something new, something that was foreign to me, something my preconceptions told me I would hate."

Simon emitted a Carpenter-like, noncommittal grunt.

"There's one other thing," Rachel said. "You need to be willing to make a fool of yourself. During the first golf lessons I took with Josh, I was a total dork. But I didn't let that bother me."

"I *am* a total dork," Simon affirmed. "And it *would* bother me."

"Forget about that," Rachel came back. "Does Frank work out?" she asked.

"Does a bear shit in the forest?"

"*You* could work out," Rachel said.

"Please. That's not going to happen."

"If Carpenter can go to a gym, so can you."

"I'm not Carpenter and have no intention of becoming Carpenter."

"I'm getting a feel for how flexible you are," Rachel goaded Simon.

Simon labored forward without saying anything for a while, then muttered, "I guess I had that coming."

"Why don't you try running," Rachel suggested. "Just think about how pleasantly surprised Frank will be when you ask him if he'd like to join you for a run."

Again, Simon fell silent. In a few minutes they would reach their office and this conversation could come to an end.

"Running? In January? If you think I'd try running in this weather, you're nuts," Simon said as they approached the door to their office building.

"You'd be surprised by what you're capable of trying," Rachel came back. "This Friday you're having dinner with Josh and me. Then we're going shopping. Bring your credit card. It's time you got outfitted."

"This just gets worse and worse," Simon grumbled, and Rachel lumped him definitively with Carpenter—that made it two grumps among her partners.

4

Sarah had taken Daisy and Rosalind outside hoping the cold would take some of the starch out of the little girls, and Daniel was racked out in an infant seat perched on Philly's second-floor office desk. Philly had been watching her son's respirations, studying his small hands, trying to figure out if he looked anything like her or Paul when her phone rang, and she answered on the first ring. Daniel hadn't stirred at the sound.

Donald Frazier had a low, soothing voice, so maybe he was an impressive salesman. "I'm in receipt of your letter and I hope that we can work this out," the elder Frazier said.

"My letter makes two very explicit requests of you. But before we get to that, do you have a lawyer?"

"The business has used a lawyer from time to time, but I haven't engaged a lawyer to deal with your letter."

"For the record, so to speak, I suggest that you engage counsel and that we continue this discussion when your lawyer is available to participate."

"Please, Ms. Sullivan," Frazier said wearily. "I do not wish to pay a lawyer if I don't have to. Your letter invited me to call you and I have. Let's proceed."

Philly had covered herself; she'd advised Frazier to obtain legal counsel. Now she opted for bluntness. "When can your son have an independent accountant view the company's underlying financial records for the last three years?"

"I really don't see why the financial reports Henry receives aren't sufficient," Frazier said.

"What you see or don't see is beside the point. Are you going to make the underlying financial records available or not? That calls for a yes or no answer. What's it going to be?"

The elder Frazier fell silent. "I don't think your demand is reasonable so I'm going to say no," he finally responded.

"Suit yourself," Philly continued with a belligerent tone. "When your son goes to court, a judge is going to require you to turn over the information. Is there anything else you wish to discuss? For example, when are you going to honor your promise to Henry that he is to take over the business?"

"I've explained to Henry that I need some additional time to do that. He's being paid as if he were CEO so he really has no cause to complain."

"Why do you need additional time?"

"I simply do."

"Anything else?" Philly asked.

"I hope that this won't result in a court proceeding," Frazier said in a barely audible voice.

'One can always hope,' Philly thought. "I suspect you'll find out soon enough," is what she said.

When Philly set down her phone, Daniel's arms and legs suddenly jerked up and out. Then, just as suddenly, his limbs relaxed, and his steady breathing resumed.

Donald Frazier had not shed any light on the positions he was taking. If Carpenter was right that the elder Frazier's actions were motivated by money, there might come a time when they needed to advise his son not to get more involved with a company that could be harboring a ticking financial bomb.

Simon felt ridiculous as Josh and Rachel looked him up and down. He had already forked over $130 for running shoes after having to endure the pair's incredulous looks when he admitted to not owning a pair of sneakers. Now they had him outfitted in a pale gray running suit with vertical, yellow reflective stripes along the pants legs and the front and back of the running jacket. What a colossal waste of money! There wasn't a chance in hell he would use this stuff, never mind that the running shoes had to be the most comfortable footwear he had ever donned. And he couldn't dismiss the image of Frank's incredulous look were he ever to suggest that they go for a run.

"If you run at night, you'll need a stocking cap," Josh said. "You can also get the kind that covers your entire face like the ones robbers use."

"I'll go for full face protection," Simon said, notwithstanding that the image of a dark mask with only eye and nose slits for openings made him cringe.

"Full face protection it is," Josh said.

The running suit was lightweight. "I'll freeze to death if I wear this outfit," Simon protested.

"You need to wear a warm layer underneath," Josh explained. "We each have a running suit with this kind of material. Once you get moving, you're going to generate heat and the suit will keep the heat in. You're going to end up sweating."

Another non-selling point. The only place Simon wanted to sweat was in bed with Frank.

"What do you say?" Rachel pressed.

She was giving him her open, innocent look that juries loved. She truly believed this running nonsense would help him. It was hard to say no to Rachel when her warm and sincere gaze was leveled at you. "What the hell," he said. "I'll take it."

"You're going to thank us," Rachel said. Simon kept silent, not wanting to disillusion her.

"We also have a present for you," Josh said, handing over a watch. "You can time your runs and check on your heart rate while you're running. We've got new watches and I had this lying around. It should be just fine for you."

“Thanks,” Simon responded. He cupped his hand over the watch face and the face glowed. While he didn’t want to disappoint his benefactors, he also didn’t want to hype their expectations. “What if running is a turn off?” he said.

“Not an option,” Josh said. “You need to get into a routine and stick to it. The weather is no excuse. The first time you go, I want you to call me in advance. I’ll run with you. I might have some pointers.”

“Thanks,” Simon repeated, now knowing what it felt like to be overwhelmed by kindness.

“Give it a chance,” Josh said.

‘A fat chance,’ Simon thought. “Okay,” is what he said.

5

A School Teacher

Philly had debated whether to engage in babysitter creativity so that she could hold her initial meeting with Sasha Barton in Boston but, in the end, the logistics were too complicated. If Barton decided to hire her, the decision likely wouldn’t be based on where they first got together. And if Barton was inclined to base a hiring decision on that factor, who the hell wanted her as a client!

Sarah had taken the kids to the third-floor playroom, and with Simon’s less than enthusiastic help, Philly had cleared up the major areas of clutter in the living room—dining room area. Barton was due to arrive any minute and Philly took the time to study her partner. “You look out of sorts.”

“I don’t want to talk about it,” Simon snapped in response.

They were seated in the easy chairs facing the couch. Simon’s leg was jiggling a mile a minute and his fingers drummed on his legal pad.

“What’s going on?” Philly pressed.

“I’m supposed to go running with Josh tomorrow night,” Simon said in a cranky tone.

“So, what’s the big deal?”

“I hate running. I let Josh and Rachel pressure me into it.”

"That's not like you," Philly said.

"It's complicated."

"What isn't," Philly said as the doorbell rang.

Philly experienced two surprises when she opened the front door. First, she was confronted with an African-American version of herself. Barton was short and compact with a helmet of tight curls. She projected a no-nonsense air and confidence bordering on defiance. There was probably only a year or two age difference between them.

The second surprise was holding onto Barton's hand, doing his best to stand behind her. He ducked farther behind Barton when Philly said hello.

"I've got my own babysitting problems," Barton said as she urged the little boy forward. "This is my son, Frankie. He's three."

"Come on in out of the cold," Philly directed, as she hugged herself to ward off the elements. She couldn't rightly complain about Barton having babysitting issues.

Philly collected coats, introduced Simon, and made an instant decision about Frankie. Philly turned to his mother. "Is it okay if Frankie plays upstairs with my daughter and another little girl? Sarah, our housemate, is supervising them."

"Sure," Barton responded after the briefest of pauses.

Philly dropped to a knee to get to Frankie's eye level. "Do you like to play games?" she asked.

Frankie didn't answer. He was a skinny kid, taller than Daisy, with a sharp nose and chin and a complexion that was darker than his mother's.

Philly pointed to the stairs. "There's a bunch of kids upstairs playing games. They also have cookies up there. Do you want to check it out?"

Frankie nodded in an embarrassed way and looked up at his mother.

It's okay," Barton said. "Go on up and see what's going on. You can come back down if you want to after checking things out."

Philly led the way upstairs. On the first landing, Frankie glanced back at his mother with an expression that suggested he might not see her again. But Frankie soldiered on and when they got to the third floor, Philly knocked twice on the door and opened it. Daisy and Rosalind were sprawled on the floor drawing, Daisy drawing roughly and Rosalind alternating between making lines and sucking on the crayons. Daniel watched them intently from his infant seat. "We have another customer," Philly said to Sarah. "Girls! Say hello to Frankie."

The girls looked up but didn't say anything. Sarah struggled to her feet and gathered together more drawing materials. "Hi, Frankie. I'm Sarah. I hope you like drawing. This is Daisy and Rosalind."

"I promised cookies," Philly confessed.

"Then you're in luck. I'll be able to keep your promise."

Sarah got Frankie settled on the floor where he eyed the girls for a time and then began to draw. Soon Daisy looked to see what he was drawing.

"Thanks," Philly said.

"Not a problem," Sarah answered.

When Philly got back downstairs, Simon filled her in on the conversation he'd been having with Sasha Barton.

"Ms. Barton was just saying that she needs a full-time lawyer," Simon said. "She's concerned that with your kids you might not be available full time."

"Is that going to be a problem if I hire you?" Barton asked bluntly.

"No," Philly replied just as bluntly. "Because of my kids, I do a lot of work at home. But I wouldn't accept any engagement I couldn't devote my full attention to. To be clear with you, there are four lawyers in our firm, and we work as a team. I'd be the partner in charge of your case, but Simon and my other partners would be working with me."

"This is not what I expected."

"This is a free consultation," Philly replied. "If anything makes you uncomfortable about me or our firm, you should seek representation elsewhere." Philly tried to be polite, but she wasn't giving an inch.

Barton took in her surroundings before settling on the couch. "When we spoke on the phone, you said Rainy filled you in on my situation."

"He did in a very general way. We'd like to hear it from you."

Barton nodded, took her time ordering her thoughts. "Do you know anything about the Parker Hill Elementary School?"

Since speaking to Rainy, Philly had gone online to find out about the school. "It's in Roxbury. It's a charter school."

"Right. I teach fifth grade. The students are mostly African American, with a fair number of Hispanic students and a lot fewer White and Asian students. There's tension between the Black kids and the Hispanic kids. Before Christmas vacation there was an incident on the playground during morning recess. A group of Hispanic kids were talking in Spanish, kicking a soccer ball around, laughing it up, when one of the Black kids, a boy in my class, walked by and made some comments about them needing to speak English and soccer being a sissy game. One of the Hispanic kids—also a boy in my class—told the Black kid to mind his own business and the Black kid came back with 'Who's going to make me?' or something like that." Barton paused, as if wrestling with the exact chronology of what happened next.

"There appears to have been some back and forth pushing between the two boys and when I got there, things had escalated and more students were involved. I stepped in and broke up the fighting. I asked what happened and was told pretty much what I just told you. I called out the two boys who started things and told them we were going to stand out on the playground until they shook hands. Which they ended up doing, although they weren't happy about it. Then recess ended and I didn't think anything more of the incident.

"After morning classes, the kids went off to lunch. I ate at my desk and was walking through the cafeteria to go to the teacher's lounge when I saw the Hispanic boy I mentioned and a bunch of other Hispanic boys eating on the floor of the cafeteria. Their food was on paper tray liners. There weren't any trays. I asked one of the Hispanic kids what the hell is going on and he tells me that Principal Clarke is punishing them for starting the playground fight. That would be Principal Samuel Clarke with an e. He's African American in case that makes a difference."

Barton had spit out the principal's name and Philly wondered whether there had been bad blood between them before the incident.

"A bunch of the Black kids were laughing at the kids on the floor, taunting them, saying things like 'You're on the floor where you belong.' A few of the Hispanic kids looked like they'd been crying. I told them to get up and go sit down at a table. I went over to the kids doing the taunting and told them I didn't want to hear another word. Then I sat down at the table the Hispanic kids had taken and had them give me more details. They told me that Clarke had ordered them to eat on the floor. I told them I wanted them to be sure to tell their parents what had happened."

"Why didn't you go to Clarke before telling the kids to sit at a table?" Simon interrupted.

"Because I didn't want those kids humiliated for another second. It was degrading!"

Philly realized that she had more than physical appearance in common with Barton: neither of them put up with stupidity and unfairness for very long.

"Clarke left word that he wanted me to see him before I left for the day," Barton resumed. "Which I did. He was pissed. He said that I had undermined his authority and disobeyed him and that I hadn't heard the last of this. I told him that if he'd ever done anything like that to my kid, I'd have ripped his heart out."

Philly struggled to keep a straight face. She could see herself doing the same thing.

"The next morning, Clarke marched into my first class and told me to come with him. He took me into his office and said I was fired and I was to pack up and leave the building in ten minutes or he'd call the police. I asked him who was going to see to my classes, and he said that wasn't my problem. So I packed up and left. Later that day I found out what had set him off. A number of the Hispanic kids' parents had called him at home and ripped him a new one. As well they should. I think some of them mentioned to Clarke that I had told their kids to tell them what had happened."

Barton sighed, leaned back on the couch.

"What's the story with Clarke?" Simon asked.

"Asshole!" Barton spat out. "The man has no tact. He's a big guy and I think that intimidates a lot of the kids. If you ask me, he's prejudiced against any kid who isn't African American. He should have done more to ease the tension between the ethnic groups a long time before now."

"Did you and Clarke have difficulties with each other before this incident?" Simon inquired.

"We don't like each other if that's what you mean," Barton responded with some heat. "He wants to do things his way and won't listen to any alternatives. We're civil to each other but that's about it."

"Do other teachers share your view about Clarke?" Simon pursued.

"There may be a few. The teacher meetings don't last very long, and I think that's because everyone knows Clarke isn't going to listen to suggestions that differ from an approach he wants to take. My guess is that most teachers won't want to get involved in my situation."

"Was there anything wrong about the Hispanic kids speaking Spanish at recess?" Philly asked.

"No. In the classroom, English is stressed at all times. One of the reasons so many Hispanic students have chosen Parker Hill is that the school's English classes have lesson plans particularly helpful to Hispanic students and word has gotten out about that. There are a bunch of carpools that drop a lot of the Hispanic kids at school."

"What are the parents of the Hispanic kids going to do?" Philly continued.

"From what I've heard, they've gotten a lawyer and are going to sue the shit out of Clarke."

"I assume that's what you want to do," Philly said.

"Why else would I be here?"

"Did Clarke's making the kids eat on the floor violate any school rule on punishment?" Simon asked.

"You can't hit a kid," Barton said, "even if a spanking would be good for some of them. But there's nothing specific saying it's wrong to have kids eat while on the floor. There's also nothing specific that says it's wrong to lock a kid in a closet with no food, light, and air. We're talking common sense here, aren't we?"

Carpenter would probably tell Barton that the law and common sense were seldom in sync. Philly saved her breath and considered legal theories that Barton could rely on. Nothing immediately came to mind. Her strongest claim might be that Barton stepped in to end an unlawful, abusive punishment being administered to students.

"Do you think I could win if I sued Clarke?" Barton asked.

Philly glanced at Simon whose expression revealed nothing. Barton was leaning forward as if awaiting a definitive answer. "I don't know," Philly admitted. "If you were to press me at this moment, I believe it might come down to whether Clarke's discipline was plainly out of line. You knew that he had ordered the Hispanic kids to eat on the floor, so you were clearly aware you were contradicting him when you told the kids to sit at a table. Clarke will claim that you disobeyed him and should have come to him before you took action."

"Well, fuck him," Barton let loose.

Philly waited for Barton's anger to cool. "How have your teacher evaluations been?" she asked when Barton seemed calmer.

"Good."

"Any disciplinary action or criticisms?"

"Nothing significant. I think a couple of years ago I was criticized because I got my grades in a day late. I'm getting the feeling you don't know whether you can help me."

"You asked whether you would win if you sued Clarke. I answered that I didn't know. We *can* help you. But whether the help will get you what you want right now is another story."

"I need to think about this," Barton said.

Philly rose from her chair. "Let us know what you decide. Let's see how Frankie's doing."

Ten minutes later Daisy and Rosalind were racing about the living room plainly on a sugar high. Philly held Daniel as the girls scooted this way and that. "Any thoughts?" she directed at Simon who appeared mesmerized by the girls' energy.

"Get me a jury with Hispanics on it and this guy Clarke is going down," Simon came back.

Philly had entertained the same thought. But the luck of the jury draw could leave a fair number of African Americans on the panel who might be prejudiced against Hispanics.

"I couldn't come up with a legal theory to help Barton," Philly said.

"Maybe Carpenter can come up with something useful when he gets back," Simon said. Again, Philly was struck by the void in their firm when Carpenter was absent.

"Do you think she'll hire us?" Simon asked. He had refocused on the girls who were rapidly approaching hyperactivity.

"I do," Philly replied without being able to point to any rational justification for her optimism.

Philly responded to a tug on her leg.

"Will Frankie come back to play?" Daisy asked.

"I don't know," Philly admitted. "Did you like him?"

"He was nice."

"His mommy was also nice," Philly said. But nice, she thought, didn't necessarily make for an easy client.

6

"This is the war room," Ralph Cray announced after they had all entered a small windowless room with a rectangular gray metal conference table ringed by gray chairs on rollers. Boxes were stacked against each wall. Affixed to each box was a colored Post-it Note. As she studied her next home away from home, Meredith vowed to maintain a neutral expression. The place was depressing: the high stacks of boxes made her feel like she was walled in. Worst of all, there was no space to pace, an activity that Meredith had found useful to relieve the boredom of examining documents in the Spenser case.

"We've color coded and labeled the boxes," Cray explained. "Red Post-it Notes are for placement office documents. Green is for the plaintiffs. Most of the boxes have a yellow tag. Yellow is for student records and we've arranged them alphabetically by year. Blue is for information on graduates. We've only got two boxes on that subject."

Meredith's rough count came to nearly a hundred boxes in the room, the majority adorned with yellow Post-its. She thought back to the Spenser lawsuit where the contents of even more boxes had to be examined.

"We decided to keep the door locked," Cray continued. "I've made three extra keys, one for each of you."

"Have you gone through any of this?" Rachel asked.

"No. I thought it best to first let you get a feel for what we've got."

Simon gestured for them to take seats. "I think it makes sense for Rachel to review the placement office documents," he said. "I'll take the first shot at reviewing the plaintiffs' files. Meredith, why don't you start with the two boxes containing information on law school graduates."

Meredith didn't have long to wonder how Simon would handle the elephant in the room—the boxes with yellow tags containing student records going back five years.

"When it comes to the student records," Simon continued, "I say we split up the task. Rachel, you take the first nine letters of the alphabet, I'll take the next nine and Meredith lucks out and only has eight letters to deal with."

"Where does that leave me?" Cray asked.

"I want you to interview Jane Snelling," Simon replied. "She's the dean's administrative assistant in charge of the placement office, right?"

Cray nodded. "What do you want me to ask her?"

"That's for you to decide. Type up the highlights of your interview and e-mail your memo to each of us."

"I've never done anything like this before," Cray said. Meredith picked up on a slight whining tone.

"Then you're in luck," Simon said. "You get to try something new. And before the case is over, this won't be the only new thing you take on."

Running with Josh tonight wasn't the only unpleasant thing facing Simon. Because the day would end on that low note, he decided to tackle an equally unpleasant chore so that by the end of the day he could put a check mark next to the two most distasteful tasks on his to-do list. Approaching deadlines meant he could no longer delay asking Christopher Blaisedell for extensions.

"Mr. Jeffries! To what do I owe the pleasure of this call?"

Blaisedell had to have already guessed the reason for this call. Simon pictured his opponent: a physically imposing young man with dark hair.

"Ms. Boyle and I will be entering our appearance for Sloan-Webster School of Law, and I'd like to talk about extensions for answering the complaint and responding to discovery."

"You mean we get to do this again?" Blaisedell responded in a cheerful tone.

"We do," Simon confirmed.

"Surely you're not expecting a similar result," Blaisedell said.

"I certainly hope that the result will be different," Simon replied, "since as I recall you prevailed in the Spenser case. You got an attorney fee award and an agreement from Spenser to make the changes to its placement office that you requested."

Blaisedell didn't respond. The plaintiffs in the Spenser case had sought tuition refunds on behalf of scores of students, but the Spenser settlement had fallen far short of that.

"You're not seriously suggesting the plaintiffs prevailed in the Spenser case," Blaisedell found his voice.

"I was more than suggesting," Simon came back. Maybe it would throw his adversary off his game if he thought Spenser believed it had been defeated. Simon paused a beat before returning to the purpose of this call. "I would like an extra forty days to file an answer and an extra seventy days to file responses to discovery."

"You were putting me on, right?" Blaisedell questioned. "You were just screwing with me, weren't you?"

"Putting you on! I've been told that I don't have a playful bone in my body. Will you agree to the extensions?"

"Sure, what the hell."

"Thanks. Ms. Boyle and I appreciate it. We'll file our appearances shortly."

The outdoor track at the Cambridge Ringe and Latin High School had a hazy look under the overhead lighting. The night was clear but bitter cold. Simon pulled his ski mask over his head and figured it was just a matter of time before he started shivering. Josh's only head gear was a wool band that covered his ears.

"We need to stretch," Josh said. "This is important. When you're on your own you need to remember to do this. Follow my lead. Tomorrow I'll e-mail you these stretching exercises."

Josh was incredibly limber; he bent over, knees locked, and palmed the track's running surface. Simon wasn't close to touching his own toes.

"Today you're going to run a mile," Josh announced.

"You're kidding, right?"

"I didn't say all at once. You're actually going to cover two miles. After each quarter mile lap, I want you to walk a quarter mile lap at a brisk pace."

"I really don't think I can do this."

"Okay, nice and easy. Let's get going."

Simon started slowly and was immediately urged by Josh to pick up his pace. Josh's exhales were visible in the night air. God only knew what was happening to Simon's own breath partially trapped behind his ski mask.

To Simon's surprise, the quarter mile ended and he was still alive. Freezing but alive.

"Walk this next lap. I'm going to run. You should be walking fast enough so that I can't complete more than two laps to your one.

Josh took off and Simon quickened his pace. He was breathing hard and his heart was racing. Josh passed him when he was halfway around the track so Simon figured he was walking at the correct pace.

"This one you're running," Josh said when he next pulled up to Simon.

Josh slowed his pace so that they ran abreast.

"Relax," Josh counseled. "You're doing great."

Halfway around the track, Simon realized that he was no longer cold. Steam was building up under his running suit.

During his second walking quarter mile, Simon felt tired. This time, Josh passed him before the halfway point.

"Faster," Josh urged.

Halfway into his third running lap, Simon didn't think he'd make it to the end.

"A quarter of a mile is long but it's not really long," Josh said running beside him. "You can do this."

On his third walking lap, Simon wondered why walking seemed harder than running. His knees hurt and he had a stitch in his side.

"Pick up the pace," Josh said as he raced by. Simon was too tired to give him the finger.

Starting the last running lap, Simon realized that he had put everything out of his mind except moving one foot in front of the other. He was definitely sweating. He fought the urge to take off his ski mask.

"Last walking quarter mile," Josh said before taking off. "Give it all you've got," he called over his shoulder."

Simon discovered he had more left that he'd anticipated. He lengthened his stride. The new running shoes really were comfortable. He got his arms pumping in rhythm with the movement of his legs and this time he had moved beyond the halfway point when Josh raced by.

Simon got to the end of his lap and bent over to catch his breath. Soon Josh was beside him, studying a stopwatch.

"This is only an approximation," Josh said. "I believe you were running at a nine and a half minute per mile pace. That's not too bad for your first time. In a month, if you keep at it, you'll shave ninety seconds off that time."

"Be still my heart," Simon said, and immediately wished he had avoided sarcasm.

"How do you feel?" Josh asked.

"Clear headed," Simon announced what he was primarily aware of.

"That's only one of the benefits of running."

Walking back to Josh's car, Simon began to feel chilled. "Thanks for doing this."

"My pleasure. Promise me you'll keep this up."

Simon didn't like to make a promise he suspected he wouldn't keep. "I'll do my best."

"Not good enough," Josh rallied back. "You really need to do this regularly. Every other day at a minimum."

"Like I said, I'll do my best."

"Think of this as being as important as your legal work," Josh replied. "For the first time in your life you're going to do something that you have doubts about but that's going to make a positive difference in your life."

Simon didn't say anything. Pep talks had never sat well with him.

7

"Should we wait until Carpenter returns before making a final decision?" Henry Frazier asked.

"That's your prerogative," Philly replied. She wasn't annoyed by Frazier's question and realized that there was a time in her life when she would have been. If Frazier was implying that he didn't trust her judgment, so be it.

"I just hate the idea of suing my father," Frazier bemoaned.

"Carpenter and I talked about this with you," Philly reminded their client. "Your father isn't going to voluntarily do what you want. Carpenter and I don't think you should be eager to take over the family business without fully understanding whether your father is holding back information that shows the business is in trouble."

Frazier fell silent. Daniel was down for a morning nap, Rosalind was under Sarah's watch, and Daisy sat on the floor of Philly's office happily paging through a picture book. Daisy was speaking softly, so softly that Philly couldn't hear the words. Her daughter probably was reciting the story which she had already proven she had memorized.

"Let me think about it," Frazier finally said. "When Carpenter returns, let's have one further call to review my options."

"Sounds like a plan," Philly responded. "I'll try to set something up the day after he gets back."

Philly set down her phone and observed Daisy. Her daughter was totally engrossed. She and Paul had discussed other day care options, which had the advantages of getting Daisy to socialize with more kids and giving Sarah a babysitting break. There would be tradeoffs. Someone would have to find the time to drop Daisy off and pick her up and Philly was the likely candidate to perform those tasks.

The unmistakable sounds of Daniel waking came from the baby monitor perched on her desk. Another country heard from, Philly thought. But the country she really wanted to hear from—Sasha Barton—had gone into radio silence.

In the war room, Simon stared at the file of the first plaintiff in the Sloan-Webster case as he catalogued his aches and pains. His knees hurt, his thighs felt tight, and a knot of soreness had lodged in his left shoulder. He'd refrained from contacting Josh about these ailments for, despite them, he felt good. He had struggled briefly to fall asleep last night but once asleep, he hadn't stirred. The clear-headed feeling he experienced at the end of last night's run was still present. He felt both calm and alert, and the thick files he had vowed to wade through before lunch were not intimidating for some reason. What was intimidating was the fact that Josh had run three miles—two of those miles at a fast clip—and wasn't winded by the effort. And what puzzled Simon was the fact that tonight, despite his present discomfort, he would give the running another go.

Simon focused on the photograph of Noah Branson, the first named plaintiff in the complaint filed by Blaisedell. He was confronted with the serious gaze of an African American with a long thin face, prominent eyes, and a wispy chin beard. This time around there would be no lily-white array of plaintiffs as had been the case in the Spenser litigation.

Branson had gone to a public high school in Michigan, earned a BA degree from Michigan State University, and graduated from Sloan-Webster in 2009 in the top third of his class. He had passed the Massachusetts bar examination on his first try. After graduating, he had worked briefly as an unpaid intern for a non-profit corporation but had yet to find a paying law-related job. According to the allegations in the court complaint, Branson had received no help from Sloan-Webster's placement office. The few times he had inquired about job openings, he had been told only that the most recent information had been posted on the placement office bulletin board.

Simon jotted down a note before the thought disappeared from memory: why had Branson sat for the Massachusetts bar instead of returning to Michigan?

Simon put off going through Branson's file in detail until he had a general read on the other two plaintiffs. Regina White's file was thicker than Branson's. White had graduated from Sloan-Webster in 2010. The black and white head shot in her file folder revealed an unsmiling woman with light hair, a studious look, and a round face. White had attended high school in Middleborough, Massachusetts, and had graduated from Colby College in Maine. She, too, had graduated in the top third of her law school class, and her experience since graduation paralleled Branson's: passed the Massachusetts bar exam on the first try, no law-related job, no constructive help from the placement office.

The third plaintiff, Marshall Hightower, graduated from Sloan-Webster in 2011 and also had yet to find a law-related position. He had attended high school in Worcester, Massachusetts, and college at the University of Massachusetts' Boston campus. He was in the top quarter of his law school class and, like the others, had passed the Massachusetts bar exam on his first attempt. Simon remembered that the court complaint contained an allegation that Hightower had met with the head of the law school's placement office who had been unable to offer any constructive suggestion as to how he might find a legal job.

Simon made a note of each plaintiff's current work experience. Branson was an administrative assistant at a Boston insurance company. White had found a secretarial position with an ad agency. Hightower worked for a landscaping company. Looking again at Hightower's photograph, Simon wondered whether the graduate's dark complexion was a product of working outdoors. Hightower's rugged features were softened by the smile playing on his lips.

This time around, Blaisedell had been careful to select plaintiffs who had participated in extra-curricular activities in law school. Branson had written an article for the law school's intellectual property journal. White had obtained clinical experience by working in a public defender's office. Hightower had participated in moot court during each of his law school years.

Outside of Branson's forsaking Michigan, Simon couldn't think of a line of attack that might undermine any of the plaintiffs. He speculated that Blaisedell had asked each of the plaintiffs the question that screeners asked potential political candidates: is there anything in your background that could hurt you if it became public? It was dispiriting to think that each of the plaintiffs was squeaky clean.

Simon took a deep breath and returned to the Branson file. There was a fair amount of paper to wade through and he was not leaving the war room until he had finished the task.

8

Meredith swiveled her chair so that she was facing away from her workstation. Carpenter looked uncharacteristically serene as he studied a document at his desk. He had color in his face, although it wasn't a color she could identify. His week in the sun hadn't produced a tan or a red hue but instead a skin tone with a hint of... could it be purple? Whatever the shade, it looked good.

It took Meredith a moment to figure out something else different about Carpenter. Whenever she'd seen him last year, he was wearing a long-sleeved, white shirt, buttoned at the neck with a tie knotted in place. At this moment, the tie knot had slid downward an inch and the top button of Carpenter's shirt was open. Clearly he had gotten too much sun and was letting himself go to hell.

"You look good," Meredith said when Carpenter looked up from his reading. "Rested."

"Maxine and I had fun," Carpenter replied. "I owe you guys for not bothering me. And I returned to the great news about being hired by Sloan-Webster."

"Rachel and Simon said the Sloan-Webster case means I get to stay."

"Yeah, it does." Carpenter paused, his mellowness disappearing for a moment before coming back into play. "I'm glad you're staying. We all are. When you first started camping out here, I had my doubts. I had always had my own office and was dreading the loss of privacy. But that hasn't been a problem. I've gotten used to having you around."

"I'm glad too," Meredith came back. "Just so you know, I think we're going to have our work cut out for us with the Sloan-Webster case."

"At some point soon, we need to have an all-hands-on-deck meeting on the case. I want to get an overview of what we're dealing with."

Meredith nodded, smiling. Was this the first time she felt totally relaxed with Carpenter? "Enough about you and your firm. I've drafted a complaint for Noreen Clark against Caryn Wheelwright that I'd like you to take a look at. I'm doing the case on a contingency. If the case is a winner, I want to pay you for your time, so keep track."

Carpenter didn't say anything. He was favoring her with an appraising look and Meredith had no idea what he was thinking.

"You're looking good yourself," Carpenter said. "I'm betting Flash has something to do with that."

"Then you would be right."

"Good. Leave a copy of the complaint on my desk. I'll get to it. Right now, I have to deal with Philly and Henry Frazier.

Meredith packed up, deciding to give Carpenter privacy. Today would be a long day. It was time to start the slog through Sloan-Webster student files.

"I would have said the same thing to Frazier," Carpenter said to Philly. "But since he wants to hear it from the horse's ass, let's get him on the line."

"You're sounding chipper," Philly said.

"The week was too short," Carpenter said ruefully. He and Maxine had fallen into a leisurely routine. Late to bed and late to rise. A buffet brunch followed by a walk on the beach. Swimming and reading. A light snack. More swimming. Dining and drinking. Some evenings, he had broken down and passed up beer for some exotic fruity-tasting concoction that could knock a horse on its ass. Maxine signed up for an exercise class every day and on two occasions had roped him into participating.

"With two little ones, it occurs to me that it'll be a long time before a week away on some foreign beach will be a reality."

"When I was married and my kids were growing up, I never even thought about a vacation like I just had. I was probably stupid. I probably should have stopped and smelled the roses. It might have saved my marriage."

Philly didn't say anything.

"Get Frazier on the line. Your ability to set up conference calls exceeds mine."

"As I see it, you have two options," Carpenter declared after telling Henry Frazier he concurred with Philly's advice. "You can do nothing. Or, you can go to court and try and get a judge to order your father to disclose detailed financial information about Elite Scripts."

"I don't like suing my father," Frazier repeated what he had said to Philly in a complaining tone.

"Then doing nothing is the direction in which you're headed," Carpenter came back. Was he being too abrupt with Frazier? Did it take one phone call with a vacillating client to undo the calming effect of a week of R&R?

"Shit!" Frazier muttered.

This time Carpenter tried to sound soothing. "I know this is hard. And doing nothing *is* a viable option. If your father has been up to something illegal and a financial audit uncovers it, you are likely going to have a duty to disclose what your father was up to."

"You mean rat him out?"

"That's one way of putting it."

"Shit!" Frazier repeated.

"If I were in your situation," Philly interjected, "I know what I'd do. I'd go to court. And the reason is, I'd want to know as soon as possible whether everything was on the up and up with your company. This is the rest of your working life we're talking about. If there's something screwy going on with the company, don't you want to know what it is so you can evaluate your long-term options?"

Philly's brief speech reduced Frazier to silence. Carpenter silently applauded his partner. Ignorance, she was telling Frazier, wasn't always bliss.

"That's a good point," Frazier acknowledged. "Okay. Draft up a complaint that I can look at. I suppose I can change my mind and opt not to file suit."

"Correct," Carpenter affirmed. "We'll need your permission before filing suit." But Carpenter regarded Frazier as being a step away from the courthouse door. Rarely did a client let the complaint he had paid for go to waste.

When Frazier rang off, Philly and Carpenter stayed on the phone, and Philly asked: "Do you want me to do the first draft? I don't have much else going on."

"What about that fifth-grade teacher you e-mailed about?" Carpenter said.

"I haven't heard back from her."

"I was thinking of taking the first cut on Frazier's complaint," Carpenter said. "That way you'll be free to deal with the teacher when she hires you."

"Is that how we're going to decide who does what? Wishful thinking that someone will hire us?"

"That's one way to look at it," Carpenter said. "But tell you what. If that teacher doesn't hire you by noon tomorrow, you get to do the first draft of Frazier's complaint."

"Deal," Philly said.

Philly had started down the stairs for some one-on-one time with Daniel when she heard her office phone ring. She sprinted back up the stairs and was able to lift the receiver before her answering machine kicked in.

"Philomena Sullivan."

"You sound out of breath."

Philly recognized Sasha Barton's voice. "That's because I had to run up the stairs to pick up the phone."

"I was wondering whether I could swing by your house tonight after dinner. "There are a few things I want to talk over face-to-face."

Philly decided to go with her instincts. "No, you can't come by after dinner. But you and Frankie can come by *for* dinner and the two of us can talk afterwards."

"If you're trying to butter me up, it's not going to work."

"Of course I'm trying to butter you up. But it's also because Daisy asked me whether Frankie was ever going to come over to play again. I'd like to tell her yes."

"No fair playing the kids card."

"Who said life was fair? What's it going to be?"

"What time do you eat?"

Raul had added a card table to the dining room table and that's where the kids were seated, their heads barely over the tabletop even with the aid of thick phone books for Frankie and Daisy and a booster seat for Rosalind. Daniel was in his infant seat placed on the dining room table within Philly's reach.

Daisy was jabbering, Rosalind was responding with her own language that only Daisy seemed to understand, and Frankie was silent, shifting his attention back and forth from his seat mates to the grownups. Frankie didn't seem nervous about being thrown into a new environment but he was taking his time, checking things out. Raul had made spaghetti and meatballs which Daisy and Rosalind treated as finger food. The girls slurped up long strands of spaghetti and giggled at the noises and splatters of tomato sauce. When Frankie joined in the slurping and giggling, Philly knew that he felt at home.

"This is nice," Barton said. She was sitting across from Philly and Paul but had directed her remark to the entire gathering.

"You can expect the girls to lose control any minute now," Sarah said. "With your son here, they've got an audience and are going to show off."

"How did you guys end up here?" Barton asked.

Isabella fielded the question. "The short version is that Philly, Raul, and I had been living together in a nearby house, kids started coming along, we needed a bigger house, Sarah was tired of living alone, and we found this place that fit our needs."

"Isabella has left out the arm twisting that she and Philly employed," Paul joined in. "Raul and I are along for the ride."

Daniel let loose with a short, piercing shriek and then fell silent.

Philly being closest to Daniel, rose, and checked inside his diaper. "All clear," she announced.

"I don't think I'm cut out for communal living," Barton offered.

"You get used to it," Paul said. "Initially I had doubts, but it grows on you. I'm glad we're together."

"As am I," Raul added. "I too had doubts. But there is a major positive. We are all busy, so it is nice to have others around to help out."

Barton shrugged, regarded Philly. "I don't see how you can practice law in this environment. That worries me."

"Philly has not slowed down in her practice," Raul said. "I don't believe any client has complained."

"And she has partners who are very smart and very capable who help her," Paul added.

"It's nice to have my press agents living with me," Philly tried for levity.

"I don't know," Barton said.

"No more talk about my law business," Philly decreed.

"I for one would like to hear about your case," Raul directed to Barton.

"Raul!" Philly exclaimed.

"I like learning new things," Raul explained. "Plus, as you know, I sometimes come up with ideas that you and Carpenter have used."

"Don't put Ms. Barton on the spot," Philly cautioned.

"No, it's all right," Barton said, and she described what had led her to seek out a lawyer.

Isabella stared at Barton wide-eyed. "That's terrible what they did to you," she blurted out.

Paul and Raul were regarding Barton with neutral expressions.

"I bet something nasty was said on the playground that provoked the altercation," Raul said.

"You may be right," Barton replied. "But the kids aren't saying anything. Nobody wants to be seen as tattling on anyone else."

"I think Raul's right," Paul joined in. "You may need to discover who said what to whom."

"I don't understand," Isabella said. "You broke up the fight and stopped kids from being humiliated. How can they fire you for that?"

"You'd be surprised. They can fire you for anything."

Philly noted that the kids had fallen silent. Frankie looked at his mother with concern, and the two girls were staring at the grownup end of the joined tables with the same wide-eyed look Isabella had just displayed.

"Hey kids!" Sarah announced. "Who wants to help me with the cookies?"

At the word cookies, Daisy and Frankie wriggled out of their chairs and Sarah freed Rosalind from her booster chair. The children followed Sarah to the kitchen. Philly was grateful to Sarah for picking up on the kids' discomfort and diverting it.

"What do you make of the tension between the Black kids and the Hispanic kids?" Raul asked.

"It's sad to see it coming from fifth graders," Barton said. "I attribute it to each group trying to show it won't be pushed around. And in case you were wondering, it's not just the boys. The girls in each group are every bit as antagonistic to each other."

"Did the Black kids resent it when you told the Hispanic kids to sit at the table?" Isabella asked.

"Probably. I think I alienated both groups by making the main protagonists shake hands."

"Do you want to keep teaching at Parker Hill?" Paul asked.

"Yes. It's a challenge and there are probably easier assignments. But I don't like being forced out. If I leave, I want it to be on my own terms."

"Cookies are almost ready!" Sarah alerted from the kitchen.

"Do you want to come up to my office so we can chat?" Philly asked Barton.

"That's not necessary. You're hired. The teachers' union has to approve but that's not going to be a problem."

"Excellent," Philly said, trying not to betray surprise at the sudden decision. "I'll send you an engagement letter in the morning."

"Here we come!" Sarah called out.

Each kid solemnly carried a plate of cookies, walking slowly, eyeing the held plate as if willing it not to drop. Sarah had given Rosalind a small plate with just three cookies. The kids' procession was according to age, Frankie leading, Rosalind bringing up the rear. Barton watched the kids advance, smiling for the first time since entering the house.

"Great job, kids!" Sarah exclaimed after the plates made it to the grownup table. "Time for dessert."

February

From Flash's Playlist

"I Love It (I Don't Care)"

Icona Pop

9

Rachel had insisted that Jane Snelling meet with her in the war room citing the need for privacy and confidentiality. Rachel's review of the Sloan-Webster placement office documents and Ralph Cray's memo following his interview with Snelling were discouraging: Sloan-Webster had not sent questionnaires to graduates to track their employment activities; Snelling had established no ties with hiring partners at either local or out-of-state law firms; when requested by law firms for information, Snelling had simply mailed out copies of Sloan-Webster promotional materials; and the law school's website contained only a one-page general description of the placement office that included a statement that job opportunities coming to the attention of the office would be posted on the placement office bulletin board. Therefore, a graduate could only get job opportunity information by actually visiting the placement office in person.

On the plus side, if you could call it that, none of the law school's promotional materials claimed that the placement office was of high quality or touted the law school's ability to place graduates in legal positions. Dean Martin had been correct: the only reference to the placement office in the law school's promotional materials had identified the office as available to try to answer students' placement questions.

Snelling must have been aware of the placement department's shortcomings for when the war room door closed behind them, she reacted as if a bolt had been shot in a jail door. She was a stout, middle-aged woman with a phlegmatic demeanor. Ralph Cray sensed that Snelling was more interested in performing secretarial duties for the dean than in working on placement office matters so she consistently put placement matters on the back burner where they usually remained. Now it was Rachel's turn to interview the woman.

"About how much of your time is taken up with the placement office?" Rachel asked.

Snelling shifted awkwardly in her chair. "It's supposed to be half my time but it's actually much less. Maybe twenty-five percent."

"How long have you been in charge of the placement office?"

"It's now about six years."

"Did you have any placement office training?"

"Not really. I followed around the person I replaced so I could get an idea what the job entailed."

"Since taking on the placement office, have you done anything to learn more about what makes a good placement office?"

"You mean like taking a course?"

"Yes. Like how to write a resumé or use the web to make contacts, things like that."

"No," Snelling replied, not having to think about her answer.

"Have you received any complaints about how the placement office is run or about how effective the office is?"

Snelling colored slightly. "There have been times when students have called me useless."

"Do you agree with that assessment?"

Snelling straightened in her chair. "I certainly do not."

"What did you understand these students to mean when they called you useless?"

"I guess they expected me to find them jobs, which, as far as I'm concerned, is *not* my job."

"Whose job is it?"

"The students."

Rachel envisioned Blaisedell arguing to a judge or jury that Sloan-Webster should have stated in its promotional materials that law school graduates were on their own when it came to finding a law-related job.

"Can you recall any instance in which you helped a student find a job?"

Snelling chewed at her lower lip. "Not really."

Did you ever check out any other law school's placement office either online or in person?"

"No."

"How have your performance reviews been?"

Snelling bristled at the question. "What does that have to do with anything?"

"It may come up," Rachel said blandly, knowing that were she in Blaisedell's position, she would raise the subject.

"They've all been satisfactory."

"Were you ever told that you needed to do more in connection with your placement office responsibilities?"

"No."

"Were you ever at a meeting where anyone raised the subject of students needing to obtain law-related jobs if the law school were to prosper?"

"I don't recall anything like that."

"You're aware of the lawsuit against the law school, correct?"

"Yes."

"Since the lawsuit, has there been any discussion about changing how the placement office operates?"

Snelling's expression turned indignant. "Not with me," she said.

Rachel consulted her list for this meeting. Given Snelling's previous responses to questions, she was able to mentally cross off most of the remaining items.

"Do you have any recollection of meeting with any of the students who are suing the law school?"

"No."

"How frequently do students contact you about placement matters?"

"I get very few inquiries. Maybe a half dozen per week."

"Do you keep a record of those inquiries?"

"Nothing formal. I may jot down a note while listening to a student. Any notes I took would be in a miscellaneous file."

"When you're on vacation or out of the office, who deals with placement matters?"

"That would be Margo Kilmer, Dean Martin's other administrative assistant."

Rachel studied her notes from this meeting. As far as she could tell, the placement office *was* useless.

"Thank you for meeting with me. I appreciate your help."

Rachel suppressed a smile at the speed with which Snelling rose and bolted from the war room. But her smile faded quickly as she envisioned the debacle of Snelling being deposed, much less being examined in court.

This afternoon, June was in charge of Sarah's babysitting duties. The teenager was helping the little girls don snowsuits, a challenging task in the case of a squirming and wriggling Rosalind. Philly marveled at June's patience. "You really like doing this, don't you?" she said.

"Yeah," June replied. "Hold still. We're almost done."

"What are you interested in at school?" Despite her piercings and wild hair, it would probably turn out that June liked something tame like history.

"English and art," June said. "They're my favorites."

"When do we get to see your artwork?"

"Next time I come I'll bring my sketch pad."

"What's the story with your friend, Cassie? She hasn't come back here."

"She quit. She said she didn't like babysitting."

"Do you sit for anyone else?"

"A few families. But I like it here best."

"I'll take that as a compliment. I know Sarah appreciates your filling in for her. You know we're going to pay you whenever that happens."

"I know. I could use the money."

"What are you going to spend it on?"

"Drawing lessons. My folks think it's a waste of time and won't help me. Okay, I think we're all set to go."

"Bathroom," Daisy announced, and looked toward June to undo the zipper on her snowsuit."

"Do you go to school with both Black kids and Hispanic kids?" Philly asked June once Daisy was freed from her snowsuit and had run off.

"Yeah."

"How do those kids get along?"

Rosalind was standing by the front door still squirming. "We have to wait for Daisy," June told her. "She'll be back in a minute." June unzipped Rosalind's snowsuit. "They get along pretty good."

"I was wondering because I've got this case I'm working on where Black kids and Hispanic kids in the fifth grade don't get along."

"Why's that?"

"I don't really know."

"One of my best friends at school, Naomi, is Black," June said. "She's good friends with an Hispanic girl. There was one time when the three of us were hanging out and the two of them were joking about how they were always fighting and didn't like each other when they were in fifth grade. So I asked them why, and Naomi said that in fifth grade they were the oldest kids in the school and each of the groups was trying to be the boss. But when they moved to sixth grade in middle school, they were the youngest kids in the school and got picked on. So they started to stick together more and found out they liked each other."

Daisy raced into the front entryway and June soon had her snowsuit back on her. "I'm ready," Daisy announced.

June re-zipped Rosalind's jacket and opened the front door. "See you."

Philly retreated to the kitchen, found a Post-it pad and jotted down a note: *5th Grade.* Under those words she wrote: *Hispanic parents petition for Barton to come back.* She wondered about the two boys involved in the altercation and what their parents were like. She had the beginnings of an idea and if it came to fruition, June would share in the credit.

Talking to Frank on the phone, Simon had to struggle to not immediately announce that he had just run a mile earlier in the evening. Well, maybe run wasn't the operative word. Jog was more accurate. Still, he had gone around the track four times without stopping at a pace faster than a walk. Frank would faint if he knew.

"I think it's great another law school hired you," Frank was saying. "Maybe you'll be the go-to guy when a law school gets sued."

The clear-headed calm Simon had felt after his run began evaporating as he thought about the Sloan-Webster case. "This is going to be a much harder case to win. The client really didn't do anything proactive to help graduates find legal jobs."

"What did the law school say it would do?"

"Not much besides saying its placement office would try to answer questions."

"So how can the law school be sued for breaking promises it never made?"

"That's basically going to be the law school's defense," Simon replied. He had been thinking about whether a defendant who made no effort to do something he never promised to do was in a better or worse position than a defendant who made an effort to do something he had promised and then did it badly.

"Nobody forced any of the students to attend this law school you're defending. If they didn't like what the law school was going to do to find them a job, they should have gone elsewhere."

Simon doubted it was that simple. "I'm prepared to argue that," he acknowledged. "But I wish I had a better peg to hang my hat on."

"I thought your buddy, Carpenter, was always saying you had to play the hand you're dealt."

"He does and you do. But you don't have to like the hand."

10

The mood in the conference room was decidedly glum. Carpenter looked more sphinxlike than usual. He hadn't changed expression during the briefings provided by Simon, Rachel, and Meredith on the Sloan-Webster case, although he had to know that the young lawyers would be looking to him for some breakthrough insight as to how to win the case. And Philly hoped that the geezer *could* pull a winning strategy out of his ear because she sure as hell was out of ideas.

Carpenter shifted in his chair. His fingers fiddled with the knot of his tie. He offered up a heartfelt sigh and Philly wondered whether he was wishing he had stayed on whatever Caribbean beach he had parked his ass.

"It appears Sloan-Webster never made a false statement on placement," Carpenter said, and Philly was relieved that he had been paying attention.

"Right," Simon said. "The school's promotional materials state the placement office will *try* to answer students' questions. There's not even a statement saying that the placement office *will* answer questions, only *try* to answer them."

Philly thought of Yoda saying that there is no try, but she held that thought. While levity was needed in the conference room, she didn't want to cause any distraction during this problem-solving session.

"What each of you is saying is that the law school didn't promise to do anything about placement and didn't, in fact, do anything about placement," Carpenter followed up.

"Right," Simon repeated. "I was talking about this with Frank. He said something like how can you be sued for breaking a promise you never made? I thought that was a good way to put it."

"The law school knew that its placement office wouldn't help anyone get a job," Carpenter went on, "and the plaintiffs say the law school should have disclosed that its placement office wouldn't place anyone." Carpenter paused. "If I were arguing for the plaintiffs, I'd be claiming that the law school lied when it said it had a placement office and used the word placement to describe the office."

'Great!' Philly thought. Here was Carpenter coming up with more arguments against their client.

"But," he continued, "simply naming an office a placement office doesn't necessarily mean that the office has to place anybody. Maybe it's okay to label an office a placement office if you're upfront about saying that the office will only *try* to answer students' questions about placement."

Carpenter was clearly playing devil's advocate with himself, and Philly found the exercise helpful.

"I hate having to use a defense that goes, 'We told you we weren't going to help you and we didn't help you,'" Rachel groused.

"Basically, I think you guys have hit on the core of the law school's defense for placement issues," Carpenter said. "The law school never said or did anything that was misleading or false. Legally, that defense should carry the day, but, between us, I doubt a jury would buy into it."

Silence and frowns greeted this assessment.

"What should the law school do going forward?" Rachel asked.

"What do you mean?" Philly said.

"Well, for example, the secretary who runs the placement office doesn't do very much. Should the law school get a qualified replacement?"

"If that happens," Simon responded, "the plaintiffs will say that the school is admitting its placement office was a bust."

"I can do some research on that," Meredith offered. "There are cases on whether plaintiffs can admit into evidence remedial measures taken by a defendant *after* an accident. Isn't there a policy to exclude such things from evidence to encourage defendants to cure something that wasn't working and possibly dangerous?"

"Put that on your list," Carpenter instructed. "We all need to be refreshed on what the law is on that issue. Make this your first priority. But remember we're not dealing with an accident."

"Do we tell the law school to change its ways?" Rachel persisted.

"We don't tell them anything until Meredith reports to us," Carpenter said.

Rachel appeared unhappy at the lack of specific direction on this issue, but Philly knew that Carpenter was right. Better to know the law before advising the school on whether to beef up its placement office.

Simon spoke up. "I'm thinking we should be taking the plaintiffs' depositions as soon as we've had time to digest whatever Freedman and McCauley come up with on them."

"Why sooner as opposed to later?" Carpenter asked.

"Because I would like to know early on whether we have any way to prevent this case from becoming a class action," Simon responded.

"That makes sense," Carpenter said.

"How's it going on reviewing the student records?" Philly directed to Meredith.

"Pretty bad. It's as tedious as it was in the Spenser case. I started going through the ones assigned to me. Nothing has jumped out at me so far. My sense is that Sloan-Webster is prepared to admit anyone who has graduated from college and taken the Law School Aptitude Test. For example, they've admitted students with C averages in college and students who didn't exactly distinguish themselves on the LSAT."

"I didn't exactly distinguish myself grade-wise in college or on the LSAT," Simon revealed.

"But your application to Spenser must have given somebody a clue you were a litigator," Rachel reacted.

"Maybe," Simon said. "I did pretty well in debate in college."

"There you go," Rachel said. She paused, discomforted. "I just want to say this. I'm concerned we're on the losing side of this case. Is it just me?"

"Yeah, it's just you," Simon said and, when Rachel appeared more dejected, he added, "just kidding."

"I tend to agree with Rachel," Carpenter said. "You know how I always suggest that we figure out which side of a case we'd like to be presenting? Right now, I'm thinking I'd rather be arguing the plaintiffs' case. But we do have a defense so we're not totally out to lunch on this."

"When do we give the law school our assessment?" Rachel asked.

"Not yet," Carpenter said. "I want to think about this some more."

Daniel had been nursed and burped, and now he lay sleeping in bed beside Philly, who considered this was probably going to be the best part of her day. She liked looking at her son when he was totally zonked out, and she wondered if her own sleep was as deep. Probably not. Currently, she was fighting to stay awake instead of taking an afternoon nap. It was so tempting to close her eyes and drift off.

Philly replayed the morning meeting on the Sloan-Webster case. The law school was relatively new but even so, why had the school shown no interest in placing graduates? A new law school should be making an aggressive effort to find placements for its graduates so that it had a selling point for future admissions. Perhaps the demand for admissions was so great that Sloan-Webster didn't need to latch onto that selling point. Was there something they were missing in connection with this client?

If she could get herself out of bed, Philly knew that she needed to finish outlining the court complaint she needed to file on behalf of Sasha Barton. Then she'd have to actually draft the document.

Philly heard Daisy and Rosalind chattering away in the living room. Sarah was on duty this afternoon and Isabella was home. Daisy was now a little person. So far, the terrible twos had not been terrible but fun. With Sarah's considerable help, Daisy was becoming one of those kids who could entertain herself.

Whether it was drawing, looking at books, putting together simple puzzles, or erecting structures with building blocks, Daisy was content to play alone or with Rosalind. And Daisy rarely whined, which was a blessing.

Philly regarded her contentedness as a kind of hubris. Giving up the fight, she set her bedside alarm for thirty minutes and closed her eyes, enveloped in Daniel's slightly damp, warm scent.

11

A Company President

Drink orders had been placed and menus were being read. Carpenter felt vindicated: forget websites; a satisfied client was the best advertising a lawyer had going for him. Last year he had assisted Clyde Atkins on being bought out of a family business, and already this year, Atkins had first referred Henry Frazier to the firm and now had persuaded Jeremiah Becker to at least have lunch to see what a lawyer had to say about his problem. Carpenter was looking forward to this luncheon since it would give him a chance to get an update on how Atkins was doing. He waited until the two men had turned over their menus before asking Atkins how the buy-out had worked out.

"No regrets," Atkins said. "I've used some of the proceeds to invest as a limited partner in a green energy company that I think has potential. As I told you last year, I'm betting on climate change. It looks like we may get a cold winter, but I'm still glad to be out of the snowblower business."

Carpenter nodded to show he did remember. Last year Carpenter had pegged Atkins for around forty years old. Today, his long, wavy blond hair appeared windblown. He had dark blue eyes and a strong chin and an air of confidence that had not always been in evidence during last year's difficulties with his siblings. He still looked forty, but a much healthier and more confident forty.

"Thanks for sitting down with Jerry," Atkins said to Carpenter before nodding at his friend. "I told Jerry how much you helped me last year. You were always direct with me even though some of the things you had to say weren't pleasant to hear. Jerry's got this issue that's bugging him, and I told him to treat us to lunch to get a feel for whether he has a legal case."

"How do you know each other?" Carpenter asked Atkins.

"We sit on the board of directors of a community hospital. Since we know nothing about health care, there are times when I'm convinced we're the only ones who make sense when the board meets."

Becker's serious expression failed to lighten at Atkins' joking tone. Becker was older than Atkins, probably in his fifties, Carpenter estimated. He was a short, stocky, brown-haired man with intense, hooded, dark eyes. Carpenter was curious about Becker's potential legal problem but judged that it was important for Becker to raise the issue. So far, outside of introductions, Becker had kept silent.

The waiter's reappearance delayed the purpose of the luncheon a little longer, and when the waiter departed with their orders, it was Atkins who picked up the conversational ball.

"Jerry's the president and a major stockholder of a company that makes air-tight, lightweight, indestructible shipping containers. They started out small and became big. They've got a patent or two and, to hear Jerry tell it, the company is doing very well."

Atkins turned to Becker, but his friend remained silent. "Take it, Jerry!" Atkins prompted.

"I'm still not sure this meeting was a good idea," Becker said.

"I think it was a brilliant idea," Carpenter said. "It's not often a lawyer gets a free lunch."

Atkins laughed but Becker remained stone-faced.

"Look," Carpenter said. "If something's bugging you, as I see it you have two choices. You can let it bug you or you can see whether you can stop it from bugging you. But I can't give you a read on the second option unless you give me a few hints as to what's on your mind."

Becker sipped at his martini. Carpenter had opted for a ginger ale to ensure focus. Atkins had also gone the non-alcohol route with iced tea. Carpenter found the drink choices ironic—he and Atkins had met in a bar.

"All right," Becker said. "My company is Safe Shipping, Inc., and we do business under the name of Ship Right Specialists. We were in negotiations to sell our company. We got approached by another company that wanted to expand and thought our company was a good fit. We reached an agreement on price pretty quickly. But when it came to the details of what would happen after the acquisition, we could never get to a meeting of the minds."

"Why not?" Carpenter asked. In his experience, price was the major hurdle to get over in the sale of a business.

"The main sticking point," Becker said sourly, "was that the buyer didn't want me or any of the other owners to play a meaningful part in managing the business and in decision making after the sale. This was a point that was important to me and a bunch of the other owners, and the point was mentioned in the letter of intent we signed with the buyer. But ultimately the buyer only wanted us to serve as advisors without any real power. There were other issues. The potential buyer wanted to let some of our employees go because they thought we were overstaffed. The name of our company would disappear, too. But the big issue was not having a meaningful role after the sale."

"There was no sale, right?" Carpenter said.

"Right," Becker confirmed. "And we're all okay with that. What we're not okay with is the legal bill we received."

Carpenter's interest in Becker's story deflated. He hoped that his disappointment wasn't visible. "Who represented you and what were you charged?" he quickly asked.

"Blake, Pennington & Dwyer. We were charged one million nine hundred thousand dollars."

Carpenter had heard of the firm. It was one of those multi-state goliaths with a Boston office. "How long did the negotiations take?" he asked.

"Four months."

"What was the sale price for your business going to be?"

"Two hundred seventy-five million."

Carpenter had never entered the big leagues of business transactions. Clyde Atkins' siblings had paid $600,000 to buy Clyde out of the family business. A significant multi-million-dollar deal had never crossed his path and, if he was to be honest, such a deal would most likely be beyond his ability to close.

"So what do you think?" Becker asked.

"Give me a minute," Carpenter said. He realized that even if he analyzed copies of all the lawyer billings received by Becker, he might not be the best person to assess whether the work being billed for was reasonable. How could he tell whether a lawyer at Blake, Pennington & Dwyer had padded his or her time on complicated business issues he knew nothing about? And assuming for the moment that the lawyer bills were excessive, did he really want to take on suing a large law firm with unlimited internal resources on the issue of excessive billing?

This last thought brought Carpenter up short. He now had three partners who might have different views on whether to take a case of this kind.

"Did you sign an engagement letter?" Carpenter asked.

"We did. And yes, we agreed to be billed for services at lawyers' hourly rates, which ranged from eight hundred dollars an hour for senior partner time to three hundred dollars an hour for associate time."

Eight hundred dollars an hour! Carpenter's hourly rate had never hit half that amount. "Were you given an itemization of the time billed for?"

Becker shrugged. "I wouldn't call it an itemization. On the first page of each of the four monthly bills there was a paragraph noting the monthly total for legal services rendered. Then behind that front page there were general descriptions of the work performed, the dates the work was performed, and the hours of service broken down by partner time and associate time. But you couldn't tell what lawyer did what work or how much time any individual lawyer spent."

"Would you happen to have copies of these bills with you?"

"You're in luck," Becker said, handing over a manila envelope. "You can take a look, but I want it back before we leave."

Carpenter opened the envelope and removed a small stack of paper. The bills were in chronological order, the earliest in front. He chose the bill for the second month of services and withdrew it from the stack. The descriptions of legal services were barebones and largely uninformative. Meetings were identified as meetings with no notation as to what a meeting was about. Most entries for telephone consultations contained no description of the subject of the calls. Over the years, Carpenter had learned that clients hated to be charged for telephone consultations, so Becker's company must have been ballistic over these billing entries where it was impossible to tell who talked to whom about what.

Choosing a date of service at random, Carpenter noticed that both partners and associates were billing for meetings and telephone conferences. That probably meant that Becker's company was being billed for internal meetings and for conference calls joined in by numerous lawyers. "Did you ask for any more detail on some of these charges?"

"You bet I did," Becker answered assertively. "The senior partner in charge of our engagement said it would take some time, but he'd put something together showing the time and charges of each lawyer being billed for."

"Did you pay any of the million nine?"

"We paid an upfront retainer of three hundred thousand dollars that as far as I can tell got used up in a matter of weeks. We haven't paid anything else."

The waiter arrived with their orders. Carpenter welcomed the distraction. Until Becker obtained further backup for the Blake firm's billings, it was impossible to determine whether the firm's charges were reasonable.

"Will there be anything else?" the waiter inquired.

Becker shook his head sullenly and took another swallow from his martini.

Carpenter considered his own firm's billings. Each partner got to comment on every bill. Writing off time was commonplace because the reality was that you couldn't charge a client for all the time you spent on a matter. When it came to phone calls or meetings involving more than one of his partners, Carpenter consistently wrote off—or at least reduced—the time of any partner not taking the lead in the case. In a large firm, Carpenter understood that associates were routinely reminded to list any and all time spent on a matter, a practice which was the source of many of the wickedest lawyer jokes. Like the one about the lawyer who billed for the time he had spent dreaming about a case. Partners in a big firm could write off or write down an associate's time, but Carpenter had no clue whether it was standard practice to do so. And he suspected that in a big firm, a lawyer who participated in a conference call for one client while typing a letter for another billed each client at his full hourly rate. Given the pressure to generate hourly billings to meet a large firm's high overhead, a lawyer able to pull off a two-for-one probably had a wet dream. In contrast, overhead was negligible for Carpenter's firm. Rachel and Simon shared Philly's old office, he and Meredith occupied his office, and they had no secretary. So they didn't need to pad billings to pay for fancy accommodations.

Becker picked at his food while Atkins ate heartily. Carpenter was hungry and followed Atkins' example. Becker was plainly bothered by the legal bill his company had been hit with which probably accounted for the man's lack of appetite.

"You haven't said anything to help me," Becker directed at Carpenter.

Carpenter had just taken a bite of food and took his time chewing and swallowing. He met Becker's glower and figured now was the time to level with the guy. "In your position, I wouldn't pay anything more on the bill until I got the backup you were promised."

"I already figured that out," Becker snapped.

"Second, when you get the backup, you can show it to me if you want, but I'm probably not the guy who can give you a feel for whether you have a case. I haven't done a transaction the size of the sale you were contemplating, so I probably wouldn't appreciate the legal tasks involved."

"Great!" Becker said disgustedly. "So you can't help me."

'Why did clients actual and potential tend to jump to that conclusion,' Carpenter thought. "That's not what I said," he responded sharply. "I said I wasn't the guy who was able to tell you whether the law firm's bill was fair. But I know someone who can, a former client who is also a lawyer. If he says you have a case, I can help you by trying to win the case for you. If he says you have a case and he is willing to be an expert witness in the case, then I would say you have a reasonable shot at winning."

"Just what I need! Another fucking lawyer!"

"Actually, that is just what you need," Carpenter retorted. "I know you're angry, but you need to lose the attitude. You need to find out whether you have a case and then make the decision whether you want to throw more money at lawyers to bring the case. If your legal position is weak, you may decide to bargain with this law firm as opposed to throwing good money after bad. But if your case is strong, if the bills you received were padded, and assuming you win, there is at least one legal theory under which you could recover the additional legal fees you spend to take your case to trial."

Atkins was smiling and Carpenter thought he knew the reason. Atkins had told Becker that Carpenter would tell it like it is, and Carpenter had.

"Who is this guy you think can tell me whether I have a case?" Becker asked.

Carpenter hesitated. There was nothing to preclude Becker from cutting him out and reaching out to Harris Burton directly. Then again, Carpenter knew that after this lunch he would pick up a phone and alert Harris about the situation. "Harris Burton."

Becker's sour disposition improved instantly. "I've heard of him."

"Most people buying and selling businesses have," Carpenter said. "That's the whole point of having him on your side."

Becker rediscovered his appetite. "See if he'll meet with me," he said, digging into his lunch.

"I can do that," Carpenter said, as Atkins flashed him a wink.

Carpenter slid the envelope with lawyer bills back to Becker. Baker slid it back. "I've changed my mind. Hang on to that for the time being. It's not like I don't have other copies."

Philly had both her kids in her second-floor home office. Daisy was absorbed in a coloring book, using the extra-thick crayons in a Crayola box of eight. Her daughter was improving—most of the colors stayed on the page, and quite a few got spread across the outlined figure to be filled in. Daisy's choice of colors was creative to say the least.

Daniel was in his infant seat on her desk, his hands moving over a plastic ruler Philly had given him as a distraction. She noticed that her son's eyes were focused as he studied the object, probably trying to figure out how to get it into his mouth. The phone rang, and for once she didn't have to race to pick it up.

"Philomena Sullivan."

"This is Lauren Goldman. I represent Donald Frazier. I've just been given a copy of the complaint you've filed against him. You've asked for injunctive relief and the hearing is in seven days. I'd like to move back that hearing an extra week to ten days."

Daisy held up her drawing. The blue and green horse was eye-catching if nothing else.

"Very nice, sweetheart."

"What?"

"Sorry. I was talking to my daughter."

Daniel began to squirm and lost contact with the ruler, which slipped off his infant seat. Philly substituted a large, pink eraser. If the ruler hadn't made it into Daniel's mouth, the eraser surely would.

"Is this a bad time?"

"Yes. But there's no such thing as a good time. Does this mean your client is opposing the injunctive requests?"

"I can't tell you definitively at this time. I really haven't had a chance to get up to speed. I'd appreciate the courtesy of an extension."

Philly had located Goldman's website. She was a sole practitioner in a space-sharing arrangement in Boston several blocks away from Philly's office on Milk Street. Goldman specialized in commercial business matters and real estate law. She had been out of law school two years. Her picture showed a young woman with straight blond hair swept back, blue eyes, and a slight smile on thin lips. Donald Frazier had opted for inexperienced counsel, which often equated to inexpensive counsel. Was this a sign that Elite Scripts was, in fact, in financial trouble?

"If I agree to an extension, will you agree to enter your appearance before the court hearing?"

Goldman didn't answer right away which made Philly wonder whether Goldman had actually been retained. She wanted Goldman to be counsel of record: better a sole practitioner with limited resources than a large firm with an attorney army at the ready.

"I can't promise that," Goldman said. "I haven't finalized my engagement and until I do, I'd prefer not to enter my appearance."

Score one for honesty, Philly reflected. Goldman had probably asked for a retainer which had yet to be received. In Goldman's position, Philly wouldn't enter her appearance in the case without money in hand.

"If you enter your appearance before the currently scheduled court hearing, I'll agree to continue the hearing another ten days."

Goldman again paused. "I'll be back to you in the next several days one way or the other. Thank you for your time."

Philly extracted the eraser from Daniel's mouth and substituted his pacifier, which he promptly spit out. Freeing him from his infant seat, she held him under the arms and stood him on her desk, which won her a grin and cascades of drool.

"I think I handled that correctly, don't you?"

Daniel began to wriggle which sent more drool flying.

"You are a very funny little person."

"Look Mommy!"

Philly received the picture of a police officer and firefighter with what she hoped was the appropriate solemnity. Times had changed since she was a kid. The police officer was a woman. Daisy had colored them both brown, uniforms and all, transforming the public servants into UPS delivery people.

"Very nice, dear. Let's find Rosalind. It's time for a snack." When in doubt, eat.

12

Meredith was pleased to be with Simon and Rachel for this meeting at Sloan-Webster School of Law. Being introduced to Dean Janet Martin was a little awkward, but the dean made light of the situation saying, "I'm glad you're on our side this time around."

"We thought it was appropriate to share some of our impressions with you," Simon said, addressing Martin and Ralph Cray. "With the exception of five years of student records, we've had a chance to take an initial look at most of the documents you've assembled. In our opinion, there's some good news and some not so good news, and I'm going to start with the good news."

Meredith thought the dean and assistant dean had been bracing themselves for only bad news.

"The good news is that we cannot find any false or misleading statement that Sloan-Webster made in connection with its placement office. In the law school's promotional materials, there is a statement that the placement office will try to answer students' questions about placement. Rachel met with Ms. Snelling and as far as we can tell, she did try to answer placement questions. That doesn't mean that she succeeded very often. And based on what we've reviewed, the law school never promised it would actually place anyone. Also, Sloan-Webster never provided any information on students placed in legal positions because that kind of information wasn't maintained.

"Therefore, we don't think the law school should be held liable for any placement office misrepresentation because as far as we can tell, nothing was misrepresented."

Janet Martin nodded while Ralph Cray wrote in his notebook.

"The not so good news—the bad news, if you will—is that the placement office appears to us to have been as ineffectual as the plaintiffs claim it was. The law school doesn't seem to have made any effort to find legal placements for graduating students. The law school can claim that it never promised to do anything in that regard, but we are concerned that a jury will look unfavorably on such a defense."

Simon paused, waiting for a reaction.

"But didn't you just point out that we shouldn't be faulted for something we never said we would do?" the dean asked.

"I did," Simon acknowledged. "But that may not be enough. The plaintiffs will claim—have claimed—that the law school should have stated explicitly that its placement office was useless and wouldn't make any effort to land a graduating student a law job. If that claim makes it to a jury—and we think it might—the law school could lose."

"And," Rachel interjected, "although the plaintiffs haven't raised this claim directly, they could end up arguing that the law school mislead students by mentioning it had a placement office when it in fact had no actual, functioning, useful placement office."

The dean sighed and leaned back in her chair. Cray leveled an unfriendly stare in the direction of the three lawyers, as if the dismal state of affairs was somehow their fault.

"We need to review further why the placement office played such a limited role," Rachel said. "Surely you were aware that placement offices at the schools you compete with were far more active and better organized than yours."

The dean slumped further in her chair. "This subject does not do credit to anyone at the law school, including me. We're a relatively new law school and our focus has been on other things such as hiring a competent faculty. We dropped the ball on placement, plain and simple. I should have focused on placement over a year ago, after I had settled in. But I didn't. I've been so intent on the law school surviving that I overlooked an area that needed improvement. I think if we can survive this lawsuit, we can turn the placement office around. But I'm concerned. A significant financial recovery by the plaintiffs might make the law school's survival problematic."

Cray regarded the dean with concern.

Rachel and Simon exchanged a glance. "Have you given any thought to trying to fix the placement office starting now?" Rachel asked.

"Won't that be viewed as an admission that the placement office needed fixing?" Cray asked.

Rachel nodded in Meredith's direction and she took her cue. "There is a legal principle that provides that evidence of improvements to cure a problem, made after the problem caused someone injury, should not be used as evidence against the defendant who allegedly caused the injury. The rationale is to motivate defendants to cure problems. There would be precious little incentive to cure a problem if the cure came back to hurt the curer."

"That sounds encouraging," Dean Martin interjected.

"Yes, but there are complications. The rule is typically applied where there's a personal injury, for example an injury due to a defect in a machine. And there are a host of exceptions to the rule I just mentioned. Evidence of placement office improvements might end up before a jury under one of those exceptions. We can't predict how the evidence will unfold or what a judge may rule."

"What do you recommend?" Cray asked, and Meredith took it as a vote of confidence that Simon nodded to her to respond to the assistant dean's question.

"We recommend that the law school make whatever changes are needed to make the placement office effective. We recognize that the changes you make could come back to bite you if this case goes to trial. But the bottom line is that you do not have a functioning placement office and fixing that problem is the right thing to do." Meredith successfully fought the impulse to limn the word *right* with air quotes.

Cray wrote vigorously in his notebook before looking expectantly toward the dean. Martin straightened in her chair and it occurred to Meredith that the recommendation had somehow energized her.

"I appreciate your directness," Dean Martin said. "Ralph and I will consider your recommendation and get back to you."

"I think we've laid enough on you for the moment," Rachel said, "but I want to go back to the question I asked you to think about the last time we met. What would you consider to be a victory in this case?"

The dean flashed a rueful smile. "Survival now seems like a good result."

"We agree," Rachel responded. "What would the plaintiffs in this case consider a victory?"

"Recovering massive damages," Cray answered.

"That's probably right, too," Rachel replied. "But what happens if a massive damage award forces the law school into bankruptcy or even closure? Would that be a win for them? How do the plaintiffs benefit from proving that the law school they attended failed? The plaintiffs claim they want legal jobs. Attaining that goal becomes a lot harder if they present themselves to prospective employers as graduates of a law school that filed bankruptcy or closed its doors."

"Where are you going with this?" Cray demanded.

"We're just talking among ourselves," Simon took over. "We need to think about what kind of financial loss the law school could sustain and still survive. We need to think about if and when to raise the possibility of the law school filing for bankruptcy."

"Do you believe that the plaintiffs will try to settle the case instead of trying to get a court decision?" the dean asked.

"I do," Simon came back. "At some time before this case goes to trial, the plaintiffs *will* try to settle the case. That's a long way off but it will happen. And the sooner we start thinking about that initiative, the better."

"Your good news doesn't seem so good anymore," the dean observed.

"Oh, it's good," Simon said. "The plaintiffs will have to consider the fact that the law school never misinformed anyone about anything to do with placement. In other words, the plaintiffs have to consider that they might lose."

"You just convinced me they were going to win," Dean Martin said.

"And we might convince a jury you should win," Simon came back. "It's a game of chicken. Time will tell who backs down first."

13

Philly arrived early for the meeting with Harris Burton, who held an of counsel position at the firm where Philip, her former fiancé and Daisy's father, had served as the managing partner. Philip's name was still on the firm's letterhead and on the front door: Sizemore led the array that included four other named partners. Below his name on the firm's stationery was the year of his birth and year of his death, 2009.

"Have a seat," the receptionist said. "I'll tell Mr. Burton you're here."

"I'm early," Philly replied. "Why don't you wait until the others arrive? I've been here before and I just want to look around."

As the receptionist reached for her phone, Philly walked down the corridor to the right of the reception desk and paused outside the door to Philip's former corner office. His managing partner position had probably earned him the choicest office in the suite. Specializing in business transactions, his firm had experienced ups and downs, struggling whenever the economy tanked and transaction work dried up. The year of his death had been a particularly rocky one for the firm.

Philly looked through the glass panel adjacent to the door. Her hope for privacy was dashed when a short, dark haired man rose from behind Philip's desk, greeted her with a wave, and headed for the office door.

"You're Philly," the man greeted her upon opening the door. "I remember you from Philip's funeral. I don't have to tell you what a sad day that was. I'm Benjamin Klein. Everyone calls me Ben. I know you're here to see Harris, but why don't you join me for a moment."

Klein held his office door open and Philly entered the spacious room. As Klein settled in behind his desk, she took the offered visitor's chair. Klein's name came after Sizemore on the office door and on the firm's letterhead. The firm had often been referred to as Sizemore Klein.

"I find this a little awkward," Klein said, and Philly observed real discomfort in his eyes. "Philip didn't exactly keep you a secret but none of his partners, including me, ever got to know you. After the funeral, we worked out money issues with the lawyer hired by Philip's family. But when it came to you, I feel remiss that neither I nor my other partners ever reached out to you."

"I wouldn't worry about that," Philly said. "The truth is I wouldn't have been receptive to any overtures back then. I was going through a hard time."

"Well, I do regret it. We were so bogged down with dealing with Philip's death and the difficult business times for our firm that we lost sight of reaching out to you. When Harris said you were coming in today, it brought back to me how lacking in grace we all were. I'm truly sorry that we didn't inquire after you or see whether we could help in some way."

Philly offered up a weak smile, not knowing what to say.

"I think you know that Philip was our leader," Klein went on. "He was our managing partner, a position I reluctantly inherited. It was Philip's vision that initially brought us all together. He wanted to form a small, high quality, business firm that would attract clients because we would outwork and undersell the large firms. It wasn't always easy, as he probably told you, but his vision is still something the current partners believe in."

"This is all very kind of you," Philly said, hoping to match Klein's graciousness.

"I don't mean to pry," Klein prefaced, "but I understand you and Philip had a baby girl. How is she?"

Philly extracted her wallet from her purse and found a color photograph of Daisy. She hesitated a moment, then handed it to Klein.

Klein stared at the photograph. "It's incredible," he whispered. "Those are Philip's eyes. I can't believe it."

Philly felt herself about to tear up. People who knew Philip and saw Daisy would unfailingly remark that Daisy had Philip's eyes.

Klein returned the photograph. "I see your wedding ring. Does that mean you've married?"

Philly nodded.

"Good for you."

Klein paused and Philly noticed his eyes were wet.

"There are times when I'm working on something or dealing with our firm's administrative matters and I find myself wishing Philip were around to give me advice. Actually, it's more than that. I find myself wishing he were still in charge. You can't imagine how we all looked up to him." Klein paused, gathered himself. "I shouldn't keep you. I know you have a meeting with Harris. He speaks very highly of you and I know we have you to thank for Harris joining us. We're lucky to have him."

Klein rose and offered his hand. "I think you know your way around, so you'll forgive me if I don't see you out."

"They're waiting for you in the conference room," the receptionist said when Philly returned to the lobby. "First door on the left."

When Philly entered the conference room, Harris Burton rose to greet her, suave as always, gray hair in place, still looking spry in his seventies. He barely hesitated before administering a hug. "Wonderful seeing you again," he said with a warm smile. "I don't see any reason why I can't hug my former lawyer."

"Then Carpenter has something to look forward to," Philly said as she took her seat.

Carpenter responded with what passed for a smile on his part. The stranger in the room had to be Jeremiah Becker, and Philly introduced herself to the potential client.

"I've never been an expert witness before," Burton broke the ice.

"Let's not get ahead of ourselves," Carpenter cautioned. "First things first. You told me you had a chance to look at the billings and the backup that just came in. I'd like to hear your general impressions."

"The backup to the originally submitted bills was sketchy," Burton began. "There was very little descriptive support for some of the charges. The additional backup provided greater detail on work performed by individual lawyers." Burton paused. "As to the reasonableness of the charges, my impression is that the law firm had too many lawyers working on the matter. That's just my impression, which may be subjective. I can only tell you that in my former firm, we would not have assigned the number of lawyers to your transaction that you were billed for. And here in my new firm, we don't even have the number of lawyers that were assigned to your matter."

Carpenter emitted a snort. "Big firms!" he muttered.

Burton laughed. "You haven't changed. You have this ingrained antipathy to large law firms that I think is unfair. My former firm was a large firm, and we took care to ensure that any bill that went out was reviewed for reasonableness by a partner who was not assigned to the case. We routinely wrote off or wrote down excessive or non-productive time, and I, for one, prided myself on providing detailed descriptions of the time that was being billed for. The same procedures are followed here."

Carpenter looked unconvinced that large law firms had any redeeming value. Philly sometimes wondered whether his instinctual dislike of large firms had to do with the fact that he was constantly butting heads with them in litigation and resented the resources they could throw at a case.

"What would your former firm have charged?" Becker spoke up.

"I can't answer that without seeing the work product that Blake, Pennington & Dwyer produced. Do you have copies of documents they prepared?"

"I printed out and saved everything they sent me. It's about two feet of paper. There were a lot of drafts of a non-disclosure and confidentiality agreement, and the letter of intent we signed. The buyer produced the initial draft of a purchase and sales agreement and Blake Pennington's initial comments doubled the size of that document. And as I said, the purchase and sales agreement never got signed."

"What was your view of the firm's legal work?" Philly asked.

Becker frowned. There was a combative air about the man, and Philly hadn't decided whether it was a help or a hindrance.

"It seemed okay to me," Becker said grudgingly. "I'm no expert but I felt they were looking out for my company's interests."

There was a long silence before Carpenter turned to Burton and focused on the purpose of this meeting. "If you look at the work product and conclude charges were excessive, is that something you would testify to as an expert witness?"

Burton sighed. "To be truthful, I have an aversion to questioning the billings of a fellow lawyer or another law firm. You may remember that I'm conflict averse. I wanted to say that up front." Burton paused. "But I've talked it over with the partners here, and they are okay with me being an expert witness. This would be something new for me, and I find that as I get older, new experiences seem more inviting. The bottom line is that I would testify if, after reviewing everything, I was of the opinion you were overcharged."

Burton's last remark was directed at Becker, who gave nothing away about his reaction to Burton's answer.

"What would you charge?" Becker asked Burton.

"You mentioned two feet of paper. Maybe I should charge by the inch. I'd estimate about five thousand dollars to review everything and provide you with a summary report."

Again, Becker showed no reaction to the figure.

"I recommend that you arrange for Mr. Burton to be retained," Carpenter said.

"That's not a problem. I'll send him a letter."

"Slow down," Carpenter cautioned. "When it comes to experts, it's preferable that your counsel engage any expert. The reason is that if a lawyer engages the expert, the discussions between the lawyer and expert are privileged. If you engage the expert, anything you and the expert say to each other can be discovered by Blake, Pennington & Dwyer."

"Wait a minute! Are you saying I've got to throw money around and hire Burton and your firm before I talk with the Blake people?"

"My recommendation is that you hire a lawyer and have the lawyer engage Harris. I'd like it if you engaged our firm, but you're under no obligation to do so."

"Jesus!" Becker muttered. "If I hire you, I suppose you'll hit me up for a retainer."

"Yes, a modest one."

"What's a modest retainer?"

"Five thousand," Carpenter replied.

"And I suppose Mr. Burton will want a retainer."

"The five thousand I estimated earlier sounds about right," Burton joined in.

"Jesus!"

Philly sympathized with Becker. He was facing more lawyer fees to contest the lawyer fee he found unfair. On the other hand, the ten thousand dollars being proposed now was nothing compared to the million nine that Becker's firm was billed.

"Screw it," Becker said. "I'll have the papers sent over to you," he gestured to Burton before turning to Carpenter. "And I'll send you a check for ten thousand dollars and you can engage Mr. Burton with half." With that, Baker rose to leave.

Carpenter saw to Becker's departure which gave Philly a brief time alone with Burton.

"It's got to be bittersweet returning here," Burton said.

"You don't know the half of it. I just had an emotional meeting with Ben Klein who now has Philip's office. I never got to know him before. We chatted for maybe ten minutes and it left me drained."

"Ben's a terrific guy," Burton said. "I still don't know how the two of us held things together after Philip died. Philip was the person I typically dealt with here. But probably to his own amazement, Ben rose to the occasion and stepped in. He hasn't exactly filled Philip's shoes, but he's done well. Currently, we're okay. It's been quite a ride."

Klein felt guilty about not reaching out to her, but Philly felt guilty, too. She hadn't contacted Harris Burton or anyone else at Philip's old firm. She had been overwhelmed by grief, her pregnancy, and the demands of her own practice.

"I take it you have no plans to slow down," Philly said.

"I make promises to slow down and proceed to break them. I don't put in the hours I used to. But I want this firm to succeed and I still enjoy the work. Sometimes I think I'll end up being one of those guys who dies at his desk."

"I know one of those guys," Philly said, thinking of Carpenter.

"Yes, you do. How are *you* doing?"

"Well. I'm married and gave birth to a boy last September. As you know, Carpenter and I have taken on two partners and that's worked out very well."

Burton fell silent, regarding her solemnly, and Philly remembered what a gentleman he was. He had challenged his former firm's mandatory age seventy retirement policy and had lost his case. Then, at her urging, he had contacted Philip and had joined Philip's firm in an atypical "of counsel" position. Usually a lawyer serving as of counsel to a firm didn't actively manage the firm's direction. But Burton was active in firm management. Philip had found his mentoring to be just what the doctor ordered for the young lawyers in his firm.

"Here's a thought," Burton said. "Have you ever thought of merging with a firm such as ours?"

Philly's mouth dropped open just as Carpenter reentered the room. "What?" Carpenter said.

Philly looked at him. "You don't want to know."

Philly slid under the comforter to Paul's side of the bed and nestled against him. It was bitterly cold outside and one of the many things Paul was good for was a source of heat.

"You've seemed preoccupied this evening," Paul said. "Everything okay?"

"It's been a draining day," Philly responded. "I had a meeting at Philip's old firm, and it brought back some very sad memories."

"That must have been tough."

"Days go by when I don't give Philip a thought, which is seriously fucked up. Then I end up spending most of this morning having people tell me how much Philip meant to them, and I want to scream at what a waste his death was."

"He's always seemed to me to be someone larger than life," Paul confessed. "It's okay to miss him and be angry. I told you I've felt guilty meeting you under those lousy circumstances. I think the best way to honor him is to soldier on. Daisy is his legacy which means his legacy isn't over. I think you know he'd be enormously proud of you."

Philly couldn't hold back her tears, and Paul drew her close. He had a sixth sense about when to shut up and she was grateful for his silence, for his simply holding her. It was at times like this that she wanted a drink, wanted to wash away the sadness that had snuck up on her today and underscored her fragility.

"Just remember you've got me, and you've got the kids," Paul whispered. "You're never in this alone."

Philly cried herself out, then closed her eyes. Her last coherent thought was that she needed to call her AA sponsor next morning.

14

Philly slid into the booth across the table from Melanie in the Brighton breakfast diner, happy to be out of the raw February wind and grateful for the coffee Melanie had ordered for her. "You look good," she said. Melanie had gained weight and had an air of confidence that had never shown itself in the early years of their relationship in AA.

"Thanks. I've been thinking about what you said on the phone. I have some thoughts. You first admitted that you had a drinking problem when you were dealing with Daisy's pregnancy on your own. I think going back to Philip's law office triggered memories of that very difficult time for you. I think you associate that difficult time with drinking."

Philly couldn't find fault with her sponsor's analysis.

"Are you still feeling a desire to have a drink?" Melanie asked.

"A little. It's not as strong this morning."

"Good. I think you need to remember that you're not alone like you were back then."

"That's what Paul said last night."

"Then Paul is a very wise man," Melanie said solemnly. "You have him, and your children, and you also have me."

Philly recalled how she had looked down on Melanie early on in their relationship. Her sponsor was not a college graduate and, for a time, had seemed incapable of offering meaningful advice and comfort. But Melanie had grown. Recently, she had been able to both advise and encourage Philly and had taken charge of their discussions when Philly needed more than her own strength. This morning, Philly felt better after listening to her.

"I think you're going to be all right," Melanie said. "You just went through an experience that dragged up old memories. If you go back again to Philip's law firm, you won't be blindsided in quite the same way. I think you'll be better prepared to face them. But if anything bothers you, please call me at once. Drinking is not the answer for you."

Philly nodded. "How many other people are you sponsoring?" she asked.

"I'm up to five. Charlie said I'm doing really well, that I've got a knack for this."

The leader of their AA meetings didn't give praise undeservedly. It struck Philly that Melanie *did* have a knack for sponsoring. "I think Charlie's right," she said.

Melanie colored. "Thanks. I think I've finally found something I'm really good at. This may sound stupid, but I think the sponsoring is why I've gained weight. I'm not so nervous about everything anymore. When I've helped someone, it makes me feel good."

"Well, you sure as hell just helped me."

Daniel was napping and Philly took charge of lunch for the girls after dismissing Sarah. Philly was struck by how Daisy and Rosalind ate anything. Today's fare consisted of small squares of whole wheat bread smeared with hummus, narrow slices of Italian cheese, and cut up lettuce and tomatoes. Before starting their finger food, each girl had knocked off half of a small, sour kosher pickle.

When Philly's cell phone sounded, she wiped her hands on her jeans. "Hello."

"It's me. What did you make of Harris bringing up a merger?"

Philly was surprised that Carpenter had waited until today to ask his question. Philly had cut out of the meeting after Burton had raised the issue in Carpenter's presence. She remembered the geezer's expression—a slight scowl, a determined set to his jaw, a hard stare. "It surprised me."

"It surprised me, too. We have to mention it to Simon and Rachel."

Philly knew that Carpenter wanted to sound her out before that happened. "My first reaction was to dismiss the idea out of hand. The more I thought about it, the more I thought it was better to keep an open mind."

"You know how much I like change," Carpenter said, and Philly laughed. His dislike of change and surprises had been a constant over the years.

"Maybe their firm is referring out a lot of litigation, and they think it would be to their advantage to bring it in-house."

"I thought of that," Carpenter said "That might be behind Harris' overture. But my instincts tell me that a small law firm should have a single purpose. A firm that did both litigation and transactions would have two independent fiefdoms. I don't see what, or how, they would share, so I don't see the point of merging."

Carpenter's instincts were often spot-on. But Philly reasoned that Harris Burton had to have thought through a plan. "I think we should ask Harris how he sees a merger working before we involve Simon and Rachel."

"So you want to follow up with him?"

"I want to better understand his thinking."

"Jesus!"

"Girls! No throwing food!"

"Am I interrupting something?"

"How'd you guess?"

Maxine sipped at her wine and studied Carpenter across the kitchen table. He had uncapped a second beer which was a reliable indicator that something out of the ordinary was bugging him. Plus, his expression was gloomier than usual so whatever was on his mind probably had nothing to do with the usual things he fretted about: work, his cancer, old age. The week they had spent in the Caribbean at the start of the year had mellowed them both out but Maxine had known the change would be fleeting in Carpenter's case. And sure enough, once he'd gotten back in the swing of work, it was as if the week's calming respite never happened. "What's on your mind?" she asked.

"Damn Harris Burton!" Carpenter muttered.

"You told me you like him."

"I do like him. I just wish he'd mind his own business."

"What are you talking about?"

"He brought up the idea of our firm merging with his. That's what I'm talking about. And Philly wants to hear him out, for Christ's sake."

Maxine worked at maintaining a serious expression. Carpenter's decision to start a firm with Philly, Simon, and Rachel had been a cosmic shift in his universe, and he was still trying to get used to his new arrangement. Coming a little over a year after starting the new firm, the idea of merging with another firm had probably shorted most of his circuits. "Do Simon and Rachel know?"

"Philly wants to hear more from Harris before we tell them."

"That makes sense," Maxine said. "For the moment, the two of you are the senior partners."

"Can you picture me with a bunch of transaction guys?"

"There was a time when I couldn't picture you in a firm with Philly, Simon, Rachel or anyone else. Yet, here you are, and you're better off because of it. Admit it."

Carpenter grunted something unintelligible which Maxine accepted as the only admission she was going to get from him. He sucked down more beer and his scowl deepened.

"Maybe Harris is turning down a lot of litigation," Maxine offered.

"That's what Philly and I are guessing. If so, he hasn't sent any of it our way."

"Maybe his clients wouldn't be comfortable with a firm as small as yours. Maybe these same clients would be comfortable if his firm had their own litigators so that Burton and his crew would be around."

"Maybe pigs will learn to fucking fly!"

Maxine decided to let Carpenter vent. She had learned to live with his sour moods. He was a quintessentially grumpy old man and she loved him enough to put up with his disposition. And as long as he was fretting, she might as well give him something else to stew over.

"If you ever did hook up with Burton's firm, do you think you'd have the need for someone involved with schools and education?"

Carpenter's jaw dropped in the classic surprise manner and Maxine could no longer keep a straight face.

"What the hell are you talking about?" Carpenter demanded.

"I'm bored. I'm rethinking retirement."

"Bored?"

"Not bored exactly. More like wanting a little more intensity and aggravation in my life. Not that you don't provide a fair share of that."

"Jesus," Carpenter muttered.

"It's something I'm seriously thinking about," Maxine explained.

"I thought you burned your old professional bridges."

"I did. I'm thinking of going over to the other side: representing students and their parents."

"I didn't see this coming," Carpenter said gloomily.

"Neither did I."

Carpenter sucked down the rest of his beer. Maxine foresaw it would be a three-beer night.

15

Meredith had never heard of the lawyer who was calling her, but she had a good idea who he was representing.

"This is John Pace. I'm an attorney in Worcester and I represent Caryn Wheelwright. Do you have a moment?"

Meredith was prepared to seize any moment that would delay today's visit to the war room to review Sloan-Webster student records. "I do."

"What will it take to make this case go away?"

Meredith had not mentioned settlement to Noreen Clark and had no clue what her client might be thinking in that regard. "I suspect an obscene amount of money," she replied.

"Give me a ballpark," Pace requested.

"No." Unless Clark gave her different instructions, she was determined to have Pace and his client make the first move.

"Do you have a demand figure?"

"No."

Pace fell silent and Meredith began to google him. For good reason, Caryn Wheelwright had not hired the firm she worked for to represent her. Pace was a fifth-year associate in a twenty-lawyer law firm located in downtown Worcester. The firm specialized in litigation. The specific information about Pace gave no indication whether he had ever tried a case. If he hadn't tried a case, that would make them even. His website photograph showed a dark-eyed young man wearing modern-styled thin glasses and an earnest expression.

"Are you willing to go back to your client and then present me with a demand figure?"

"No."

"Is your client willing to settle the case?"

"I don't know."

"Are you willing to circle back to your client and let me know if settlement is a possibility?"

Meredith decided to maintain a hard line. "It's possible to settle any case. I intend to report this call to Ms. Clark. If your client wishes to present a specific dollar proposal, of course I'll relay the figure to Ms. Clark."

"If the case can be settled, I think it makes sense to do so at the outset," Pace said. "That would avoid excessive legal fees on both sides."

"Yes, it would."

"I'm assuming that when it comes to settlement, you're not prepared to make the first move.

Meredith decided to throw Pace a bone. "That's a reasonable working assumption."

"Get dressed," Dr. Specter directed, and Carpenter was only too happy to oblige. He dreaded the checkup sessions with his oncologist, certain that if he were feeling good, the physician's news would be bad.

Specter sat down before the computer in the examining room and began typing away. "Is it my imagination or are you crankier than usual?" she asked, without taking her eyes off the monitor.

"How would you rate my usual crankiness?"

"On a scale of one to ten with ten being the crankiest, I would say you typically turn up at seven point five. This morning you're at least a nine."

"I've got a lot on my mind."

"Don't we all."

Carpenter was quickly reminded that Specter had a bedside manner as unsympathetic as his own.

"There we go," Specter said as she exited from Carpenter's medical record. "You're now officially updated in our system. The news is all good. You remain stable. Your white blood cell count remains in a tight range with no sign of a sudden spike. Your lymph nodes are normal. Your weight is about where it should be. Putting aside your grouchiness, you *look* good. Any questions?"

Carpenter couldn't resist asking the question he had been debating whether to ask if nothing untoward turned up at this examination. "I've been stable for a while now," he said. "Does that mean I have a chance of beating this thing?"

Specter seemed poised to reply and then appeared to check herself. Carpenter had yet to get a complete read on his young, blond physician whose quirky personality was at times as prickly as his.

"We can't predict the direction that chronic lymphocytic leukemia will take. You already know that. It's encouraging that you've stayed stable. You should be heartened by these stable results. That doesn't mean you should read more into the results than is there. Keep doing what you're doing. I told you I believe that exercise is important, and you've kept that up. Don't stop. You said your sex life has improved with Viagra. Don't stop having sex." Specter paused. "Have I answered your question?"

"Yeah," Carpenter groused.

"So what the hell is bugging you?"

"Possible changes at my law firm. My significant other is thinking of going back to work instead of retiring. It just seems like a lot of little annoying things are surfacing at the same time."

Specter studied him. Carpenter willed himself not to look away. Specter had a way of looking at you that made you think she could see through any bullshit you'd direct her way.

"None of those things sounds little to me," Specter said. "Each item you mentioned has stress associated with it. Have you ever meditated?"

Carpenter shook his head. Who the hell had time to meditate? The last thing he needed in his life right now was touchy-feely nonsense that would further stress him out. Although, to be fair, in the past he had tried relaxation exercises.

"Give me your e-mail address. I'm going to send you something and I want you to read it."

Carpenter provided his e-mail address with misgivings.

"I'm serious," Specter said. "I want you to read what I'm going to send you and call me. And be advised that when you do call me, there's going to be a pop quiz."

"Why don't you try it," Maxine said, sipping at her wine.

Carpenter took a greedy gulp of beer. The "it" was meditation, and now he was kicking himself for mentioning Dr. Specter's recommendation. He could see this discussion morphing into one of those give-and-takes where Maxine talked sense to him, and he responded with a two-year old's stock response of no.

"Just the thought of meditation turns me off," Carpenter said. "Right now, I just don't have the patience."

"That's pretty lame," Maxine fired back. "When we first met, you were using relaxation techniques that were a lot like meditation. Remember?"

Carpenter muttered under his breath. Maxine had the memory of a goddamn elephant.

"What?" Maxine prompted.

"Yeah, I remember," Carpenter owned up. He had tried various visualization exercises to slow down, calm down. The damn things worked. He remembered his favorite: closing his eyes, shutting out all extraneous thoughts and picturing an array of numbers starting with 100, and imagining the numbers disappearing, one by one. The best he had done was reach somewhere in the 70's before thoughts of work intruded.

"Why did you stop?" Maxine asked, genuinely curious.

"Damned if I know." At the moment, he couldn't recall precisely why he had started on the number exercises or why he had given them up.

"I think you should listen to Dr. Specter on this," Maxine persisted. "You've described her as an odd duck, but she's steered you right so far. The exercising she recommended has been good for you. You're probably too pigheaded to admit it, but I think you enjoy going to the gym."

"The gym's all right," Carpenter said, and this caused both of them to laugh out loud. Saying the gym was all right was the closest he would come to admitting he liked going there.

"It's more than all right," Maxine kept up her momentum. "We both know that. So tomorrow, you need to finish going over what Specter sent you and call her back about what she wants you to do."

'Game, set, and match,' Carpenter thought.

16

Philly planned to use her free time this morning to draft a court complaint for Sasha Barton. For the moment, she didn't have to worry about Henry Frazier's case. Lauren Goldman had filed her appearance on behalf of Donald Frazier and therefore was entitled to extra time to answer Henry Frazier's complaint and to extra time before there was a court hearing.

Philly had outlined the claims she would make on behalf of Barton. She turned her attention to her computer monitor, typed and centered the word **Complaint**. For a moment she suffered writer's block. Her thoughts of Barton's narrative were jumbled. Begin with what the case is about, she heard Carpenter advising. She began to type.

> *"This is a legal action for damages and injunctive relief brought by an elementary school teacher who was illegally fired for successfully breaking up an altercation among fifth grade students and for successfully intervening to protect fifth graders from the abusive and humiliating punishment of being forced to eat their lunch off the school cafeteria floor. Her firing also stemmed from her advising the abused students to report the abusive treatment to their parents."*

Philly reread what she had written. It was a start, and she could now visualize a path to the finish. She would raise a breach of contract claim on Barton's behalf and also throw in a claim that Barton's firing was against public policy because her termination resulted from helping students who were being treated abusively. Repeatedly using the phrase *abusive treatment* was necessary to show Barton in a sympathetic, courageous light. If the complaint survived a motion to dismiss, Philly would depose Samuel Clarke, the principal who had fired Barton. If Clarke had a justification for making students eat lunch on the floor, Philly wanted to hear it.

"What amount would you recommend I accept?" Noreen Clark asked.

Meredith still hadn't come to grips with how she would answer Clark's predictable question. She had conveyed to Clark how important it was for Caryn Wheelwright to make the first move when it came to broaching a settlement figure. But now, understandably, Clark wanted an idea of what would be a suitable financial settlement. Meredith didn't want to admit ignorance or display uncertainty, but on this occasion, she believed she had no choice.

"I'm not sure. I'm interested in seeing what figure, if any, Wheelwright comes up with. I understand that what she puts on the table shouldn't necessarily influence what I think is fair. But if she offers an amount, it may affect my thinking."

"Wouldn't she offer something low to start off?" Clark followed up.

"Probably. We need to be patient and see what she comes back with."

"I really don't want this to drag out," Clark said. "I sort of had mixed feelings about bringing suit against her personally, what with the big payoff from Sloan-Webster."

"They're really two different matters. Winning something from the law school doesn't address Wheelwright's behavior. If she makes a settlement proposal, you can always make the case go away by accepting it even if the proposal is low. But this may be one of those cases where going to trial makes sense as a way of getting the biggest recovery. Remember, Wheelwright denied under oath that you told her the article you submitted for publication was not a final draft. Sloan-Webster settled with you because you were able to recover a more complete draft and show that you did in fact obtain citations for your final document. That's why Sloan-Webster settled with you. The law school knew that you hadn't plagiarized anything. But it was Wheelwright who made the plagiarism allegation in the first place—one she knew was false. And Wheelwright lied under oath. A jury might sock it to her for trying to ruin you."

"I really don't want to go through a trial. I've got money in the bank from the settlement. I like my job. Everyone at my firm is nice. I'm back with my old boyfriend, Kevin, who you met last year and who testified for me, and we're doing well. I know I should feel vengeful against Wheelwright, but I don't. And besides, even if a jury were to give me a large damage award, what makes you think Wheelwright can pay it?"

Meredith sympathized up to a point. After all, she herself had accepted a settlement from her former law firm rather than litigate over her improper firing. But in this instance, she didn't understand Clark's seeming willingness to throw in the towel so soon.

"We need to take this one step at a time. During discovery we'll find out what assets she has. If she has few assets, then that's going to play a part in figuring out what a proper settlement might be. I reported to you what Wheelwright's lawyer said to me, and the ball is in his court on getting back to me."

Clark sighed as if she had the weight of the world on her shoulders. "Okay, get back to me if you hear anything new."

Meredith put down her phone and wondered what she was missing. As a plaintiff, Clark had a strong case on liability. Why would she not be pressing the matter? Maybe Carpenter had some ideas.

Simon checked the stopwatch Josh had given him. Eighteen minutes. He'd made it around the quarter-mile oval eight times, so that meant he was master of the nine-minute mile. It was mind boggling to think that highly trained athletes could knock off mile after mile at a four-minutes-plus pace. And then there were those Africans who would sprint the final miles of marathons. Simon considered that for him, running two miles in eighteen minutes might be the equivalent of some tall, skinny Kenyan running two miles in eight minutes. Was that a farfetched comparison? Maybe not. A Kenyan didn't have to run in slush.

Simon didn't want to embarrass himself the first time he went running with Frank. Frank could probably run a mile in six or seven minutes, and Simon didn't want to hold him back excessively. Was lowering his time even possible? The eighteen minutes had left him spent. Simon didn't want to be a pest, but he saw no alternative to calling Josh for advice.

And then there was the subject of his recent purchase. Would he ever crack the cover of *Football for Dummies*? Well, if he did, at least it would be inside.

17

Meredith loved waking up at Flash's place. He rented the top floor of a three-story house in East Cambridge that had a separate entrance and consisted of a single spacious living area that flowed from kitchen to dining area to work area to bedroom with no dividers. The only door in the unit was to the bathroom adjacent to the kitchen. If you woke in the night and needed to use the bathroom, you had to navigate past a good-sized table and a minefield of computers, computer parts, wires, nuts, bolts, tools, and soldering equipment littering the floor area. Paradoxically, this is what Meredith liked about Flash's unit—the mess and clutter that was so unlike her own orderly one-bedroom apartment where everything had its place and dust bunnies had a half-life measured in seconds. Flash had no trouble with nighttime maneuvering, but he had mercifully placed a flashlight by her side of the bed in case she needed to use the bathroom. This precaution had probably spared her a number of nasty bumps and bruises. Flash's bed had taken some getting used to—a king sized mattress laid on the floor with the head flush against the wall farthest from the kitchen. Being so close to the floor made getting out of bed awkward; Meredith had never appreciated how accustomed she had grown to sitting up while swinging her feet down to the floor.

Waking up this morning, Meredith found Flash staring at her. He consistently woke first, and sometimes she wondered whether he slept at all. Today he was favoring her with a serious, appraising gaze that she found impossible to read. His amused look was nowhere in evidence. "What?" she said.

"My hair," Flash said, reaching behind his head and moving his ponytail where it rested on a naked shoulder.

"What about your hair?"

"When we're making love, you always undo my ponytail."

"So what?" Meredith came back, but she knew where this conversation was heading.

"It seems to excite you when my hair's undone. What's up with that?"

Meredith figured it was only a matter of time before this subject came up. She had a lame, evasive explanation at the ready, but opted for honesty. She was damned if she was going to screw things up with Flash by pretending to be someone she wasn't.

"I'm bisexual. When your hair is freed up and drapes over your shoulders, it's a turn on. I can't explain it but there it is."

Flash continued to regard her without expression. The word bisexual usually got a reaction from people, but Flash seemed to accept that declaration as nothing unusual.

"Is it because it makes me look like a woman?"

"I don't know. Like I said, I can't explain it."

Flash moved closer.

"Did I just turn you off?" Meredith wondered aloud.

"Why would you say that?"

"Because a bisexual orientation isn't always accepted."

"It made me think of a threesome. Why would *that* turn me off?"

Meredith returned Flash's smile. The threesome idea had occurred to her during the first week they had dated. "I'm not ruling anything out."

"I suppose I need to learn more about this," Flash said.

"Good," Meredith said, relieved that Flash hadn't been turned off.

"I do have one question," Flash said. "How does this orientation fit in with your ideas of family and kids?"

"Why are you asking?"

"I want kids."

Kids were not high on Meredith's wish list. There were times when she visualized her life playing out without kids. She remembered the first time Philly brought Daniel to the office. Rachel had fussed over Daniel, eager to hold him. But Meredith had had no desire to pick up the baby.

"I haven't decided about kids yet."

Flash flipped his ponytail back off his shoulder, his expression serious.

"Family and kids are important issues with me. Very important. I've told you my dad was a cop. He was on the force with those two guys you use as private investigators. He kept the weirdest hours and wasn't around a lot. I was a handful growing up. We didn't see eye to eye on a lot of things which probably had to do with me pissing him off every chance I got. I've got four brothers and sisters and home life was a circus. But even with my dad and me at odds a lot of the time, I was always conscious that I had a home. I want to make a home for my kids. But unlike my dad, I plan on being around for them. I'm in the perfect business to do that. I make my own hours."

In the time they had been together, Meredith couldn't recall Flash making such a long speech. "Message received," she said.

"Good," Flash came back, and Meredith was relieved when he smiled.

18

Carpenter was thinking about when the hell he could carve out fifteen minutes twice a day to relax his body, starting with his toes and working his way up to his head, all the while entertaining a calming vision of his choosing. During working hours, was he supposed to lie down on the floor of his office and close his eyes? What if Meredith was around? And who the hell would want to lie down on a carpet that undoubtedly harbored deadly microbes? Which left the morning and the evening to do what Dr. Specter had recommended. He didn't jump-start well for early morning activities, and after a day at work he didn't want to be *obligated* to do anything, even to think happy thoughts. And just how the hell were you supposed to relax your head?

There was one saving grace. Carpenter knew the calming vision he would select. Evenings during their Caribbean vacation, he and Maxine would sit in low beach chairs at the water's edge, their feet in the water, their eyes on a horizon turning from burnt orange to purple to black. Those moments had been so restful that sometimes he wanted to drop off and sleep through dinner.

Carpenter's phone sounded and he started. "Carpenter."

"It's Harris Burton. Am I interrupting something?"

"Not really," Carpenter said. "I was just sitting at my desk thinking about how much hard work was involved in learning to relax."

"You don't seem like a guy who gets bothered by much," Burton said.

"A lot you know. I'm a fucking wreck. And now I have to work at chilling out. Where have I gone wrong?"

"Stop complaining and feeling sorry for yourself. I have some news that I think even you will agree is good. I do think Jeremiah Becker's company *was* overcharged for legal services. His law firm had an army of lawyers involved in matters that probably could have been handled by two or three lawyers. There were internal meetings for which six or more lawyers billed for their time. There are other examples, but that's one pattern that comes to mind."

Carpenter eased back into lawyer mode. "Any ballpark figure on how much the overcharge was?"

"Ballpark? I'd put it at about seven hundred thousand dollars."

Carpenter did the easy math. "That's a little over a third of the one point nine million bill."

"Right."

"Have you told Becker?"

"I will. But I wanted to tell you first."

"Thanks. I want to ask you something that's been bugging me," Carpenter changed subjects.

"Something's bugging you besides relaxing?"

"Very funny." Since when did Burton become a wit? Carpenter remembered his former client as prim and proper. "There's a shit-load of stuff bugging me besides relaxation. But what I wanted to talk to you about was this merger notion you floated to Philly and me. I suppose you're going to tell me you're serious about that."

"I am serious about it," Burton said. "I wouldn't have mentioned it if I weren't."

"Does that mean you guys are turning down litigation and referring it out?"

"There's a bit of that, but not a particularly high volume. The litigation referrals are not the most important factor."

"What might that be?"

Burton paused. Carpenter recalled his thoughtful, deliberate approach to legal matters.

"You know that Philip Sizemore's vision was to create a boutique business transaction practice that could undersell large firms and provide the same quality as large firms. I came to the firm to generate business and provide some overall supervision for the deals the firm was handling. I think Philip's vision is viable, but it's risky. I don't like the idea of putting all of a firm's eggs in one basket. I view creating another basket as a hedge against transactions slowing down. I think litigation is an attractive second basket because business deals go south and then the parties head for court. Ben Klein, the current managing partner, agrees with me."

Carpenter found no flaws in Burton's general reasoning. But the devil lay in the details.

"We have no overhead to speak of," Carpenter said. "Why would we want to take on more overhead?"

"Do you like your current offices?" Burton asked.

"Not particularly," Carpenter admitted. "The lawyers have doubled up and that's only possible because Philly works from home. We're cramped. And the place has a worn look. But I don't give a rat's ass for appearances."

"I know you don't. Remember, I was a former client. When I first saw where you worked, I had to fight the impulse to walk out the door."

"I'm sure we've lost business because of the way our offices look. But I don't care. If someone is turned off by a barebones operation, he can go somewhere else and get gouged."

"We have space here for more lawyers," Burton noted.

"That would help *your* overhead, not ours," Carpenter rejoined. "And here's another thing. I don't like the idea of a firm with two areas of focus that are unlikely to intersect. It sounds to me like there would be two independent kingdoms. After a while, nobody would know or care what was going on in the other half of the firm, and it could lead to trouble."

"I've thought of that," Burton said, "and it's a fair point. The solution that Klein and I have come up with is bi-monthly meetings where both transactions and litigation get discussed."

Carpenter suppressed his standard rant against time-consuming meetings.

"In the last couple of years, have you guys ever been hurting for business?" Burton asked.

Burton had raised a sore point but was entitled to an honest answer. "Yeah. We started this year with not much inventory but we're seeing some pickup."

"Then a broader base might help you as well as us," Burton observed.

"But if transaction work was carrying all of us, that would drive me up a fucking wall."

"Ben and I haven't completely thought through how we'd deal with money. At my old firm, as you may remember, partners were paid based on a formula and on how the firm's management committee allocated thirty percent of net income."

"Right now, we pretty much split everything four ways," Carpenter said. "I'm not a fan of a formula that awards points for bringing in business and points for working on business."

"Then that could be a problem," Burton said. "I'll give some more thought to the compensation issue and let you know what Ben and I come up with. If anything."

"Why us?" Carpenter asked.

"Because I like, respect, and trust you and Philly," Burton replied. "You're the first people I thought of when it came to expanding."

Carpenter wondered who occurred to Burton as a second thought. "That's very kind, Harris," is what he said.

March

From Paul's Playlist

"Carry On"

Fun

19

Meredith had forgotten how huge Barney Freedman and Herb McCauley were. It looked like you couldn't fit another chair on their side of the office suite's conference table, while she and Simon and Rachel were sitting comfortably on the other side. Meredith would always have a soft spot for the two retired Cambridge detectives. Freedman and McCauley had helped in her own suit against her former employer, and they were the ones who had made the suggestion of a computer expert that had brought Flash into her life during Noreen Clark's suit against Sloan-Webster.

"It's good to see you guys," Simon led off. "You haven't changed much."

"That's because we're taking aging in place to a new level: we're calcifying," Freedman fired off. "Give us a few more years and we'll be immobile."

"Speak for yourself," McCauley said, smiling. "We're doing fine. Thanks for asking. We appreciate the business."

Meredith smiled at the investigators' back and forth. The two men were probably around Carpenter's age. Freedman, with his salt and pepper buzz cut and grouchy disposition, came across as the more formidable of the duo. But despite his softer features, McCauley had as much steely resolve as his partner.

"Let's start with Noah Branson," Rachel said, referring to the first plaintiff named in the suit against Sloan-Webster School of Law.

McCauley consulted a notebook and Meredith remembered that of the two private investigators, he was the record keeper.

"The Branson kid is from Michigan," McCauley said. "His family is lower middle class on the economic front. The kid did well in high school and got a small needs-based scholarship to Michigan State. He did okay academically and graduated in the top quarter of his college class. He had no extra-curricular activities but that was probably because he worked part-time during college. His parents had to take out a loan to make the tuition payment for his last college year, and they're still working that off. Something out of the ordinary occurred in his senior year at the end of the term preceding graduation. There was a cheating concern involving an economics course. It was one of those large lecture classes and, as best I can tell, Branson was taking the course to fulfill some distribution requirement he had let slip. The final exam was multiple choice, and there was an investigation into whether the exam questions had been leaked."

"How in the world did you find all this out?" Rachel asked.

"I flew out to the university," McCauley said, "and looked at copies of old student newspapers and asked around."

Meredith registered the surprise on her colleagues' faces.

"You should have cleared that expense with us," Simon said when he recovered.

"Who said I'm going to charge for the expense," McCauley said. "You're jumping to conclusions."

Meredith enjoyed seeing Simon at a loss for words.

"I've heard of going beyond the call of duty," Rachel said, "but nothing like this."

"We had some cash in our business account and we were bored," McCauley explained. "So we cut cards and I won."

"I'm dying to see your business plan," Rachel said.

"You think that's our problem?" Freedman turned to his partner. "When you go into business, you're supposed to have a plan?"

"That would explain a lot," McCauley deadpanned.

"I'm glad you guys are enjoying yourself," Simon interrupted. "What else do you have for us on Branson?"

McCauley turned serious. "I had lunch with a woman who is the administrative assistant for the economics department. She's been in that position for ages. She remembered the investigation. There were a hundred questions on the multiple-choice test. Twelve students got ninety or more questions correct and Branson was one of them. The next highest mark was eighty-six. The twelve who scored highest hadn't exactly distinguished themselves academically in any other course and that includes Branson. This woman I spoke with said that the investigation ultimately fizzled because there was no pattern. Each of the twelve high scorers missed a different set of questions. The high scorers were all interviewed and most of them—including Branson—said they guessed on a lot of questions."

Simon broke the silence following McCauley's narrative. "I don't see what this gets us."

"According to this administrative assistant I spoke with, the professor who gave the test was convinced someone had gotten hold of the questions. Some of the high scorers missed questions that were easy. But ultimately, the college couldn't prove anything. The administrative assistant had worked with the professor on the investigation. Her theory was that something *was* going on, and she believed that the twelve high scorers had worked out a plan to miss different questions."

"I still don't see how this helps us," Simon repeated.

"That's for you to figure out," McCauley said. "I'm just reporting in and telling you what I found out."

"We were wondering why Branson left Michigan and went to law school here in Massachusetts," Meredith spoke up. "Do you think this test business had something to do with that?"

McCauley shrugged. "I couldn't tell you."

"Were the twelve high scorers ever told they were suspected of cheating?" Meredith asked next.

McCauley nodded. "The administrative assistant confirmed that."

"Did the twelve high scorers know each other?" Rachel asked.

"A few knew of each other, but none of them were close friends."

"Were any of the other high scorers Black like Branson?" Rachel continued.

McCauley smiled. "I actually thought to ask that question but don't ask me why. Three of the other high scorers were Black. There were also four Asians, two whites, and two Latinos."

"Was anyone suspected of stealing the test questions?" Meredith asked.

"A teaching assistant named Corey Addison was suspected, but no one could prove anything, and the guy denied it."

"What was the teaching assistant's race?' Meredith asked.

McCauley laughed. "Another question I thought to ask. The guy was Black."

"What was the sex of the high scorers?" Meredith pursued.

"Six men and six women."

Even though the high scorers were largely minorities so that perhaps the racial mix of that group might be significant, Meredith agreed with Simon: this narrative didn't appear to help Sloan-Webster. It might be worth asking a deposition question about the incident to observe Branson's reaction. But Branson's denial was predictable.

Simon surveyed the table. "Let's turn to Regina White," he said.

"Now there's a piece of work," Freedman let loose.

"What are you talking about?" Simon exclaimed. "I remember her photograph. She was basically nondescript. She had this serious, studious look that made me wonder whether she ever smiled."

"Wonder no more," Freedman said. "I can tell you from firsthand knowledge that she smiles."

"Let's hear it," Simon requested.

"During law school she worked on and off as an exotic dancer at this place in Lynn that's just off of Route 1. While she's been looking for a legal job, she's continued to dance. If you call what she does dancing."

"A girl's gotta eat," McCauley observed.

"Wait a minute!" Simon interrupted. "I thought she was working as a secretary for an ad agency."

"That's her day job. I'm talking about her night job."

"This place she dances at. What kind of place is it?" Simon asked.

"Kind of a hard-drinking, blue collar place," Freedman elaborated. "Pole dancing. Stripping down to a G-string. There's some lap dancing that goes on in private rooms."

Meredith calculated that McCauley and Freedman were two for two—this was the second time that they had reduced Simon and Rachel to silence.

"What kind of money does she make?" Meredith asked.

"Thirty to forty thou a year," Freedman supplied. "Depends on the lap dancing."

"Does White have a Facebook profile that mentions any of this?" Meredith followed up. These days, prospective employers checked job applicants out via social media, and she figured an employer discovering White's sideline would be turned off.

"She's on Facebook but this doesn't turn up," Freedman responded. "The only reason I learned this was I followed her for a couple of days."

Rachel was shaking her head and Meredith interpreted the gesture as Rachel's concern for how much time Freedman had spent on the assignment. Freedman must have picked up on Rachel's unease. "I was bored and had some spare time," he offered with a shrug. "It doesn't mean I'm going to charge for all my time."

"Did you find anything out about her law job searches?" Simon reentered the discussion.

"I overheard her on her cell phone after she went on an interview," Freedman said. "I was sitting next to her in a Starbucks, and she was saying that the interview sucked, that she thought the guy interviewing her had written her off and kept on talking to be polite."

Rachel was writing. "This from a woman who thinks it's polite to take off her clothes in a bar," she said after completing her note taking.

"It gives us something to go after her with," Simon said, and Meredith had to agree.

"Do you think White declares her dancing income on her tax returns?" Simon asked, and Rachel again began writing when Freedman shrugged.

"That leaves Marshall Hightower," Simon said.

"I would describe him as a free spirit," Freedman said. "He's doing landscaping work, which is pretty slow in the winter. But his company got lucky. It's got a fairly big job getting the grounds of a large estate cleared and ready for some serious spring planting. At night, the few times I followed him around, he did a fair amount of partying and a fair amount of bar hopping."

"What about pursuing a law-related job?" Simon questioned.

"Couldn't tell you what he's up to on that front. I can tell you that he didn't seem down in the dumps because he didn't have a legal job. He seemed happy go lucky, as if he didn't have a care in the world."

Meredith didn't find Freedman's report on Hightower helpful. If there was a way to go after the last of the three plaintiffs, they would have to find it somewhere else.

Rachel looked up after rereading her notes. "The way I see it, you gave us something to work with on White and very little to work with on the two guys."

"That was our impression," McCauley said. "We'll think about the two guys some more and get back to you if we come up with something."

"How come you guys aren't busier?" Meredith asked, curious. "You do good work."

"It must be because we're so selective when it comes to clients," McCauley responded.

"Or," Freedman added, "it could be we're idiots without a business plan."

20

Meredith was in the Sloan-Webster war room, unable to concentrate, trying not to get depressed by the file boxes of student records she had yet to wade through. 'Fucking Flash,' she thought. He had to bring up kids. Why didn't he have the self-restraint to delay raising that issue until the time they couldn't get enough of each other had passed? During much of last year she had publicly and privately bemoaned the fact that there was no one in her life. Now Flash was front and center, a guy whose good looks and quirkiness intrigued and excited her, and yet she was reduced to wondering whether she was about to experience a be-careful-what-you-wish-for disaster. Why couldn't he accept, for the near term, a relationship where they hooked up at the end of each workday and screwed each other silly?

Meredith couldn't envision a life in which she had to make room for kids. Yet, women survived in law firms—even made partner—while rearing families. How the hell did they do it? There was no one at her former firm she could ask for advice. Her lawsuit burned that bridge. But there was one person she could ask.

Meredith left the war room, where cell phone reception was hit-or-miss, and made her way to the student lounge on the first floor. An array of vending machines lined one wall. The interior was filled with roomy leather chairs and most of the chairs were occupied by students banging away at laptops, snacks and drinks within easy reach. For the most part, the students looked like slobs, the women as unkempt as the men. Personal hygiene and presentable attire had taken a back seat to a uniform grunge look marked by stained, mismatched, and torn clothes, greasy hair, and unhealthy pallor. Meredith had let herself go during her law school days. But hopefully not to this extent.

Meredith found a chair in the corner of the lounge that afforded a measure of privacy. She worked her cell phone.

"Philly Sullivan."

"Hi, it's Meredith. Do you have a moment?"

"Hold on. Give me a second."

Meredith was brought up short by Philly barking orders that came through loud and clear.

"Daisy, make sure you share that. Rosalind needs a turn."

"Good grief, Daniel! You may think that's cute, but it's also disgusting."

"No, Rosalind! Now we're going to have to clean you up before lunch."

"Hey," Philly said, getting back on the line. "This is a nice surprise. It's a little crazy here, but what can I do for you?"

"I want to know how you do it," Meredith said.

"Do what?"

"Deal with practicing law and having kids. I don't see how you manage."

"Is this why you called?"

"Pretty much."

"What brought this on?"

Meredith didn't answer straightaway. She didn't know Philly that well, and rarely dealt with her in person. Most of her face-to-face contact was with Carpenter and Simon and Rachel.

"Is it this Flash guy?" Philly asked.

"Yeah," Meredith said, deciding to be direct. "He was sounding me out on the subject of kids. He wants them—he made that pretty clear. I basically pleaded the fifth. I don't know what I want. I can see myself without kids. But maybe that's because I have a vision problem."

"Not in the mouth, Daniel! Hold on a minute."

Whether she knew it or not, Meredith thought, Philly was making the case for no kids.

"Sorry. Where were we? Oh, I remember. Daisy was not a planned baby. After I discovered I was pregnant, I told Philip, my fiancé, that motherhood was not on my radar screen. You've met Maxine, Carpenter's lady friend? Well, she came to see me and said I'd regret it the rest of my life if I didn't go through with the pregnancy. She was right. So I got out of the way of my own pigheadedness and told Philip it was a go. I've never regretted it."

"But how do you do it?"

"The practice of law suffers," Philly said. "We ended up with bright, young lawyers who do the real work so I can coast."

"Do you really feel that way?"

"Sometimes. But I've come to terms with it. The four of us are a team and we essentially sink or swim together. It seems to be working. The thing is, the kids come first."

"I don't know if I can do that," Meredith admitted.

"You'd be surprised what you can do," Philly came back. "Now that we're talking about this, I remember this guy I was interested in before I met Philip. He was a lawyer working for the US Attorney's Office in Boston. He asked me whether I wanted kids. It was an awkward moment seeing as how we were at the top of this indoor rock-climbing wall. I told him I hadn't made up my mind. Hold still for a moment, Daniel. I need to clean you up a little."

Meredith didn't see how she would make time to review records in the war room if she had a kid to take care of. Then again, maybe Flash would be on kid duty.

"Sorry about that."

"What happened to the guy on the rock wall?" Meredith asked.

"He dumped me. He said he didn't want to waste time with a woman who had any doubts about wanting kids. I had gone through this elaborate plan to get him in the sack and he turned me down."

Would Flash do that? Meredith wondered, and as soon as she asked herself this question, she knew the answer: Flash *would* dump her.

"That's harsh," Meredith said.

"That's what I thought at the time. You wouldn't believe how pissed I was at the guy. But now that we're talking about it years later, he had a point. Kids are a big deal. A really big deal. It's an issue that's important to get on top of if a relationship is serious. Have I helped you?"

In truth, Meredith was more conflicted now than before the call. "Yes and no," she replied. "You've focused the issue for me. But I still can't picture how the juggling kids with career thing works."

"On the career side, you need to be with the right people and get lucky. There's no clear answer." Philly paused. "Here's a thought. What if you woke up tomorrow and found out you were pregnant?"

"I thought you were trying to help me?"

"I am."

After ending the call with Philly, Meredith stayed seated in the student lounge, unable to face the war room. Philly's last question had stayed with her, bugging her. She pictured telling Flash she was pregnant and his elation at that news. Which probably meant, at least on his part, that there was something going on between them that involved more than great sex. But if she told Flash that she was pregnant and had no intention of keeping the baby, Flash would be devastated. So she could only tell Flash she was pregnant if she intended to keep the baby and stay with Flash for the long haul. But did she know him well enough to be able to make an intelligent decision about a long haul?

There was also the question of women. If she was serious about Flash for the long haul, she'd have to give up women. She and Flash could joke about threesomes, but threesomes would become divisive over a long haul. Did she really want to give up women?

Philly was part of a law firm with partners who would help her out in a work crunch. Meredith was freelancing, not a partner or an associate, so Philly's situation didn't count for her. Would she feel differently if she were an actual associate with Philly's firm? Maybe, but who knew? And if she had to take time off to deal with a delivery and a new baby, could Flash support a family? She had no idea how much money he made.

Meredith rose and made her way to the bank of elevators in the lobby. The unthinkable had happened: the war room looked attractive.

21

Philly had incorporated helpful suggestions from all her partners in the complaint she had drafted for Sasha Barton and then e-mailed what she hoped was the final draft to her client. Next on her list was to contact Carlos Ibanez, the lawyer representing the punished Hispanic students who were suing Parker Hill Elementary School and its principal, Samuel Clarke. Ibanez was a sole practitioner in Chelsea and he picked up on the first ring.

"This is Carlos Ibanez, attorney at law. How may I help you?"

Philly smiled at Ibanez's warm greeting, a far cry from Carpenter's curt "Carpenter" whenever the geezer answered the phone.

"My name is Philly Sullivan. I represent the Parker Hill teacher Sasha Barton, and I'm about to file a court complaint on her behalf against the defendants in the suit you have brought. Do you have a moment?"

"But of course. I was wondering when Ms. Barton would seek legal redress."

"That's about to happen. I was wondering whether anything significant has happened in your case."

"The defendants have filed an answer denying any wrongdoing," Ibanez said. "That was to be expected. I have asked for extensive discovery and I expect to be fought at every turn."

"I take it the school system is backing Principal Clarke."

"Yes. I don't know what the school officials are thinking, but for the moment they are taking a united hard line."

"Did they say anything that would justify making your clients eat on the floor?"

"No, nothing specific. One of my interrogatories asks for all of the justifications for that degrading punishment. It remains to be seen what the defendants will come up with."

"One of your clients is Xavier Acevedo, the Hispanic boy who got in a fight with the Black student. Did I pronounce his name correctly?"

"Close enough. What about Xavier?"

"I would like to meet with him and his mother in your presence. If possible, I would also like to have Stanley Brown present, the boy who fought with Xavier. And of course, Stanley's mother."

"I don't think that's such a good idea. The two boys dislike each other intensely. What would be the purpose of such a meeting?"

"One purpose would be to get the two boys to patch things up. Another purpose would be to get Black parents behind our lawsuits."

Ibanez sighed. "Those are admirable objectives but, in my humble opinion, they are doomed to fail. The two boys are enemies. I cannot envision them patching anything up. The Black parents are going to rally around the Black principal. They won't assist our lawsuits and may end up opposing them."

"You may be right," Philly admitted. "But I've got a few ideas on how to accomplish both of my objectives. Hear me out," she requested and Ibanez, perhaps curious, perhaps being polite, didn't interrupt as she outlined her plan.

Jeremiah Becker hadn't wanted to take up time with another face-to-face meeting, which Carpenter thought was unfortunate. Over the phone, it would be difficult to determine how serious Becker was about litigating to solve his company's problem.

"I think my best bet is to call the partner who was the lead attorney representing my company and try to negotiate a deal about their fees," Becker led off. "Is there any problem with that?"

"Are you going to mention Mr. Burton?" Carpenter came back.

"Absolutely. That's one of my strongest negotiating points. I want to put the fear of God into those bastards right off the bat."

"I've got experience with negotiating," Carpenter said evenly. "Ordinarily, I believe it makes sense for a lawyer to negotiate on behalf of a client, and that's what I recommend here. But you're the one who has the relationship with the Blake Pennington lawyers. If you think that relationship is such that it makes sense for you to take the first stab at a settlement, then so be it."

Becker fell silent. Carpenter resolved to let the man do battle with himself. If Becker couldn't win a negotiation with himself, he was almost certain to come up short in a negotiation with a firm of lawyers.

"I might as well make the call," Becker finally said, morosely. "Since Mr. Burton thinks we were overcharged by about seven hundred thousand, I guess I should start by asking them for a bigger reduction off our bill."

Carpenter saw no way around it and went into his negotiation approach. "So," he concluded, "I favor putting on the table what my client is really looking for. The approach of starting with a higher number than you're really looking for can cause negotiations to be protracted and, in some cases, to blow up."

"I don't agree with you," Becker said.

'Now there's a surprise,' Carpenter thought. "I'm simply telling you how I approach these kinds of situations," he said, trying to stifle his irritation and sound reasonable.

"Okay, enough pussyfooting around," Becker said. "I'll call Morgan Carmichael at Blake and get back to you guys."

"Sounds like a plan," Carpenter said. 'Not a great plan,' he thought, 'not even a good plan. But a plan.'

"Ten thousand dollars," John Pace said, and Meredith glared at her cell phone and let the figure hang in the air while she let her anger subside. During her own case against her former law firm, she had learned about negotiating strategies from Carpenter. Pace's offer on behalf of Caryn Wheelwright was a lowball offer—ridiculously low.

Meredith took several deep breaths. She was standing in an empty corridor outside the war room at Sloan-Webster. "I'll present that figure to Ms. Clark."

"Is it something you're prepared to recommend?"

Meredith's irritation returned. She thought about answering honestly, telling Pace to shove the offer up his ass. But honesty wasn't always the best policy, so she took several additional deep breaths and paused until she was in control of her emotions again.

"I'm not prepared to discuss with you any recommendation I might make. Rest assured I will convey the offer you've made, and I hope to be back to you with a response shortly."

When Pace disconnected, Meredith tried to predict Noreen Clark's reaction. Wheelwright had tried to damage Clark's legal career permanently, but retribution didn't seem to be on Clark's mind. Clark had been reluctant to bring suit and might simply accept the lowball offer. More likely, she would opt for an inadequate counter proposal—something in the $25,000 neighborhood—and Wheelwright, if she had a brain in her head, would jump at such a figure.

Meredith believed it would be a mistake on Clark's part to accept any settlement proposal until Wheelwright had been deposed. Absent a deposition, Clark would never know why Clark had lied to Sloan-Webster officials about Clark's journal article. There was always the chance that Wheelwright's lowball offer would enrage Clark and energize her to pursue litigation. But Meredith viewed that chance as slim.

Clark was the client, Meredith reminded herself. And to quote Carpenter, a client could be dumber than dirt.

22

Carpenter looked up to find Meredith staring at him. She had swiveled her chair so that her back was to her workstation, and he sensed that she had been waiting for him to come to a stopping point.

"What?"

"Noreen Clark," Meredith said with some heat, and she reported on the settlement proposal put forward by Caryn Wheelwright's attorney.

"What's the problem?" Carpenter asked. "You're going to advise Clark to reject the offer."

"But she might accept it," Meredith complained. "For some reason, she's not interested in vigorously pursuing this case. I want to depose Wheelwright. I want to understand why she lied about Clark's article. I may never get the chance."

Carpenter sympathized with Meredith's predicament. When a client took an absurd position, sometimes all the reasoning a lawyer could bring to bear on the situation failed to turn the client around.

"Your job is to advise Clark. If she accepts this first offer, then she's got a serious screw loose. But if she directs you to accept the offer, you ultimately have no choice. If that happens, I strongly advise you to write Clark a cover-your-ass letter outlining why you think accepting the offer is a mistake."

Meredith frowned. She was sitting upright in her chair, chewing on her lower lip. Carpenter was struck anew by her presence, by her determination and forcefulness which was evident even in this moment when she was dealing with a client's frustrating vagaries.

Carpenter's phone sounded and he reached for the receiver. "Got to take this," he said as Meredith turned back to her workstation. "Carpenter."

"It's Jeremiah Becker. Have you got a moment?"

"I do. What's going on?"

"I spoke to the Blake partner in charge, Morgan Carmichael. He heard me out and then basically told me to pound sand. He said the firm had put in the time and that the time was reasonably spent."

Carpenter was not surprised by the response. "I take it Mr. Carmichael was not impressed by Harris Burton's analysis."

"You've got that right. He clearly knew of Burton, but he dismissed him. He said something like Mr. Burton is entitled to his opinion, but it doesn't mean much to me."

Becker sounded irritated which Carpenter viewed as propitious. "Where do we go from here?" he asked.

"Sue the bastards," Becker let loose. "Fuck them. I was right to question their bill. Burton's assessment backs me up. We'll take our chances."

Carpenter debated whether to bring up a point that might either dampen or stoke Becker's belligerence. He decided to raise the issue in part because Becker was the kind of guy who might be angered by a subject not being aired promptly.

"I want you to think about something," Carpenter said. "The total bill from Blake, Pennington & Dwyer was a million nine. You've paid three hundred thousand already, so that leaves a million six. Harris Burton says you've been overcharged by seven hundred thousand, so that leaves nine hundred thousand that you pretty much agree that you owe to Blake."

"Where are you going with this?"

"Just stick with me. There are a number of ways to play this. One way is to do nothing—pay nothing. This would essentially force the Blake firm to sue your company for a million six.

"A second approach is to pay the balance you think is really owed—the nine hundred thousand—and inform this guy Carmichael that your company disputes the seven-hundred-thousand-dollar remainder of his bill and isn't going to pay it. That approach would probably result in Blake Pennington suing your company for the disputed seven hundred thousand they say you owe.

"A third approach is for Ship Right to bring suit against Blake Pennington asking the court to determine whether your company's been overcharged and, if so, by how much. Your company could pay Blake Pennington the nine hundred thousand it doesn't dispute and let the court decide how much, if anything, you owe on the remaining seven hundred thousand in dispute. As part of any suit, your company could pay the entire unpaid amount—either one million six or seven hundred thousand—into court and ask the court to determine who gets what."

Becker didn't respond to these proposals and Carpenter wondered whether he had overloaded the man's circuits.

"Wouldn't we be able to put pressure on them by not paying anything until the court decides what's fair for us to pay?" Becker asked.

"You're right," Carpenter said. "That would be a pressure tactic. But I wouldn't advise going that route. You want your company to be perceived as being fair. I'm leaning toward paying the Blake firm the nine hundred thousand that Burton believes is reasonable and initiating the court action to determine whether the seven hundred thousand is owed by your company. I want to think about this some more. But I'm bringing this subject up now so that it gives you time to consider the options before we get into crunch time."

"I have to say Clyde Atkins was right about you," Becker said. "You're very direct. I'm glad you've brought this issue up now. I wouldn't have been a happy camper if I had to deal with it on short notice."

"Okay," Carpenter said. "I've given you enough to think about. Get back to me after you've considered what we just discussed."

When Carpenter set down his phone, he found Meredith again staring at him.

"What?"

"When I call Noreen Clark," Meredith said, "I want you on the line. Remember, if I win her suit, I'm paying you for your time. That's the deal."

"I think you should talk to Clark alone," Carpenter replied, ignoring Meredith's wanting to pay him. "The way you've described her, I think she's going to take another lawyer being on the line the wrong way. She's going to think you're trying to pressure her."

"Shit, you're probably right. She needs to be pressured, but I guess I get to do that by myself."

Carpenter had gotten Maxine's okay for a later dinner than usual. Before leaving the office for the day, he wanted some quiet time to review the firm's active cases and where they were heading financially.

Simon and Rachel had filed an answer to the complaint against Sloan-Webster School of Law. Shortly, they would be responding to the voluminous discovery requests that Christopher Blaisedell had unloaded on the law school. Meredith had been largely responsible for reviewing student records even though Simon and Rachel had agreed to divide the work with her. Once Blaisedell's discovery requests were dealt with, Simon intended to depose the plaintiffs. Carpenter grinned. The case was a proverbial cash cow that would be producing steady billings throughout the year.

Philly had just filed a court complaint for the elementary school teacher who had been fired. The teacher's union was paying for the litigation, so this case provided another steady vehicle for billable hours. Philly had laid out her plan to rally parents and students behind her client, and Carpenter backed her initiative. Her approach would never have occurred to him.

Henry Frazier's dispute with his father was another billable hour lawsuit. An answer had been filed by Donald Frazier. Philly would shortly be going to court to try to pry loose the financial records for Elite Scripts. She had asked Carpenter whether he wanted to handle the court proceeding, and he had trusted his instincts to let Philly do the honors.

Last but not least was the legal fee dispute between Jeremiah Becker's company and Blake, Pennington & Dwyer. Carpenter saw his challenge as keeping charges modest for the work that he and his colleagues did. It made no sense for Becker's company to pay hundreds of thousands of dollars in new legal fees to chase $700,000. Carpenter again assessed whether Becker's company could recover its legal fees. There was a chance, he concluded, provided Burton was believed as an expert witness.

Carpenter liked the inventory of the firm's active cases. For the most part they were challenging and—best of all—involved billable hours. That was a very comfortable difference from some years in the past. One downside involved reliance on the Sloan-Webster litigation to keep most of the partners busy. Also, any case could end abruptly and, if one of their active matters did, there wasn't anything to pick up the slack. So, while for the moment they were all occupied, their reality hadn't changed: they needed more business.

Carpenter turned off his computer and closed his eyes. He hadn't gotten around to meditating this morning but now, in the evening, he had no excuse to avoid that task. He took several deep breaths. Then he began to will his body to relax starting with his feet and working his way up to his head. This order seemed wrong—it made more sense to start with relaxing your head and working your way down. But what did he know? And, at the moment, his degree of knowledge was a moot point. He couldn't relax a goddamn thing.

23

Judge Martin Cornell briefly surveyed the lawyers in front of him before resuming his review of the papers that had been filed in Henry Frazier's suit against his father and Elite Scripts. His expression gave no indication whether he was intrigued by or indifferent to the son-father dispute. Cornell was painfully thin and his pale complexion, sandy colored hair, and hazel eyes gave him a washed out look.

Donald Frazier was not in attendance and his counsel, Lauren Goldman, did not appear troubled by her client's absence. The young, blond woman displayed the slight smile that Philly remembered from her website photograph.

"I've read the complaint filed by the plaintiff, the affidavits filed by the parties, and the legal memoranda submitted by counsel," Judge Cornell said. "The plaintiff desires access to Elite Scripts' underlying financial information. The defendants claim that the plaintiff has been provided with the company's financial statements and that no further financial information need be furnished. Let me ask you this, Ms. Sullivan. Does your client have an issue with any item on the financial statements he has received?"

Philly rose. It had been some time since she'd been in court, and she took time to collect her thoughts. "My client can't point to a specific item on the financial statements that he has a problem with," Philly conceded, heeding Carpenter's advice to directly answer any question posed by a no-nonsense judge, a label that seemed to fit Judge Cornell. "Rather, my client has a general problem with all of the financial statements because he doesn't trust the accuracy of any of them. May I please explain further, Your Honor?"

The judge gave a curt nod.

"My client's father promised my client control of the family business and that promise has not been honored. The frustration arising from this broken promise is heightened by the fact that my client has not been given a specific reason as to why the promise has not been honored. The inference that my client draws from these circumstances is that the defendants are concealing something about the financial condition of the company. Until the records underlying the financial statements are reviewed by a financial consultant, my client cannot rely on the veracity of any figure set forth in the financial statements."

"The defendants note that the financial statements were issued by an accounting firm," Judge Cornell pointed out. "Isn't that sufficient?"

"Respectfully no, Your Honor. The company's accountants did not perform an audit. The notes to the financial statements state that the accountants merely performed a review that relied on the information provided to them by company management. In other words, the accountants have confirmed that they did not go behind the figures given to them by the defendants."

"Ms. Goldman," Judge Cornell shifted focus. "Why hasn't the plaintiff been given control of the family business?"

Goldman stood promptly and made eye contact with the judge. "Donald Frazier's affidavit acknowledges that he did make the promise to turn over the control of the business to his son but has had second thoughts about the timing of that move and has put the move on hold."

"What are these second thoughts?" the judge inquired.

"As Mr. Donald Frazier states in his affidavit, he regards the timing of the transfer of control as inappropriate. Nonetheless, Mr. Frazier has ensured that his son has not suffered financially from this delay by increasing his salary to what it would have been if the transfer had occurred."

"And just why is the timing of the control transfer inappropriate?"

Philly was right. This was a judge who wanted his questions answered.

"I'm not able to add to Mr. Frazier's affidavit," Goldman replied, "except to say that it involved a business judgment made by Mr. Frazier senior."

"What is the harm to the defendants if underlying financial information is provided to the plaintiff?" the judge asked next. "The younger Mr. Frazier is a minority stockholder in the company. Why shouldn't he have access to underlying financial records?"

"Because the younger Mr. Frazier hasn't made a case for obtaining further financial information. As his counsel has conceded, the plaintiff cannot point to a single item on the financial statements that gives him cause for concern."

The judge paused, became lost in thought, and Philly wondered whether Goldman had successfully put him off the scent.

"When it comes to concessions, you and Mr. Frazier senior have conceded that the elder Mr. Frazier has not honored his promise to turn the business over to his son. That tells me that the younger Mr. Frazier, the plaintiff, has a valid breach of contract claim that he is likely to win. Have the books of this company ever been audited?"

"I don't believe so," Goldman said.

"Then maybe it's time they were. The plaintiff states that he is prepared to front the cost of a financial audit although he reserves the right to have that cost reimbursed to him if he wins this case. Therefore, giving the plaintiff access to the company's financial records won't be a financial drain on the company. Do you agree, Ms. Goldman?"

"No, Your Honor. The company will have to divert man-hours and incur costs to deal with whatever financial consultant the plaintiff employs to conduct an audit."

Judge Cornell nodded, apparently acknowledging that Goldman had made a fair point.

"Are the parties present in court today?" the judge asked.

"The plaintiff is present," Philly answered.

"The senior Mr. Frazier is not in court," Goldman advised.

Judge Cornell wrote briefly in his trial notebook. "Both counsel have made valid points," he declared, "but when I apply the standards for a preliminary injunction, I conclude that the plaintiff has made a case for injunctive relief."

Philly relaxed for the first time since she had taken her seat before the bench.

"I've already indicated that the plaintiff's breach of contract claim is likely to succeed," the judge resumed. "When it comes to irreparable harm, I conclude that the defendants will not be harmed by turning over underlying financial information to the plaintiff. In contrast, the plaintiff is subject to the risk of irreparable harm if there is something in the financial records of Elite Scripts that is improper. Frankly, I find the reasons for the defendants' refusal to turn control of the company over to the plaintiff unconvincing and vague."

The judge consulted his trial notebook. "The defendants have asked for certain safeguards in the event the plaintiffs are afforded injunctive relief, and I find that some of these are appropriate. The plaintiff's financial consultant is to conduct any audit at the office of the company. The consultant may not remove original papers. If the consultant makes copies of any documents, the consultant is to provide the defendants with a list of the documents copied. Lastly, the consultant is only to share his or her findings with the plaintiff and plaintiff's counsel. I'll have the order drawn up and sent to counsel by fax. Any questions? No? Court is in recess."

"Nice job," Goldman said as she offered Philly her hand.

"You too," Philly responded. Goldman had done her best with the hand she'd been dealt.

Philly gestured for Henry Frazier to join her as she stowed her papers.

"What happens now?" Frazier asked when he drew near.

"We're going to get you an accountant to look at the company's books. We have someone in mind who has helped us in a number of cases. She doesn't miss much. We'll see if she's available and willing to take this on. If she is, we'll arrange for you to meet her." Philly knew she'd be disappointed if Lily Tompkins refused the case.

"What do you make of my father not showing up?"

"I think he didn't want to face questions from the judge about why he wasn't honoring his deal with you."

"Do you really think my father has something to hide?"

"The judge thought so, and that's what counts."

24

Xavier Acevedo and Stanley Brown glared at each other from opposite ends of Philly's living room. The fifth graders really didn't like each other. They were skinny, wiry, dark complexioned kids, and each looked like he wanted to be elsewhere. Their mothers were eyeing each other without the hostility displayed by their sons, but there was no sign of friendliness in their expressions. Xavier's mother was pale skinned so her son must have gotten his coloring from his father. Stanley had his mother's looks; they shared broad features and deep-set dark eyes.

Philly was holding Daniel. She had made the decision to let Daisy and Rosalind run loose in the hope that their antics would reduce tension. When the fifth-grade boys had first entered the living room, the little girls became quiet. But in a matter of minutes, they had resumed their activities—Daisy running around and Rosalind with mixed success determinedly trying to keep up with her—as if the boys weren't there. Philly caught the boys directing sideways glances at the girls, but there was no change in their dark looks. Still, Philly believed that her decision to hold this meeting at her house was correct. No one would relax in a lawyer's office.

Following a knock, the front door opened, and Carlos Ibanez entered, along with a chilling blast of March wind. Xavier's mother seemed to relax at his appearance, while Stanley's mother drew closer to her son. Philly approached Ibanez, introduced herself and pointed out the entryway closet where he could leave his parka and gloves. The lawyer for the Hispanic students earned points with her by grinning and waving at Daniel before seeing to his coat. He was a young man, slightly overweight, with a receding hairline that would leave him with a fringe of hair in short order.

Sasha Barton emerged from the kitchen and Philly positioned Daniel so that she could clap loudly for everyone's attention. Even Daisy and Rosalind looked up.

"Thank you for coming. I want you all to make yourselves at home. We won't take up much of your time. There are some drinks and cookies on the dining room table so please help yourselves. My name is Philly Sullivan. I'm a lawyer and I represent Ms. Barton, who had been teaching Xavier and Stanley. Mr. Ibanez is also a lawyer and he is representing the Hispanic students who were involved in an incident where they were told to eat their lunch on the school cafeteria floor. When Ms. Barton told them to eat at a cafeteria table, she was fired from her teaching job."

When Daniel began to wriggle, Philly set him down on the floor.

"Before the cafeteria incident, there had been a playground argument and some pushing and shoving between Xavier and Stanley. I've heard that there is some tension between the Black and Hispanic students at Parker Hill Elementary School." Philly turned to the boys. "The reason I wanted you both to come today is because I want you to listen to what some middle school students have to say about that kind of tension. While the middle school students are talking to you boys, the grownups will be in the kitchen. When you finish listening to the middle school kids, they'll send you up to the third floor and come and get us."

She turned to the two mothers. "Is that all right with you?" After a brief pause, the mothers nodded. The nods weren't enthusiastic, but they were enough. "Okay," Philly pressed on. "Any questions?"

The boys weren't happy with what was to unfold but with their mothers on board, they didn't have much choice. Philly suspected that their unhappiness would ratchet up a notch when they discovered the middle school students were girls.

Philly scooped up Daniel. "Daisy!" she called out. "Rosalind! We're going to the kitchen."

The kitchen was cramped. June and her two friends and Sarah stepped aside so that the grownups and kids all fit.

Philly moved next to June. "This is June, who babysits for my kids and for Rosalind. These are her friends, Naomi and Lucinda. The boys are ready for you," she directed at June. "Play it by ear but you might want to sit at the dining room table where I've put out cookies and drinks."

"We know what to do," June said as she led her friends to the living room.

Philly kept hold of Daniel. She knelt and whispered to Daisy and Rosalind. "You need to go upstairs with Sarah. Try to be very quiet when you go past the living room and climb the stairs."

Philly smiled as the girls held hands and followed Sarah out of the kitchen with Daisy trying to tiptoe.

"You really think your babysitter's friends are going to smooth things over with the boys," Stanley's mother spoke up as soon as the adults were alone. "That's not going to happen. First of all, they're girls."

"I don't know what's going to happen," Philly started with a disclaimer. "But June's friends had racial issues with each other—it was a Black-Hispanic thing—and now they're close friends. The boys might learn something from them."

"You're dreaming," Stanley's mother retorted. "I don't know why I agreed to come here."

"My son won't talk to me about the fight he got into with your son," Xavier's mother said. "I still don't know what started it."

"Me neither," Stanley's mother said sourly. "So what's the point of all this?" she added, making an arm motion that took in the kitchen.

Daniel began to squirm. Philly nodded to Ibanez to field the question as she tried to calm her son.

"Ms. Sullivan and I want to enlist the parents of all students to support our lawsuits. Xavier and Stanley seem to be the leaders of the Hispanic and Afro-American fifth grade boys. Ms. Sullivan and I thought that if we could bring them closer together it would help with all parents getting behind us."

"You've got to be kidding me." Stanley's mother didn't bother to conceal her irritation. "You're trying to get principal Clarke in trouble, maybe get him fired. If you think I'm going to get behind a movement against a Black principal, you've got the wrong woman. Save your breath."

"What's your opinion of Mr. Clarke?" Philly asked.

"He seems all right to me," Stanley's mother replied with less heat. "I've never had a problem with him."

"He made my son eat off the floor," Xavier's mother interjected. "So I've got a problem with him."

"That has nothing to do with me," Stanley's mother rejoined.

"I think it does," Sasha Barton spoke for the first time. "These kids are ten to eleven years old. I don't care what color they are or what their race is. And whatever they did, humiliation isn't the answer. No kid should be embarrassed the way Mr. Clarke embarrassed the Hispanic kids. If Stanley had been told to eat off the floor, think about what your reaction would have been. Also, at this age, they're learning to imitate the adult men in their lives, especially about how to treat other people. They're deciding what kind of men to be. So, what goes on now matters a lot."

Stanley's mother didn't respond straightaway. She stared at Barton, and Philly wished this meeting of the grownups hadn't taken the direction it had. The last thing she wanted was for Stanley's mother to feel ganged up on.

"What do *you* think of principal Clarke?" Stanley's mother directed at Barton.

"I think we've gone a little off course," Philly said, not wanting her client to prejudice her lawsuit.

"I don't mind answering," Barton said, as if reading Philly's mind. "We don't get along as well as I wish we did. We have a difference in approach which sometimes puts us at odds. Mr. Clarke is a disciplinarian and I'm not saying there isn't a place for discipline. When he took over as principal, discipline was needed. But as time has gone on, I think he tends to take discipline too far sometimes. I tend to favor a softer approach than he applies. When it comes to discipline, he's more rigid than I am."

"I will say that Xavier seems to be learning," his mother said.

Stanley's mother nodded. "Same with Stanley. Stanley's always got a book in his hands."

"That's because I'm a great teacher," Barton said and, when the laughter subsided, "well, *was* a great teacher," she qualified.

Xavier's mother moved closer to Stanley's mother. "I understand what you're saying about the principal," she said. "If we were dealing with an Hispanic principal, I wouldn't want to do anything to cause the principal to lose his job. But I think Mr. Clarke was out of line when he embarrassed my son and the other Hispanic kids. If you're the kind of parent you seem to be, you wouldn't put up with that kind of treatment of your son."

"You have no idea what you're asking me to do," Stanley's mother said. "The answer's still no. I'm sorry this happened, but I'm not going to do a damn thing that would make Mr. Clarke look bad."

June appeared in the kitchen doorway. "The boys are up on the third floor. They're not too happy about being thrown in with Daisy and Rosalind."

"Let's go back to the living room," Philly said, and June led the way.

June joined her friends at the dining room table while the adults took seats in the living room. The girls huddled and began giggling. Naomi and Lucinda looked normal compared to June. Today June's hair featured green and pink spikes. She had a gold stud in one nostril and a silver stud in the other. In contrast, Naomi and Lucinda had no added colors to their dark hair and wore no jewelry except for identical charm bracelets.

"Anything to report?" Philly asked the girls.

Naomi got up from her seat. "Lucinda and I told them about how we became friends in sixth grade. We told them how we didn't like each other in fifth grade but became friends when we went to middle school because nobody liked to be bullied by the older kids and we decided to stick together. We found out we had more in common than we thought."

"I don't think they were convinced by anything we said," Lucinda added as she also got to her feet. "I think if we were boys, they would have been more impressed."

"Did you find out anything about the fight they had gotten into?" Ibanez asked.

The girls again huddled. Philly wondered why a conference was necessary to answer Ibanez's question.

"They told us what happened," June said, "but they made us promise not to tell anyone."

"I'm sure you can share some details," Ibanez said, in a tone that Philly found ingratiating to a fault.

"We gave them our word," Naomi said, shaking her head.

The girls huddled for a third time, and Philly could only make out a word or two of their whispering.

"There was some name calling before the fight," June said. "That's all we're going to say."

"Thank you, girls," Philly said, anxious to head off another probing question from Ibanez. "Why don't you rescue the boys."

The girls raced up the stairs.

"We need to find out about this name calling," Ibanez said.

"None of us can mention that we know there was name calling," Philly cautioned.

"I disagree," Ibanez said.

"The girls gave their word," Philly reminded the gathering. "June was trying to be helpful to us, but we need to respect their word."

"I agree," Xavier's mother joined in. "I will talk to Xavier. Perhaps you can talk with your son," she added to Stanley's mother. "If you wish I will call you with what I find out."

"Okay," Stanley's mother said, and she read off her phone number while Xavier's mother entered the number on her cell phone.

The boys returned to the living room keeping distance between them.

"Thank Ms. Sullivan for the cookies and drinks," Stanley's mother urged her son.

"Thank you."

"Xavier?"

"Thank you."

As the visitors began to leave, Philly signaled Sasha Barton to remain behind. Daniel had fallen asleep and she deposited him in her bedroom before rejoining her client. "Any impressions?" she asked Barton.

"I'm guessing here, but I believe there were probably some racial epithets thrown around before the fight."

Philly considered that scenario. If Xavier had landed the first blow, did that mean that Stanley had initiated the racial slurs? Or was it the other way around? "Maybe their mothers can get to the bottom of this."

"If racial slurs caused the fight, I don't see how that's going to change anything, let alone help me," Barton observed.

"That might depend on what Clarke knew when he made Xavier and his friends eat on the floor," Philly responded.

"What happens now?" Barton asked.

"We've thrown some bread upon the waters and we'll see what comes back to us. We'll be going to court to try to get you your job back and, with luck, maybe we'll have some parental support through affidavits."

"It would take a miracle for Stanley's mother to help us."

"Stranger things have happened," Philly said.

25

"I've thought about what you said," Noreen Clark said over the phone, and Meredith braced herself for the punch line. She was alone at her workstation in Carpenter's office.

"I think you're probably right that Wheelwright's offer is too low," Clark continued. "I'm okay with you rejecting it. But if they don't come back with a higher figure, I'm thinking of accepting it later to make the case go away."

Meredith let her frustration dissipate. She decided to be direct with Clark but wanted her tone to be neutral. "You've changed, Noreen," she said, deliberately using Clark's first name. "When I first met you, you were down in the dumps but determined to fight to clear your name. Now you're pretty much resolved to throw in the towel. The fight's gone out of you."

"I told you," Clark said defensively. "The settlement you got for me was huge and I want to put this behind me. My life is good right now, and I don't want to be sidetracked by negative situations. This is a negative situation."

"With all due respect, your attitude doesn't make sense to me. I think we need to find out why Wheelwright lied to Sloan-Webster about your article. Until we know what motivated her, we're never going to have a handle on what a fair settlement might be."

"This is no longer about the money," Clark replied. "I just want to put this behind me. It really is that simple."

Meredith stifled her ready response which was to point out that until Noreen knew why the other woman had lied, she wasn't likely to be able to put this behind her. But Noreen didn't seem to want to hear this, and there was no point to permanently antagonizing her. "Okay. I'll call Wheelwright's lawyer and reject the offer. He'll ask me whether I have a counteroffer, and I'll tell him no because his offer was so low that settlement appears unlikely. We'll see whether that produces a higher offer."

"Okay," Clark replied grudgingly. "But if no higher offer comes after a while, I want to take the ten thousand dollars."

"I could increase the chance of a higher offer coming back by sending out a deposition notice for Wheelwright," Meredith said.

"I'm not sure I want to escalate things at this time," Clark replied.

"It's not really an escalation if you don't intend to go through with the deposition and intend to accept the rejected offer."

Clark remained silent. "I guess that's right. Okay. You can send out a notice to take Wheelwright's deposition."

Meredith set down her phone and took a moment to explore her own motivations. She had agreed to take Clark's case on a one-third contingency. That meant a $3,333 legal fee if Clark accepted a $10,000 settlement. After paying Carpenter for his time, her fee would be negligible. Even a $20,000 settlement—assuming Wheelwright doubled her offer—would produce only a modest legal fee. But Carpenter was right. If Clark insisted on accepting a lowball figure, there wasn't a damn thing she could do about it.

Carpenter was sitting at his desk obsessing about his firm's need for new business when his phone rang, and Jeremiah Becker provided a welcome distraction.

"I've thought about what we discussed and I'm okay with paying Blake, Pennington & Dwyer nine hundred thousand dollars. Also, I think my company should be the one to bring suit."

"I think that's the right move," Carpenter said. "Hold off on sending the nine hundred thousand until we're ready to file the complaint. I'll try to get you a draft soon."

"Sounds like a plan," Becker said. "I've got to run."

Carpenter set down his phone. Now he had to come up with a complaint in short order. Stop complaining, he told himself. You wanted more business and you just got your wish.

For this meeting, Sloan-Webster's dean had journeyed to the war room. Janet Martin had Ralph Cray in tow and neither looked happy. Rachel and Simon faced the law school administrators across the small conference table.

"We think we have the proper candidate to run the placement office," Martin led off. "We've done a search and some networking and interviewed three candidates. We think that Neil Taylor is a cut above the other two."

"Neil heads up the placement office at a small law school in the Midwest," Cray elaborated. "His wife has ties to Massachusetts, and she's been pressuring him to move back east. He's ready to make the move."

"Did you fill him in on the situation here?" Simon asked.

"We did," Cray confirmed. "He claims that he's not afraid of the challenge. He wants a year and half salary guaranteed and we're prepared to meet that request."

"How soon can he start?" Rachel asked.

"He needs to give a month's notice," Cray said. "But he's prepared to be in contact with us during that month to try to get some changes in place. His first priority is to come up with an electronic record keeping system that can track the law school's placement efforts for students during their time in law school and after graduation. He seems to be saying the right things."

"We're prepared to make Taylor a written offer," the dean said, "but before we do, we want to go over again whether we're shooting ourselves in the foot in the lawsuit."

Rachel had reviewed Meredith's research on the issue before this meeting. "As we explained previously, upgrading the placement office could come back to haunt you in the litigation. We will try to prevent post-suit placement office changes coming into evidence against you, but we may not be successful. This is not like a typical situation where, for example, a customer injures herself in a dark corner of a store and the store later adds lighting to the area which the store patron claims is an admission the accident scene was dangerously dark. In your position, I would assume a worst-case scenario where Taylor's hiring and any other move you make will be allowed into evidence at trial. But that doesn't mean you shouldn't go ahead, as long as you know the risk."

Dean Martin frowned and Cray muttered something unintelligible. Rachel believed she had covered her firm's collective ass to even Carpenter's satisfaction.

"What do you think, Ralph?" the dean asked her assistant.

"I think Ms. Boyle is right. If something bad can come out of this, then I think we need to assume it will."

"All right," the dean said wearily. "I suppose this is why I get paid the big bucks. Send Taylor the offer. Right now, our placement office isn't doing anything productive and that's got to change. This is the right thing to do even if it costs us."

Rachel silently applauded the dean's final decision. Simon's expression revealed nothing.

"We'll be responding to the plaintiffs' discovery shortly," Simon said. "Then we plan to take the plaintiffs' depositions."

"Something else to look forward to," the dean observed gloomily.

As soon as Philly sat down at the dining room table, she heard her upstairs office phone ring. She regarded evening meals with the entire household assembled as a time without interruptions. There was something about the evening meal ritual that was both settling and rejuvenating. "Shit," she muttered.

"Go," Raul urged her. "We will start without you. Perhaps it is Carpenter."

Philly sprinted up the stairs, hoping that she would pick up the phone before her answering machine kicked in.

"Philly Sullivan," she gasped.

"This is Sonia Acevedo, Xavier's mother."

It took Philly a moment to get her bearings. "Of course. How are you?"

"I hope I am not interrupting your dinner."

"No, not at all. What can I do for you?"

"I have spoken to Xavier and Stanley Brown's mother has spoken to her son. The two of us have talked. We would like to meet with you and Mr. Ibanez at his office tomorrow afternoon at two if possible. We have more details about how the fight started on the playground."

Philly could juggle tomorrow's schedule to make the meeting. "Are you able to fill me in on what happened?"

"We'd prefer to speak with you directly. This is all very sensitive."

"I'll be there," Philly said.

April

From Simon's Playlist

"Catch My Breath"

Kelly Clarkson

26

Carlos Ibanez shared an office suite with five other lawyers. There was no conference room so Ibanez had brought extra chairs to his office. Philly was flanked by Sonia Acevedo and Carmen Brown in front of Ibanez's desk. Neither mother looked upbeat.

"I have to admit I'm curious," Ibanez said, nodding slightly in Acevedo's direction. "You told me that you have information about the playground altercation, but you did not wish to discuss the information over the phone."

"Is what we say here confidential?" Brown asked.

"No," Ibanez said. "You are not my client and neither of you is represented by Ms. Sullivan. Only my private conversations with Ms. Acevedo would be protected by the lawyer-client privilege because she is my client."

Acevedo looked troubled. "I was afraid of that."

"What do you want to do?" Brown asked.

Acevedo shrugged.

"There are two lawsuits pending," Philly noted. "If depositions are taken in the lawsuits, the information you have is likely to be discovered. The school could take your depositions and could take the depositions of your sons. For that matter, I could take your depositions on behalf of Sasha Barton."

Acevedo put her hands to her temples, as if she had a bad headache.

"I think we should tell them," Brown said. "Especially if it's all going to come out eventually."

"All right," Acevedo said after a long pause. "We each talked to our sons. Xavier and some of his friends were kicking around a soccer ball on the playground during a morning recess." Acevedo leaned forward past Philly to catch Brown's eye and received a head nod to go on. "Stanley and his friends made fun of soccer, saying it was a sissy game unlike basketball or real football. Xavier and his friends said that Stanley and his group should mind their own business and that they were too chicken to play soccer which required real skill. The talk escalated and I am sorry to say Xavier used the n-word. Stanley then used the s-word. Then the fighting started."

Ibanez showed no reaction to the revelations. He nodded at Acevedo and wrote on his note pad.

Philly, too, nodded slightly, her suspicions confirmed. "Just so we're clear," she said, "I assume we're talking about the words 'nigger' and 'spic.'"

Acevedo nodded. "I didn't raise Xavier to be bigoted. I'm mortified."

Philly heard Carpenter's voice telling her to think like a lawyer. "Does the school principal—Clarke—know what was said on the playground?"

"He knows the n-word was used," Brown supplied. "One of Stanley's friends was called into Clarke's office over something else, and Clarke questioned him about the playground fight."

"Did Clarke learn the n-word was used before or after he ordered the Hispanic children to eat on the floor?" Philly followed up.

"Before," Brown said. "Stanley said his friend was called into Clarke's office immediately after Ms. Barton broke up the fight. Clarke was aware that there was a fight and asked Stanley's friend what had happened."

"Did Stanley's friend mention the s-word to Clarke?" Ibanez inquired.

"According to Stanley, he didn't."

"Well, that might explain Clarke's chosen punishment," Ibanez said.

"Maybe, but it doesn't justify it," Philly said. "Clarke needed to be even tempered and not act out of anger."

"Perhaps our lawsuit is less certain of victory," Ibanez addressed Acevedo.

"I don't buy that," Philly said. "The punishment was uncalled for. I continue to believe that my client did the right thing in telling Xavier and his friends to take seats at a table."

"So where does this leave us?" Ibanez threw out to the gathering.

Ibanez's question hung in the air until Brown looked at Philly and spoke. "I have something to say. I thought about what was said when we met at your house. "Sonia was right. I would have been furious if Clarke had made Stanley eat on the floor. If that had happened, I'd have wanted Miss Barton to step in and stop that punishment. So I'll help Ms. Barton now. You want an affidavit from me, and I'm okay with that. But I want to limit the affidavit to Ms. Barton being brought back to the classroom. I'm not going to criticize Mr. Clarke."

"Ms. Barton will be very grateful," Philly said, opting for diplomacy.

"You're probably wondering why I changed my mind," Brown said. When Philly nodded, she continued. "Stanley doesn't like the new teacher. He says he's bored in class. That was not a word he used when Ms. Barton was teaching his class."

"Ms. Barton will be pleased to hear about your son's assessment of her teaching," Philly strove for a light tone.

"But what do we do about our boys?" Acevedo addressed Brown. "I've talked to Xavier and tried to explain how inappropriate his behavior was. He keeps telling me he understands but, truthfully, I have my doubts."

"I have the same situation with Stanley," Brown replied. "He claims he's learned his lesson when it comes to taunting, but I'm not so sure."

"You could surprise your sons," Philly suggested.

"What do you mean?" Acevedo asked.

Philly spelled out what she had in mind. The mothers' cool reception had only thawed slightly when she finished.

"I don't see that happening," Brown said.

Philly shrugged. "What else have you got?"

Carpenter sat at his desk reviewing the complaint drafted for Jeremiah Becker's company. The initial draft had been well done. Rachel and Meredith had researched cases in which lawyers' fees were challenged as excessive, and while legal precedent was skimpy, the women had come up with cases in which lawyers' charges to clients had been cut back because the client was billed for duplicative tasks. Philly's edits had improved the document. Carpenter didn't know whether to feel disappointment at being superfluous or relief that he had so little to offer in the way of further revisions. In the end, he opted for relief, put the document in final form, and sent it on to Becker.

27

Meredith, alone in Carpenter's office, had just taken stock of her situation and realized that she was at another turning point. She had completed her review of student records in the Sloan-Webster case and prepared drafts of the law school's responses to the plaintiffs' requests for documents. Simon and Rachel wanted to withhold some kinds of information initially, forcing the plaintiffs to make their case for disclosure before a judge. So the hardest task had been to compose a list of the documents that were being withheld from disclosure or that were being provided with redactions, and to set forth a justification for why each document was being withheld or partially blacked out. The principal reason for withholding student information had to do with the privacy rights of students. Did the plaintiffs have the right to discover notes made by a professor meeting with a student or student health history information that had made its way into a student's file?

Meredith agreed with the strategy. But now that her task was for the most part completed, she foresaw the hours she had been spending on the Sloan-Webster case dropping dramatically. This was a replay of her role in last year's Spenser School of Law litigation; after her involvement with discovery issues had come to an end, few further work assignments came her way. Perhaps the partners had already discussed when she would be leaving Carpenter's office.

The phone at her workstation rang and John Pace announced himself. "My client is willing to double the settlement amount she had put on the table," Caryn Wheelwright's lawyer said. "I'm authorized to propose a twenty-thousand-dollar figure."

'I'll bet you are,' Meredith thought. Doubling a previous offer might sound like a grand gesture but, when the first amount was absurdly low, doubling it didn't do the trick.

"I'll report the new offer to Ms. Clark," Meredith said, dreading that call because Clark would be eager to accept the new figure.

"Will you recommend it?"

"No."

"May I inquire why?"

Were Carpenter present, he'd be drawing an imaginary zipper across his lips. And maybe the less said the better. Meredith would have been more inclined to do things Carpenter's way if Noreen Clark wasn't so willing to take a small amount of money and run. She decided to be more forthcoming with Pace. "Your client was prepared to destroy my client's professional career. In my judgment, twenty thousand dollars doesn't come close to redressing that malicious intent."

Pace fell silent. "Is there a figure that you would recommend to your client?" he finally asked.

"I haven't come up with one," Meredith was able to answer truthfully.

"I would like to postpone my client's deposition while this new offer is pending," Pace said.

"That's agreeable. We can set a new date when I respond to your proposal."

"If your client is thinking of a six-figure settlement," Pace said, "then this case isn't going to settle."

"I'll report that to Ms. Clark," Meredith said tersely.

Meredith set down her phone and decided to hold off on making a call to her client. Maybe Carpenter had some advice about how to proceed. She'd have to own up to not following his advice during her discussion with Pace, but it was worth a rebuke to hear what he had to say.

28

"Christ, how long has it been?" Lily Tompkins brayed at Carpenter across the conference room table. "It's got to be years. You must be desperate to bring me into a case."

This opening salvo reminded Philly that Lily was one of the few people who showed Carpenter no mercy and got away with it. The accountant hadn't changed much since Philly and Carpenter had last worked with her. She was a large woman who favored dresses that accentuated her bulges, and lipstick of a garish color, today's hue a variant of mauve. Optics aside, Carpenter did not trust many people, but when it came to accounting, he trusted Lily.

"Nice to see you too, Lily," Carpenter said.

"What the hell were the three of you thinking?" Lily followed up with amused glances directed at Philly, Rachel, and Simon. "You actually partnered-up with this old goat. What'd he do, hold a gun to your heads?"

"The gun theory sounds good," Philly said, producing smiles from Rachel and Simon.

"What's the problem about that you dragged me down here for? You weren't very descriptive on the phone."

Carpenter filled Lily in on the court order requiring Donald Frazier to turn over the financial records of Elite Scripts to his son, Henry. Lily was all concentration as Carpenter narrated.

"I'd have to go to the company and figure out what records need to be copied," Lily said. "That'll add to the cost."

Carpenter nodded. "I'm thinking you'll need to view records before you'll be able to get a read on the costs and your fees."

"What do you think the father is hiding?" Lily asked.

"That's what we want you to tell us," Carpenter responded. "I don't want to put any ideas into your head."

Lily tapped the side of her head. "My brain's not full-up yet. I can squeeze a few more ideas inside." She stared at Carpenter a long moment. "I've just got to ask," she said. "What happened to the lone wolf, the guy who would never join a firm?"

"It was never the right time or the right people," Carpenter said.

"I'm impressed. I always thought you'd be the kind of guy who died at his desk. At least with partners, somebody might find your body before rigor mortis set in."

Carpenter shook his head resignedly. "Love your images, Lily."

There was a knock on the door and Henry Frazier entered the conference room.

"Saved by the bell," Lily said.

"Lily was a big pill for Henry Frazier to swallow," Rachel observed later when the four partners were alone. Their client had been put off by Tompkins' off-color humor and blunt questions about his father.

"But he swallowed it," Carpenter pointed out, "and he's going to be glad he did." Carpenter paused. This was the first time that all four partners had been together in a while. He glanced at Philly, who nodded, before he turned to the others. "Philly and I need to fill you in on something that came up a short while ago. We should have met to discuss this earlier, but the truth is I wanted to think about it and anticipate your questions."

Rachel felt a stab of worry. She didn't want anything to rock the firm's boat which, in her opinion, was moving in a direction she liked.

"You'll remember that Philly and I had a meeting with Harris Burton over at the firm where he's of counsel. We were sounding out Harris on being an expert for Jeremiah Becker's company and he's agreed to do that, as you know. When we were alone, he brought up the idea of our two firms merging."

Rachel couldn't hide her surprise. She probably looked like an open-mouthed idiot but so what? Carpenter and Philly couldn't be serious about a merger proposal. They all had a good thing going here.

"I almost don't know where to start," Carpenter said. "First, I'm going to remind you that the firm we're talking about was founded by Philly's former fiancé, Daisy's father, Philip Sizemore."

Did that mean Philly was in favor of a merger? Rachel wondered. Did she feel some duty to the memory of Daisy's father to become part of the firm he had founded?

Rachel took several deep breaths to calm down as Carpenter began to provide background information about the other firm and how it was currently farming out the litigation that came its way. She started to take notes and the notetaking calmed her.

"My initial reaction was negative," Carpenter disclosed. "Joining up with you guys, as Lily alluded to, was a big step for me. I figured the last thing I wanted was a business relationship with a bunch of lawyers who weren't litigators. Plus, our overhead would go up. Our place isn't exactly a dump but it's nothing special; Christ, we don't even have a secretary. But because our costs are so low, we're able to pocket most of what we take in. Then there's the whole corporate culture clash issue. We know each other and we have a common specialty. In a merger, we'd be outnumbered and could be outvoted. This firm has twelve lawyers, and I didn't like the idea of hooking up with people in a different specialty, business law, where I wouldn't be able to understand let alone control what these folks were up to."

"For me, the culture issue is a big deal," Philly joined in. "My reality is that I'm going to need to work from home for a long time. With you guys, I don't feel guilty about it, because I view us as a team. But I'm worried about partnering up with new lawyers who might not be sympathetic to my situation."

"In a merger would we be partners?" Simon asked.

"That's my assumption," Carpenter said. "I'm embarrassed that I didn't ask Harris that directly." He kept a further embarrassment to himself: not thinking to ask whose names were to be on the door of a merged firm.

"How many partners do these guys have?" Simon followed up.

"Eight," Carpenter said. "That brings up another point. A merged firm would have twelve partners and only four associates. That's not a great mix."

"Right now," Simon said, "we pretty much split profits evenly. Would that continue?"

"In a true merger," Carpenter said, "I doubt it. If the four of us somehow remained independent from their eight partners, we might be able to keep splitting litigation profits four ways. But then we wouldn't be talking about a true merger."

"I don't know what to say," Rachel said. "This is so out of the blue."

"I just wanted to get this out on the table," Carpenter said. "We're not under any time deadline to respond to Harris. But ultimately, we owe it to him to get back to him."

In the silence that followed, Rachel studied Simon. He had not taken any notes during Carpenter's briefing and, as was often the case, his expression gave no clue to what he was thinking. Rachel resolved to find some time alone with him to get a read on his reaction to the merger idea.

"Here's something," Philly said. "When we represented Harris Burton, he was fighting his former law firm's age seventy retirement policy. Today's he's over seventy-five. He's a key figure at this firm even though he's technically of counsel. Given his age, he may not be with the firm very long and, if he wasn't in the picture now, I don't think I'd be considering a merger."

"You said that Burton was of counsel to this firm," Simon noted. "How can he talk about a merger when he's not a partner?"

"The firm's managing partner is a guy named Ben Klein," Philly said. "I talked to him briefly. I had gone to look at Philip's old office and Klein has taken that over. He seems like a nice guy, and Harris mentioned to me that Klein is aware of the merger proposal."

"As I said, we don't have to decide anything right now," Carpenter said. "If any of us has questions to ask these guys, I suggest an e-mail listing the questions. If anyone doesn't want any part of a merger, that would be helpful to know. Our partnership agreement only requires a majority vote on issues like this, but I wouldn't be comfortable pursuing this if we weren't all on board."

"To be continued," Philly said.

29

Meredith couldn't put off calling Noreen Clark any longer and phoned her client at work. Carpenter had not come up with any brilliant suggestions on handling this call. He agreed that Clark should be advised not to accept $20,000 in settlement, but he reiterated that Clark was the client and had the right to accept a lowball offer.

"Twenty thousand!" Clark exclaimed. "Wow! That's great. Go ahead and accept it. I never thought she'd double her original offer."

Meredith briefly covered up her phone so Clark wouldn't hear her deep sigh. "Noreen, please listen to me. I suspected this would be your reaction, but I want you to hear what I have to say."

"I've made up my mind on this," Clark said, peevishly.

"Please listen for a moment. I'm recommending that you not accept the offer. The new proposal might seem like a big concession, but it isn't. True, Wheelwright doubled the previous offer. But that previous offer was so low, doubling it doesn't get you near to where you deserve to be."

"Why are you fighting me on this?" Clark said with some heat. "I've explained to you that I simply want this done with. Weren't you the one who told me that you settled your lawsuit against the law firm that fired you because you wanted to move on? Well, I want to move on."

"There's a big difference between my case and yours. In my case, I made a settlement demand which was largely met. In this case, you haven't made any demand."

"I don't see that as a significant difference."

"If you were to make a demand, I would advise you to make a demand for six figures."

"If I do that, I don't see the case settling," Clark said.

"Wheelwright's attorney would agree," Meredith replied. "He asked me for a demand figure, and I said I didn't have one. He said the case wouldn't settle if you were looking for six figures."

"Well, I'm not looking for six figures."

"Wheelwright's lawyer asked me whether I would recommend that you accept the twenty-thousand-dollar offer. I told him no. He asked why and I decided to level with him. I told him that his client had tried to ruin your legal career and that twenty thousand was inadequate to compensate for such a malicious act."

Clark appeared to have run out of indignant comebacks, but Meredith doubted that she had turned her client around.

"I don't want to see the offer of twenty thousand taken off the table," Clark finally said.

"We could do what we did last time," Meredith threw out. "I could reject the offer, decline to make a counteroffer, and reschedule Wheelwright's deposition. If that doesn't get them to budge, you could always decide to accept the twenty-thousand proposal before the deposition goes forward. There is a risk that if you reject the twenty thousand, Wheelwright might not put that figure back on the table down the road. But that's the risk you took last time and I still regard it as a negligible risk."

Clark didn't say anything, and Meredith wished there were a way to climb inside her client's head to discover what was going on there.

"Okay," Clark said. "We'll play this game one more time but it's the last time. I don't want to have this conversation again if they come back with a higher figure."

"Let's not jump ahead of ourselves," Meredith cautioned. "One step at a time."

Walking back to the office from the Sloan-Webster war room, Rachel decided to sound out Simon on the merger proposal. She grabbed the sleeve of his lightweight coat and led him toward a Starbucks. "My treat," she said when he pulled back. "Besides, I want to talk to you."

"It's the merger that's on your mind, isn't it," Simon said when they had settled in at a table with their lattes.

"Why would you say that?" Rachel asked, knowing the answer to her question.

"Because when Carpenter first said the word, you looked like you were going through a near death experience."

"Was I that obvious?"

"Let's just say poker should not be your game."

Simon's smile cheered Rachel and emboldened her to be frank. "I was thinking of these last years and what a wonderful ride it's been. It seems like only yesterday that I was working as a paralegal and you were waiting tables."

"I agree we've taken a remarkable turn for the better."

"I don't want to give up what we have," Rachel said. "I'm happy. I don't want to jinx anything."

"I know what you mean," Simon replied, and Rachel felt her frustration mount: Simon still hadn't stated his position. "What's your view of this merger business?" she pressed.

"I'm keeping an open mind," Simon said.

"What does that mean?"

"Just what I said—I'm keeping an open mind. I haven't decided I'd want to do something like that but I'm not dismissing it, either."

Rachel had been looking for a black or white response, not some gray musings. She decided to probe further. "What appeals to you about a merger?"

"I'm talking generally," Simon responded. "We don't know the first thing about the people in this law firm that's been mentioned, so what I have to say doesn't mean I'm thinking positively or negatively about this group."

"Fair enough," Rachel said, thinking of the endless process of getting to know partners in another firm.

"Right now, we're reasonably busy," Simon said. "The Sloan-Webster case is filling up our time and Meredith's time. Without that case, things wouldn't be so rosy."

"Where are you going with this?"

"I worry about maintaining a steady stream of business. If we had another practice area through a merger, that might provide some financial stability and might get us some extra litigation that wouldn't otherwise come our way."

Rachel had to admit that she seldom took a long view when it came to the financial success of their firm. If money was coming in at the moment, she rarely looked beyond the moment.

"Here's something else to think about," Simon continued. "This guy Harris Burton is around seventy-five. Carpenter's past sixty-five. How long is Carpenter going to be around?"

"Lily Tompkins thinks he's going to die at his desk."

"I wouldn't be so sure. Carpenter admits it was a big deal for him to form our firm. So he's open to change and maybe he's rethinking what he's going to do as he gets older."

Simon didn't really need to mention Carpenter's health issues. Rachel knew.

"And if Carpenter goes, we'd be missing a source of business and a mentor," Rachel voiced the implication of Simon's comments.

"Exactly. And there's something else I've been thinking about."

Rachel was taken aback by how Simon had analyzed the merger issue in ways she wouldn't have considered.

"Remember how Carpenter was saying our office was low cost? Of course, he's right. But there's a price that comes with low cost. The place is a dump. You and I are working in a cramped space and the same goes for Carpenter and Meredith. I'm willing to bet that this guy Burton's firm is a lot nicer than ours. I don't know about you, but I'd be willing to make less money to have a nicer office."

Rachel accepted the defects of their office as a given. Simon didn't. "I'm impressed," she said. "You've really given this some thought. The thing you said that really scares me is the prospect of Carpenter not being around. And what scares me even more is that I didn't even think of that." For all her smarts, there were times like this when Rachel wondered whether she had a practical brain in her head.

"I think Philly would be the first to admit that she couldn't fill all the roles that Carpenter plays," Simon said. "And what happens when you and Josh have kids?"

Rachel felt herself redden. She and Josh had talked about marriage and she knew it was only a matter of time before he proposed formally and she accepted.

"For that matter, what happens if I decide I want kids with Frank?"

Rachel tried to wrap her mind around the concept of Simon as a father. Why was that? Did his aloofness and reserve cause her never to think of him as a parent?

"I'm just saying that each of us will be going through major changes in the years ahead. Even if we don't merge with another firm, our own firm isn't going to be just the way it is now. And maybe a different work environment than we're used to will be better for us."

Rachel appreciated the plural pronoun. Her firm had four partners and at the end of this year they would all be equal partners. But the fact remained that she and Simon would be the new kids on the block for a long time to come.

"What do you see as the next step on this merger?" Rachel asked.

"I'd like a meeting with Burton and the managing partner Philly mentioned, Ben Klein. I'd like to meet them and hear them out."

Rachel couldn't believe that in the time it took to down a latte, her thinking had taken a U-turn. "Okay," she said. "Why don't you suggest that in an e-mail to Carpenter and Philly. You can say that I'm on board."

30

Carpenter sat at his desk relieved that Meredith was out of the office. He attributed her brooding mood to the impending drop off of her billable time in the Sloan-Webster case. Whatever was bugging her, he needed alone time to assess Harris Burton's merger overture.

When he and Philly had brought up Harris' proposal with their young partners, Rachel had been adamantly against the idea. True to form, Simon had given no indication what he was thinking but Carpenter should have realized that despite Simon's bland expression, he might have an interest in Burton's proposal. In any event, here were his two youngest partners requesting to meet with Harris and the managing partner of Sizemore Klein.

Maybe Simon and Rachel had the right idea. After all, there was no harm in talking—talk was cheap. But Carpenter had the nagging feeling that he and his partners were being somewhat disingenuous. Was it kosher to meet with a firm about a possible merger when they couldn't even keep Meredith busy with billable work? 'What the hell,' he thought. 'What's another meeting!'

Carpenter refocused on the firm's active case likely to require immediate attention: Ship Right Specialists' suit against Blake, Pennington & Dwyer. With the complaint filed and the law firm paid the $900,000 not being contested, the Blake firm would file a counterclaim against Jeremiah Becker's company seeking to be paid the $700,000 it had yet to receive. Then the firm would likely file a motion for summary judgment claiming that there were no facts in dispute and that under the parties' engagement letter, Ship Right owed the

$700,000. To oppose that motion, Becker's company would need an affidavit from Harris Burton and a legal memorandum opposing the motion. Perhaps drafting the legal memorandum was a task to entrust to Meredith. That might brighten her mood. And perhaps that assignment would prove that Meredith could be kept busy.

In Brighton, Philly spent the morning preparing for the court hearing in which she would seek an injunction ordering Sasha Barton returned to her job with pay. Sonia Acevedo and Carmen Brown had provided supporting affidavits. Sonia Acevedo's affidavit supported Barton's intervention on behalf of her son and his friends. Carmen Brown's affidavit focused on Barton's teaching and stressed that the replacement teacher lacked Barton's ability to engage her son in his coursework. Brown had not leveled any criticism at the principal, Samuel Clarke, but Philly was pleased with what she'd gotten. Sasha Barton had submitted an affidavit setting forth her version of events. Barton would attend the court hearing. Philly had invited the mothers to attend but neither had committed to showing up. After reviewing her one-page oral argument outline, Philly decided she was ready for the court hearing.

Just before noon, as Philly descended the stairs to the living room-dining room area, she heard Daisy and Rosalind shrieking with laughter and Daniel crying. Sarah was holding Daniel and looked relieved when Philly appeared.

"The marines have landed," Sarah said, handing over Daniel. "I think he's hungry."

"Mom! Look!" Daisy implored.

Philly dutifully admired the coloring book page featuring a pink turtle. "I need to feed Daniel," she told her daughter.

Philly lay down with Daniel in her bedroom. Her son *was* hungry. Philly closed her eyes while he nursed but willed herself to stay awake. She was on lunch duty this afternoon and, besides, Sarah needed a break. If they merged with Philip's old firm, would she and Daniel be able to share a moment like this?

Philly had been surprised by Simon's e-mail suggesting a meeting with Harris Burton and Ben Klein. Mostly she was perplexed by Rachel's joining Simon's willingness to meet because Rachel had seemed totally opposed to a new affiliation when the partners had discussed the matter. She herself was ambivalent on the subject. On the one hand, she wanted to do what was best for their newly formed firm. On the other, she would not agree to an arrangement where she couldn't care for her kids as she was now doing, at least for the next few years.

Daniel stopped sucking. His eyes were closed and he was breathing deeply. "Wish I could join you," Philly said, disengaging.

It was always impossible to drive in downtown Boston on Patriots Day, so Simon, Rachel and Meredith had an early lunch followed by a brisk walk to Sloane-Webster for a video conference with the newly hired director of placement. Simon had pictured Neil Taylor as a bookish, middle-aged guy with little pizzazz, but his Skype image showed a young man with sandy hair, a broad, natural smile, and a healthy dose of nervous energy. "Great seeing you all," Taylor said enthusiastically after the dean introduced Simon, Rachel, and Meredith. "It's a little scary when the lawyers outnumber the administrators," he joked.

They were in a small conference room with the dean and Ralph Cray. By now the dean knew that Sloan-Webster would only be billed for one lawyer's time. Simon wondered whether his firm's billing practices were off the mark: just look what Blake Pennington had billed Ship Right.

"Did you get all the materials I forwarded?" Taylor asked.

"You've been busy," the dean said, "and you're not even on salary here."

Taylor shrugged resignedly. "I do feel like I'm working two jobs. Finishing up here is taking more time than I thought it would. But I want to hit the ground running when I get to Boston."

"We're entering the spread sheet information you requested," Cray said. "Also, I'm making progress on getting you the list of hiring partners at Massachusetts law firms."

"Excellent. I'm planning on sending out a letter to each of them introducing myself. Of course, I'll run the letter by you."

"You asked for a copy of the court complaint we're dealing with," the dean said. "Any reactions?"

The dean's question had a dampening effect on Taylor's enthusiasm. "I thought we were only going to talk about pleasant things," he said without much attempt at humor.

"We're curious," Martin said.

"All right. To be blunt, your placement office hasn't been working at all on placing students."

"We never said we would," Cray came back.

"Then why have a placement office? Look, it's hard for students to find legal jobs on their own. That's why law schools have placement offices. It's a different environment out here in the heartlands, but I've had decent success in landing our students legal jobs. At freshmen orientation, I give a short speech. Every freshman knows that I'm available to review any student's resumé and that my preference is to review any resumé before it's mailed out to anyone." Taylor paused. "One of the reasons I do that is because a poorly done resumé reflects badly on the whole law school, not just the student who sends it." Taylor helped himself to water before continuing. "During freshman year, I make it a point to meet one-on-one with each first-year student. I intend to do these kinds of things at Sloan-Webster."

Janet Martin circled back to her original topic. "We sent you our answer to the complaint. What do you think of our defenses?"

"I think that's a question for your lawyers," Taylor responded. "The gist of your position is that you never said anything that was untrue. I get that. And maybe as a legal defense, that position will carry the day. But a placement office needs to be proactive. That didn't happen as far as I can tell. And I think a case could be made that Sloan-Webster's placement office needed to be particularly proactive because the law school hasn't yet reached prestige status. That's the situation of the law school I'm currently at, too.

"And there's something else I've been thinking about. Sloane-Webster admits a lot of students who don't have high-achieving records. That's okay. In fact, it's potentially something you could build your own reputation on *if* your graduates find jobs and succeed. But if they don't, then the school could dry up. So, having a placement office—and a really good one—is essential. And, with all due respect, you don't have one now."

Although the group in the conference room had discussed these deficiencies, Simon found the shortcomings especially disheartening coming from a newcomer such as Taylor, and he was glad when Taylor changed the subject.

"We've got a place to live," Taylor said. "My wife's Massachusetts connections have been useful. The house has to pass an inspection and we need to actually see the place, but our deposit is taking the property off the market."

"That's good news," the dean said, sounding like she meant it.

Simon tuned out on the ensuing small talk. Taylor's sobering assessment suggested that Sloan-Webster's simply telling the truth about the placement office might not amount to much of a defense in the end. He could hear Christopher

Blaisedell's opening argument to a jury beginning with, "This is a case about a law school placement office that never placed anyone and never tried to place anyone."

Rachel and Meredith were subdued, too. Simon wondered if they were entertaining the same dark thoughts. Was a new game plan necessary? Maybe they needed to turn from trying to right the sinking ship of the placement office to undermining the individual plaintiffs. Simon had never liked a blame-the-victim approach but, as Carpenter was prone to say, you played the hand you were dealt.

It was just after midnight when Philly heard the front door open and she sped to the entryway. Paul looked drained and shaken. For a long moment, they held each other.

"This is just the beginning," Paul whispered. "I'm going to be flat out for a while."

It wasn't until after the kids had finally been put down for the night that the grownups had allowed themselves to watch the horrible images on the television news. Bombs had exploded at the finish line of the Boston Marathon, and the casualty count mounted as they watched. Philly had to look away sometimes. The announcement that a little boy had been killed by one of the bombs had reduced her and Isabella to tears.

Paul removed his coat, sank heavily into one of the living room chairs, and closed his eyes. "I wouldn't mind a beer," he said.

Philly fetched a beer thinking that this was one escape she wasn't allowed. She settled onto Paul's lap. "Any leads?" she asked.

"Not yet. A lot of films are being studied, and the Boston police are interviewing anyone who might have seen someone. There's an eyewitness description of someone that's being looked at. A bunch of cities and towns are being briefed. I'll know more tomorrow morning."

"Are you in charge in Cambridge?" Philly asked.

"No. I'm part of the team being kept in the loop."

Philly nestled against Paul's chest.

"I can't really finish this," Paul said, setting his beer bottle on the living room floor. I'm zonked."

Philly took the bottle to the kitchen, emptied it, then followed Paul to their bedroom.

"What's this?" Paul asked.

Daisy and Daniel were sleeping in the middle of their bed and Philly slipped into bed on her side.

"I wanted us all together tonight," Philly said.

"Good thinking," Paul said as he began to shed clothes.

31

The door to the rear of the courtroom opened, and Philly got her first look at Parker Hill Elementary School principal Samuel Clarke. The guy was huge—all muscle and no fat—and his dark suit dropped off his broad shoulders in straight lines. It made Philly think of the movie where Arnold Schwarzenegger played a kindergarten teacher. Fifth graders were bigger than kindergarten kids, but Clarke had to be intimidating to any grade school student.

Philly had already met the defendants' counsel, Miranda Hernandez, who reminded her of Isabella. Like Isabella, Hernandez had a natural elegance, tall and lithe and impeccably turned out in a blue suit. Unlike her housemate, Hernandez was fair-skinned and had light hair, which was arranged in a complicated bun. Philly had to hand it to the other side; by choosing an Hispanic attorney they delivered a message to the judge that Principal Clarke was not racially prejudiced.

The courtroom itself was unusually quiet. Philly attributed the subdued mood to the Marathon bombing. The shocking events on Patriots Day had changed the mood and feel of daily life. Yesterday the courts had been closed altogether, and few people and cars were about. Today Paul was assigned to help Boston police conducting interviews of people who had been in the crowd near the finish line. She couldn't bear to think about him assigned to pursue leads. The whole city was terrified, and that included Philly.

She heard the courtroom door open again and turned in that direction. Carmen Brown and Sonia Acevedo joined Sasha Barton, who was sitting in the rear of the courtroom. Barton rose and the three women joined in a group hug.

"Court!" the bailiff announced, and Judge Raymond Wu ascended the bench. Carpenter had been before this judge several times and had stressed to Philly that Wu enjoyed byplay with lawyers and tended to be fair. The judge had close-set, dark eyes, which panned the courtroom methodically as the court clerk called the case.

"I have before me the plaintiff's motion for a preliminary injunction supported by a legal memorandum," the judge stated. "The plaintiff is seeking an order permitting her to resume teaching at the Parker Hill Elementary School. She has submitted an affidavit. In addition, her request for an injunction is supported by affidavits from two mothers whose children are in her fifth-grade class.

"The defendants oppose the plaintiff's injunction request. That opposition is supported by a legal memorandum and an affidavit from the school's principal, Mr. Clarke, who is a named defendant in the case."

Judge Wu addressed Philly. "Would you agree, Ms. Sullivan, that the irreparable harm the plaintiff must demonstrate to obtain an injunction is absent in this case because, as the defendants' point out, your client can be made whole financially after a trial?"

Philly rose thinking of Carpenter's admonition that it was always a bad sign when a judge directed his first question to you. "No, Your Honor, I would not agree. Ms. Barton is harmed each day she is not present in the classroom. Those are classroom teaching opportunities that cannot be restored after a trial. Moreover, as established by the parent affidavits you mentioned, the students that Ms. Barton bonded with before she was fired are harmed each day she is not in the classroom. The parents make the additional point that Ms. Barton's substitute does not measure up to Ms. Barton's excellent teaching abilities."

"Do you agree, Ms. Hernandez, that the plaintiff's teaching performance was not in question before she was fired?"

Philly sat as Hernandez rose. "That is correct, Your Honor. But I would add that while two parents would prefer the plaintiff to be back in the classroom, her replacement has been a long-term teacher with both experience and expertise. The defendants disagree that there has been any drop-off in learning in Ms. Barton's classroom."

"The mothers who have submitted affidavits say their sons are bored," the judge said, "and that they weren't bored under the plaintiff's tutelage."

"The defendants have replaced the plaintiff with a competent, trained individual whose past performance shows her to be an effective teacher," Hernandez replied. "The defendants have discharged their duty. They can't be faulted if two students prefer a previous teacher."

"Ms. Sullivan," the judge said, and Philly realized that this would be one of those court hearings where the judge switched targets constantly. "Principal Clarke states in his affidavit that one of the disciplined students used a particularly derogatory racial epithet offensive to African Americans. While the punishment employed by the principal may be unusual, wasn't the punishment reasonable to drive home the unacceptability of what the student said?"

"I would disagree with characterizing the punishment as simply unusual," Philly began. "I submit that degrading is a more appropriate description. In addition, there was more than one racial epithet uttered during the students' altercation, as one parent affidavit establishes. That second epithet was offensive to Hispanics. Yet only Hispanic students were singled out for degrading treatment, and the degrading treatment was not limited to the student who used the epithet. The mother of the Hispanic student involved in the altercation makes the point that forcing her son and other students to eat off the cafeteria floor was excessive and degrading no matter what epithets were used. And I would also point out that literally adding insult to injury, the punished students were taunted and ridiculed by other students while the punishment was going on."

"Would you agree that principal Clarke was aware of only one of the epithets used in the altercation?" the judge continued.

"That is what he claims in his affidavit. But the fact is that he didn't investigate the incident before insisting Hispanic students eat off the floor. If he had investigated fully instead of rushing to judgment and humiliating a group of students, we might not be here today."

The judge turned to Hernandez. "Besides hearing from one of the African American students involved in the altercation, what else did Mr. Clarke do to learn what had happened during the altercation?"

"As his affidavit states, he did not make any further investigation," Hernandez replied.

"Did any of the Hispanic students admit that the n-word was used?"

"Not specifically."

"In fact, none of the other Hispanic students said anything when confronted by Mr. Clarke. Is that correct?"

"I believe that is correct," Hernandez confirmed.

"Did Mr. Clarke do anything else before imposing punishment?"

"I don't believe so."

Judge Wu glanced at his notes and turned toward Philly. "Isn't it true, Ms. Sullivan, that when the plaintiff told the Hispanic students to eat at a cafeteria table, she knew that Mr. Clarke had directed the students to eat on the floor, and she wasn't aware that any of the Hispanic students had uttered a racial epithet?"

"Yes," Philly said. "May I elaborate?"

"You may," the judge said.

"As Ms. Barton's affidavit makes clear, when she entered the cafeteria, she encountered the Hispanic students eating on the floor and being ridiculed by African-American students. She properly found the situation intolerable and quickly restored dignity to the Hispanic students while at the same time cutting off the ridiculing comments of the other student group." Philly paused, met the judge's stare, and decided what the hell, she might as well go for it. "There is only one person who distinguished herself during this unhappy situation. That person is Ms. Barton. She's the one who broke up a playground altercation between two student groups. She's the one who directed the students leading each group to shake hands. Later on, the only person who acted with compassion, with common sense, was Sasha Barton. Firing her for exercising compassion and defusing a situation that was causing humiliation and bullying is simply wrong. If Mr. Clarke wanted to punish the person who used an inappropriate word, then why did he end up punishing students who never said anything inappropriate?"

Philly had deliberately put emotion into her brief speech but whether her tone resonated with the judge was uncertain. Judge Wu regarded her without expression and she recalled Carpenter mentioning that he was difficult to read.

"Ms. Sullivan characterizes the chosen punishment as demeaning," the judge said to Hernandez. "Why did Mr. Clarke choose that punishment?"

"As Mr. Clarke states in his affidavit, he wanted to send a message that racial insults would not be tolerated."

"I will point out," the judge said, "that Ms. Acevedo, in her affidavit, states that her son and his friends were ordered to eat on the floor without explanation."

"Mr. Clarke denies that, as set forth in his affidavit," Hernandez responded. "He is present in the courtroom in the event Your Honor has questions."

Philly had to admire Hernandez's nerve. In her position, she might not have offered her client up to the judge for questioning. But her adversary's ploy called for a response on her part.

"The plaintiff is also in the courtroom," Philly said, "as are the two parents who have submitted affidavits."

Judge Wu continued with Ms. Hernandez. "Ms. Sullivan points out that the plaintiff directed the Hispanic students to eat at a table because they were being taunted and bullied by the African American students. Why wasn't her action appropriate in these circumstances?"

"Because, Your Honor," Hernandez responded, "she knew that her superior had ordered the discipline in question. Her proper course of action would have been to consult with him. She didn't consult with him even after she countermanded his disciplinary decision."

Judge Wu stared at Hernandez who calmly met his gaze. "There appears to be a fair amount of racial tension at this elementary school," he observed. "One might conclude that Mr. Clarke's punishment—or disciplinary action to use your words—contributed to that tension. No matter what happens in this case or in the lawsuit by the Hispanic students that Ms. Acevedo mentions in her affidavit, somebody needs to get a handle on the underlying causes of this racial tension and do something about it."

The judge leaned over and briefly conferred with his court clerk. "I believe I've heard enough," the judge said when the conference concluded. "I'm taking the plaintiff's motion under advisement and you may expect a decision on the motion shortly. The court is in recess."

Philly made it a point to shake hands with Hernandez before moving to the rear of the courtroom where Sasha Barton and the parents had lingered.

"How do you think it went?" Barton asked.

"The judge didn't seem to miss much," Philly replied. "I think the defendants' lawyer got the harder questions. But as I've said to you, it's difficult to get an injunction. We'll just have to wait and see."

"This sucks," Barton said. "I've been doing a lot of subbing, but it's not the same. I want to be back in my classroom where I can feel the day-to-day continuity of my work."

"Keep your fingers crossed," Philly said. "What about the boys?" she directed to the mothers. "Is anything in motion?"

"See for yourself this afternoon," Carmen Brown said. "Stanley's about to find out if soccer *is* a sissy game."

"Can I bring my kids?" Philly asked, thinking she'd probably need babysitting help with three little ones.

"The more the merrier," Sonia Acevedo said.

The soccer field was better maintained than Philly expected. It sat amidst two- and three-family houses in Chelsea and had somehow escaped development. There were goal posts with nets at either end. A white chalk, rectangular boundary line defined the playing field. The grass was mostly green, but brown spots showed, particularly in front of the goals.

Philly turned Daisy, Rosalind, and the stroller over to June, who thankfully had the afternoon free. They were told to stay along the white line and started off at a quick pace, pretty much heeding that instruction. Philly held Daniel under his armpits and began "walking" him, an activity that she knew from experience would tire her out before her son.

Xavier's team was the visiting team. They wore matching, long-sleeved, green jerseys and black shorts. The home team's jerseys were yellow. Philly saw Carmen Brown marching her son to the green team, gripping an arm above the elbow, practically dragging him forward. He was wearing jeans and sneakers; Xavier's mother was ready for him with an extra green jersey. Stanley's unhappiness with this arrangement was matched by Xavier's. "What's he doing here?" she heard Xavier complain as she drew closer to where the green team was warming up.

"You have a new teammate for today," Sonia Acevedo told her son. "I expect you to welcome him and treat him like your other teammates."

"I bet he's never played before."

"Then help him out on the field."

The green team formed a circle and kept three soccer balls in motion. Philly was amazed that the balls didn't strike each other. Stanley Brown lacked the smoothness of the rest of the team but, to his credit, he returned passes when a ball came his way.

June and the girls had circled the field by the time the game started. Philly set Daniel down in the stroller and paid attention to the field. Xavier and Stanley were forwards: she knew that much about soccer.

The boys' mothers joined her, and Philly reintroduced them to Daisy and Rosalind and to June. The little girls looked at the women with solemn expressions, but Philly was pleased that they held their ground and didn't seek refuge behind her legs. Carmen Brown checked with Philly, then lifted Daniel up and tickled him under his chin; he responded with a silly, wet smile.

"This is hard for Stanley," his mother said. "He really doesn't know this game."

"I'm counting on Xavier to show some class," Sonia Acevedo replied.

Philly paid attention to the game. It was fast paced. Coaches called out instructions from the sidelines and the boys, for the most part, had skills. Stanley appeared out of place, but at least he was trying.

At the half, there was no score. The green team huddled and were given a pep talk by their coach. Stanley Brown was bent over, clearly gassed.

"I think it's been a while since Stanley had to run like that," Carmen Brown observed.

Philly noticed that all the green team players except Stanley were drinking from water bottles. She was about to point this out to the mothers when she saw Xavier walk toward his antagonist. Xavier held out his water bottle and Philly watched Stanley's internal debate. In the end, Stanley accepted the bottle; he tilted it up and began to drink greedily before Xavier snatched the bottle out of his hands. "You need to sip it," she heard Xavier say. "You don't want to cramp up," he added as he returned the bottle.

The mothers had observed this exchange and shared smiles.

"Does Xavier know he's playing basketball tomorrow?" Carmen Brown asked.

"I haven't broken it to him yet," Sonia Acevedo said. "There's just so much a kid can take at one time."

32

Henry Frazier eyed Lily Tompkins with trepidation, as if he expected unpleasant news. They were sitting in the office suite conference room, Tompkins at the head of the table flanked by Frazier and Carpenter. Philly sat beside her partner, poised to take notes.

"Okay, I'm just going to jump into this without beating around the bush," Tompkins said, and Philly figured that this blunt introduction had probably ratcheted up Frazier's blood pressure. "Your father's expense account was the only area I have concerns about."

Tompkins removed three sets of documents from a leather satchel and handed one set to Frazier and a second set to Carpenter. Philly moved her chair closer to Carpenter's so that she could look on.

"These are documents relating to your father's personal expense account for October of 2012, last year. As you can see, the total is a little over ten thousand dollars. The other monthly expenses for 2012 were reasonably close to this figure."

"Wow!" Frazier exclaimed.

"There's nothing wrong with expense accounts that are reimbursed by a company," Tompkins explained. "But there is a problem when there is no backup for claimed expenses."

Philly wrote the words *Donald Personal Expense Account* on her notepad and waited for the punch line.

"For a lot of your father's expense reports, there are credit card receipts and credit card statements that show what was purchased. But as this month shows, there are no receipts—and no description of the purpose—for exactly eight-thousand-dollars-worth of expenses. Each undocumented expense is listed as a client expense without disclosing precisely what the money was spent on or for which client. Also, these undocumented expenses are in even amounts. For the month you're looking at, October, we're talking about three expenses in the amounts of four-thousand, three-thousand and one-thousand dollars."

Frazier seemed poised to intervene but then sank back into his chair as Lily Tompkins continued.

"If the IRS ever audited the company, it would demand backup for all expense account items. An IRS auditor would go over personal expense items with a fine-tooth comb because, obviously, any undocumented expenses reduce the company's income and tax liability. You need to find out what these expenses are about, and why there's no paperwork to back them up," Tompkins concluded as she set her copy of the October information down on the conference room table.

Philly jumped to what she believed was an obvious conclusion: Donald Frazier was putting money into his pocket.

"I can't believe this," Frazier said in a weak voice.

"What don't you believe?" Carpenter asked.

"Our business isn't big on socializing. We have business meals where we pick up the tab and we'll do some modest going out for drinks with clients and prospective clients. But we don't have major expenses to the tune of thousands of dollars a month."

"In that case," Carpenter said, "it looks like your father is skimming money."

"I can't believe that either," Frazier said with emotion.

"You may not *want* to believe it," Carpenter came back, "but that's a working hypothesis we can't dismiss at this stage. Do you have a different theory?"

Frazier glumly shook his head.

"Where did these undocumented expenses show up on the financials that were sent out by the company?" Carpenter questioned Tompkins.

"They were buried under miscellaneous operating expenses. Also, there's a similar issue in earlier years. In the earlier years we're talking about less than eight thousand dollars. However, in those earlier years the total monthly amount in question was also always an even thousand-dollar figure such as six thousand dollars."

"Did the miscellaneous operating expenses line ever strike you as too high?" Carpenter put to Frazier.

Frazier colored, his look sheepish. "To be honest, I never thought about the figure one way or the other. I guess I more or less accepted the financials that were given to me."

Carpenter took in this admission with a head nod. "I don't think you should contact your father," he said. "My recommendation is that I contact your father's lawyer and ask for detail on the missing documentation for October."

"I think I should talk to him," Frazier said.

"I disagree," Carpenter replied with some force. "One reason people hire lawyers is to put someone in the middle so that they don't have to deal directly with their adversaries. Think of us as a buffer. You're too worked up emotionally to deal with this situation largely because it involves your father. Let me deal with his lawyer."

"I think he'll talk freely if he's dealing with me," Frazier said. "He'll probably tell his lawyer to clam up."

"He hasn't dealt freely or fairly with you up till now," Carpenter observed. "It's better if I deal with his lawyer. I'll deliver the message that if backup information isn't provided, we'll be back in court seeking a court order to get the information. It's better if your father hears that threat from his lawyer, not from you."

Frazier hung his head. "All right," he said grudgingly. "But before you do anything further in court, I want to review and approve what you have in mind."

"Of course," Carpenter said. "You're the client."

"There goes an unhappy client," Tompkins said when Henry Frazier left the conference room. "You haven't lost your knack, Carpenter. You continue to leave clients more depressed after you meet with them than they were before they showed up in your office."

Lily's jibe never penetrated Carpenter's demeanor. He had his game face on. "Do you think it's as simple as the father putting money in his own pocket?" he asked.

"Nothing's simple," Tompkins fired back. "That's one of the few things we agree on. But in this case, simple makes sense."

"There is another way to look at this," Carpenter said.

"I'm listening," Tompkins replied.

Carpenter shook his head. "I want to think about it some more. One step at a time."

"Did the father really think we wouldn't focus on these undocumented expenses?" Philly asked.

"Stupidity is highly underrated," Tompkins said, delivering a line that Carpenter might have uttered.

After glancing at the caller-ID, Meredith picked up the phone at her workstation in Carpenter's office. "I assume you're getting back to me to reschedule Ms. Wheelwright's deposition," Meredith said to John Pace. When she had rejected Pace's twenty-thousand-dollar offer they had left it that Pace would get back to her on a new date for Wheelwright's deposition.

Pace didn't respond immediately. "Frankly, I'm both frustrated and annoyed that you haven't put forth a demand figure," he said finally.

"You'll just have to live with that," Meredith said. "What works for you as a deposition date?"

"What if I were to tell you that I'm prepared to recommend to my client a thirty-thousand-dollar settlement? Or a fifty-thousand settlement for that matter? Are you at least prepared to tell me what you will recommend to your client?"

Meredith had some sympathy for Pace. In his position, she would be trying to settle the case because of the potential for a whopping verdict against Wheelwright. "If you give me a figure you're prepared to recommend to Ms. Wheelwright, I'll tell you whether in turn I'll recommend it to Ms. Clark."

"Why do I have the feeling that you won't recommend any figure I put forward?" Pace said dejectedly.

"Probably because way back I told you that this might be one of those cases where it made sense for a plaintiff to have a jury decide what the damages are," Meredith said, thinking that there was something surreal about this conversation. Pace would be less put out if he knew that Noreen Clark would take any number he put on the table, including the recently rejected $20,000. Yet Meredith had to play hardball with Pace to get for her unenthusiastic client what she believed to be a fairer figure.

"I'm prepared to recommend thirty thousand dollars," Pace said.

Meredith paused. She was about to reject the figure out of hand. But then she realized that there was nothing stopping her from telling Pace what she would recommend. Given Noreen Clark's attitude, this might be a way to go. Carpenter was wrapping up a meeting with a client. She wanted to run her thinking by him.

"Are you thinking about it?" Pace prompted.

"Sorry. Something's come up. I need to call you back."

When Carpenter returned to his office, he was so lost in thought that Meredith doubted he was aware of her presence. He sat down at his desk chair and closed his eyes. His jaw muscles were grinding away, a signal that meant no interruptions.

Meredith resumed proofreading the assignment Carpenter had recently given her. Because he was certain that the law firm sued by Jeremiah Becker's company would file a motion for summary judgment, he wanted to start work immediately on an opposition to the anticipated motion.

Meredith was grateful for the assignment for two reasons. First, she'd be paid for the billable hour work and could defer, for the moment, her fears that the firm had no further use for her services. Second, it was an interesting assignment.

Ship Right Specialists had ten stockholders and Becker's ownership interest was among the highest at seventeen percent. The other owners were a mix of technical types and investor types. The company's product, air-tight, lightweight shipping containers, was protected by several patents and had achieved a decent-sized market niche.

The engagement letter agreement between Ship Right Specialists and Blake, Pennington & Dwyer was lengthy and detailed. When Meredith had worked for a large Boston firm, she had been kept in the dark about the firm's business arrangements with clients. However, on one occasion, a copy of the firm's engagement letter had been included in a file she had been assigned to work on. She had taken the time to study her former firm's standard engagement letter and found Blake Pennington's engagement letter similar.

The letter spelled out that the sale of Ship Right Specialists would involve business, corporate, tax, labor, and real estate issues and therefore would be handled by these various departments within Blake Pennington. Morgan Carmichael would be the partner in charge of the engagement, and he would have overall supervision of all attorneys working on the engagement, regardless of department. Because the Ship Right sale was a major transaction due to close in a short period of time, Blake, Pennington & Dwyer would devote the necessary manpower to ensure that the deal's closing would occur timely. Nowhere did the engagement letter specify or limit the number of attorneys who would be assigned to the transaction. The letter contained a boilerplate pledge by the firm to provide services efficiently and economically. Meredith remembered that in her former firm's engagement letter, there was a commitment to use associates where feasible so that lower hourly rates would apply; there was no such commitment in the Blake Pennington letter.

Carpenter had drafted an affidavit for Harris Burton to sign, and Meredith had relied on it to complete her own assignment, making the obvious points: too many lawyers were assigned to the transaction; charges for multiple lawyers should not have been billed, particularly in connection with internal and outside meetings and conference calls; and attorneys provided duplicative services and billed for services that were not meaningful.

In addition to these points, she had come up with another contention, one that Carpenter had not touched upon in drafting Burton's affidavit. The deal had fallen apart because Ship Right and its prospective buyer couldn't agree on a purchase and sale agreement. Meredith had added a contention that a lot of the legal services provided by Blake—particularly relating to taxes and real estate—should have proceeded slowly or not been started until there was a signed purchase and sale agreement. Of course, Blake Pennington would argue that advance work on these subjects needed to be done because of time pressures to close the deal. But so what! Let them make that or any other argument they wished to make. Carpenter would ultimately decide whether her position had merit and whether it should be included in the document.

"How's it going?" Carpenter asked.

Meredith swiveled her workstation chair to face Carpenter's desk. "It's going," she said. "I'll give you that Becker case pleading you assigned to me shortly."

"Good. I appreciate that."

Carpenter was staring at her; his jaw muscles were at rest, but it still seemed to Meredith that he had something on his mind.

"Let me ask you something," he said, and he proceeded to recount what had occurred at his meeting with the accountant hired in the Frazier case. "So what was the father up to?" he asked.

To Meredith, the conclusion was obvious. "It looks like the father was putting money in his own pocket so he didn't have to declare it as income and pay personal taxes on it."

"But let's say that he didn't put the money in his pocket," Carpenter posited. "What would he have spent it on that had no documentation?"

Meredith decided that she was being used as a sounding board. Which was not a complaint; in fact, she was pleased. "I'm thinking it would be some kind of illegal cash payment."

"Exactly," Carpenter said, punctuating his concurrence by slamming an open hand on his desktop. "The question becomes, what kind of illegal cash payment?"

Meredith drew a blank. "A bribe," she said tepidly.

Carpenter nodded. "That makes sense."

"Who would he be bribing?" Meredith wondered aloud.

"Shit," Carpenter muttered.

"What?"

"I've got to call Lily Tompkins back," Carpenter said. "Twice in one day I've got to listen to her give me shit."

But judging from his tone of voice, Carpenter didn't seem put out that he would be subject to the accountant's abuse; his rueful smile gave him away. Meredith wanted his ear while he maintained a modicum of good humor. "Can I ask you something?" she said.

"Yeah, sure."

Meredith summarized her thinking on how to proceed with the negotiations in Noreen Clark's case. Carpenter listened impassively as she began, but it wasn't long before his jaw muscles were in motion.

"So you're going to hold off on telling Clark about this guy Pace saying he'd recommend thirty thousand?"

"That's what I'm thinking," Meredith confirmed.

"What are you going to tell this guy you will recommend?"

Meredith hesitated. "Sixty thousand," she said, going on instinct.

"How'd you come up with that figure?" Carpenter questioned.

"It just feels right. I kind of pulled it out of my ear."

"Are you prepared to go lower?" Carpenter pursued.

"Yes, but I'm not going to tell Pace that."

Carpenter nodded. "Do you think Pace already has Wheelwright's consent to settle at thirty thousand?"

"I don't know. If you were to push me, I'd say no. He seemed to be trying to get me to throw out a number before he talked to his client. I haven't given him any figure yet."

"And Clark, your client, would take the twenty thousand you just rejected, right?"

"Right."

"Which is why you're keeping her in the dark about Pace saying he'd recommend thirty."

"Right again."

"And you only came up with the sixty thousand figure because Clark is willing to settle for short money. It's not a number you think is fair to Clark, right?"

"Right. I think she'd get more at trial, but she doesn't want to go to trial."

Carpenter drummed his fingers on his desktop. "You know what," he finally said. "Given Clark's unwillingness to roll the dice and go to trial, I think you'd be doing the right thing mentioning sixty thousand to Pace. That amount feels right to me, too."

"Thanks," Meredith said.

"Don't you just love these little talks?"

"You bet I do," Meredith said, meaning it.

"How's Flash, my favorite expert witness?"

"Flash is doing well, thanks for asking. At least he better think he's doing well if he knows what's good for him."

Philly snuggled against Paul. They had kept the kids with them four nights running before returning them to their own room, and the bed now felt strange without them. But then, the whole world had felt strange as local, state and federal agencies searched the city for the two suspects, finally named. When the drama finally ended with the death of one brother in a shootout and the arrest of the other a few hours later, Paul had returned home completely exhausted.

"A while back I met that MIT cop who was killed two nights ago," Paul said. "It was a chance thing. He was at the Somerville Police Department and I happened to be over there when he put in an appearance. One of the Somerville cops introduced me."

Philly drew closer. Paul had been running himself ragged since the bombings, and the arrest was just the beginning of the investigation, which could go on for months. Paul seldom talked about the details of his work, but Philly sensed that tonight, and for the next several nights, he'd make time to talk.

"This MIT cop was a tremendous hot shit. He had such a lot going for him. It's going to come out that he was one of these thoughtful, considerate guys who truly wanted to help people."

Philly believed Paul was describing himself.

"What a fucking waste!"

Philly stayed silent. Paul was dealing with what he had experienced in his own way. Last year he'd gotten counselling after he shot an armed man who pointed a pistol at him, but she didn't think he'd opt for counseling for the Marathon events, even though they too had touched him personally.

"I've never favored the death penalty," Paul said. "But this asshole who was taken alive last night? I'm rethinking my position."

Philly and Paul had been listening to a talk show on the radio before dinner. A caller had made the point that while the Marathon bombing was an unforgivable act, what about our country's numerous drone strikes that killed civilians as well as suspected terrorists? "Do we even care what the parents of blown-up children are going through?" the caller wanted to know. Maybe there was a time to talk about that with Paul, but it wasn't tonight.

"It makes me want to scream!"

Philly kissed Paul and settled against him. "Try to sleep," she urged, knowing that his mind would keep on racing.

33

The day's mail brought Carpenter the expected motion by Blake, Pennington & Dwyer for summary judgment in the Ship Right case. The motion was supported by a legal memorandum and an affidavit by the Blake partner in charge of overseeing the engagement, Morgan Carmichael. Carmichael had attached to his affidavit his firm's engagement letter with Ship Right and the billable hour detail that underlay the firm's charges. Carmichael swore under oath that the hours billed for had been expended and were reasonable given the size and complexity of the transaction and the short time frame the parties to the transaction had imposed for the deal to close.

In addition, the firm had filed an answer to the Complaint as well as a counterclaim against Ship Right seeking damages for the $700,000 in unpaid legal fees plus attorney fees and costs.

Carpenter took a moment to reflect on the defendant's choice of counsel. Brian Murphy and Sarah Warren were from the large Boston firm of Dudley, Atkins & Tyng. The pair were formidable litigators. With Philly's invaluable help, he had gotten the better of Murphy in an employment case a little over five years ago. But hiring Murphy and Warren was a signal that Blake Pennington was playing for keeps.

In front of a judge or a jury—but particularly a jury—Murphy had the talent of simplifying complex cases and coming across as a straight shooter. He was a good showman but, unfortunately for opponents, his flamboyance never came across as elitist or exaggerated. Carpenter himself never tried to charm a jury, a tactic that would appear false and forced, given his personality. But he knew he had an ability to connect with a jury if he stayed focused and serious and spoke to jurors as equals.

True, there was a benefit to having Murphy and Warren on the other side. They were fun to do battle with. Over the years, Carpenter and Murphy had developed a shtick. In private, any discussion between them would include each telling the other to go fuck himself.

Carpenter began to make PDF copies of the Blake Pennington pleadings. So far, he'd used Meredith to get a jump on responding to the Blake firm's motion for summary judgment. Philly might also want to get involved now.

Frank had just arrived for an overnight stay and had one immediate destination in mind—the bedroom. Simon resolved to hold him off. "We need to do something first," he said. "Here, put these on."

Frank peered into the shopping bag that Simon had tossed him. "What the hell!" he exclaimed after extracting a running suit.

"Get dressed," Simon repeated before heading for his bedroom.

Frank's jaw dropped when Simon emerged in a matching running suit, and Simon savored the moment. "I knew your size," he explained.

"What the hell got into you?" Frank exclaimed.

"What's the matter? Are you afraid you won't be able to keep up?"

"Fat chance of that."

"We're wasting time," Simon said as he headed for the door.

"Where are we going?"

"You'll see."

Simon held his apartment door open for Frank. Outside the dusky sky was a mix of burnt orange and deep purple. There was a lit bicycle path nearby that afforded a non-hilly course. Simon had gotten his time below eight minutes a mile for a three-mile run, a pace Frank would find lame, but so what?

"What brought this on?" Frank asked.

"You," Simon said. "That is, at first I was doing this for you, but now I'm not so sure. I actually look forward to it."

"All right," Frank said. "You get to show me what you've got."

May

From Meredith's Playlist

"Blurred Lines"

Robin Thicke

34

"Hey, asshole," Brian Murphy said when Carpenter picked up his phone. "Let's get the pleasantries out of the way. Go fuck yourself."

Carpenter lost the fight to suppress laughter. "The feeling's mutual," he said when his laughter subsided.

"You know why I'm calling, right?" Murphy said.

"Right," Carpenter confirmed. He pictured Murphy, a broad shouldered, barrel-chested redhead, grinning mischievously in his posh office.

"What amount do you think I'm going to hit you with to end the litigation?" Murphy asked.

Carpenter knew what he would do in Murphy's position. "One hundred thousand," he said.

"Bingo!" Murphy sounded. "Do we have a deal?" he asked neutrally.

"Not if I can help it," Carpenter replied. The amount was large enough so that it had to be taken seriously, but nowhere near what Carpenter felt he could recommend as a settlement given the $700,000 in dispute. Murphy and Warren had to be working on an hourly-rate basis and had probably advised their client that legal fees would be steep if the case went to trial. The timing of Murphy's initiative was also predictable; it came after his firm had filed a motion to dispose of the case and before Carpenter had spent considerable time, at Ship Right's expense, to oppose the motion.

"You realize, Carpenter, that you're a disgrace to the legal profession," Murphy pronounced.

"That's probably true, and no doubt you're about to provide me with specifics as to my shortcomings."

"You're going to end up wearing a scarlet A for asshole."

"I can live with that."

"What the hell are you thinking? The position you're taking, if successful, might irreversibly set back lawyers' ability to gouge clients when it comes to fees. We can't have that!"

"Does that mean your own firm would have charged what Blake, Pennington & Dwyer charged for the legal services we're fighting about?"

This time Murphy laughed. "I'm just a litigator. I have no idea what's reasonable when it comes to a business transaction."

"Yeah, right," Carpenter said. "Now who's the asshole?"

"You realize that if this case goes to trial, our respective legal fees will make the amount in dispute look like chump change."

"Maybe your fees will," Carpenter said while silently acknowledging the truth of Murphy's comment. Even the winning side could find itself with a pyrrhic victory unless the judge's award included attorney fees.

"I can't help it if you continue to charge fees so low they disgrace the legal profession."

"How much did you say your rent was per square foot?" Carpenter asked, remembering the last time he had been in Murphy's swank office.

"I see you're still in that dump on Milk Street," Murphy retorted.

"It's home," Carpenter said. "All right," he decided to end the back-and-forth. "I'll get back to you on the hundred thousand."

Murphy paused. "Since I know you, I'm just going to give you an off-the-record heads-up that the hundred thousand is pretty much it."

Carpenter received this intelligence without comment. He didn't believe Murphy was posturing, but he also knew that Murphy wasn't above doing so. "Like I said, I'll get back to you."

Carpenter set down his phone. The next conversation with Jeremiah Becker would need to be about strategy, and it could get complicated. If Ship Right Specialists had been routinely billed for every lousy minute an attorney even thought about the case, then the bills were certainly padded. Even if Blake Pennington eventually won, it wouldn't want the trial making it public knowledge how many of its lawyers got to charge a client for one conference call or meeting. It could be worth a small pile of money to avoid having that talked about in open court. So before that conversation with Becker, Carpenter needed to think about the options they had, what amount a jury might award, and what amount of money Blake Pennington would be willing to pay to avoid the whole mess. During that conversation, he foresaw asking Becker if there was a figure that would be acceptable to Ship Right to avoid litigation and further legal fees. Carpenter predicted that Becker would come back with $500,000. Which meant settlement was going nowhere. In the event Becker asked him for a settlement recommendation, Carpenter would mention $250,000, a figure pulled out of his ear in a manner similar to the way Meredith had arrived at a $60,000 figure in the Clark case. Becker would balk at that number, probably dismiss it out of hand. So even if Blake Pennington might seriously consider a $250,000 figure, settlement was not on the horizon.

Carpenter decided to switch gears and punched in the phone number for Donald Frazier's lawyer. Lawyers were bugging him; now it was time to return the favor.

"Lauren Goldman speaking."

"This is Carpenter, Henry Frazier's lawyer. Do you have a moment?"

"I do."

According to Philly, Goldman had done a good job at the previous court hearing. She was a sole practitioner, relatively new to the practice of law. He remembered his own days in those circumstances. Of course she had a moment.

"This concerns Donald Frazier's personal expenses that were reimbursed to him by Elite Scripts," Carpenter set the stage, and went on to summarize Lily Tompkin's research so far, promising to send her a copy of October 2012 information that would explain what he was looking for. "So, bottom line," he concluded, "we want the documentation for items for which there appears to be no backup at all."

Goldman didn't answer for a long moment. "I'm writing," she said. There was another pause. "Okay. Send me an e-mail and attach the October information you mentioned. If I have questions, I'll contact you."

"Works for me," Carpenter said. He set down his phone thinking that if Goldman had a brain in her head, she'd be considering Donald Frazier's possible tax fraud.

Meredith was holed up in the law library at the Spenser School of Law reviewing the pleadings unloaded on Carpenter in the Ship Right case when her cell phone vibrated and displayed John Pace's name. She and Pace had been playing telephone tag, and since she was seated at an isolated carrel, she didn't think fielding the call would disturb anyone. "Mr. Pace. I'm glad we finally connected."

"What can I do for you?" Pace said brusquely.

Meredith didn't like his tone. True, she had been driving him nuts by not presenting him with a demand figure. But she had no doubt that were their positions reversed, he would be using the same tactic on her.

"You asked me if there was a figure I would recommend to settle the case that Noreen Clark has brought against your client. I do have a figure."

"Let's hear it," Pace said, his tone bordering on hostile.

"Let's get two things clear," Meredith said, deliberately opting for a sharp tone. "First, the figure I'm about to give you has not been presented to Ms. Clark and she hasn't authorized me to present it." That statement was technically accurate, although its implication that Clark might require more was probably not. Meredith paused, deciding to let Pace stew for a moment. "Second, the figure I'm going to give you is a bottom-line figure as to what I'm prepared to recommend. It's not a figure that is deliberately set high as a prelude to any back-and-forth negotiation. Are we clear on that?"

"We're clear," Pace said, sounding more subdued.

"Sixty thousand," Meredith said.

Pace fell silent, and Meredith decided to wait him out.

"I mentioned a while back that I was prepared to recommend a thirty-thousand-dollar settlement to Ms. Wheelwright," Pace said. "I now have authority to present that figure."

"I'll let my client know, but obviously I won't be recommending it," Meredith said.

Pace again paused. "I'm pretty sure sixty thousand won't fly with my client," he broke the silence.

"It may not fly with *my* client," Meredith responded. "But if you tell me that the case will go away at that figure, I will try to sell it." She opted to keep the pressure on Pace. "If none of this works out, we need to set a firm date for your client's deposition."

Meredith heard Pace sigh. He was doing what he could to ensure that Caryn Wheelwright was never placed under oath.

"I'll get back to you," he said.

Meredith ended the call. She had a duty to report the $30,000 proposal to Clark, but she wasn't about to do so until she heard back from Pace. Maybe she was violating some professional canon of ethics by delaying but, at least for the moment, she didn't care.

35

Philly had Daniel in her lap as she reviewed the Ship Right pleadings. Daniel was busy gumming an orange-colored ring with the consistency of a fortified gummy bear, and his chin was covered in drool. His dark hair pointed every which way and his eyes swept across her computer screen from time to time. "Maybe I can bill for your time," she whispered to her son.

On balance, she suspected that Carpenter wouldn't be happy having Murphy and Warren as his opposing lawyers He respected them but had to know that the trial of the Ship Right case would involve a hard-fought contest with no quarter given on any point, small or large.

Philly had been briefly involved with Murphy and Warren some five years ago. At a deposition, Warren had thoroughly shredded one of their clients. Another time, when Carpenter was out of the country, she had filled in for him and obtained an injunction for one of his clients that had been opposed by Murphy and, when the case went to trial, she'd helped Carpenter litigate the matter. Carpenter's client had prevailed, but it had been a hard win.

Well, one thing was a given—the Ship Right litigation wouldn't be dull.

Philly's home office phone rang, and she reached over her drooling child to answer it.

"This is Philly Sullivan."

"You got a decision in that teacher case of yours," Carpenter said.

Philly tensed. Carpenter would leave it to her how she wanted to receive the news. She decided to tear the bandage off with one, swift, violent tug. "Lay it on me," she said, her throat tight.

"You got your injunction with conditions," Carpenter revealed.

Philly began to relax. How bad could conditions be?

"Barton can return to the classroom to teach her fifth grade class," Carpenter said. "If she is aware of a matter on which she knows that the principal—Clarke—made a decision, she may not act in any way to undermine the decision, although she may inform Clarke of her views. For the remainder of the school year, she and Clarke are to meet outside of regular school hours twice a month for at least fifteen minutes to discuss any matter they wish to discuss. During one of the first two meetings, she and Clarke *must* discuss this book called *Racial Stereotypes in the Classroom.* During the summer, they've got to talk on the phone twice a month for at least fifteen minutes. That's pretty much it."

Philly tried to get her bearings. "I've never heard of a decision like that."

"What's with Judge Wu?" Carpenter asked.

"Beats the shit out of me. Have you ever seen an order like this?"

"No. Sounds like Wu wants to send a message."

"That's one way to look at it." Philly couldn't imagine which party would be more put off by the forced discussions. If the judge was trying to start a dialogue on the racial tensions among students at Parker Hill Elementary, he had come up with a curious way to achieve that objective. She changed the subject. "Are you looking forward to another battle with Murphy and Warren?"

"Yeah," Carpenter said, and he proceeded to fill her in on Murphy's most recent call.

"Let me know how you make out with Becker," Philly said.

"I'm going to throw work to Meredith on this, but I want you involved."

"Are you kidding?" Philly said. "With Murphy and Warren in the picture, I wouldn't miss it."

In the war room at Sloan-Webster Rachel was trying to figure out what was different about Simon. He had mentioned that Frank had come up to Boston for several nights, which might account for his laid-back manner. But he looked different. It wasn't anything he had done with his hair—still combed straight back, slicked down—or anything to do with the way he dressed—he had on one of the black suits he favored. There was just something… changed.

"So we agree?" Simon was saying. "The first deposition will be the second named plaintiff, Regina White."

Rachel nodded. Regina White was the only plaintiff for whom something potentially embarrassing had been unearthed: her nighttime career as an exotic dancer.

"I figure to go with Branson next. I'll bring up that college cheating incident McCauley and Freedman discovered, even though nothing ever came of it."

"Sounds like a plan," Rachel said. "Do you want me to do one of the depositions?" She expected Simon to say no, remembering that in the Spenser case, he had been a bit of a control freak.

"Sure," Simon said. "Why don't you take Hightower. I should have suggested that earlier. Sorry."

'Maybe Frank should visit Boston more often,' Rachel thought. "We can expect Blaisedell to start with depositions while ours are going on. In his position, I would start with Jane Snelling, the soon-to-be or maybe already ex-placement office head."

"I agree," Simon said. "I want you to defend that deposition. You've met with her. I think she's got to stick to the theme that the placement office would try to answer placement questions which is what the law school's brochure said it would do."

Snelling's deposition would be painful. She was likely to become defensive, and Rachel knew it would take considerable coaching to have her come across as matter-of-fact with nothing to hide.

"Okay," Simon said. "We have a plan."

"Have you put on weight?" Rachel asked.

"Why do you ask?"

"You look different. You don't look as thin."

"I've been exercising," Simon confessed. "This is all Josh's fault. I seem to be adding some muscle."

"Just don't lose your boyish charm."

"No chance of that."

So far, Carpenter's call to Jeremiah Becker was right on script. "A hundred thousand dollars!" Becker let loose. "Fuck that."

"I was going to recommend that Ship Right reject that offer, albeit in less graphic terms," Carpenter responded.

"Morgan Carmichael's got a fucking nerve!"

Carpenter waited for Becker to calm down before going on. His combativeness that had surfaced at their first meeting now had a new reason to manifest itself. "If I had been on the other side, I would have tried the same tactic. A hundred thousand dollars is serious money and Carmichael probably factored in what he'd have to pay lawyers if the case went to trial."

"Carmichael can still go fuck himself," Becker said with less force.

Carpenter paused again in the hope that Becker would wind down even farther. "You and Ship Right have several options in responding to an offer like this. One option is to accept the offer, and that's not going to happen here. So the first realistic response is to reject the offer and do nothing else."

"That's what I want to do," Becker jumped in.

"Another approach is to reject the offer and make a counteroffer," Carpenter continued as if Becker hadn't responded.

"I suppose if they were willing to reduce their legal fee by five hundred thousand dollars, I'd be nuts not to take them up on it."

'Still right on script,' Carpenter thought, taking no satisfaction from Becker voicing the number he had predicted Becker would put forward. "A further approach is to not reject the offer but make a counteroffer without rejecting the offer."

"Why would we do that?" Becker said, recapturing some of his heat. "I can understand making a counteroffer, but I don't understand not rejecting the original offer since we're never going to accept it."

"I'm just going through the options," Carpenter explained.

"Well, some of those options just plain suck!"

"If you were to make a counteroffer, what would it be?" Carpenter asked, not put off by Becker's belligerence.

"I don't know. I suppose the five hundred thousand figure I just mentioned."

"Let's come back to that," Carpenter said. "There's one other wrinkle I need to tell you about first. There's a court rule that permits either party to a case to file a dollar figure with the court. Let's say that Ship Right did that and the dollar figure it filed was three hundred thousand dollars. Under the court rule—Rule 68—Ship Right would be saying that it would accept three hundred thousand dollars off the outstanding bill in settlement. If the Blake firm agreed to that figure, the case would be over. If the Blake firm rejected that figure and the case went to trial, Ship Right could recover its attorney fees from Blake if it won a verdict in the amount of three hundred thousand or more. The attorney fees Ship Right could recover would be for legal services beginning when the Blake firm rejected the three hundred thousand. The Blake firm could also file a figure with the court and Ship Right, if it rejected the figure, would thereafter have to pay the Blake firm's attorney fees from the date of rejection if Blake received a verdict equal to or less than the figure it filed with the court."

Becker didn't immediately respond to this briefing. As a matter of practice, Carpenter disliked employing the court rule on behalf of a client. Nevertheless, Becker needed to be informed as to how the rule worked. It might help Becker's thinking on whether to propose a counteroffer and, if so, in what amount.

"Are you saying we should use this court rule?' Becker asked.

"No, not at this time. But I wanted you to be aware of it."

"Does this rule get used a lot?"

"Not in my experience."

"It's fiendishly clever," Becker acknowledged.

"I agree," Carpenter said.

"Christ! I don't know whether I'm coming or going. I would need to think about it. What do you think I should do?"

"I think you should reject the Blake firm's one hundred thousand dollar offer and make a counteroffer."

"In what amount?" Becker pressed.

"Before we started talking today, I was going to propose two hundred fifty thousand dollars. But I've changed my mind. I would propose three hundred thousand dollars. I'm trying to factor in the vagaries of litigation and the possibility of losing the case as well as winning the entire seven hundred thousand."

"Where did you come up with that?" Becker asked with a mixture of frustration and pique.

"Where else?" Carpenter came back. "I pulled it out of my ear."

"Very funny."

"I wasn't entirely joking because none of this is an exact science," Carpenter said. "The three hundred thousand figure does have an element of guesswork in it. At this stage of the litigation, if Ship Right could save itself three hundred thousand and avoid further litigation costs and end the matter, that might be a good result. I was also thinking about that court rule I just told you about. If, later on, you were okay with filing a figure under the court rule, I was thinking in general terms of going with a figure in the three-hundred-thousand-dollar range. There's seven hundred thou in dispute, and I would want to come in at less than half that figure in case the jury decided to divide the baby in half."

Becker took his time digesting this reasoning. "You know," he said after a time, "you've given me a fucking headache, but I think I understand what you've said. I need to let it settle in. Let me call you back."

"That's fine. I know this is a lot to take in."

"You know what my initial reaction is?" Becker said, sounding engaged. "I'm probably going to want to make the counter offer three hundred twenty-five thousand. And if Carmichael doesn't like it, then I'm seriously thinking of using that number under that court rule you just told me about. If I remember right, Harris Burton thought that roughly three to four hundred thousand of the seven hundred thousand had to do with too many Blake lawyers billing for the same call or meeting. I think we're going to win that issue."

Becker had correctly recalled Burton's estimate of duplicative time billed for calls and meetings. Although a busy guy, Becker was still able to focus on key aspects of the litigation. All of which reinforced Carpenter's assessment that Becker was smart. "Okay," Carpenter said. "Call me when you're ready. You know where to find me. And by the way, we're putting together the opposition to the Blake firm's motion to recover the full seven hundred thousand and dismiss your suit. I'll be sending you drafts of what we put together."

"Christ!" Becker muttered. "I've got lawyers tying me up every time I look around. It's a fucking infestation."

"Just doing our job."

Meredith returned to the office from the law library at the Spenser School of Law to find a message that John Pace had called. She had been researching the legal authorities in the court memorandum filed by Blake Pennington's lawyers hoping that their cases had been incorrectly cited. Unfortunately, they had not.

Meredith glanced Carpenter's way. He was seated at his desk, alternately writing on a notepad and pecking away at a calculator. She debated whether to call Pace back in private and decided not to. As long as Carpenter was grinding his teeth, he wouldn't focus on a thing she said.

"I'm returning your call," Meredith said when Pace picked up.

"Did you present my thirty-thousand-dollar offer to Ms. Clark?" Pace asked.

"No," she said. "I simply haven't gotten around to that. But I know what she's going to say." Meredith *did* know what Clark would say—Clark would tell her to take the thirty thousand, but Pace didn't have to know that. "Besides," she added, "you've probably figured out what she's going to say."

"Yeah," Pace muttered, and it sounded to Meredith that Pace had taken to heart her rhetoric about Caryn Wheelwright viciously trying to destroy Clark's legal career. Pace might be convinced that a jury would render a six-figure verdict in Clark's favor.

"Okay," Pace said with a resigned weariness that was unmistakable. "If you were to propose sixty thousand dollars in settlement, my client would accept that figure."

Meredith stopped herself from blurting out that they had a deal. After all, she had promised to try to sell the $60,000. "Thanks for your efforts with your client," she said. "I'll try to sell the sixty thousand and make this happen. In any event, you'll be hearing from me shortly."

Meredith set down her phone and made some notes on her legal notepad. She would call Clark tomorrow. She wanted Pace to think that she *was* selling the $60,000.

Meredith turned in her chair to find Carpenter staring at her.

"Well played," he said.

"I guess so," Meredith said. The constraints Clark had put on her ability to negotiate still rankled.

"You're putting twenty thousand dollars in your pocket," Carpenter pointed out. "That's not too shabby."

"No, it's not." The money would come in handy especially if billable hours from Carpenter's firm dried up. Meredith scribbled a reminder to pay Carpenter for the time he had put in helping her.

"Are you going to tell Clark about the thirty-thousand-dollar offer?" Carpenter asked.

"Yes," Meredith said. "I think I'm ethically bound to do so."

"I'd agree with that. But you might want to mention it *after* you tell Clark about the sixty-thousand-dollar deal."

Meredith nodded. 'Timing *was* everything,' she thought. She assembled her Ship Right legal research and set her work down on Carpenter's desk. "No surprises here," she said. "Their cases hold up."

"That figures," Carpenter replied. "Tomorrow I hope to finalize Burton's affidavit. "Why don't you shoot for tomorrow to give me your final draft of the legal memorandum we need to file. Remember to copy Philly and Rachel and Simon."

"Okay." Meredith thought what the hell and decided to be nosy. "What is Ship Right going to do about the one-hundred-thousand-dollar offer?" she asked.

"Reject it," Carpenter said.

"And then what?"

"I need to hear back from Becker, and then I'll fill you in. This could get interesting."

36

"Principal Clarke and I had our first fifteen-minute meeting," Sasha Barton said. "Talk about awkward."

"Give me a second," Philly said. She set her phone down and observed the three rug rats on the floor of her office. Daisy, with Rosalind's uncoordinated help, was turning Daniel onto his back and then the two little girls squealed with delight when he flipped onto his stomach. This was a game that could go on indefinitely. "Girls! I need you to use quiet voices while I'm on the phone." But the din persisted; quiet was a lost cause.

Philly moved into the hallway where the noise level was down slightly, but where she could still see the kids. "I take it you met early, before class," she said.

"Yeah. I've still got twenty minutes before my first class, so I thought I'd try to fill you in. Is this a bad time?"

"There's no better time. What did you guys talk about?"

"Not much," Barton admitted. "There were a lot of awkward silences. Clarke was not happy. He finally said that he hoped I understood that he had reacted to the n-word when he punished the Hispanic kids. I told him I had read his affidavit and that I did understand what he said about reacting as he did. But I told him he overreacted. You can imagine how he liked that."

"What's this book the judge wants you to discuss?" Philly asked.

"I'm halfway through it and it's pretty much what the title says it's about: racial stereotyping in the classroom. But what's interesting is that it approaches racial stereotyping from the points of view of teachers—white teachers, African-American teachers, Hispanic teachers, and Asian teachers. So, for example, when it comes to African-American students, white teachers might have different stereotypes in mind than Hispanic teachers do. The idea is to sensitize each racial group to its unique stereotyping pattern when it comes to students of different racial groups."

"Remember the judge commenting on the racial tensions at Parker Hill Elementary?" Philly reminded Barton. "It seems to me that he wants to get a dialogue going to address those tensions, and he's chosen the two of you to begin the process."

"Great!" Barton said. "Clarke comes on like I've betrayed my race when I stopped his punishment of the Hispanic kids."

"I've heard from Sonia Acevedo, Xavier's mother," Philly said. "Xavier had to play basketball on Stanley Brown's home turf. I'm told it was a humbling experience, almost as humbling as when Stanley had to play soccer on Xavier's team."

"There's been a change between them in class," Barton said. "They've stopped glaring at each other, and I've actually seen them nod when they run into each other."

"The mothers are arranging for the families to have dinner together," Philly revealed her latest intelligence.

"Wow!"

"This is all good," Philly said. "It shows there's hope for you and Clarke."

"Aren't you the optimist."

It might be too early to broach the subject of settlement but maybe there is never a good time for some things, so Philly dove right in. "With your permission, I'd like to talk to the school's attorney about settling your case."

"What are the terms you have in mind?" Barton didn't sound put-off.

"You get your job back with back pay for the days you didn't work less what you earned subbing. The firing is eliminated from your record and there's nothing adverse to you about this in your personnel file."

"What about money damages?" Barton asked.

"I don't see that happening in a settlement, but I can ask. What figure did you have in mind?"

"Ten thousand dollars. Also, I would like them to pay the union back for your fees."

Philly evaluated her client's conditions. In the grand scheme of things, $10,000 was a modest figure. As for her legal fees, she hadn't charged for a lot of the time she had spent with the Acevedo and Brown families, so those costs were also relatively modest at this juncture. "Okay," she said. "I'll add those items to the list."

"This is all fine and good," Barton said, "but talking settlement is a waste of time right now."

"Why?"

"I've got some friends on the faculty and the scuttlebutt is that the school and Clarke can't settle with me until the suit by the Hispanic kids is settled."

Philly wondered what sort of settlement deal Carlos Ibanez would be looking for. "Maybe I should talk to the kids' lawyer first."

"I'd go along with that."

An unhappy, tired cry came from Philly's office. Daniel apparently had decided that being treated as a rollover toy had lost its appeal. "I've got to go," she said. "I'll be back to you when I have something to report."

"Whatever you say, Mommy."

The receptionist at Noreen Clark's law firm put Meredith through to her client.

"Tell me this is over," Clark said out of the box.

"It can be if you want it to be," Meredith said.

"We've been through this a million times. You know that's want I want."

"Okay, then. I'll tell Wheelwright's lawyer we have a deal."

"Did they move off the twenty thousand?" Clark said.

"They did."

"What's the final number?"

"Sixty thousand dollars."

"No kidding?"

"I have to tell you a few things," Meredith said. "First, Wheelwright's attorney had upped her offer to thirty thousand. During that discussion, I told him that I wouldn't recommend the thirty thousand to you, and he asked me whether there was a figure I would recommend to you in settlement. I told him I had to think about it, and I called him back and told him I would recommend sixty thousand dollars to you. He asked me whether I had presented the thirty-thousand-dollar offer to you and I told him I hadn't gotten around to doing that. We had some further discussion and he ended up telling me that the sixty thousand dollars would be acceptable if you agreed to it."

"You delayed telling me about the thirty-thousand offer," Clark said.

"Delayed is not the word I would use. As I told Wheelwright's attorney, I simply hadn't gotten back to you on that. I've been busy on other matters."

"Yeah, right."

"Are you complaining?" Meredith asked. She was tempted to tell Clark that she was free to reject the $60,000 and retreat to $30,000.

"What else do you have to say to me?" Clark said, without answering Meredith's question.

"Even though I told Wheelwright's lawyer that I would try to sell sixty thousand, I'm reminding you that I advised you not to accept a settlement of less than six figures. I'll be sending you an e-mail specifying my previous recommendation."

"You're just covering your ass," Clark said heatedly.

"There's some truth to that," Meredith said neutrally. "Frankly, when it comes to this case, I don't understand your motivations, so I want my previous advice to you to be clear."

"All right," Clark said, her annoyance evident.

"Does that mean I may accept the sixty-thousand-dollar settlement offer on your behalf?"

"Yeah."

"Okay. I'll get that e-mail out to you as soon as we ring off, and I'll accept the offer tomorrow, first thing."

"No," Clark said. "I want you to accept it today. I'll say that when I respond to your e-mail."

"Works for me," Meredith said, and ended the call. Honestly, she had expected Clark to thank her, or at least to be happy to be getting several times the amount she'd first been offered. Instead, she just seemed pissed at Meredith. Carpenter was right: there was just no accounting for some clients.

While Carpenter waited for his call to be put through to Brian Murphy, he thought about Jeremiah Becker. The more he interacted with Becker, the more he liked the man. The value of a client who listened to and weighed legal advice, was not afraid to make a decision, and came up with helpful suggestions of his own, was incalculable.

"Hey asshole," Brian Murphy greeted him.

"You know what I have to say to you," Carpenter responded.

"That I do and the feeling's mutual."

"Now that that's cleared up, my client rejects and pisses on your one-hundred-thousand-dollar offer."

"What's the counteroffer?" Murphy asked without hesitation.

"Am I that predictable?" Carpenter came back.

"This is your logical next move is what I'm thinking."

"Then you're in for a surprise. My client has no counteroffer at this time."

Murphy didn't say anything for a long moment, perhaps not expecting this comeback. Becker had decided not to make any counterproposal until the court ruled on Blake Pennington's motion for summary judgment, betting that the motion would be denied and that he'd be in a better position if that occurred. Carpenter thought the bet was a reasonable one.

"I suppose I should have expected something unpredictable with you on the other side," Murphy said.

"Just livening up your day."

Murphy laughed. "Do you have to keep reminding me what a pain in the ass you are?"

"All part of the job."

When the call concluded, Carpenter jotted down a few notes. If he was going to play the role of pain in the ass, there were a few things he could do at relatively low cost that would get Brian Murphy's and Sarah Warren's attention. If he wasn't careful, he might soon be having fun with this case.

37

"I have a question for you," Carpenter directed at Simon after asking his young partner to his office. "You said you were willing to talk to Harris Burton and Ben Klein about their suggestion of a merger. What are you hoping to take away from this meeting?"

Simon decided that Carpenter was entitled to a frank answer. "I'm curious and want to understand what they're thinking. They must have more details as to how an association would work. Also, I want to see if what they have in mind would be a plus for the four of us. I get it that we run a lean and mean operation with almost no overhead. But our offices pretty much suck, no offense. I don't think that bothers you, but it could bother clients, and it does bother me. If Philly were back full time, we couldn't keep going the way we are now. I want to understand what we'd have to give up to get nicer offices."

"I can tell you what you'd have to give up," Carpenter responded immediately. "You'd have to give up money. You'd have to pay more attention to billable hours because of the increased overhead. You'd be giving up independence, too. For example, you might not be able to take on a case like Philly did with Sasha Barton. And you might be giving up decision making authority to a bunch of people none of us really know."

"I understand all that," Simon said. "But I still want to hear what these guys have to say. If our litigation case load increases, then we may not have to give up money."

Carpenter frowned. "You and Rachel were right to want to have a meeting," he said. "I'm trying to keep an open mind. But you know what I'm thinking."

"The devil's in the details," Simon supplied.

"Exactly."

"We want money," Carlos Ibanez said to Philly. "Lots and lots of money."

Outside the window of her office was a clear, sunny day. With the window slit open to let in some cool air, Philly could hear Daisy and Rosalind laughing in the backyard. Sarah had probably sat Daniel on the new grass and would have to keep track of what he put in his mouth. Philly had put Ibanez on speaker phone and perhaps that had been a mistake—with both ears free the girls' laughter called to her.

"Rumor has it that I can't settle my case until your case is resolved," Philly said, refocusing.

"I haven't heard that rumor, but it makes sense. If I were representing the school and Clarke, that would be my position."

"Is there any prospect of your case getting resolved?"

"I haven't brought up settlement," Ibanez replied. "When I represent a plaintiff, I don't like being the one to start settlement discussions."

"I have a partner who feels that way." Philly wondered whether she should have touched base with Carpenter before making this call. "How much money are you looking for?"

"Six figures and the first digit is not a one. I think a jury will stick it to Clarke and the school."

Philly kept her opinion to herself. Ibanez might achieve a big score. But the racial composition of the jury would be a wild card and might ultimately be the determining factor in any damages that would be awarded in the case. And damages only came into play if the plaintiffs won. Philly wasn't about to dismiss the possibility of a jury accepting Clarke's discipline even though his punishment was unusual—if not extreme. Her own limited experience with juries mirrored Carpenter's: you never really knew what a jury would do.

"Are you looking to get Clarke fired?" Philly asked.

"I wouldn't lose any sleep if that happened. Between you and me, what he did makes him unfit to be a principal."

"What about a settlement that includes an apology on his part?" Philly threw out.

"Everything I've heard about Clarke tells me that's not going to happen. Besides, I'd rather have the money. I think a substantial judgment will have a more positive, lasting effect than any apology."

Philly disliked Sasha Barton's limited options. Barton's most attractive, immediate course appeared to be doing nothing active on her case and making sure her classroom performance was beyond criticism so that her injunction stayed in place.

"Do you disagree with my approach?" Ibanez queried.

"Not really," Philly said. "I just wish it were different so that my client could put her own case behind her."

"I'm going to put you on speaker phone," Meredith heard Carpenter say and when she turned in her chair and looked his way, Carpenter motioned her to take the visitor chair at his desk.

"I've got Meredith Sweeney listening in," Carpenter continued, "so I have a witness to your latest round of bullshit. Meredith, say hello to Brian Murphy, asshole extraordinaire."

"The pleasure's all yours," Meredith decided to get into the spirit of things.

"Where do you find these people?" Murphy questioned. "Whoever you are, Meredith, your career took a turn for the worse when you hooked up with Carpenter. He's not content to screw up his own career. He's on a mission to screw up the career of any young lawyer he comes in contact with."

"I'll keep that in mind," Meredith said.

"I'm returning your call," Murphy said, pleasantries over.

"Right. I'm giving you a heads up that we're about to notice a bunch of Blake Pennington depositions and request some documents in connection with the depositions."

"Which I will dutifully oppose until our motion for summary judgment is acted upon," Murphy replied.

"Understood," Carpenter said. "Since you moved for summary judgment you can't very well ask for discovery. I don't have that problem. We hope to respond to your summary judgment motion shortly."

"I appreciate the heads up on discovery."

"My pleasure."

"Then may the best asshole win," Murphy ended the call.

"You actually like this guy?" Meredith asked when Carpenter disconnected.

"Yeah, I do. You've taken depositions, right?"

Meredith nodded. At her former firm, depositions were her closest experience to actual trial work.

"Then you're about to take a lot more."

"Who am I deposing?"

"Lawyers. Lots of lawyers."

Meredith began to take notes as Carpenter explained what he had in mind. He had a wicked gleam in his eyes as he went over his strategy. He was enjoying himself.

"There are no other documents to provide to the plaintiff," Loren Goldman said over the phone to Carpenter.

This response from Donald Frazier's lawyer, took Carpenter aback. "Then what was the money spent on?"

"You can ask that question in interrogatories or you can depose Mr. Frazier," Goldman said. "To the best of my knowledge, all written financial information has been provided to your consultant."

"What if we were to talk off the record?" Carpenter proposed.

"At the moment, I'm not prepared to do that," Goldman responded.

"Aren't you the cryptic one," Carpenter allowed his frustration to show.

"Anything else?" Goldman asked.

Carpenter remembered his manners. "No, thanks for getting back to me."

Henry Frazier would now start lobbying to talk directly to his father. Carpenter resolved to do whatever was necessary to prevent that course of action but, ultimately, father and son could elect to converse regardless of what their lawyers advised.

"Am I missing something or are you actually happy?" Maxine asked.

They were in their condo's small kitchen, seeing to the dinner dishes, Maxine washing and Carpenter drying, the division of labor that kept arguments to a minimum.

"I had fun today," Carpenter owned up. "It was one of those days when I got to see human nature in action in a lot of different circumstances." The best part of practicing law, he had long ago decided, was hearing a problem for the first time, because you got to play voyeur and brainstorm simultaneously. But days like today were a close second, filled with occasions when clients and opponents had to decide on a course of action, faced with directional choices ranging from wild, circuitous, possibly self-destructive tangents to straight lines with helpful signposts.

"Anything you want to share?"

Carpenter took the events of the day in chronological order. As he replayed them, he couldn't help smiling and Maxine joined him.

"*I* have some news," Maxine said, when Carpenter was finished. "I've taken on my first new case."

"Good for you," he said, still uncertain whether the end of Maxine's retirement was a good or bad thing. "What's it about?"

"A family trying to get a private school placement for their son. The kid has some ADD issues. Their case is a long shot."

Maxine looked happy and that made him smile.

"I have in mind ways to keep that smile on your face," Maxine said.

"As you know, you need to give me an hour, and I'll see what I can do."

"I'm aware of that. That was a heads up in case you missed it."

38

Meredith stared with mixed feelings at the settlement check drawn on John Pace's client account. On the minus side, it was a lousy deal for Noreen Clark. On the plus side, the damn case was over and she got to put some money in her pocket. There would be no celebratory lunch marking the end of this lawsuit. Clark was probably as sick of her as Meredith was sick of her client. And nagging questions would remain unanswered: why had Caryn Wheelwright accused Clark of plagiarism, and why was Clark willing to let her accuser off lightly when it came to monetary damages? When she had vented to Carpenter, he had reminded her that Clark had given her reasons for wanting the case to disappear—the desire to put to bed anything to do with the law school plagiarism charge that had been leveled against her—and suggested that Meredith accept that explanation at face value. "Worry about something you can do something about," he had counseled. But Carpenter's advice, however sound, was not easy to take. She had also disliked his refusal to accept payment for the time he had put in on the case. "You've paid me back in other ways," he had insisted.

So Meredith turned her attention to the legal bills submitted to Ship Right by Blake, Pennington & Dwyer. A total of thirty-nine attorneys had worked on the Ship Right sale, and backup information identified the hours spent and the work performed by each attorney. Carpenter had charged her with making a chart identifying each attorney who had worked on the Ship Right sale, whether the attorney was a partner or associate, the attorney's hourly charge, and the total billable time spent by the attorney on the engagement. Meredith double-checked her findings.

The ten attorneys who spent the least amount of billable time on the Ship Right matter spent between 15 and 90 hours each on the case, and their billable time totaled $120,000. For the most part, the billable time for these ten lawyers involved attending meetings and participating in conference calls. Carpenter wanted those ten lawyers deposed immediately. He estimated that each deposition would take twenty minutes and that all the depositions could be completed in one day. He had reasoned that the lawyers who spent the least amount of time on the Ship Right sale would be the least likely to be able to point to any document they had generated on behalf of Ship Right or to identify any positive contribution to Ship Right's representation.

Meredith thought that Carpenter was probably right. With one exception, the ten lawyers she had targeted were associates. For the most part, their time had been billed for attending internal and external meetings and for conference calls during which it was likely that the firm's partners, not associates, did the heavy lifting.

Meredith printed out her findings and set the work down on Carpenter's desk. She was thrilled that he was entrusting her with the depositions; yet she wondered why he wasn't doing the first deposition himself so that she could pick up pointers from his approach. Still, she wasn't about to question his trust in her. There were some things you just couldn't ask.

Philly placed a call to Miranda Hernandez, the attorney representing Parker Hill Elementary School and its principal, Samuel Clarke. If Hernandez wasn't prepared to settle with Sasha Barton until the Hispanic students' suit was resolved, Philly wanted to hear it straight from the horse's mouth.

"What can I do for you?" Hernandez asked in a business-like tone.

"Are you prepared to talk settlement in Ms. Barton's case?" Philly tried to match Hernandez's brusqueness.

"No."

"Is that because there's no possibility of settlement, or because your clients are not in a position to settle while the other lawsuit is pending?"

"The latter."

Philly considered ending the phone call; her question had been answered, and Hernandez wasn't in a forthcoming mood. Still, nothing ventured, nothing gained. "If the other suit wasn't in the picture, what kind of settlement would you consider?"

"I really haven't given it any thought."

This was like pulling teeth, Philly thought. "Is there anything I can do to facilitate a resolution of Ibanez's case?" she asked.

"I'd be open to any suggestions you might have," Hernandez said.

"Ibanez's clients want money," Philly noted.

"Don't we all!"

"Have you talked about a monetary settlement with Ibanez?"

"No."

"Is it in the cards that you will discuss settlement with him?"

"Not at the moment."

"Do you think it would be helpful if there was a meeting of all the parties and lawyers involved in the two suits?"

Hernandez didn't respond. Philly decided to wait her out.

"I'm not dismissing the idea," Hernandez said, "but I'm having difficulty picturing how a meeting would advance anything."

"We won't know unless we try," Philly rejoined. "My suggestion is that you broach the idea to Mr. Clarke. If he shows any interest in a meeting, let me know and I'll try to set it up. Ibanez may nix the idea, but maybe not."

"All right. I'll let you know if there's any interest."

Philly concluded the call. She would be hard pressed to explain why she had proposed a meeting. And Hernandez was probably right that a meeting wouldn't advance resolution of the pending cases. Still there had to be some worthwhile reason the meeting notion had popped into her head. If only she could figure out what it was.

39

"Have you cornered the market on suits against law schools?" asked Jeannie Smith, Carpenter's stenographer of choice, as she set up her equipment.

Simon wondered whether it was his imagination or whether Smith's fingers really were working in slow motion as she arranged her equipment to her liking. Smith was old, approaching eighty, the obvious giveaways being her unruly mass of white hair that appeared to be thinning in spots, wrinkled skin, and pendulous jowls. But this was the first time Simon sensed that she might be slowing down. "We should be so lucky," he responded to Smith's question.

"As usual, I expect to be entertained," Smith said.

"On this one, you may get your wish," Simon came back.

There was a knock and Christopher Blaisedell held open the conference room door for Regina White, the second named plaintiff in the lawsuit brought against the Sloan-Webster School of Law. Blaisedell introduced his client, an unsmiling woman with light brown hair and a round face, probably only an inch or two over five feet tall. Having learned she was an exotic dancer, Simon had anticipated that her law school photograph would prove not to have done her justice. But the photograph was on the mark. Guys attending her strip club to watch a well-endowed, curvaceous woman would be disappointed by this flat-chested and skinny young woman. She looked even smaller next to her counsel. Simon had forgotten that Blaisedell was even bigger than Frank. With his black hair, blue eyes and half-moon eyeglasses, Blaisedell looked studious but he had the body of a brawler.

After Smith swore in White as a witness, and Simon and Blaisedell agreed on the rules for the deposition, Simon's initial questions brought out what he already knew: White had graduated in the top third of her law school class, had yet to land a law-related job, and had found the law school placement office to be of no help in obtaining a legal position. Simon quoted from the complaint and confirmed that White was currently working as a secretary for an ad agency.

"How many times have you contacted the placement office?" Simon asked.

White considered the question composed and thoughtful.

"I believe it was about three times."

"What happened during each of those contacts?" Simon followed up.

"The first time I called the placement office, I asked if it offered help with resumés. I'm pretty sure I spoke with Ms. Snelling. She said that her office didn't assist students or graduates with resumé drafting. She said that she would send me copies of articles that discussed resumé writing, and she did send me the articles." White paused. "We may have talked about something else, but that's all I remember right now. The second time I called the placement office I spoke with someone who said she was filling in for Ms. Snelling who was on vacation. I asked her to send me any information on legal job openings. I explained that I hadn't been successful in landing a job. I was told that the placement office didn't routinely send out that kind of information and that any job opening that came to the attention of the placement office was posted on the placement bulletin board.

"About a week later I went to the placement office and wrote down all the job openings that were posted. While I was at the placement office, I dropped in on Ms. Snelling and explained my situation to her. I asked her if she had any proactive suggestions for me and she said no and that it was a tough market to try to find a legal job."

White glanced at Blaisedell who was busily taking notes.

"Have you finished your answer?" Simon asked.

"No. I tried calling the job openings that I had written down, but I gave that up after the first six calls I made because each of the positions had been filled. I called Snelling back. I guess that makes four contacts with her office. I was angry and told her that I had wasted my time contacting law firms and agencies that had already filled positions. I asked her whether she followed up with job openings and took them down from the bulletin board when they got filled, and she said something like she hadn't done that recently." White paused. "Now I'm finished."

"Did the placement office ever tell you anything or provide you with any information that was untrue?" Simon next asked.

White again didn't respond immediately. "Just those job openings I mentioned," she finally said. "I was led to believe the jobs were still open, but they had been filled."

"Did each of the job openings that you made a note of list a date when the job opening was posted on the placement office's bulletin board?"

White frowned in concentration. "I'm not totally sure but I think there was a date listed."

"Would you agree that the possibility existed that between the date of the posting of a position and the date you called about the position, the position could have been filled?"

"I guess that would have been possible."

"As we previously discussed, the plaintiffs' complaint states that you work as a secretary in an advertising office. Isn't it true that you have additional employment besides that secretary position?"

White colored slightly and Blaisedell looked up from his note taking.

"Yes."

"Why didn't you mention your non-secretary work in the complaint?"

"My primary job is my secretarial position and that's what is mentioned in the complaint."

"Have you ever listed your other employment on your resumé?"

"No."

"What is the nature of your non-secretary employment?"

"I work as an exotic dancer," White said smoothly, and Simon noticed that her brief flash of color had disappeared. Blaisedell's jaw dropped and his blue eyes widened as he stared at his client.

"How long have you worked as an exotic dancer?" Simon asked.

"It's been years. I was doing it in law school."

"Do you take your clothes off during your performances?"

"I do."

"Have you had occasion to give lap dances?"

"Yes."

"Would another name for this job be stripper?"

"It's not the word I would use, but others may use that word."

Simon wondered whether White's composure had to do with the nature of her nighttime work. Maybe taking your clothes off instilled calm and self-possession. She certainly didn't appear embarrassed by her nighttime job.

"Have you ever told a prospective employer about your exotic dancing?"

"No."

"Why not?"

"It had nothing to do with any position I applied for and it concerned my private life."

"Your private life," Simon repeated. "What is private about taking off your clothes in a public place?"

"It's how I choose to spend my own, private time and I don't regard it as anyone else's business."

"What made you start exotic dancing?" Simon asked, curious.

"Initially it was a way for me to earn money to pay for law school so I wouldn't be saddled with large student loans."

"You said initially. What did you mean by initially?"

"You asked me what got me started with exotic dancing. Initially it was the money. But very early on, I found that I enjoyed performing."

"Does that mean that you would be continuing with exotic dancing if you found a legal job?"

"I can't tell you for certain, but I haven't ruled out continuing with it."

Blaisedell hadn't taken a note in a while. He was looking at his client with regret.

"Do you know whether any employer to whom you have applied for a legal job was aware of your exotic dancing?"

"I don't know."

"Would you agree that some people regard exotic dancing, in which the dancer removes her clothes, in a negative light?"

"I don't know for sure, but I suspect that's true."

"Do you agree that an employer seeking to fill a legal job might view exotic dancing in a negative light and might decline to offer an exotic dancer a legal position?"

"I suppose that's possible, but I have no way to agree or disagree with your statement."

"Is it true that you have received rejections from all the employers you have applied to for a legal position?"

"Yes. I believe I mentioned that previously."

"Is it true that for all you know, every one of those rejections may have been due to your exotic dancing job?"

"I don't know one way or the other whether that's true."

"Did you ever follow up with an employer who rejected you for a legal position as to what the reason for the rejection was?'

"No."

"Do you have any theory as to why you have been rejected for each of the legal positions you've applied for?"

"No."

"How much do you earn from your exotic dancing?"

"On average about thirty to forty thousand dollars a year."

"Do those figures include tips?"

"Yes."

"Do you declare your exotic dancing income for tax purposes?"

"Yes."

"Do you have any outstanding law school loans?"

"No. I had a loan outstanding when I graduated from law school, but I've paid that off."

"Is it true that you've left exotic dancing off your resumé because you knew that an employer seeking to fill a legal position would have a negative reaction to exotic dancing?"

White regarded Simon evenly. "I've already answered your question. I didn't include it on my resumé because I didn't think it needed to be mentioned and because it concerned my private life."

"Do you think that including exotic dancing on your resumé would help or hurt your chances of getting a law–related job from a prospective employer?"

"I couldn't tell you," White replied. "I suppose it would entirely depend on the employer."

"What is your preferred legal position?"

"Litigation," White responded.

'Figures,' Simon thought. "Let's take a five-minute break," he said.

Regina White's deposition had concluded, and now Simon was watching Jeannie Smith as she stowed her equipment in a wheeled carrying case. Smith had to know that Simon would ask her for a postmortem; this was a ritual that she and Carpenter had adopted, and Simon followed that tradition last year during depositions in the Spenser School of Law case. "Any comments?" he asked.

Smith leveled a flinty gaze his way. Simon opted for a neutral expression.

"She was a cool customer," Smith said. "She showed no embarrassment over her exotic dancing. Now there's a euphemism."

Simon agreed. White's mousy appearance gave no hint that she had a backbone and resoluteness that would probably serve her well as a litigator.

"But her lawyer," Smith continued, "was about to shit a brick."

Simon again agreed. Blaisedell had to be pissed off at White's failure to mention her night job. Probably when Blaisedell had asked her whether there was anything that might surface to undermine her status as a lead plaintiff, she had simply said that there wasn't.

"What did you think about her testimony concerning the placement office?" Simon asked.

"It didn't sound to me like much of a placement office," Smith responded. "She got no help from anybody. It doesn't look good that the placement office posted jobs that had been filled. You made a good point about the job postings being dated when posted, but it didn't sit well with me that outdated postings were on that bulletin board and that a graduate had to actually return to the law school to look at potential job openings."

Simon believed that jurors might come away with Smith's impressions of the placement office. "What did you think about her efforts to find a legal job?" Simon changed the subject. After the five-minute break he had pressed White on the details of her search for a legal job.

"I think she was pretty diligent after graduating and passing the bar," Smith said. "But over time, I think the rejections started to wear her down."

Simon had the same impression.

"It's got to be tough spending three years going to school for a job you can't land," Smith observed. "I felt sorry for her. I thought she had some spunk to go for that exotic dancing. I liked her."

Simon realized that he had as well. He remembered how miserable he was after graduating from Spenser School of Law and having to wait tables to make ends meet because no law firm would hire him. He couldn't imagine White naked, but the image of her gyrating in front of drunk guys in a seedy dive was sad and bleak. It did pay pretty well, though. He had done the math. With her daytime and nighttime jobs, White had probably made more money than she would have made as a law firm associate. From a big picture point of view, Simon figured that White probably couldn't prove that she was entitled to money damages, and that wouldn't sit well with Blaisedell. But White would score points for the plaintiffs' claim that the Sloan-Webster placement office was pretty much a sham. And despite everything, a jury might find her a sympathetic witness.

"Do you know how long it would take me to make twenty thousand dollars?" Flash asked.

Meredith treated the question as rhetorical and kept silent.

So Flash answered his own question. "About four months."

Meredith wondered if she had made a mistake telling him what her fee came to in the Noreen Clark case. Depositing her fee had made her feel flush, made her appreciate Carpenter's description of a contingency fee coming in as found money, and made her want to do something with Flash that was a splurge. She and Flash had never discussed money and she wondered whether money was an ego thing for him. He had resisted her urge to splurge and so they had gone to his place, had Thai food delivered, and headed for the bed. And now here was Flash bringing up money when he should have been on her side of the bed cuddling. What was the point in telling him that she had worked more than four months to get Clark's case settled? What was the point in trying to convey to him the aggravation of getting to the settlement? And then there were taxes—it wasn't as if she was putting the full $20,000 in her pocket.

"I'm not complaining or begrudging you anything," Flash said. "I'm sorry if I gave that impression. In fact, I'm impressed. I'm proud of you."

Meredith's irritation dissipated as Flash drew close and began to snuggle. She thought of all the hours she had put in on the Clark case and figured that it was best to forget about hourly rates that probably were around the minimum wage rate. Stick with the found money concept.

"You feel like going out for a drink?" Flash asked.

"I thought you didn't want to do anything fancy. It was your idea to stay in."

"There's this bar I know has a live band. There's dancing."

"You dance?"

"I've been known to dance. I'm told I have a unique style."

"Okay. This is on me."

"No," Flash said. "I'll get this one. I insist. You can get the next one."

"Twenty-five thousand dollars!" Josh exclaimed, staring at the check Rachel had brought home as if it were a miracle.

After receiving checks from the Sloan-Webster School of Law and Ship Right Specialists, Rachel and her partners had decided to take a major pay day. She would have to pay taxes on her share but there was no denying the significant size of the check. Now, Rachel was second-guessing herself for showing Josh the check, fearing that the amount made him feel threatened or inadequate in some way. Since moving in together they had shared expenses. Rachel dealt with the bill paying and Josh gave her a check for his half at the end of each month. They'd never had a money talk, and neither had brought up opening a joint account.

"Let's do something fancy tonight," Rachel suggested. "We could go to a really nice restaurant."

Josh pondered the proposal in that serious way he had, frowning in concentration, nodding his head almost imperceptibly as if he were adding up the pros and cons of what she had suggested.

"I've got a better idea. You're not the only one with money in his pocket." Josh rummaged in his wallet and extracted a check. "We finally paid off our startup costs and this is our first profit split," he announced. "I'm taking you out."

Josh's new sports instruction venture had been picking up business. Recently, he'd had little free time.

"What'd you have in mind?" Rachel asked, unable to make out the amount on the check Josh was holding and pleased that he seemed to have gotten beyond the amount on hers.

"Can you cut out of work early on Friday?"

"I think so," Rachel said.

"We're going to New Hampshire," Josh announced. "There's a bed and breakfast I've checked out that looks pretty good and is reasonable. I say we spend two nights. There are hiking trails nearby and a mountain bike path that's supposed to be good for running. It's the perfect time—before the bugs come out."

"You've been doing research."

"I have. I wanted to surprise you. We can even work in a nice dinner." Josh held his check aloft. "I think three hundred and fifty dollars should cover all that."

"Are you still running?" Frank asked.

"I am," Simon replied. He was eating a late dinner in his cramped kitchen, his cell phone on speaker resting on the small kitchen table. He wished Frank were with him. He remembered telling Rachel their office was a dump, and he was struck by the fact that at this moment, the same could be said of his apartment.

"Any chance of you coming down here this weekend?" Frank asked.

"Let me think about it," Simon said as he stared at the check for $25,000 that lay next to his cell phone. It was a payday he wanted to share with Frank but held back. Frank was still in college, subsidized by his parents. How would he react to news of this windfall? Would Frank think he was boasting if he mentioned the amount?

"What's there to think about?" Frank pressed.

Simon thought he had put the age difference between him and Frank out of sight, out of mind. But maybe when it came to money, the nine years between them mattered.

"You're right," Simon said. "There's not much to think about. I'll cut out of work early on Friday and see you Friday night. I could get us a room."

"So my dorm room isn't good enough for you?"

"It leaves a little to be desired."

"Fine, get us a room."

"I'm on it," Simon said, deciding to splurge.

"Damn!" Paul exclaimed, returning the check to Philly. "That's a lot of money."

"I know," Philly agreed. "It's going to come in handy."

"I'll say."

They were sitting in the living room on the couch, Paul holding Daniel, bouncing him on a knee, the girls playing quietly on the floor with Daisy "reading" a picture book to Rosalind that she had pretty much memorized. Raul and Isabella were having dinner out and Sarah was spending the evening with friends.

"Alone at last," Philly said.

"Very funny."

Philly took a last look at the check, then stood up quickly and stowed it in the back pocket of her jeans. She and Paul had made all their accounts joint with one exception. Even the Fidelity investment account that Raul had started for Philly and into which she had religiously continued to deposit a hundred dollars a month, was in their joint names. But Paul had insisted that the money from Philip Sizemore's family remain in Philly's name only, since the money was intended to be used for Daisy's needs.

"I feel like we should splurge on something," Philly said.

"We just did," Paul said, and he reminded her of the baby carriers they had just bought for each of their bikes.

"No, something else," Philly said.

"Let me think about it. Are we talking with kids or without?"

"Good question," Philly said.

"I vote for with," Paul said as Daniel let out a squeal.

"With it is," Philly seconded, pleased with Paul's choice.

"I want to do something nice," Carpenter said. He had told Maxine about the firm's recent partner draw but hadn't mentioned the amount. They continued to share expenses without hassle, and he had concluded that they would never open a joint account. They alternated months—this month it was his turn to pay the bills and Maxine's turn to reimburse him half.

"You don't have to twist my arm," Maxine said. "I like nice."

"Let's get the hell out of town," Carpenter suggested. "How about we drive down to Woods Hole on Friday and take a ferry over to Nantucket or the Vineyard. We could spend a couple of nights."

"You'd leave work early on Friday?"

"I'm thinking of blowing off Friday completely."

"Would we take the car on the ferry?'

"I'm thinking we pack light and take bicycles."

"You're surprising me," Maxine said.

Carpenter was surprising himself. Was feeling momentarily flush causing him to walk on what, for him, passed as the wild side? In a couple of months, after no major infusion of cash, he'd be back to hunkering down. Maxine had better take advantage of his adventurous spirit while it lasted. Tomorrow was another day.

June

From Josh's Playlist

"Get Lucky"

Daft Punk

40

Henry Frazier was delivering a hard sell for the opportunity to confront his father over the business expenses lacking backup information, and Henry's sale's pitch had to be working. Carpenter was seriously considering abandoning sound judgment by agreeing to a father-son talk, since acquiescence would shut Henry up. 'Get a grip,' he told himself.

"We need to take your father's deposition," Carpenter said when Frazier paused. "I don't want you talking to him because, even assuming he will tell you the truth, knowing what he's been up to limits your options."

"That makes no sense," Frazier said. "If you take his deposition, you're going to tell me what he said, right?"

"Right," Carpenter had to agree. "But it's a lot better for you if your knowledge is based on something your father said under oath, which was reported to you by your lawyer instead of on something he said in a private conversation with you that he could deny."

"I think that's a ridiculous distinction," Frazier replied with some heat.

Carpenter couldn't summon up a calming thought to ease his irritation. "Look," he snapped. "I'm advising you as to what I think is best for you. I can't make you take my advice, but I'm recommending that you do. You're free to disregard anything I tell you and go your own way, but I hope you won't."

Frazier didn't respond immediately, and Carpenter hoped his client was thinking things over.

"I'll call you back on this," Frazier said before ending the call.

'Can't wait,' Carpenter thought.

"You were expecting this, right?" Meredith asked Carpenter, pointing to her copy of the motion Brian Murphy had filed in the Ship Right case to delay the ten depositions Meredith had scheduled for Blake Pennington lawyers. Murphy argued that if the Blake firm was awarded summary judgment, the case would be over and there would be no need for the depositions or for document production related to the depositions.

"Yes," Carpenter replied. "You were listening in when Murphy told us he would do this."

Meredith was seated in his visitor's chair, rocking slightly back and forth. "I don't see how a judge can order summary judgment," she said. "Harris Burton's affidavit shows that there are facts in dispute and when facts are in dispute, summary judgment isn't permissible."

"You're right, of course," Carpenter said. "And assuming some judge doesn't go off the rails, I think we're going to defeat the summary judgment motion. Maybe Murphy is sending a message that we're going to have to fight for every inch of ground we have to cover."

"I would have thought he'd pick his spots," Meredith countered. "A judge might think he's stalling."

"We can always hope," Carpenter said. "I'm going to argue against the motion for summary judgment. I'd like you to prepare an opposition to Murphy's motion to delay discovery. And if the judge decides to hear oral arguments on that motion, I'd like you to do that argument."

"Thanks," Meredith said with feeling. Carpenter had to struggle to keep a neutral expression in the face of her enthusiasm. It occurred to him too late that Philly might want to argue the motion he had just assigned to Meredith, so he needed to reach out to Philly to make sure he hadn't been out of line.

"I don't believe Samuel Clarke," Sasha Barton said.

Philly repositioned her cell phone in the hope that it would improve reception. She was in the backyard keeping an eye on Daisy and Rosalind, who were using toy plastic rakes to make a pile of debris they found in the yard. The girls were actually doing a good job. They had amassed a small stack of twigs and leaves. Daniel observed the girls from his seat in a round, plastic device on wheels that had bells and whistles on a plastic bar within his reach. Daniel would be dangerous when he figured out that his legs touched the ground and by moving them, he would be in motion.

"Did you talk about that book about racial profiling?" Philly asked.

"I did most of the talking. He felt it was degrading to have to read the damn thing, and I doubt he read all of it."

"Did you reach any common ground?"

Barton took her time with the question. "I'm not sure," she finally said. "He's cagey. I'm pretty sure he acknowledged that you shouldn't rush to judgment when meting out discipline, but it didn't come out quite that clear."

"I'm out of ideas on how to try to resolve your case informally," Philly admitted. "Clarke's lawyer won't talk settlement in your case until the Hispanic kids' case is sorted out, and she hasn't gotten back to me on whether Clarke would agree to a meeting of all parties and their lawyers."

"Shit." Barton muttered. "I don't like this hanging over me. But I suppose I shouldn't be complaining as long as I'm in the classroom."

If Barton's case couldn't be resolved without a trial, then maybe Philly should press for a trial. "I could file a motion for a speedy trial," she said, wondering how Miranda Hernandez would react to that proactive move.

"I've got a better idea," Barton said. "I think it's time you had a party at your house. Frankie's been asking when he can play with your daughter. Invite Xavier and Samuel and their mothers. Invite that Ibanez guy. Invite Clarke and his lawyer. Put everyone's name on the invitation. You know, one of those 'you're invited' invitations. Worst case, we have ourselves a good time."

"Do you think Clarke will come?" Philly asked.

"I don't know," Barton said. "I'm going to tell him that he and his lawyer are getting an invitation to a party and he better damn well show up."

Philly figured Clarke's attendance was a long shot. Everything she had heard about the principal painted a picture of a stubborn, rigid man.

"Besides," Barton continued, "it will give you a chance to observe Xavier and Samuel. You did a good thing with them. They now talk to each other. The families having dinner at Xavier's house helped."

"Okay," Philly said. "E-mail me a date."

"And throw in an invite to that babysitter of yours and her friends. Who doesn't love a party?"

41

Rachel silently acknowledged that the conference room at Sizemore Klein put theirs to shame. The large, rectangular room was painted a soft white, and black and white photographs of early twentieth century Boston were artfully arrayed on the longer walls. No faded Japanese prints here. The mahogany conference room table at which they were seated accommodated twelve roomy, comfortable chairs with black and white cushions. A decanter of ice water and a half dozen glasses were centered on the table. On a small corner table was a coffee urn, and china cups. Rachel didn't want to credit Simon's charge that their own offices were a dump but she had to admit that based on a conference room comparison, they were nothing to brag about.

"I'm so glad you could join us," Burton said, and Rachel wondered why Ben Klein, the firm's managing partner, wasn't handling the introductions. "We're here," Burton continued, "because I threw out to Carpenter and Philly the idea of our firms merging. What I had in mind was a merger that would result in one firm where two firms had been before. I'll be very frank why I raised this with Carpenter and Philly."

Burton paused to pour himself some ice water and took a sip. "Our firm, as you know, focuses on business transactions. I'm sure each of you checked out our website. Our basic pitch to clients is that we're cheaper than the large firms, but equal in terms of quality work. We have no litigators so obviously we don't do litigation. Since I've been serving as of counsel to our firm, we've been asked to consider taking on cases that involved litigation and following the close of transactions, we've had clients asking us to represent them when litigation arose. These are all litigation opportunities that we've had to refer out. With the competition out there being so tough, I'm sure Carpenter can tell you that no lawyer likes to refer any piece of business to someone else. This is where you folks come in."

So far, Rachel hadn't learned anything new. Burton was reiterating what he'd said to Carpenter.

"I want to be clear," Burton said. "The litigation opportunities I've mentioned are sporadic. There hasn't been a steady stream that we've turned down. Also, as you all know, even if a potential client meets with a lawyer about a litigation matter, there's no guaranty that the potential client will hire the lawyer.

"My own background before coming to this firm was with a big Boston firm. I've enjoyed myself tremendously here and learned that smaller firms can be really good. But even though bigger is not always better, bigger has advantages, and the main one is that a big firm has many areas of practice so it's not dependent on the temporary fortunes of one niche area of the law. As everyone knows, in 2008 and 2009, transactions dried up when the economy tanked. This firm struggled because we're a transactions firm, pure and simple. We didn't have another leg to stand on. I don't know if your litigation practice has had peaks and valleys but, if that's been the case, I suspect that during the valleys you wished you had work to do that wasn't purely litigation. So in addition to some possibility of referrals from our transactions business, joining us could also provide some buffer for you when times are lean for litigation."

Burton glanced briefly at Klein who responded with a head nod.

"A second advantage that I see—and this is for both firms—is that you end up with more people to bounce ideas off. That can only be a good thing particularly if you're getting a new perspective. As business lawyers, we might have ideas for you when it comes to litigation that involves business and, conversely, you might have transaction ideas for us based on your litigation experience."

Rachel regarded her partners. None of their expressions had changed during Burton's remarks. Carpenter's stony look was in place. Simon hadn't blinked for some time. Philly's look was solemn. Had Burton ever before confronted such an unenthusiastic audience? If so, he didn't show it.

"A merger would only work if there's a consensus on structural issues," Burton resumed. "By structural issues, I would include governance, compensation, personnel, and firm cultures."

Rachel didn't know about the culture of Sizemore Klein, but would choose "loosey-goosey" if pressed to provide an apt description of her firm's culture. The four partners had no scheduled partnership meetings, no billable hour requirements, no marketing or business plan, no budget, and no managing partner, notwithstanding that Carpenter was de facto in that role. Any work that came to the firm got done. Somehow, it had always been clear which of them was to take the lead on a new case. All papers generated on a case were routinely sent to all partners for review and comment. She and Simon wouldn't be full partners until next year but, to date, had been treated as equals by Carpenter and Philly. Harris Burton and Ben Klein were in for culture shock, she decided.

"How do you see a merged firm being governed?" Simon asked the first pointed question.

"Does one of you serve as a managing partner for your firm?" Klein came back with his own question.

"Carpenter fills that role," Simon replied, "but refuses to take the title."

"Basically, I'm the managing partner here," Klein said. "I deal with the day-to-day running of the firm's business and I don't consult with any of my other partners on the day-to-day stuff. I sign the checks paying our expenses. I work with our bookkeeper to produce monthly financial statements. I give the other partners a heads up on any check over five thousand dollars before the check gets mailed. The partners meet once a month—that is a scheduled meeting—but we get together more often if there's a need. We think we're pretty informal."

'You don't know the meaning of informal,' Rachel thought.

"How do you deal with compensation?" Simon next asked.

"Seventy percent of profits are divided evenly among the eight partners. Harris isn't a partner—he's of counsel—and we deal with him separately when it comes to money. As managing partner, I allocate the other thirty percent. It's somewhat subjective but I look at each partner's billable hours, cash receipts, business generation, and other factors. I send out my proposed partner distribution and each partner gets to comment. If there are comments, I consider them and make a final distribution. My decision is final."

"Are you anticipating that we would become a part of that kind of system?" Simon asked.

"That's certainly one approach," Klein said. "We're open to other suggestions. We're keeping an open mind on this."

"We've pretty much been splitting profits four ways," Simon said. He glanced at his partners and seeing no objection to his disclosure, continued. "Income is often uneven in terms of when it comes in, particularly when it comes to contingency cases. Billable hours are recorded but we don't have a minimum billable hour requirement. We seem to have come to a consensus that if the work gets done, we share in the upside regardless of who does the work."

"That's very democratic," Burton observed. "I can see how contingency cases don't fit neatly into our model. But for a business transaction firm, we need more structure than you're describing."

"What if our firms stayed independent," Simon threw out, "and we worked out some kind of mutual referral arrangement. For example, if we became aware of a business transaction that was beyond our reach, we could bring you guys in."

Rachel glanced at Carpenter. He was sitting sphinxlike, content to have Simon take the lead at this meeting.

"That opens up the issue of referral fees," Klein said. "If our firms refer business to each other there doesn't have to be a referral fee. But in the absence of a referral fee, there's not much incentive to refer business. Harris and I have discussed this issue in some detail. Both of us would prefer not to get involved with referral fees. For one thing, if there is a referral fee arrangement, the arrangement needs to be disclosed to the client. If there exists a unified firm, the subject of referral fees goes away."

"Your offices are nicer than ours," Simon said forthrightly. "We run a bare bones operation with an extremely low overhead. If we became partners in your firm, we'd be taking on more overhead. Why would we want to do that?"

"You might not want to do that," Burton responded. "You may decide that a boutique litigation practice is the niche you wish to remain in. I believe it's prudent to take a long view. For us, obtaining litigation capabilities makes sense. After that, I would be interested in obtaining intellectual property expertise. Frankly, I look at the Internet and software products and everything that goes with those areas as essential for any law firm in the near future, not just because it's a separate line of business, but because issues about electronics and the Internet are going to come up in almost every case, no matter what the case is supposed to be about."

"How big do you want to become?" Simon asked.

"I don't know," Burton said. "I have no desire to become part of a firm as big as the one I left when I was forced to retire because of my age. But I believe for our current firm to succeed, we need to engage in measured growth in certain areas."

"How long do you expect to keep practicing?" Simon directed to Burton, and not for the first time, Rachel admired Simon's fearlessness.

"I have no plans to stop practicing," Burton said. "Ben and his partners have been very gracious and generous to me. I don't put in the hours that I used to. My role here is to generate business and to provide overall guidance and supervision on the business transactions we handle. It's an ideal situation for me."

Rachel wondered whether Simon would ask the next logical question. She needn't have wondered; Simon forged ahead.

"Would you agree," Simon asked, "that we should take the long view you were talking about and envision this firm without you?"

"Of course you should," Burton replied. "Just as we would need to envision your practice if Carpenter wasn't in the picture. If our discussions go further, these are two interrelated questions that need to be addressed. I will tell you that I've been grooming Ben on the business development side. On the transaction side, Ben and his partners don't need my guidance and supervision as much as I may have implied. They're very good at what they do. But admittedly, sometimes I'm able to draw on my experience and help out on occasion."

Rachel was pleased that Burton's and Carpenter's ages had surfaced, but she didn't want the discussion to go any farther. She and Simon and Philly had never pressed Carpenter on his long-term plans. They should do that. But it was a discussion the four of them needed to hold in private.

Simon drew a piece of paper from the inside pocket of his suit jacket and took his time perusing it. "I don't have anything further at the moment," he announced. "My thought is that we review what we've discussed and get back to you. Do you have any questions for us?"

"I have one general question," Ben Klein spoke up. "Is a type of merger something you view positively or negatively?"

"I don't know," Simon said, and while Rachel had no idea what Carpenter and Philly were thinking, she felt that Simon had spoken for her.

When the meeting had concluded, calls had been made and significant others informed to go ahead with dinner on their own. Now, the four partners were seated in an Italian place, making inroads on two large pizzas and washing down the food with beer and, in Philly's case, diet soda. Carpenter had suggested going out for dinner so that they could talk, but as they ate in silence, Rachel saw no indication that their elder statesman was about to start the discussion. She borrowed a page from Simon's book and jumped directly into the deep end of the pool. "How long do you plan to keep practicing?" she asked Carpenter.

"I don't know," Carpenter said after finishing off a piece of pizza crust and taking a slug of beer. "It's funny. Right before turning sixty, I thought I'd keep going for another ten years before retiring. I figured I'd grind along by myself and I was okay with that. Then, after I turned sixty, I started working more and more with Philly. And after the few investments I had took a hit in 2008, I figured I would turn out to be one of those guys who never retired. More recently, I've been thinking that dying at my desk is not the way to go out and retirement at some point makes sense." Carpenter took another swallow of beer. "And Maxine may have something to say about when I pack it in. We haven't had that discussion yet. So I guess the answer is that I don't know."

"Burton has to be over seventy-five," Rachel said. "A health event could put him out of action."

"The same could be said for any of us," Simon noted.

"But he's the oldest player in this game," Rachel pointed out, "so we have to get a handle on how his firm currently functions with him, and how it would function without him."

"I think we can take it as a given that his firm would take a hit if he wasn't in the picture," Carpenter said. "As he said, one of his roles is to generate business, using his contacts and his reputation. It's because of his stellar reputation that we're using him as a witness in the Ship Right case."

"I worry about what *we* bring to the table," Philly said. "We have very few active cases. I'm working on Sasha Barton's case, but it's not enough to keep me busy. The Sloan-Webster case is what's really keeping us afloat." Philly paused, sipped at her diet soda. "Really, we could use some referrals. But if we had more volume, I'm not sure I'd want to share it with anyone."

Simon spoke up. "I think Burton's overall point is valid," he said. "I'm talking about a firm not having all its eggs in one basket such as litigation. Taking that long view Burton was talking about—say seven to ten years—I think there's something to be said for a firm that has some diversity."

"I'm not sure I have any interest in getting involved in the transaction work these guys do," Philly responded.

"I don't think Burton or Klein was suggesting that we do," Simon answered.

"But I think if we're involved with transaction lawyers and they outnumber us," Philly came back, "we're going to want to know what they're up to."

"Here's something to think about," Carpenter said. "Some years ago, there was a firm that had litigators and business lawyers under one roof. Eventually, the two groups went their separate ways. The rumor was that the business lawyers were focused on billable hours. The litigators didn't want to be tied down by billable hours and wanted flexibility to take on contingency cases. Plus, the litigators were doing a lot of defense work where insurers were on the hook financially, and the insurers refused to pay the hourly rates that the businesspeople were charging. Reading between the lines, my guess is that money caused the split."

"That doesn't sound promising," Rachel said, wondering why Carpenter hadn't mentioned this situation previously. "What's your read on referral fees?" she asked Carpenter.

Carpenter shrugged. "Over the years, most of the lawyers who referred cases to me didn't ask for a referral fee. A few did, and I never had trouble paying it. I figured that without the referral, I wouldn't have gotten the case. When it comes to referring a transaction case to the firm we met with, I'm wondering whether that kind of business will even come our way. It seems to me that they would be doing most of the referring and not the other way around."

Rachel agreed with Carpenter. She couldn't remember any business transaction coming their way that needed to be referred out. "Listening to this," she said, "I think the negatives outweigh the positives." Rachel wasn't sure whether her partners agreed.

They ate for a time in silence.

"If we could dictate the terms of an association, what would they be?" Simon asked.

'It was a fair question,' Rachel thought. They had been considering what they would give up in an association. But maybe the way to come to a decision was to list what *they* needed to get.

"Don't all answer at once," Simon joked. "My impression is that we would want to stay pretty much the way we are even though we'd be under the same roof with new lawyers who practiced in a different specialty." Simon paused but no one else jumped in. "To me," Simon continued, "that means we operate as an independent litigation department, we only pay for the overhead we utilize, we throw back money at the business department for litigation they direct our way, and we divvy up profits as we currently do when and if they come in."

"Then the only upsides for the business department would be getting referral fees for litigation they steered our way and us picking up some of the overhead like rent," Rachel said.

Simon nodded. "That's pretty much it."

"That's not the kind of merger Burton was envisioning," Philly pointed out. "It sounds more like two independent firms under one roof."

"But maybe that's necessary to avoid the situation of that firm Carpenter just told us about," Rachel observed.

"This is giving me a headache," Philly said. "We haven't even gotten to issues like me working from home."

"But if we go the independent firm route," Rachel said, "the business firm would have nothing to say about you working from home or about anything else."

Rachel found Carpenter's silence disconcerting. The partner with the most practical experience had yet to say anything about what he himself wanted. "Do you think we're looking at this correctly?" she asked him.

"Pretty much," he said. "I think this has been helpful."

"Do you have any preferences you can share?" Rachel pressed.

"You know me," Carpenter replied. "I'm slow to embrace any kind of change."

"If it's not broke, don't fix it," Rachel supplied one of Carpenter's maxims.

"But our offices are sort of broke," Simon put in. "If Philly ever spent more time in Boston, we'd have no place to put Meredith, and I don't see Philly working at Meredith's workstation in Carpenter's office."

"We're never going to find bigger quarters for the same price," Carpenter pointed out.

"Is there any chance we could take over the office of the title examiner or the administrative law judge?" Simon asked.

Carpenter shrugged. "We could raise that with them. The guys are never around, and I still have no idea why they keep a Boston office in our suite."

"What if Burton and Klein agreed to independent fiefdoms?" Simon asked. "Would we be interested?"

"That depends," Carpenter said. "I'd want a clear idea of how much new overhead we'd be taking on." He paused. "Let's do this in stages. I'll ask the title guy and the ALJ if they're interested in moving out. Let's let the independent fiefdom concept percolate for a bit. It's not like we have to get back to Burton and Klein tomorrow."

"Sounds like a plan," Simon pronounced. "All in favor!"

"Aye!" came the chorus.

42

Carpenter took an early morning call from Henry Frazier hoping the man had come to his senses. That hope quickly crashed and burned.

"I talked to my father," Frazier said. "I probably should have listened to you, but what's done is done. It's not good. Remember when we first met, and you or your partner said something to the effect that in the age of computers and the Internet, how did a company specializing in high end stationery make money?"

"Yes, Ms. Sullivan made a comment to that effect," Carpenter confirmed.

"Well, she was right, it turns out. A lot of companies that do what we do have gone out of business and while there's still a need for high end stationery, the competition for the business that remains is intense."

Carpenter understood the phenomenon. Technology negatively changed the demand for a product or a service, and those businesses that survived began chasing a piece of a pie that was continually shrinking.

"We've got a client that's roughly fifty percent of our business," Frazier went on, and Carpenter regarded that statement as containing another recipe for disaster. Any company—including a law firm—dependent on one client, would suffer a major hit if the client bolted. He made a mental note to inquire whether Sizemore Klein had such a lynchpin client.

"This client is called Event Planning Specialists Unlimited. As their name implies, they arrange weddings, funerals, fundraisers, business retreats—you name it—and we do the stationery for the announcements, programs and mailings that go with the events. So maybe seven years ago, the vice-president of this company tells my father that he's thinking of going with a different stationer but he's willing to stay with Elite Scripts if my father can think of a way to make it worth his while. My father saw this for the shakedown that it was, but he was scared of losing the business, so he agreed to pay this vice-president, a guy named John Harrison, a thousand dollars a month. At the beginning, he took the money out of his own pocket. Of course, Harrison kept upping the ante. It's now eight thousand a month. But keeping the client keeps us profitable, and we're doing pretty well even with the payments. My father's been trying to get Harrison to back off on the payments without success."

"Has your father told his lawyer about this?"

"That didn't come up," Frazier said. "Knowing my father, he hasn't told his lawyer."

"Are you still interested in taking over the family business?"

"Not with my previous enthusiasm. I really don't want this kind of aggravation in my life. I mean it's illegal to bribe someone, right?"

"I can't answer you definitively," Carpenter admitted. "Some things are wrong but not illegal. I need to ask Lily Tompkins some questions first." Lily Tompkins was going to love this.

"What's there to think about?" Frazier let loose. "These are under the table payments for Christ's sake!"

"Let's say a guy goes to an illegal bookie, places a bet and wins a thousand bucks," Carpenter hypothesized. "Has the guy committed a crime?"

"How the hell am I supposed to know? You're the lawyer!"

"If the guy declares the thousand dollars on his income tax return, I'm not sure he has committed a crime," Carpenter answered his own question, ignoring Frazier's outburst.

"Are you saying my father did nothing wrong?"

"I'm not saying anything. I need to ask around about this. Do you think this guy Harrison declared your father's payments on *his* income tax returns?"

"Probably not," Frazier said in a frustrated tone. "My father paid the guy in cash. He's going to deny he ever received anything."

"That may be. But before I start advising you, I'm going to talk to Lily Tompkins and generally ask around."

"And what am I supposed to do while you're playing with yourself?"

"Do what *I* do best—nothing. But if you want something more to think about, think about this. For the month of October 2012, your father claimed three separate expense items that totaled eight thousand. Did he actually pay this guy Harrison in three installments or did he make one eight thousand payment to the guy and try to disguise that by listing it as three expenses?"

"Shit!" Frazier exclaimed.

'My sentiments exactly,' Carpenter thought.

"I suppose the guy you're deposing this morning is some kind of porn star," Jeannie Smith said in a flinty tone. "Or are we in for another exotic dancer?"

"You should be so lucky," Simon replied, wishing he could open some can of worms in Noah Branson's life that would cause Christopher Blaisedell to wish he had chosen a different lead plaintiff to sue Sloan-Webster.

Smith's stenographic equipment was ready to go when Blaisedell, on the stroke of ten, entered the conference room with Branson. Simon shook hands with Branson and directed him to a chair opposite Smith. The man hadn't changed much from his 2009 law school picture—long, narrow face, close-cut Afro, prominent dark eyes. Gone, however, was the wispy chin beard, which Simon had thought provided a touch of flash. Branson was tall and thin but didn't look like he possessed an athlete's body.

Once the rules of the deposition were established, Simon began with background questions. Branson had worked as an unpaid intern for a charitable organization after graduating from law school. When he had passed the Massachusetts bar, he had hoped to be hired full time. But a full-time position was never offered to him, and he had taken a position at an insurance company as an administrative assistant.

"You grew up in Michigan and went to college in Michigan," Simon summarized. "Why did you decide to go to law school in Massachusetts?"

"I had more or less had it with Michigan," Branson answered. "It's a lot colder there than here. And I wanted to try living someplace else. You know... expand my horizons. I figured I could always return to Michigan to practice law."

"Was there any other reason why you wanted to put some distance between you and Michigan?"

Branson frowned at the question. "I'm not really sure what you're getting at, but no."

"During your senior year at Michigan State, were you involved in the investigation of an alleged cheating incident concerning a survey economics course you took?"

Branson's jaw dropped and his eyes opened wide. Simon noticed that Blaisedell had stopped taking notes and was staring at his client. Branson rubbed his chin, perhaps searching for the chin beard that was no more. Simon had been right to ask his question out of the blue. He had hoped to produce a reaction with his question but hadn't anticipated Branson becoming unglued.

"That whole thing was total BS," Branson said, agitated. "Nothing ever happened with that because nothing happened period."

"Isn't it correct that you were told that there was a concern that the final test questions and answers had been leaked and that you were a suspect because of your high score on the test?"

For a moment, Branson seemed unable to speak. There was both anger and fear in his look, and Simon judged that fear was narrowly winning out.

"I think everyone who got a high score on the test was told something like that," Branson found his voice.

"Then you were told that, correct?"

"Yes."

"Did you cheat on that economics test?"

"How dare you?"

"Please answer my question," Simon said neutrally. He was certain that Branson had never before had to answer the question under oath.

"No," Branson said.

"To what do you attribute your high score on the economics test?"

Branson flashed a rueful grin. "Luck," he said. "It was a multiple-choice test, and frankly I had to guess at a lot of the answers."

"Luck," Simon repeated. "Do you know someone from your college days named Corey Addison?"

Branson flinched at the name of the teaching assistant who was suspected of leaking the economics course test questions and answers.

"The name sounds vaguely familiar," Branson said tentatively.

"Was Corey Addison more than an acquaintance to you?"

"I can't really place the name," Branson said.

"Does it help you to recall Mr. Addison if I tell you that he was the teaching assistant for the economics course you took that involved the cheating investigation?"

Branson seemed to be making an effort to show he wasn't concerned by the question. "Not really. It was a large lecture course. I'm not sure I was even aware that there was a teaching assistant."

"If Mr. Addison were to say that he supplied economics course test questions and answers to a small number of students, would Mr. Addison be telling the truth?" Simon gambled.

"Objection for the record," Blaisedell said.

Branson again reached for his chin. "How the hell would I know? I don't know the guy."

"What have you done to find a law-related job since you graduated from law school?" Simon again changed the subject abruptly.

Branson took a deep breath and let the air out slowly. "I've checked in with the placement office, which is totally useless. I've actually gone to the law school to look at the placement bulletin board, but most of the openings they've listed are stale. I look through the positions being offered in the weekly lawyers' newspaper, and I've sent my resumé out for positions I think might suit me. Things like that."

"Have you ever looked for a law-related job in Michigan?"

"No."

"Why not?"

"Like I said before, I'd like to settle someplace else. I like Boston. I'd like to find something near the city."

Simon consulted his deposition outline and the handwritten notes he had been taking. "You mentioned that the placement office was useless. Has the placement office ever given you any information that was incorrect?"

"They haven't ever given me *any* information that was useful."

"That's not my question," Simon persisted. "Has the placement office ever given you any information that was incorrect or untrue?"

Branson pulled at his chin. "Not that I recall. But like I said, they have never offered me any information that was useful. So that's why I said the office was useless."

"For the record," Simon said, "I'm going to move to strike the answer after the words 'not that I recall.'"

"Objection to your motion," Blaisedell countered.

"Let's change the subject," Simon said. "Have you had personal contacts with the placement office?'

"Yes."

"Let's go through them one at a time. When was the first personal contact you had with the placement office?"

Following the departure of Blaisedell and Branson, Jeannie Smith checked with Simon about the spelling of some names that had come up in the deposition. Then Smith began packing up her equipment.

"Any impressions?" Simon asked the stenographer.

"If the guy wasn't Black, we would have seen him turning red when you asked him questions about that economics course."

"I thought he was lying," Simon said. "I think he knew that teaching assistant he claims he never heard of."

"That was my take," Smith said. "But where does that get you?"

Simon wasn't sure. "It's better than nothing," he offered up. "Maybe it will give his lawyer something to think about."

"But it doesn't address the elephant in the room," Smith kept her focus.

"The elephant?"

"The placement office was useless for this guy just as it was useless for the exotic dancer. When he got to talking about his contacts with the placement office, it came out that they did nothing for him."

"Oh!" Simon feigned surprise. "That elephant!"

"Holy shit!" Lily Tompkins let fly after Carpenter filled her in over the phone. "I think we both knew that we'd be headed in a direction like this."

"I had my suspicions," Carpenter said. "What's the father guilty of?"

"Elite Scripts should have given this guy Harrison 1099 forms listing what he was paid," Tompkins said. "If the IRS audits Elite Scripts, it will never allow the undocumented payments to this guy Harrison as an expense."

"Let me stop you there," Carpenter interrupted. "Let's say there is an audit and the father is asked to come up with documentation for the payments to Harrison. What happens if the father tells the auditor the truth that there is no documentation because Harrison insisted he be paid in cash."

"I don't think that would fly for an auditor," Tompkins opined. "I told you before that auditors live and breathe documentation. But what the hell do I know! In any event, Elite Scripts still should have sent 1099 forms to Harrison. Also, if the father did make one eight-thousand-dollar payment to Harrison, and then listed three separate payments on his expense account, the father looks like he was trying to conceal what was going on."

Carpenter brought up Henry Frazier's question. "Was it a crime to pay this guy Harrison cash money under the table?"

"There's an argument that it wasn't," Tompkins said. "But I'd want to hear that from some hot shit, white collar, criminal defense lawyer who's never lost a case."

"This guy Harrison is a vice-president," Carpenter noted. "I wonder whether the president of the company knows about these payments." Carpenter jotted down a note to ask Henry Frazier how Elite Scripts got the account.

"Let's say the president doesn't know," Tompkins hypothesized. "So what?"

"I need to think about that," Carpenter returned.

"What's the son going to do?" Tomkins asked.

"Let's just say he's conflicted. He's not as eager to own the majority of stock in the family business."

"Can't fault him there," Tompkins said.

"Can you get me a definitive answer on whether the father committed any crime?" Carpenter asked.

"Let me see what I can do," Tompkins said.

"I appreciate it."

"You know," Tompkins said, "there is one thing the father could do. I'm not recommending that he do this, but he could send this guy Harrison 1099s for all the years he made payments to the guy. I'm sure there will be IRS penalties for missing deadlines, but maybe better late than never."

"These would go to the IRS, right?"

"Right."

"That's one way for Elite Scripts to lose its main client."

"It's hard to predict how this will all shake out," Tompkins said. "But I'm guessing that no matter what he does, the father is going to risk losing that client."

43

Philly was grateful for nice weather. The cloudless sky, warm sun, and faint breeze meant that everyone could enjoy the outdoors, and the kids could run loose. True, the afternoon could prove to be a bust if the real people of interest failed to show up at the party. She hadn't requested any RSVPs so there was a distinct possibility that she and Sasha Barton would be talking to Acevedo and Brown family members and to no one else. Samuel Clarke and his lawyer were the most likely no shows, and it was far from a sure thing that Carlos Ibanez would put in an appearance.

"This is nice," Sasha Barton said, surveying the small backyard.

Barton had brought a supply of folding chairs for the grownups, and Philly had set up a picnic table where she could lay out sandwiches, paper plates and plastic knives, spoons, and forks when the time came. A cooler with soft drinks was positioned under the table. Xavier Acevedo and Stanley Brown were playing keep away with a soccer ball, a game that was sure to tire their pursuers: Frankie Barton, Daisy, and Rosalind after a fashion. Philly saw it as a good sign that the two fifth graders were smiling at the little kids' antics.

"I can't tell what I'm worried about most," Barton said. "It's a tossup between Clarke showing up, or Clarke not showing up."

"I think he's going to show," Carmen Brown said, joining them. "But then again, maybe his lawyer will tell him not to."

"Then there's my lawyer," Sonia Acevedo said. "He said he would try to make it, but he wouldn't promise."

"Hi, Mrs. Sullivan?"

Philly returned June's friendly wave. June and her friends—Naomi and Lucida—made a beeline for the fifth graders. Xavier surrendered the soccer ball to the little kids and he and Stanley seemed, not happy exactly to see the older girls, more like okay with it. Soon the five youngsters were talking animatedly.

"Is your babysitter going to pump the boys for information?" Carmen Brown asked.

"Of course," Philly responded. "I've given her specific instructions."

"I think our sons are getting on better," Sonia Acevedo directed to Brown.

"They might actually be friends," Brown responded. "But I don't think either will admit it."

"You should be proud of your sons," Barton said. "They've done a lot to tone down the tensions at school between the two groups."

"Hello!" Carlos Ibanez called out as he pushed open the back screen door. "I was ringing the bell, but I guess no one heard."

"That's because I'm a lousy hostess," Philly said. "Welcome."

"Am I correct that Mr. Clarke has not put in an appearance?" Ibanez asked.

"You are," Philly replied.

"I suppose my client is the guest of honor," Miranda Hernandez said as she emerged from around the side of the house, leading Samuel Clarke to where the grownups had assembled.

"Thanks for coming," Philly addressed the latecomers warmly. She noticed that Xavier and Stanley had stopped chatting with June and her friends and were giving the principal hard, guarded stares. Clarke looked uncomfortable, and Philly wondered what Hernandez had said to get him to attend.

"Let's make time later to talk about the lawsuits," Philly said. "For the moment, I suggest we simply relax and mingle." She pointed to June and her friends. "That's my babysitter and her two friends. The babysitter is the one with the pink and blue hair and nose studs. In fifth grade, her two friends felt the same kind of hostility to each other that Xavier and Stanley were going through. We had the three girls talk to the boys, and I hope, Mr. Clarke, that you will talk with the girls to learn about their experience. They have an interesting story to tell which they have shared with Xavier and Stanley. There are drinks under the picnic table, and I'm going to excuse myself and bring out some food."

"I will assist you," Ibanez said, and Hernandez quickly offered her services, too.

"What are you hopping to accomplish?" Hernandez asked in the kitchen as she helped Philly arrange sandwiches on a serving tray.

"I want your clients to settle the pending lawsuits," Philly replied.

"On what terms?"

"My client is permanently rehired with no negative mark on her record or in her personnel file," Philly said. "Plus, her legal fees are taken care of and she is paid some money."

"What about you?" Hernandez directed at Ibanez.

"My clients want money to be compensated for their humiliation."

"And why should my clients agree to any of that?" Hernandez demanded.

"Because," Philly said, "we're going to make Mr. Clarke into a symbol of tolerance and fairness that will make his career."

Philly ignored Hernandez's quizzical look.

"I'll deny I said this," Hernandez said, as she and Philly picked up the sandwich trays, "but you've got your work cut out for you."

After making sure that everyone had what they needed, Philly joined June who was sitting on the grass with the younger children. Daisy, Rosalind, and Frankie were poking holes in the sandwich bread, inserting their fingers and giggling. Egg salad coated the girls' sweatshirts and tuna fish cascaded down the front of Frankie's jacket. June was holding Daniel and managing a sandwich.

"Anything to report?" Philly asked, relieving June of Daniel.

"Xavier and Stanley are doing okay," June said. "I think they like each other but they're boys so they kind of keep it to themselves. Seeing each other's home was a big deal. I told them that the next time I checked in with them, I wanted to hear that they had apologized to each other for what was said on the playground."

"Do you think that's going to happen?"

June shrugged. "If it does, it's going to be when they're alone."

"Excellent." Philly noticed that Naomi and Lucida had buttonholed Clarke. "How's that going?" she asked, pointing in the direction of the group.

"I'll let you know later. Naomi and Lucida can be pretty persuasive."

Philly watched Clarke while calming Daniel, who had started to fuss. The principal towered over the girls and didn't look happy, but at least he was listening to what they had to say.

Philly got to her feet holding Daniel under his armpits. "I think this guy's hungry."

Philly had settled Daniel down for a nap, and Isabella had returned home and was keeping an ear out for Daniel while seeing to Daisy, Rosalind, and Frankie in the living room. Emerging from the back door, Philly saw that the groupings had changed. Hernandez and Ibanez had moved to a far edge of the yard and were in earnest conversation. When Clarke moved to join them, Hernandez waved him away. Philly approached the principal who appeared to be the odd man out. All the other attendees were grouped around the food table where Naomi and Lucinda were holding court, Lucida with a hand on Xavier's shoulder, the adults and June listening intently.

"Thanks for coming," Philly said to Clarke. "I'm guessing it wasn't something you particularly wanted to do."

"You're right," Clarke said, and Philly wondered if the man ever permitted himself a light tone.

"What got you into education?" Philly asked, searching for a neutral subject.

"Shouldn't my lawyer be present if you're going to question me?"

Philly didn't think Clarke was joking. "That's up to you," she said.

Clarke shrugged. "I suppose it doesn't matter. My parents were teachers, and I got a taste for teaching growing up. When a knee injury ended my football career, I figured why not, and decided to follow in my parents' footsteps."

"Do you enjoy it?" Philly asked.

"What kind of a question is that?"

"The reason I'm asking is that I don't think I've ever seen you smile. I admit we're not meeting under circumstance likely to make anyone smile. But still… "

"Yeah, I enjoy it," Clark said with some heat. "I wouldn't stay at something I didn't enjoy."

Clarke was staring down at her and Philly searched for something to like about the man. "I saw you talking to Naomi and Lucida. They're friends of my babysitter, June." Philly pointed in June's direction.

"That's one weird looking babysitter."

"But since you've talked to Naomi and Lucida, you know that appearances can be deceiving."

"Don't you think you're laying it on a bit thick?"

"You tell me," Philly rejoined.

Clarke glared at her and Philly met his gaze, opting for an ingratiating smile. "You've got a mouth on you," the principal said.

"This will probably shock you, but you're not the first person to point that out."

Clarke's gaze softened and he gave in to a laugh. Philly wondered whether his students had ever been given a glimpse of this side of him.

"Now that I've loosened you up," Philly said, "I have a favor to ask you. Talk to your lawyer about what Naomi and Lucida had to say to you. Then ask her to call me."

"I'll think about it," Clarke said, and there was no edge to his words. For the first time, Philly entertained the notion that there could be an end in sight to Sasha Barton's case.

44

Philly was sitting in the first row of spectator seating in the Superior Court courtroom. She didn't have a problem with Meredith assisting Carpenter with this hearing, but since Brian Murphy was representing the other side, she wasn't about to miss the first round of court action in the Ship Right case.

Judge Woodrow Hart arranged the case papers in front of him and turned his attention to the lawyers who had previously introduced themselves. He was a relatively young superior court judge, an African American who had spent six years in the public defenders' office before moving on to a mid-sized Boston law firm that specialized in criminal defense work. There was a touch of gray in the judge's close-cut hair and Philly thought that his black-framed glasses gave him a slightly nerdy look.

"I have before me the defendant's motion to dismiss and the defendant's motion to delay discovery," the judge declared. "There are affidavits opposing and supporting the dismissal motion. I've looked at the papers including the legal memoranda. Since the motion to dismiss is accompanied by an affidavit, I will treat the motion to dismiss as one for summary judgment. Frankly, Mr. Murphy, the affidavit opposing your client's motion raises substantial fact questions about whether your client's billings to the plaintiff were reasonable. How can I allow your motion in these circumstances?"

Brian Murphy rose smoothly and paused briefly before addressing the judge. He had aged since Philly had last seen him. She remembered his barrel chest but now he had a bit of a belly. Murphy's red hair was less alive than she remembered, probably because gray had made inroads.

"Actually, Your Honor, there are no *material* facts in dispute. The affidavit from Attorney Burton offers an opinion that Ship Right was charged for too many lawyers. But Mr. Burton nowhere rebuts Morgan Carmichael's sworn statements that the transaction was a complicated transaction involving many areas of the law, and that Ship Right was pressing for the sale of its business to be completed in a short time frame. These facts were specifically pointed out to Ship Right in the engagement letter that company signed."

Philly knew Carpenter would view it as a bad sign that the judge was writing.

"Mr. Carmichael was the Blake, Pennington & Dwyer partner in charge of the Ship Right transaction. As he explains in his affidavit, in order to meet the client's expressed desire to close a complicated transaction promptly, Mr. Carmichael employed a team approach that involved keeping attorneys from many departments up to speed on all aspects of the transaction so that knowledgeable manpower could be directed to problem areas as they arose. There was nothing improper about this approach given Ship Right's insistence that the transaction close promptly. Ship Right was billed by Blake, Pennington & Dwyer only for the necessary resources that had to be brought to bear to ensure that Ship Right was sold on schedule. None of the forgoing is disputed."

"What's your response, Mr. Carpenter?" the judge inquired.

"Mr. Murphy's characterization of Harris Burton's affidavit is inaccurate," Carpenter began after he rose. "Mr. Burton, one of the most experienced and respected transaction attorneys in the commonwealth, viewed the defendant's charges as unreasonable, even given the nature of the transaction and the timing of the potential sale. His affidavit provides the specifics, and the specifics do not pass the smell test. An excessive number of attorneys participated in internal meetings and phone calls and there is no indication of what, if anything, many of the attorneys contributed substantively to the Ship Right transaction. Calling this a team approach doesn't take away from the fact that Ship Right was billed for the services of numerous lawyers who appear to have provided nothing of value. This so-called team approach would justify all the lawyers in the defendant's firm to bill for time on the Ship Right matter, and that would have been absurd."

"What do you say, Mr. Murphy, to the plaintiff's claim that your motion is premature because discovery has not taken place? The plaintiff wishes to take the depositions of ten lawyers at the defendant firm and has also requested the firm to produce documents reflecting the ten lawyers' work on the transaction in dispute."

"That position is misplaced," Murphy responded at once. "From the plaintiff's most recent comments, one could infer that discovery is being conducted to determine whether certain of the defendant's attorneys provided services that advanced the transaction. That focus does not accurately portray what Blake, Pennington & Dwyer was engaged to do. The law firm was engaged to complete the transaction timely and promised to devote sufficient resources to accomplish that objective. Keeping lawyers in reserve and updated on the transaction was absolutely necessary for Blake, Pennington & Dwyer to honor its obligations under the engagement letter signed by the parties. If the transaction had succeeded, I submit there would be no objection to any fees. In fact, if the transaction had not concluded because Ship Right was not prepared to close the deal, Ship Right would be claiming that Blake, Pennington & Dwyer was responsible for the delay and should have marshaled more troops to meet the four-month deal deadline."

"Your response, Mr. Carpenter," the judge requested.

"I'll be responding to Your Honor's questions on the defendant's motion to prevent discovery," Meredith said, rising, and Philly liked her forceful tone, her commanding presence before the judge. "Your Honor asked about discovery, but much if not most of what we just heard had nothing to do with discovery. Discovery would clarify facts in dispute such as how Blake Pennington attorneys really spent their time and what their concrete contributions to Ship Right really were. Once that is known, it is for a jury to decide whether it was reasonable for a law firm to include six or more lawyers on a host of calls and in a host of meetings, and to bill for their services, where there is no indication that the lawyers produced anything of value. A jury might well conclude, as it should, that such piling on of bodies is gouging.

"Mr. Murphy's speculations as to what action Ship Right might take as to the law firm's bills had the transaction failed to close due to the firm's lack of readiness is just that—speculations. There is no reason to believe that Ship Right would have accepted an out-of-line, inflated bill whether the transaction failed to close or did close."

Meredith looked at her notes. "Mr. Murphy has referred to a team approach. Discovery is necessary to determine whether, if there was something we may call a team, the team contained deadwood, individuals who contributed nothing, said nothing of substance, wrote nothing, and played the role of potted plants during calls and meetings to bump up billable hours. Again, it is for a jury to pass judgment on whether there was a team and, if so, whether the team was overstaffed and padded with so-called players who were really just benchwarmers. In that regard, one of the points that Ship Right makes is that in various areas such as, for example, taxation, there should never have been a full-blown manpower effort to close a transaction prior to the existence of a signed purchase and sale agreement by the seller and buyer. That is also for a jury to determine."

Meredith took her seat and Philly silently applauded her effort. She understood Carpenter's willingness to trust Meredith at this hearing.

"I've heard enough," Judge Hart pronounced. "I'll take the two motions under advisement. We're in recess."

"All rise!"

When the judge left the bench, Philly passed through the gate separating spectator seating from counsel tables and drew near to Carpenter and Meredith. "Nice job, guys."

Carpenter grunted. Meredith said, "Thanks."

Philly next advanced on Murphy who was stowing his papers into a litigation briefcase. "You know what I have to say to you," Philly said, trying to mimic Carpenter.

Murphy looked up, smiled when recognition dawned. "Ms. Piper. What a joy."

"It's Ms. Sullivan to you," Philly came back. "I'm married now."

"Where does Carpenter find these women he persists in unleashing on me? First there was you, and now it's Ms. Sweeney."

"What can I say, Carpenter's a chick magnet."

Murphy laughed. "You're still a pisser whatever the hell you're calling yourself."

"Was it my imagination, or were you and Carpenter more formal than usual?"

"Sometimes you've got to go with your instincts," Murphy said with a shrug. "I didn't have a read on this judge, and he didn't look susceptible to humor."

"Carpenter must have had the same read," Philly remarked.

"Who knows what that old goat is thinking."

"No consorting with the enemy," Carpenter said as he drew near with Meredith in his wake.

"I thought we were best buddies," Murphy responded. "Nice job," he said, offering his hand to Meredith.

"Thanks."

"Anytime you want to work for a real law firm, give me a call."

Philly remembered when Murphy had thrown a similar suggestion her way. "No poaching the talent," she said.

"Seriously," Murphy directed at Meredith. "Hang around Carpenter long enough and you'll become a shell of your former self. You're still young. You can still save yourself."

Meredith showed no reaction to Murphy's overture, but Philly figured that she would think about it later.

"Any side wager on how these motions will be decided?" Carpenter asked.

"I'll pass," Murphy said. "But when it comes to the final outcome of the case, let me know what you have in mind."

"Let me give it some thought," Carpenter replied. "You know what I have to say to you."

"Indeed I do," Murphy said with a smile.

45

Carpenter paused before picking up his phone. Whatever Lily Tompkins had to tell him would have to be passed on to Henry Frazier. Frazier would ponder the new information and call him back and that would lead to another call to Lily. Clients could throw hissy fits over being charged for telephone calls, but Carpenter believed that lawyers weren't paid enough to be put through telephone hell.

"It's pretty much what I told you," Lily said after Carpenter picked up. "First, Elite Scripts should have sent that guy Harrison 1099 forms. The company will end up having to pay penalties if it belatedly sends out the 1099s. Second, the chances are slim to none that an IRS auditor would allow a personal expense account item that lacked documentation. That's particularly the case where undocumented items dwarf the total of documented items. Third, the father, Donald Frazier, may not have violated any law by paying Harrison under the table. But nobody I spoke to is a hundred percent sure of that because what the father did looks, smells, and feels bad. Going back to the tax side, a few of the people I talked to brought up that because of the lack of documentation, Donald might be subject to a criminal tax fraud charge. As might Harrison."

"Okay," Carpenter said. "I appreciate this. I'll pass it on to Henry Frazier. Frankly, I don't know what to recommend to the guy. I suppose one option is for Henry to walk away from the family business and leave his father with the mess. Another option is for both father and son to go to the president of Event Planning Specialists, the client, and tell the guy what's been going on."

"I'm an accountant so I don't know shit about anything but numbers," Lily said. "But the first question I would ask the son is whether Elite Scripts is profitable without this major client. I'm thinking the answer is no because the client accounts for half its business."

"I'm inclined to agree. Do you have a second question?"

"I would ask what above-board financial concessions Elite Scripts could make in order to keep its main client and still make a profit."

Carpenter made a note of Lily's second point. "All right. I'll let you know how this plays out."

It was Rachel's turn to take a deposition in the Sloane-Webster case, and she wished that her outline for Marshall Hightower's deposition weren't so skimpy. She would have to play it by ear and hope that Hightower's answers to questions opened up new areas of inquiry that were helpful to Sloan-Webster.

"Your partner kept me amused with the last two depositions," Jeannie Smith said. "I expect you to follow suit."

"Don't get your hopes up."

After the usual preliminaries, Marshall Hightower answered background questions with an amused, cocky look on his face as if Rachel's questions were a minor nuisance that he would handle without breaking a sweat. Rachel had no idea how to knock Hightower off his high horse. Blaisedell had yet to take a note.

"The plaintiffs' complaint states that you met with the head of the placement office," Rachel said. "Was that your only contact with the placement office?"

"Yes."

"What happened at that meeting?"

"I told Ms. Snelling that I needed help with finding a legal job. She referred me to the placement office bulletin board. I told her that I had looked at the bulletin board and didn't find it particularly helpful and asked her what else she could do to assist me. She basically told me that there was nothing else she could offer. She said that the placement office was there to try to answer students' questions, and to post any job opportunities that came to her attention."

"Do you recall anything else about that meeting?"

Hightower paused. He was a big, rugged looking guy with broad shoulders and muscular arms. His blond hair, cut short and gelled, curled up at the back of his neck. He had come to the deposition dressed in stylish jeans, a white dress shirt, and a dark blue blazer. "No," he said. "I can't recall anything else."

"What have you done to obtain a law-related job?"

"I look at the weekly lawyers' newspaper for job openings and send out my resumé if there's something I'm interested in. That's pretty much it. If you have other suggestions, let me know."

"What are you interested in?" Rachel asked next, ignoring Hightower's request.

"Criminal law mostly."

"Have you applied for a public defender position?"

"No."

"Why not?"

"They don't pay particularly well."

"Do they pay more than your current landscaping job?"

"No."

"What do you make at your current landscaping job?"

"In 2012, I made fifty thousand dollars."

Rachel found the figure high. She had pictured Hightower as a day laborer who wasn't paid particularly well.

"What do you do for the landscaping company?"

Hightower gathered his thoughts. "I work jobs for the company. Sometimes I'm in charge of a job. When the owner's gone on vacation, he's put me in charge. Last year, I revised the company's standard contract with its clients, and I reviewed the company's contracts with its vendors."

"How long have you worked for this landscaping company?"

"Since the fall of 2011."

"Haven't you been given a lot of responsibility for a relatively recent hire?"

"I guess that's right. But keep in mind I'm familiar with landscaping. It's what I did during summers in high school and college, so I know the business."

"The contract reviews you just mentioned. Is it correct that that involved legal work?"

"Yes."

"Have you been offered a permanent job with this landscaping company?"

"I have a permanent job with the company as far as I'm concerned. But I'd prefer to practice law full time."

"Have you considered opening your own law office?'

"I considered that."

"What did you decide?"

"I decided not to go that route. It was too uncertain, and I didn't think I could make sufficient money at it. I was pretty sure I couldn't have matched what I made at the landscaping company."

Rachel reviewed the few notes that she had made during the deposition. A subject had come up twice, she noted. Not unusual, but perhaps worth pursuing. She regarded Hightower and Blaisedell. Neither showed concern. In Blaisedell's position, she would be pleased with the way the deposition had so far progressed.

"You mentioned that you didn't try for a position with the public defenders' office or decide to go out on your own because of concerns about not being paid enough. Do you have any extraordinary expenses that you need to defray?"

"Objection," Blaisedell said.

"I'll rephrase the question," Rachel said before Hightower could offer an answer. "Was the concern you previously expressed about money in connection with a public defender's job and going out on your own due to any expenses you need to meet?"

"Normal living expenses," Hightower amplified. "Plus, I'm paying back a law school loan."

"How much is the law school loan for?"

"Twenty-five thousand dollars?"

"What are the monthly payments?"

"Four hundred twenty dollars and change."

"Where do you live?"

"In Medford?"

"Do you rent?"

Hightower nodded. "Yeah."

"What is your monthly rent?"

"Seven hundred fifty."

"Is that for an apartment?"

"It's basically a studio apartment."

Rachel did some quick math in her head. Then she thought back to her own post-law school expenses. "Do you basically need the fifty-thousand-dollar salary you make with the landscaping company to live?" she asked.

Hightower shrugged. "I could probably live on less," he said.

"What salary would you need from a law-related job to have enough to live on?"

"I'm guessing here," Hightower said, sounding annoyed. "Forty thousand give or take."

Rachel had graduated from law school without student loans. But even on the $32,000 a year that she'd made on her part-time paralegal pay, she could have managed a four hundred dollar a month loan repayment.

Rachel scanned her notes, which provided no inspiration for further questions. "Nothing further," she said.

Blaisedell stood. "Then the deposition is concluded."

Jeannie Smith finished packing up her stenographic equipment and looked up to regard Rachel. "This is where you're supposed to ask me if I have any impressions?" Smith said.

Rachel laughed. "Sure, why not. Any impressions?"

"I don't think you got any dirt on the guy," Smith opined. "He was kind of smug, but maybe he had a right to be."

"I think you're right," Rachel said. "There was nothing to work with really."

"Where were you going with all those questions about the salary the guy needed to live on?"

"Probably nowhere," Rachel admitted. "The guy was definitely concerned about money. I was just fishing around."

"I don't think you got a bite," Smith said.

"I'd have to say you're right," Rachel replied. But there was still one more thing she could try. She'd run her idea by Simon.

46

"What a mess." Henry Frazier grumbled over the phone.

Carpenter didn't disagree with his client's assessment. He had filled Frazier in on his conversation with Lily Tompkins and then listened, more or less patiently, while Frazier thought out loud, trying to figure out what to do. Frazier had made one decision that Carpenter regarded as sound: so long as under-the-table payments were being made to John Harrison, Frazier had no intention of taking over the family business. Frazier had also produced one useful piece of intelligence; his father had yet to inform his own lawyer, Lauren Goldman, about the payoffs.

"What did your father have to say about disclosing everything to Event Planning's president?" Carpenter asked.

"He can't bring himself to do it."

"What do you know about Event Planning's president?"

"I met the guy once. His name is Warren Anderson. He's an older guy who's been running Event Planning for years. If he knows about the payments to Harrison, then he's got to be sharing in them. But if I had to guess, I'd guess he doesn't know about them. I probably shouldn't be forming an opinion of someone based on one meeting, but from what I remember of the guy, I think Anderson would be pissed off at Harrison's side business. He struck me as a strait-laced kind of guy."

"Let's see if we agree on your options," Carpenter said. "You could resign from the family business, which would leave you without a job. You could remain in the family business until you find a job. You could pressure your father by writing him a letter demanding, as a minority stockholder, that he confront Warren Anderson with John Harrison's shakedown scheme. Or you could confront Anderson yourself."

"What do you recommend?" Frazier asked.

"Well, there's a potential for unpleasant consequences whatever you do, but I'm thinking that approaching this guy Anderson might be the best of a host of lousy alternatives. If you go that route, you have to be prepared to lose Event Planning as a client because if Anderson really is a play-it-by-the-book guy, he could fire Harrison and stop doing business with Elite Scripts. So you need to assess whether your company could survive that loss. And if you go that route, I think it would be best for your father to approach Anderson, rather than you, since he may have a personal relationship with Anderson that's developed over the years. But if your father won't do it, you could approach Anderson yourself. If an approach is made to Anderson by either one of you, I see no reason why Elite Scripts wouldn't send Harrison 1099 forms for all the years he never received them."

Frazier didn't respond immediately. "I'll talk to my father," he finally said. "I guess the lawsuit I filed stirred the pot. But in the lawsuit, I asked to hold my father to his promise to put me in charge of the family business. Until this mess with Harrison is fixed, I don't want what I asked for."

Carpenter had been thinking the same thing. Be careful what you wish for.

47

'Meditation couldn't be all it was cracked up to be,' Carpenter thought. He'd been meditating reasonably dutifully, counting on the practice to help him deal with the sudden onset of a stressful situation, but here he was with his heart pounding and his blood pressure probably close to a personal best high. He used a scissors to slit open the mailing from superior court.

Judge Woodrow Hart's rulings in the Ship Right case were handwritten on the first pages of the motions. The judge had denied the motion to dismiss filed by Blake Pennington because material facts were in dispute that needed to be resolved by a jury. He also denied the motion to delay discovery and noted, "*discovery to commence forthwith.*"

Two for two, Carpenter thought, feeling calm return. And against Brian Murphy no less. Time to turn Meredith loose on depositions.

"We need an Asian girl," June said. "Then we'd really be diverse."

"If you want diversity," Lucida said, "we need an Asian *boy*."

"Forget guys," Naomi said. "I want this to be all girls."

Philly stayed silent. She favored Naomi's view, but had resolved to butt out of their deliberations.

"I agree," June said. "Let's make this a girl thing."

"Fine," Lucida conceded. "What the heck."

They were seated on what passed for grass in Philly's backyard, gathered in a shady spot, sipping from juice boxes.

"It feels funny coming here and not having to look after the kids," June said to Philly.

"You're off duty," Philly replied. "So, do you think you can come up with a written outline of what you might say?"

June nodded. "The other night I wrote down what I remembered from what Naomi and Lucida told Xavier and Stanley. I remembered a lot. I'll finish up what I was writing and get it to you guys."

"Sounds like a plan," Philly said. "Speaking of Asian girls, do you have one in mind?"

"Ding-a-ling!" the girls chorused and broke out laughing.

"Ling Li," June said in response to Philly's puzzled look. "Everyone calls her Ding-a-ling. She's very funny."

'Great,' Philly thought. Just what the project needed—a comedienne.

"Not to worry," Naomi said. "She's also very smart."

June produced a drawing pad which she handed to Philly. "You wanted to see my drawings."

Philly began to flip thought the drawings, which were mostly pencil drawings of faces. There was Daisy. Philly saw her daughter's blue eyes even though there was no blue on the page. And here was a drawing of Philly herself, capturing her hard stare. Philly wondered whether she had ever presented a softer look for June to draw. "These are good. I don't know much about drawing, but I think you have talent."

"When it comes to drawing, June and Ding-a-ling are the best," Naomi said.

"When do I get to meet Ding-a-ling?" Philly asked.

Carpenter reread an e-mail from Henry Frazier. Father and son had talked, and Donald Frazier had agreed to a meeting with Warren Anderson, the president of Event Planning, provided his own lawyer attended. 'Why the hell not?' Carpenter thought, as he drafted a responsive e-mail giving his okay to the course of action. 'In for a penny, in for a pound.'

"You think we're getting too old for this?" Herb McCauley asked.

"If you have to ask, then *you're* getting too old for this," Barney Freedman retorted.

This was the second night the two private detectives had spent tailing Marshall Hightower. Last night, Hightower headed out to a Cambridge bar at about eight in the evening. He had left the bar three hours later with a woman, and they had made a beeline back to his apartment.

Tonight, Hightower had driven to Somerville, parked just off the city center, and set out on foot. Herb lucked out, found a parking space near where Hightower had parked, and now he and Barney were following the man on foot.

"He's heading for the bars," Herb said. "This is probably going to be a repeat of last night."

"You ever think it's easier for a young guy to get laid these days than it was back in our day?" Barney asked.

"Don't go there," Herb responded. "It's not productive."

They were keeping about two hundred feet behind Hightower, more than a safe distance, but Herb wondered whether any precaution was worth the effort. He and Barney were big guys, hard to miss, and they surely stood out among the young people making the rounds of the city center bar scene.

"Twisters," Barney said, and because they had been partners and friends for so long, Herb didn't need Barney to elaborate. Things might be looking up.

Hightower stopped before Twisters and glanced back the way he had come. Herb saw no reason to slow down—they were far enough away that stopping would have attracted more attention than maintaining their slow advance. By the time they passed the bar's entrance, Hightower was inside.

"How do you want to play this?" Herb asked after they stopped before the entrance to the next bar on their side of the street.

"I could go in now," Barney offered. "Check it out."

Herb shook his head. "Let's wait till he comes out. If he's dealing with Two Tone it shouldn't take long, and then we can go in and ask some questions."

Barney nodded and moved out toward the street where he could lean up against a lamppost and keep an eye on the entrance to Twisters.

Herb joined his partner. "When's the last time you saw Two Tone?" he asked.

"It was right after we resigned from the force. I was doing some shopping or something and there was Twisters. I went inside and Two Tone was at that booth he does business at and when he saw me, he began shoveling papers into a briefcase. He thought I was there to roust him, and I don't think he knew we had left the force. I went to him real slow and asked him if it was necessary for me to read him his rights. He gets all indignant, says he hasn't done anything, and I cut him off and start reading him his rights. He was nervous as hell and finally I cracked up.

I told him I had just popped in to say hello and wish him well. He asked about you and I told him we had both left the force. Then he became all chatty and wanted to buy me a drink. I declined and told him to keep to the straight and narrow."

"Like that was going to happen," Herb said.

Twister's front door opened and Hightower exited, moving quickly, heading back in the direction of his car.

"Let's get this over with," Barney said.

Barney and Herb slid onto the vacant bench of a booth already occupied by a man of rather indeterminate old age, not particularly imposing and rather forgettable except for the two white patches—one on each cheek—that marred his dark complexion and had gained him his nickname. The booth was in an isolated spot away from the bar proper, and Herb noticed that only one other booth was occupied. The man across from them didn't look up directly. He was taking his time, writing on a sheet of lined notepaper, acting as if he had no interest in who had come to join him. When he did look up, his nonchalance disappeared. "I do not have to talk to you," he said, in a pleading voice very faintly tinged with an Indian accent. "You are no longer police officers."

"I thought we were friends," Barney said. "Since when do you refuse to be sociable with old friends?"

"We have never been friends," Two Tone said with some bitterness. "I would like you to leave me alone."

"Not going to happen," Barney said as he reached out and grabbed the piece of notepaper that Two Tone had been writing on.

"Hey! That is my personal property!"

Barney took his time reading what was on the notepaper. Herb couldn't help feeling sympathy for Two Tone. When they had been with the Cambridge Police Department, he and Barney had occasionally leaned heavily on him for information. Two Tone was middle management in one of the larger bookmaking operations that continued to do business in the Cambridge-Somerville-Medford area. The man was reputedly a whiz with numbers. His family had emigrated from India and settled in Cambridge when Two Tone was a little boy. Herb could neither spell nor pronounce his given name, and it always surprised him when Two Tone showed no embarrassment about his nickname. Herb had never understood how such a mild-mannered individual had ended up associated with men who were both dangerous and violent.

"This is interesting reading," Barney said when his perusal of the notepaper had concluded.

"I would like it back," Two Tone said with what, to Herb, was unaccustomed forcefulness.

"Of course," Barney said. "But first we need some information from you."

"I told you. I do not wish to talk to you."

"A man just left here," Barney said, ignoring Two Tone's protest. "A young guy, white, big, muscular, with a lot of gel in his blond hair. Did you meet with him?"

"I do not have to answer your questions."

"That's right, you don't," Barney acknowledged. "That would be a shame, however. Because if you don't answer our questions, I'm going to have to drop this piece of paper off at the Somerville Police Department and tell them it fell out of your pocket at Twisters. They may ask you to explain the numbers on this paper. I can't figure them out. I have my suspicions, but I'm not sure."

"This is not right," Two Tone said indignantly.

"Put a sock in it," Barney erupted "All you have to do is tell us if you met with him and, if you did, whether the man owes any money."

Two Tone slumped against the rear of the booth. They all knew that he would eventually answer their questions, but Herb grudgingly admired him for not caving in immediately.

"This is not something I am permitted to discuss."

Barney set the piece of notepaper down on the table before him, keeping it covered by his massive hands. "You don't have to say anything," Barney said. "If you just met with the man, all you have to do is nod your head."

Two Tone became lost in thought. Then his head inclined downward several inches and sprang back to its former position.

"Does the man owe money?" Barney next asked.

Again, a pause followed by a barely perceptible nod.

Barney pushed the piece of notepaper across the table. "Your cooperation with former officers of the law is appreciated," Barney said. "If there's ever anything Herb or I can do for you, all you have to do is ask."

Herb exited the booth and Barney followed. Outside they huddled.

"We'll need two or three photographs," Herb said.

"You still have that fancy camera?" Barney asked.

Herb nodded. "Hightower probably puts in a regular weekly appearance. I'll take next week and you take the week after that if necessary."

"A division of labor," Barney said. "No wonder we get along."

July

Philly's Untitled Playlist

"Demons"

Imagine Dragons

48

This year, Philly's July Fourth party had been a zoo. Both usual and unusual suspects had attended: her parents had driven up from Fall River; Philip's parents had been chauffeured from North Andover by Philip's best friend, Tom Grange; Paul's daughter Jennie from his first marriage had come with one of Paul's brothers and his family; Rainy and Monica and their child had arrived early and stayed late; friends of Raul and Isabella had put in an appearance; Carpenter, Rachel, and Simon had brought their significant others; Meredith and Flash arrived early and were among the last to leave; and Sarah invited a guy she had met at the senior center who soon fit right in helping Paul and Raul man the grill.

Philly had stolen away from the cleaning-up efforts and retreated to her second-floor office for some privacy. Now she sat at her desk chair and stared at the envelope given to her by Tom Grange. "This is for Daisy," Tom had said. "I'd like you to give it to her if and when appropriate. Take a look when you have some down time alone. This is something I should have given you a while ago."

Tom's appearance had jolted her, just as it had when he showed up at the July Fourth party celebrating Daisy's first birthday. Tom's physical resemblance to Philip was still disconcerting, both tall, blond, and blue-eyed. Philly and Tom each felt a bit sad and awkward whenever they were together. She had lost her fiancé and Tom had lost his best friend.

Tom hadn't sealed the envelope. The words "To Daisy" were handwritten on the front. Philly removed a letter and began to read.

Dear Daisy,

I know you have a Daddy but I wanted to tell you a few things about the Daddy you never saw. I think it's important that you know something about your other Daddy so here goes even though I'm not much of a letter writer, as your Mommy will tell you.

Your other Daddy was my best friend growing up. We were in school together from kindergarten through the twelfth grade. We lived two blocks away from each other but were always spending time at each other's house. We had too many sleepovers to count. We were such good friends that it felt like we were brothers.

Your other Daddy was the smartest guy I knew. It wasn't so much that he got good grades in school, which he did. It was more that no matter what happened, he knew the right thing to do. I probably should have kept my mouth shut and done whatever he said. I always knew the wrong thing to do; if we followed my advice, sometimes, we ended up in trouble.

Your other Daddy was generous. He liked helping people and when he helped them, he had a way of doing it so people didn't feel like they owed him anything. Lots of times they didn't even know it was your Daddy who helped them. That's pretty hard to do as you will learn. In high school, he and a bunch of other kids helped out kids who were having trouble with a class. Your Daddy came up with a list of kids who would help out, and any kid could call anybody on the list for help. I wasn't on the list because I kind of goofed off during high school and never got good grades. And of course I was too proud to ask for help from anybody on the list. Your other Daddy helped me out anyway.

Your other Daddy loved the outdoors. He liked to run and bike and swim and ski. In high school, he was a runner on the track team. He was especially good at the two-mile race. He was tall and had long, strong legs and he would keep near the leaders of the pack until the final lap, and then he would sprint for all he was worth. It was a pretty good strategy—he ended up as one of the best runners in the state. I liked the water more than land. In high school I was on the swim team. I still like the water. Today I'm an oceanographer and I'll leave it to your Mommy to tell you what that is.

We were different in other ways, too. Your other Daddy was the serious one. I was the one who joked around and tried to get people to laugh. In fact, I was one of the few people who could make your other Daddy laugh. I'll let you in on a secret. Your other Daddy was actually a pretty funny guy, but he tried to keep that quiet. Being so different made us even better friends.

When your other Daddy died, I was off on a ship and never got home to say goodbye to him. There are not too many things I wish had turned out differently, but your other Daddy dying in a stupid accident and me not getting home for his funeral are two of the things I wish I could undo.

I've been putting together a photograph album that I want you and your Mommy to have. I've been collecting pictures from your grandparents and from my parents and I never realized there were so many. It's hard to choose what to put in the album so it's taking me some time to finish this project. But I think I'll have it ready for your fourth birthday. I'm writing descriptions next to each picture so you will know what you're looking at. When I'm through, you're going to have a book that will help you to know your other Daddy.

I've said this to your Mommy and I need to say this to you. If you ever need me for anything, all you have to do is ask. I will always be there for you.

Love,

Tom Grange

Philly set her head on her desk and wept. That was how Paul found her. She handed him Tom's letter and kept on crying.

49

Alan Rule was a second-year associate at Blake, Pennington & Dwyer assigned to the firm's real estate department. As the young lawyer answered background questions, Meredith felt her age. Rule was a kid, a skinny, bespectacled, scrawny guy with a sallow complexion and a mop of long, black hair that he was constantly pushing off his glasses. Meredith hoped she hadn't had the same look of someone adrift in the adult world when she had joined a large Boston firm straight out of Spenser School of Law.

Rule had graduated from Harvard Law and gone directly to Blake Pennington. He claimed to be enjoying his work which, as far as Meredith could elicit, was limited to drafting and reviewing complex business leases. Meredith marveled at the guy's threshold of pain. If she'd been fed a steady diet of lease documents early on in her legal career, she'd have seriously considered switching professions.

For this first deposition in the Ship Right case, Carpenter sat beside her, and Meredith was grateful for his presence. Carpenter had so built up the abilities of Brian Murphy and Sarah Warren that Meredith wanted the crutch of his presence in case they came up with a tactic that was out of her depth.

This was Meredith's first look at Sarah Warren, who was defending Rule's deposition. Meredith guessed Warren to be in her mid-fifties. She was trim, almost gaunt, and her black hair, cut short, was losing the battle against gray. She might have come across as severe if it weren't for her dancing, hazel eyes.

Ship Right had been billed just under $6,000 for Alan Rule's services, which consisted of participating in conference calls and attending internal firm meetings.

Meredith had the documentation showing the charges for Rule's time marked as a deposition exhibit, and directed his attention to the first conference call he participated in.

"Do you remember this call?" Meredith asked.

"Not particularly. Not specifically."

"How did you come to participate in this call?'

"I would have been told to participate in the call by Jack Pender."

"Who is Mr. Pender?" Meredith asked, quickly concluding that Rule had been well-schooled and would only answer the question he was asked.

"He's a partner in the firm's real estate department."

"Was Mr. Pender the partner in charge of the real estate aspects of the Ship Right transaction?"

"I believe so. That was my impression. But you'd have to ask him to make certain. There may have been another real estate partner in charge as well."

"Were you told by Mr. Pender or by anyone else why your presence was required for this conference call?"

"Not that I recall."

"Who was the conference call with?"

"Attorneys at our firm and representatives of Ship Right."

"Where were you when you participated in this conference call?"

"I was in a conference room at our firm."

"Who else was in the conference room?"

"I don't remember for sure. Mr. Pender was there and so were other lawyers from the firm."

"Were the other lawyers from the firm limited to the real estate department?'

"No."

"What other departments of the firm were represented at that conference call?"

"I think there were corporate and tax department lawyers present, but I'm not totally sure."

"Were you and Mr. Pender the only lawyers from the firm's real estate department who were present for the call?"

"I don't think so, but I'm really having trouble remembering who was there."

"How many lawyers were present in the conference room in connection with the call we're discussing?"

"I'm not sure of the exact number. Ten to twelve maybe."

"Ten to twelve," Meredith repeated. She directed Rule's attention to the amount billed for his time on the conference call. "Am I correct that for this conference call we're discussing, Ship Right was billed for an hour and twenty minutes of your time?"

Rule studied the document. "I've never seen the firm's bills. It looks like that's what was billed for my time, but I don't really know how billing for my time was decided upon."

This didn't surprise Meredith. During her years with a large Boston firm, she and other associates were kept in the dark about actual bills. "At the end of each day did you record the time you spent and submit the time spent to your firm's billing department?'

Rule nodded, looked relieved. "Yes, that pretty much was it."

"This bill we've been discussing lists your hourly rate at three hundred dollars. Is it your understanding that this was your hourly rate?"

Rule appeared discomfited. He swept his hair off his glasses and glanced briefly at Warren. "I don't believe I had a fixed hourly rate."

"What's the basis for that belief?"

"I was told once that my hourly rate would be determined for each firm engagement, and that if pressed for a specific figure, I was to say approximately two hundred seventy-five dollars an hour subject to change by a partner."

"Who told you that?"

"I don't remember."

"Did you speak during the conference call I've asked you to focus on?"

"No."

"Did Mr. Pender speak?"

"I know he spoke at conference calls I participated in, but I can't tell you whether he spoke during this particular call."

"In advance of this call, were you given any documents to review to prepare for the call?"

"No."

"Were you given any advance notice of what the conference call was about?'

"I was told that it involved the sale of a business that included real estate matters."

"Who told you that?"

"I believe it was Mr. Pender."

"Was real estate the only subject discussed during this conference call?"

"No."

"Assuming that the conference call lasted one hour and twenty minutes, how much time during the call was spent on real estate matters?"

"I couldn't really give you a specific figure. I don't remember."

Meredith had another document marked as a deposition exhibit. "Do you recognize this document?"

"It appears to be my notes on the call we've been discussing."

"Please take a moment to review your notes."

Meredith glanced at Warren. The woman's features were a mask.

"I've reviewed my notes," Rule said.

"Does your review help you answer how much time was spent on real estate matters during the call?'

"It doesn't appear to be very much time. There was some discussion of Ship Right leases that would terminate if Ship Right sold its business."

"Again, please assume that the call we're talking about lasted one hour and twenty minutes. Would you agree that less than a quarter of the time spent on the call was devoted to real estate matters?"

Rule took his time with the question. For a nerdy, unprepossessing guy, Meredith had to acknowledge that Rule was handling himself well, answering truthfully in difficult circumstances.

"That seems like a reasonable estimate," Rule said. "But like I said before, I can't tell you for sure."

"Following this call we've been discussing, were you given any assignments to work on?"

"No."

"Did you draft any document as a result of this call?"

"No."

Meredith reviewed her deposition outline. "I'm going to try to speed things up, Mr. Rule. Did you speak at any conference call involving the Ship Right transaction?"

"No."

"Did you speak at any meeting, including your firm's internal meetings, that concerned the Ship Right transaction?"

"No."

"Did you draft any documents in connection with the Ship Right transaction your firm was working on?"

"No."

"You mentioned that there was some discussion about Ship Right leases that would terminate if Ship Right sold its business. Are you aware of any conclusion reached by your firm on that issue?"

"No."

"Did you ever receive a memorandum or other document from Mr. Pender or anyone else concerning the Ship Right transaction?"

"No. I believe the transaction didn't go forward."

"Why do you believe that?"

"I think I was told that."

"By whom?"

"I don't remember."

Meredith leaned toward Carpenter, shielding their faces with her notepad. "I'm pretty much done," she whispered. "Let's take a five-minute break and we can discuss what else I should ask."

"No need," Carpenter said. "As far as I can tell you're done." He had a sheet of notepaper in front of him that contained a list. Each item on the list had been checked off."

"Thank you, Mr. Rule," Meredith said. "No further questions."

"You're looking good, Sarah," Carpenter said, after Rule left the conference room. "I'm impressed that you're covering these depositions with your A-team, instead of using Murphy."

"Flattery will get you everywhere," Warren joked. "You don't look half bad yourself. You look like you've lost some weight."

"It's an illusion," Carpenter responded.

"Aren't you at retirement age?" Warren asked, and Meredith was curious what his answer would be.

"What age might that be?" Carpenter replied.

"Sixty-five is recognized by the Social Security system," Warren pointed out.

"You mean the system that's supposed to go broke if it's not fixed soon? Why would I accept any retirement age figure from that losing outfit?"

"It's coming back to me," Warren said laughing. "Your warm and fuzzy personality. God, how I've missed you."

"You don't need me," Carpenter said. "You've got Murphy to babysit."

"Don't remind me." Warren turned to Meredith. "Who's next? she asked.

"Patricia Cloverdale, another real estate department associate."

Carpenter rose. "I'll see if she's in the reception area and, if she is, I'll send her in. I'm going to excuse myself. You two ladies have a great rest of the day."

50

Rachel was probably more nervous about Jane Snelling's deposition than Snelling was herself. Rachel had prepped the former director of the Sloan-Webster placement office for the hard questions she thought Christopher Blaisedell would ask, and Snelling had been obviously uncomfortable when she knew that an answer made her look bad. But now, at the actual deposition, Snelling was solemn and didn't appear to be ill at ease. Her all-business attitude was emphasized by a dark blue pants suit, a white blouse, and a severe bun containing her graying hair.

As he did in the Spencer School of Law case, Blaisedell was using the offices of Shapiro & Morales for this deposition. There were no conference rooms in the two-man law firm's office suite, so the deposition was being held in Morales' cramped, drab office. Blaisedell sat behind Morales' desk with the stenographer beside him. Rachel and Snelling were seated in the office's visitor chairs.

Blaisedell moved through background questions quickly. Rachel thought she was prepared for the worst but hearing Snelling under oath recount her lack of placement experience both before and after her appointment, drove home to Rachel the magnitude of the liability she would be at trial.

"In all your years as placement department head, did you ever place a Sloan-Webster graduate in a legal position?" Blaisedell asked.

"I may have," Snelling responded.

"What do you mean by that answer?"

"From time to time I would try to answer graduates' questions. Typically, I wouldn't get feedback from graduates, but it may have been the case that an answer I provided led to a legal job."

Rachel silently applauded Snelling's attempt to find a silver lining in her placement efforts. She must have recently come up with her last answer on her own because it wasn't a response she had offered during their practice runs.

"Does that mean you are not able to name a single graduate who you successfully placed in a legal position?" Blaisedell challenged.

"If you're asking whether I can provide the name of someone I placed, the answer is no."

"During your placement office tenure, did you ever try to determine what placement offices did at other law schools?"

"No."

"Would it be correct to say that while you served with the placement office, students and graduates would approach you requesting specific suggestions on how to obtain a law-related job?"

"Yes."

"Were you ever able to answer such a question with a specific suggestion?"

"I may have but I can't recall any instance. However, I would typically direct people to our placement office bulletin board and to the job offerings listed in the weekly lawyers' newspaper."

"Did you ever report to anyone at the law school about your inability to answer requests for specific suggestions on how to obtain a law-related job?"

"No."

"In the absence of a specific suggestion from you, what did you think would happen to a student or graduate who had asked you for a specific suggestion on how to obtain a law-related job?"

"Objection," Rachel said.

"Do I have to answer?" Snelling asked.

"Yes," Rachel instructed.

"I'm not sure I fully understand your question, but I assumed that an individual would continue to contact prospective legal employers and continue to review job opening opportunities posted on our bulletin board and in the statewide weekly newspaper for lawyers."

"Did it bother you that you weren't able to provide specific suggestions to students and graduates when they asked for specific suggestions on finding a job?"

"Objection," Rachel said to break Blaisedell's rhythm and hopefully to cause Snelling to think before she answered.

"Yes and no. The law school's placement office was not elaborate, and this was spelled out in the school's printed materials. I did my best to try to answer students' and former students' questions, which is what the printed materials said would be done. So I wouldn't say it bothered me that I did my best to try to answer questions that came to me. But I'm sure it did bother me not to be more helpful than I was able to be."

Rachel was pleased with Snelling's answer. It would have been a disaster if she had said she wasn't bothered by her inability to provide specific direction to students and graduates.

"When you ran the placement office, did the office have a website that listed potential job openings?"

"No."

"Did you ever consider creating such a website?'

"No."

"Did you ever remove a job opportunity from the placement office's bulletin board?"

"Yes."

"What would cause you to remove a job posting from the bulletin board?"

"When I put up a job posting, I would note the date. Every month or so, I would contact the sources of the job postings to see if the positions were still open. If a position had been filled, I would remove the posting."

"Is it true that you have been relieved of your duties with the placement office?"

Snelling colored slightly. "I wouldn't say relieved. Recently, the law school brought in a new, full-time director of the placement office and I now devote my full time to being an administrative assistant to the dean and to the assistant dean of students."

"Did you ever inform anyone at the law school that your part-time position with the placement office needed to be full time?"

"No."

"Is it your view that the position should have been full time during the period you held the position?"

"I don't have a view one way or the other. That was something that the dean and the board of the law school would have needed to address."

Blaisedell turned over a page in his trial notebook. "Has your replacement at the placement office instituted any changes that weren't in place while you were in charge of the office?"

"Yes."

"What are those changes?"

"The new director has expanded the placement office's website so that job openings are posted. He intends to speak to each incoming class about the placement office. And I believe he's tried to make personal contact with the hiring partners of Massachusetts law firms. There may be other changes, but these are the ones that readily come to mind."

"Why weren't these changes made by you during your placement office tenure?"

Rachel was relieved they had gone over, in detail, a question similar to the one Blaisedell had just asked.

"The law school's administration has redefined the placement office's function. For example, I mentioned that the new director is full time. Until administration redefined the office's function, the changes that have been made weren't a matter of discussion."

"Do you think the new changes are positive changes?"

"Objection," Rachel said. When Snelling looked at her questioningly, she nodded for her to proceed.

"Time will tell," Snelling said.

"Does the new director have experience with a law school placement office."

"Yes."

"While you ran the placement office, did you keep statistics on law school graduates obtaining law-related jobs?"

"No."

"Were you aware that competitors of Sloan-Webster kept statistics on law-related jobs obtained by their graduates?"

"I was aware that other law schools in Massachusetts kept such statistics, but I wasn't aware of the numbers."

"If you were aware that other Massachusetts law schools kept such statistics, why didn't you have Sloan-Webster maintain such statistics?"

"This was not something that the law school's administration asked me to do. If I had been directed to come up with statistics on any subject, I would have done so."

Rachel suspected that Blaisedell's evident irritation had to do with Snelling passing the buck to unnamed administrators. It was probably only a matter of time before Blaisedell deposed Janet Martin.

"Being aware that other area law schools kept statistics on law-related jobs of graduates, did it occur to you to be proactive and ask Sloan-Webster's administration for authority to maintain similar statistics?"

"Did it occur to me?" Snelling asked.

Blaisedell requested the stenographer to reread his last question.

Snelling paused. "No," she finally said. "I don't recall that occurring to me."

"Would you agree that one indication a law school placement office is doing a good job is the number of graduates that find legal positions?"

"That might be an indication."

"Why do you say *might*."

"Because a placement office might have played no role in a graduate finding a legal position."

"Do you think that the changes put in by your successor will make Sloan-Webster more successful in placing graduates with legal jobs than was the case during your placement office tenure?"

"I wouldn't know. It's certainly possible. Again, time will tell."

"This might be a good time for a brief break," Blaisedell said.

Rachel stood and beckoned for Snelling to join her outside the office. Blaisedell might have a few surprises left, but she believed the worst was over for Snelling and, on balance, Snelling had made the best of a bad situation.

Carpenter and Meredith were in the office suite's conference room with transcripts of the first round of depositions from the Ship Right case on the table between them. Carpenter had read all the transcripts. "This is about as good as we could have hoped for," he said. "Nice job."

"Thanks." Meredith was pleased. For some reason, getting a compliment from Carpenter meant more to her than any acknowledgement of good work from a partner at her former law firm.

"I did some quick math," Carpenter said. "We've got evidence of about a hundred thousand dollars in legal fees billed for lawyers who sat in on calls and meetings and never said a word or wrote a word. Do I have that right?'

Meredith smiled. "It's ninety-eight thousand three hundred dollars," she corrected.

"I think we should schedule another ten depositions," Carpenter said. "Even if they turn out half as good as these, it would be a plus."

"Okay," Meredith said. "I'll call Warren as a courtesy and see if there's a date that works for her."

Carpenter nodded. "If you were Murphy and Warren right now, what are you telling your client?" he asked.

Meredith had been around Carpenter long enough to know that he liked to stand in the shoes of his opponent. "I wouldn't like the results of these depositions," she said, pointing to the transcripts. "I'd ask my client what they were thinking and, if the firm came back with the team approach response, I wouldn't be particularly pleased."

"And would you schedule Jeremiah Becker's deposition?"

"Yes," Meredith said. "I'd probably decide it was worth a shot to try to get something damaging out of Becker, or about Ship Right, to use either in litigating the case or in settlement discussions. I'd figure there was nothing to lose by deposing Becker."

Carpenter again nodded. "That's more or less what I was thinking." He sat for a moment, drumming his fingers on the stack of transcripts. "Do you think we're now in a position to file a Rule 68 motion?" Carpenter next asked. "Becker liked the idea, using a figure of three hundred and twenty-five thousand."

Meredith had been thinking about this. "I'd like to see how the second set of depositions goes before filing the motion."

Carpenter frowned. "Then Ship Right couldn't recover legal fees for the second round of depositions under the court rule."

"We still have a legal claim that could get us legal fees," Meredith pointed out.

Carpenter went into his faraway look, jaw grinding mode. "I could go either way on this," he said after a long pause. "I'll call Becker and make sure he's okay about taking another round of depositions before filing the motion. Anything else?"

Meredith hesitated only briefly. "The way you had described Sarah Warren, I thought she was going to give me a tough time at these depositions. I'd been worried about her and was glad you sat in at the first deposition."

"There really wasn't much she could do with the questions you asked," Carpenter responded. "Between Murphy and Warren, I'd say Warren is the more reflective, less impulsive of the two. Warren and Murphy *are* formidable. You're going to run up against formidable lawyers throughout your career, and from what I've seen, I don't think you need to worry about them being tough on you. I suggest you develop the mindset that they should worry about you being tough on them."

'Another compliment,' Meredith thought. Two in one day. Not too shabby.

51

Today was one of those half-days of school when the students were let out early so teachers could focus on administrative tasks. In the Parker Hill Elementary School, chairs had been placed upside down on all but two of the tables in the cafeteria. Philly was the second to arrive for the two o'clock meeting. Already seated, Sasha Barton sent a nervous wave in her direction.

"Smile," Philly counseled, as she squirmed her way into a child-sized chair next to her client. It was going to be interesting to see how Clarke managed to seat himself.

"What if this doesn't work?" Barton said.

"You need to convey the attitude that the outcome doesn't matter to you," Philly advised.

"So you want me to lie? This does matter to me!"

"Why do clients think their lawyers are advising lying? No, I want you to project a certain attitude. You can do this."

Barton slumped in her chair, her attitude tentative, her posture conveying uncertainty. Philly was relieved to see the other attendees approach their tables. Carlos Ibanez lent a supporting arm to Sonia Acevedo, and Miranda Hernandez preceded Samuel Clarke. Ibanez was the only one of the four who looked at ease. For this meeting, he had selected Sonia Acevedo as the sole representative of the Hispanic students who had been punished. Hernandez looked all business, and Philly couldn't decide whether that boded well or ill. Principal Clarke appeared to have steeled himself for a difficult meeting.

"It's nice to see everyone," Ibanez said as he awkwardly took his seat. "Ms. Sullivan and I are pleased that you were able to make time to meet with us." Ibanez nodded in her direction and Philly took her cue.

"I'm going to distribute a pamphlet to each of you which I want returned to me at the end of our meeting. The material is marked copyrighted as you will see. I think you will find it interesting. At least I hope you will."

Philly passed out the document to the attendees. Clarke had solved his seating problem by moving two chairs together. His knees were up by his chin. He took his copy of the pamphlet and regarded it skeptically. The children's chairs had an oddly equalizing effect. Everyone's posture was just this side of ridiculous, and it made it hard for anyone to look stern.

Philly studied her own copy. She liked the title: *What You Don't Know About People You Know.* The subtitle was less catchy: *Avoiding Bias and Stereotyping.* When June, Naomi, and Lucida had seen the finished product of their work, their looks of wonderment quickly gave way to a giggling, group hug. At the bottom of the first page, Sasha Barton was listed as Teacher Advisor. No name was listed as Principal Advisor.

Ibanez and Acevedo nodded approvingly as they read the document. The expressions of Clarke and Hernandez gave nothing away. Ibanez had briefed Hernandez on what was coming, but he had reported to Philly that Hernandez had not offered any comment.

Philly took charge when everyone resumed looking her way. "I'm going to make a proposal to settle Ms. Barton's lawsuit and the lawsuit brought by Mr. Ibanez. In the case of my client, her firing would be rescinded, and her record would be wiped clean. She would be paid ten thousand dollars plus back pay, and the teachers union would be reimbursed for the attorney fees paid to me." Philly paused, expecting a question on how much she had been paid to date, but when Hernandez remained silent, she continued.

"Mr. Ibanez's lawsuit would be settled by each of the children he represents receiving ten thousand dollars, and the school reimbursing his legal fees." Philly again waited for questions, but none were forthcoming.

"If these terms are agreeable, Mr. Clarke would be listed as the Principal Advisor on the pamphlet I've distributed. If these terms are not agreeable, Mr. Ibanez and I and our clients will listen to and consider any objections, but I need to tell you that this is pretty much a take it or leave it proposal. I know that sounds uncompromising, but the defendants in these cases need to understand that the plaintiffs are willing to take the cases to trial. The plaintiffs have made what we believe is a fair and reasonable proposal and we urge you to give it serious consideration.

"Also, if these terms are not agreeable, the student authors of this pamphlet will seek a different Boston school principal to be the Principal Advisor listed on the pamphlet. The student authors will be submitting this pamphlet to the superintendent of schools with a proposal to make a presentation at each Boston middle school. At any presentation, the authors will be accompanied by a fourth student, an Asian girl. If the program works smoothly, the students will explore expanding the program beyond Boston." Philly consulted her notes. "I think I've covered everything."

"Returning to the broader settlement, no defendant would admit any liability," Ibanez amplified. "We envision side agreements of settlement and dismissals of the lawsuits with prejudice."

Philly saw Hernandez glance at Clarke. Hernandez had heard these details previously, and Philly wondered whether she had briefed her client on the proposal before this meeting. From the look on the principal's face, Philly believed that he was hearing the settlement proposal for the first time. In Hernandez's place, Philly would have made the same tactical decision.

After a brief pause, Hernandez spoke. "Mr. Clarke and I and school officials will consider your proposal. I'd appreciate it if you would provide me with figures on legal fees incurred to date and an estimate of future legal fees. We'll get back to you."

Philly had noticed that during the presentation, Barton had straightened in her chair and adopted a more confident look. Now she was gazing at Clarke as if trying to gauge his reaction. Clarke was frowning, looking like he wanted to be elsewhere.

"Samuel," Barton said. "We are due to have another conversation shortly. I propose we have it sooner rather than later. One of the things I would like to talk about is what the lawyers presented this afternoon."

Clarke appeared momentarily nonplussed and Philly wondered whether Barton had ever previously addressed him by his first name.

"Sure," Clarke said, sounding both defeated and disgusted. "Why the hell not."

'Don't sound so enthusiastic,' Philly wanted to say, but she kept silent. Miranda Hernandez flashed her a brief, weak, enigmatic smile. Was the school attorney signaling that Clarke could be brought around or that there wasn't a chance in hell of that happening?

52

Carpenter had advised Henry Frazier to keep a low profile during this meeting with Event Planning's president, Warren Anderson, but now he doubted whether his client would heed this advice. Waiting for Anderson to arrive, Frazier appeared to be champing at the bit. In contrast, the elder Frazier sat composed, and Carpenter wondered whether the looming end of years of dissembling had brought some relief to the man. Lauren Goldman also appeared relaxed; she sat motionless, a notepad and pen resting before her on the conference room table.

This was Carpenter's first look at his client's father. He saw no clear physical resemblance. The elder Frazier could pass for a male Barrister at Carpenter's ritual, Sunday morning breakfasts with fellow lawyers: a balding, slightly overweight guy with thinning hair. He certainly didn't resemble his tall, muscular son, much less the next man to arrive.

"Sorry I'm running behind," a wiry, gaunt, gray-haired man declared as he entered the conference room and took a seat at the head of the table. He was joined by an athletic-looking woman wearing dark slacks and a dark blazer over a purple blouse. Warren Anderson introduced himself and his counsel, Sophie Teague.

"I have to say I'm curious as to what this is all about," Anderson said once introductions concluded. "I certainly hope I don't really need a lawyer."

"This is both awkward and embarrassing for me," Donald Frazier said, "so I think I just need to say what I came to say and let the chips fall where they may."

Anderson's expression didn't give anything away.

"For a number of years, I've been making under-the-table, monthly cash payments to John Harrison. Years ago, John told me that he was thinking of making a change in vendors, and he asked whether I could come up with something to change his mind. One thing led to another and I began paying him a thousand dollars a month. His demands increased. Currently I'm paying him eight thousand dollars a month. I asked for this meeting to inform you about what's been going on and to tell you that the payments are going to stop. I'm also going to be sending John 1099 forms for all the years I've been paying him. Finally, I want to apologize to you. I should never have given in to John. I'm ashamed that I did."

Carpenter was relieved that Donald Frazier's account sounded heartfelt.

If Anderson was aware of the payments to his vice-president or shocked by their existence, you couldn't tell from his reaction to the elder Frazier's disclosure. "This is deeply disturbing," he said, stating the obvious as he turned to his lawyer.

Teague wrote for a brief time on her notepad. "Is there a reason why you didn't ask for Mr. Harrison to be present?" she asked.

"Since the payments were in cash, I expect him to deny that he received them," Donald Frazier said. "But I have no problem repeating what I just said to John if that's what you prefer."

Teague leaned toward Anderson and the two engaged in a whispered exchange shielded by Teague's notepad.

"We may ask you to repeat what you said in Mr. Harrison's presence at a later date," Teague said. "Obviously, what you've said *is* disturbing as Mr. Anderson noted. Event Planning needs to think about this and decide what to do. All options are on the table including severing business ties with Elite Scripts."

Carpenter leaned toward Henry Frazier. "Don't say a bloody word," he whispered.

"I asked my son and his counsel to be present today," Donald Frazier said. "Henry had nothing to do with my payments to John and didn't know about them until very recently. Henry and I have talked about transitioning the business to him, and should we reach an agreement, I may be dropping out of the picture at Elite Scripts."

Neither Teague nor Anderson showed any reaction to the takeover scenario.

"May I say something?" Henry Frazier requested.

Carpenter squeezed his client's knee and whispered "shut up" in his ear, all to no avail.

Anderson nodded at Henry to proceed.

"I hope you will give serious consideration to continuing the relationship between our companies. We believe our work is excellent, and nothing that's been said here is going to change that. We can talk about changing the terms of the relationship but I, for one, would hope that the relationship continues."

Carpenter didn't think that Henry had come across as begging. But maybe Anderson and Teague saw it differently.

"Duly noted," Teague said, and Carpenter began to wonder whether the lawyer was more hard-nosed than Anderson.

Carpenter passed his business card to Teague, and Goldman followed suit with her card.

"Excellent," Teague said. "Now I know how to reach you."

53

Simon took the visitor's chair in Philly's old office. Rachel sat in what used to be Philly's office chair and together they read over copies of the motion filed by Christopher Blaisedell to have his lawsuit certified as a class action. Blaisedell wanted the three plaintiffs he had selected to represent a class comprised of all graduates of Sloan-Webster School of Law who had tried and failed to obtain a law-related job. Simon had informed the dean that this motion was coming, but its arrival was sobering, and he foresaw a number of hand-holding sessions with Janet Martin and Ralph Cray.

"He's seeking a very broadly defined class," Rachel observed. "At a minimum, for placement office claims, shouldn't the class be limited to individuals who requested but didn't receive help from the placement office?"

"Not necessarily," Simon answered. "The plaintiffs claim that the placement office never placed anybody, and the school made a misrepresentation by saying it had a placement office. Also, for non-placement office claims such as falsely claiming a top-notch faculty, the class may not be overbroad."

Rachel sighed.

"I think we both know what we have to do to oppose this motion," Simon said.

"Trash the three named plaintiffs," Rachel said. "We have to show they are not suitable to represent the class Blaisedell wants the court to recognize."

Simon nodded. Of the two of them, Rachel would usually have the strongest misgivings about taking the low road in a case. Yet here he was—uncharacteristically—harboring misgivings of his own.

"Let's go over what we've got," Rachel suggested. "There's the exotic dancer. Does being an exotic dancer disqualify a person from representing a class of law school graduates who can't find a legal job?"

"Not necessarily, is the logical answer," Simon threw out. "But since when does logic come into play? I think we're forced to make the argument that an exotic dancer shouldn't represent the class because most employers seeking to fill legal positions would have negative reactions to anyone in that line of work."

Rachel slumped in her chair. "Since when did we become the bad guys?"

"Since we became litigators and pledged to represent the interests of a client," Simon answered. "Then there's the Black guy, Noah Branson. Basically, we've got nothing on him except the fact that he would have jumped up and run out of the room if he were able when I started asking about cheating on that Michigan State economics test. I'm telling you Branson has something to hide."

"But since we don't know what, we're nowhere," Rachel countered.

"The only thing I could come up with was to try to scare Branson," Simon revealed.

"What do you mean by scaring him?"

"We ask the judge to hold a hearing devoted solely to the cheating incident before making any determination that Branson may represent a class."

Rachel frowned as she mulled over Simon's suggestion. "So we have to be scumbags?" she finally asked, glumly.

"I don't see any way around it," Simon said. "Doesn't Carpenter constantly say that you've got to play the hand you're dealt?"

"Great!" Rachel said dispiritedly. "Carpenter strikes again."

"And lastly," Simon continued, "we've got the guy who's probably into a loan shark, Marshall Hightower."

"I still can't believe that," Rachel said.

"You deserve a lot of credit on that one," Simon said. "You picked up on the guy's need for money. I don't think I would have caught that let alone thought of asking Freedman and McCauley to look into it."

"I was grasping at straws," Rachel confessed.

"Good thing you did," Simon came back. "So, are we agreed? Our best chance to defeat this motion is to smear the plaintiffs."

"You're right," Rachel said grudgingly. "I don't see any other option."

"You drafted the opposition to the class action motion in the Spenser case," Simon noted. "How about taking first crack at the opposition to this motion?"

"Sure," Rachel said dejectedly. "I can't wait."

"Here's another cheerful thought," Simon said. "We're assuming that Sloan-Webster is going to be okay with trashing former graduates. We may be in for a surprise on that front."

"Well, whatever the law school decides," Rachel said, "it better decide right away."

54

Philly and June and Ling were sitting at a card table placed in a shady spot on the blacktop in the backyard. Recently, June had been coming over to the house even when no babysitting was scheduled. Philly guessed that she needed a place to hang out and was okay with the unannounced visits. Sometimes June volunteered to spell Sarah and watch the kids. When Philly had asked June whether everything was okay at home, the girl had shrugged and let loose with a one-word response: "Parents!" According to June, her parents didn't understand her and were making no effort to try. Philly had been surprised to discover that June hadn't mentioned the stereotyping project to her parents. "They wouldn't get it," June had declared.

For this visit, June had brought Ling, the fourth member of the team that would present the program on stereotyping if the superintendent of schools approved the project. Ling was a talker. At the moment, she was complaining about the heat, bemoaning that in Massachusetts it was either too hot or too cold, never just right. Ling had a round face and dark eyes. Unlike June, she had no noticeable piercings. But her black hair was cut short and the hair on either side of the middle part was dyed a hot pink.

"Do you speak Chinese?" Philly asked in the hope of getting Ling to stop going on about the weather.

"No!" Ling said with some heat as she folded her arms across her chest. "It's all my parents' fault. When I was growing up, they never spoke Chinese to me. They wanted me to be totally American. Now they want me to be Chinese. Last year they wanted me to take Chinese lessons. I said if learning Chinese was so important, why didn't they speak it to me at home when I was little? That shut them up."

"Do you have any brothers and sisters?"

"No. I am an only child with a tiger mom. What did I do to deserve that?"

"I told you Ling was funny," June said.

"Your parents must love what you've done to your hair," Philly said, making a mental note to hide any photographs of her own teenage hairdo with spiked curls, each dyed a different color. Daisy did *not* need to see that.

"This is what a tiger mom deserves," Ling said, running a forefinger along the part of her hair. "It is very important for the child of a tiger mom to rebel," she added with the authority of a sociological expert.

"What do your parents do?" Philly asked, now curious. She didn't think a lot about her own parenting style one way or the other. Daisy was continuing to evolve into one of those kids who could entertain herself. When Philly told Daisy to go play, her daughter typically found something to do. She and Rosalind were currently absorbed in their new passion—croquet. Daisy could barely manage a mallet, while Rosalind had to settle for rolling the heavy croquet balls. Every once in a while, one of the older girls had to scoop up Daniel to move him out of the way so he wouldn't get hit by a rolling ball.

"My mother is a lawyer like you," Ling said. "June told me what you do. My father is a stay-at-home dad. He should be the tiger mom, but he does what my mom wants."

"What kind of law does your mother practice?"

"She's a corporate lawyer at a big Boston law firm that has a lot of names. You ask me, my mother needs a lawyer. I hear her complaining to my father. They don't like to tell me things, but I keep my ears open. My hearing is very good."

Philly debated whether to pry. It was no contest. "Why do you think your mother needs a lawyer?"

"She thinks she's not being treated fairly because she's an Asian woman. She says she's a good worker and brings in lots of money, but she doesn't get recognized for what she does. My father says she needs to try harder and not rock the boat. But my mother says she can't try any harder."

"You can tell your mother that if she wants to talk about her situation, I'm available."

"No, no. You don't understand. I can't tell my mother that. She doesn't know I overheard them."

"Okay," Philly said.

"Why don't you get your mother to pick you up here?" June suggested.

Ling nodded sagely. "I like that. Then maybe my mother's problems will come up in conversation."

"Why do you say your mom is a tiger mom?" Philly asked.

"Are you joking!" Ling exclaimed. "Do you think she would like it that I'm sitting here in your backyard when I could be improving my mind? How would you like to have to explain a B on your report card? Do you think I like to go to soccer practice and take ballet lessons? I hate that stuff. But my mom doesn't care. She wants me to go to a good college. That's all I ever hear. She says you've got to be well-rounded to go to a good college and make something of yourself."

"What do you like?" Philly asked.

"Fashion," June answered for her friend. "Ling designs clothes. And she really knows how to draw."

"Well, your parents must be proud of you for working on the stereotype project with June and Naomi and Lucida," Philly said.

"Are you crazy? Do you think I'd tell them about that? They'd say it's too controversial, especially my father. And my mom would throw a fit because it would take time away from my schoolwork. My mom especially would forbid me from taking part if she knew."

'Tiger mom it is,' Philly thought.

Janet Martin and Ralph Cray looked defeated. Rachel felt for the law school administrators. Simon had previously explained to them the ramifications if the suit against Sloan-Webster turned into a class action. But now that Blaisedell had actually produced a motion to do that, the possibility of each member of the designated class being awarded monetary damages was sinking in.

"That would bankrupt us," the dean had said.

"Shit!" Cray had muttered, the first time Rachel had heard him use vulgarity.

Simon was now in the process of calming the administrators, and Rachel rated his efforts as only partially successful. She wished they were occupying a spacious conference room. Huddling together in the dean's small office only furthered the sense that the law school was under siege.

"So," Simon was saying. "I've gone through our strategy for opposing the class action motion. Is there anything you wish to add or clarify?"

"Is it wise to attack our former students?" Cray asked.

"It's less than ideal for Sloan-Webster to try to discredit any graduate," Simon answered, "but in this situation, yes. Believe me, I'm aware that the wise choice here is unpleasant. But the wise course is to go on the offensive, because that is the law school's best chance to defeat the class action motion."

"Maybe now is the time to discuss settlement," the dean offered. "If this case becomes a class action, what incentive would the plaintiffs have to settle?"

"That's a fair point," Simon acknowledged. "But we need to view that point from various perspectives. Right now, Blaisedell would probably view a settlement proposal as a sign the school regarded its case as weak, and he would likely make exorbitant demands."

"I thought our case *was* weak," Cray interjected.

"The law school's position is weak in various areas," Simon conceded. "But it's never a good strategy to give any indication that weaknesses exist, and in this case we think it's particularly unwise to do it until the class action motion is ruled on."

Rachel was grateful that Simon was the one to address their client's pointed questions.

"Let's say," Simon resumed, "that the class action motion is denied. If that occurred, the law school might fare better in a settlement than it would have fared in a settlement hammered out now."

"So how we do in settlement is likely to be a function of what happens on the class action motion," the dean concluded.

"Yes, but it's complicated," Simon replied. "In any settlement before trial, it would be desirable to have the case be a class action so that the settlement was binding on all Sloan-Webster graduates who couldn't find a legal job. A settlement with the three named plaintiffs alone might cost less, but it wouldn't prevent other graduates from also suing the law school. Also, keep in mind that a settlement means that a jury will not decide the case. We have no idea what a jury would do in this case. A jury might rule for the law school, but also could deliver a verdict for the plaintiffs that might be higher than any settlement amount."

The dean looked thoughtful. "That all sounds bleak. But suppose we did decide to engage in settlement talks now. What would you propose? What would you recommend the settlement terms be?"

Rachel was disappointed that she and Simon hadn't come to any resolution on what was reasonable for the law school to offer in settlement. Simon felt that a jury would not be sympathetic to the law school given the lack of effort from its placement office. If the law school had a million dollars to throw at a plaintiff class, Simon was prepared to recommend doing so. Rachel believed that a million-dollar figure was excessive; however, she had trouble marshalling arguments for a lesser settlement figure.

"Rachel and I would want to confer with our partners before answering that question," Simon answered.

"Give me a ballpark figure as to what you think we'd have to pay," the dean pressed.

"It could be a million-dollar figure if you were to proceed with settlement discussions now," Simon answered.

"Jesus!" Cray swore.

"That's the money part, the hard part," Simon amplified. "In terms of reforms, the law school is already making changes to the placement office and job postings and it could agree to those reforms in a settlement agreement."

"I feel sick," Cray said, and Rachel noticed that Janet Martin wasn't looking her best. But at least the dean wasn't going to pieces the way Cray was.

"It's a mistake to decide anything today," Simon said. "We think that we should devote our immediate efforts to opposing the class action motion, which we have to do in any event. Once that's done, we can revisit the question of broaching settlement before the class action motion is actually heard by the judge."

"Great!" Cray exclaimed. "We get to kick the can down the road a little longer so we don't have to make a decision."

"There's a lot to be said for kicking the can down the road," Simon replied.

55

A Corporate Lawyer

Ling Li's mother looked nothing like her daughter. The long black hair that flowed over the back of her dark business suit showed no sign of gray and certainly no sign of pink, and the woman's long face was nothing like Ling's round, fleshy features. When Philly answered the door and invited her to wait inside, Ling's mother hesitated, glancing nervously at her watch before reluctantly entering.

"I'm Philly. What's your name?"

Philly was greeted with a quizzical look. "What kind of name is Philly?"

"It's my nickname. Everybody calls me Philly. And you are… "

"Ai."

"Ai," Philly repeated, sure she had mangled the pronunciation. "Let me tell Ling you're here," she added, according to plan.

Philly moved through the kitchen and out the back door. "She's here."

June extracted a math problem book and calculator from her backpack. She and Ling drew chairs close together at the card table placed on the blacktop. "Go," June said.

Philly retraced her steps. "Your daughter's helping her friend June with some math problems. They should be done in a few minutes. Would you like something to drink?"

"No thank you," Li said, again glancing at her watch.

"Your daughter said you were a lawyer," Philly began her effort to direct the conversation. "I'm a lawyer as well. What kind of law do you practice?"

"Corporate law."

This was going to be like pulling teeth, Philly decided. Li hadn't offered up the name of her firm. "I'm a litigator," Philly said. "Mostly plaintiff work. I've been involved in all kinds of cases: contract disputes, tort cases, employee terminations, discrimination cases. I remember one case where we represented an Asian guy who claimed he was fired because he was Asian." Philly paused, saw no sign of interest from Ling's mother at her unsubtle reference to discrimination. "We won," she added and that caused Li to make eye contact. "Are you sure I can't get you something to drink?"

"No thank you," Li repeated.

"At least have a seat," Philly pointed to the living room.

"I really have to be going," Li said.

Philly retreated to the living room and sat down on one of the easy chairs. "Take a load off," she said, pointing to the other easy chair.

Li advanced hesitantly into the room and took a seat. "Maybe you should check on the girls," she said.

Philly ignored the request. "What firm do you work for?"

"Hazelton, Kauffman, Garfield & Smith."

"Are you the only Asian there? I ask because that case I just mentioned—the discrimination case we won—our client was one of two Asians employed by the company that fired him."

"I am the only Asian woman who is a partner," Li said.

"I'm sure you know this," Philly said with a smile, "but that gives you job security for life. If you were ever treated differently than other partners, you could always claim that it was because you were the only Asian woman partner in the firm. You're in a great position."

Li regarded her neutrally. Philly wondered whether she would take the bait; she had laid it on a bit thick but had figured she had no choice—Li was in a hurry.

"What do you mean by treated differently?"

"I meant less favorably," Philly clarified. "I'll give you an example. It's probably an example that doesn't fit your firm because I know nothing about your firm. But let's say you brought in a client that produced a certain amount of revenue to the firm, and let's say that a male partner who was your equal brought in a client that produced less revenue. If the other partner was given a bigger financial bonus than you were with respect to bringing in new business, that would be the kind of unfair discrimination I was talking about."

Ai Li said nothing. She glanced about the living room, again looked at her watch. "Where is your office?" she asked.

"Our office is in Boston. I've got three partners. But my primary office is upstairs here at the house. There's another family that owns the house with me and my husband. And there's another owner, an older woman, who does babysitting for the rest of us. That's how I met your daughter's friend June. June took a babysitting course from the woman who takes care of our kids, and we use June to babysit when she's free."

Ai Li's lips pursed. "I don't see how you can stand the lack of privacy."

"I wouldn't have it any other way," Philly came back.

Li stood up. "I really need to be going. Please tell Ling that she needs to leave now."

Tell her yourself, Philly wanted to say. Instead she said, "I'll be right back."

Outside the girls sat close together. The ruse of doing math problems had evaporated; Ling was drawing an evening gown while June was playing angry birds on her handheld.

"How'd it go?" Ling asked.

"I did the best I could. But I'm not sure I got through to her. You need to go. Your mother's getting impatient."

"What else is new?" Ling pouted.

"Nice meeting you," Philly said when she and the girls returned to the living room. She held out one of her business cards to Ling's mother. "Do you have a card? You never know when I might need a corporate lawyer."

Li extracted a card from her purse and traded it for Philly's card.

"And you never know when you might need a discrimination lawyer," Philly added, deciding to beat that dead horse one more time.

56

Carpenter was in and Meredith was out—just what Philly had hoped for. Carpenter was facing away from the door to his office, doing his hunt and peck technique on his computer, and Philly slipped silently into his visitor chair. When Carpenter finished his typing and turned his desk chair, he started.

"Jesus! Don't sneak up on me. You scared me half to death."

"Only half? Good. You got a minute?"

"Yeah, I got a minute. It's always good to see you, even when you go into ninja mode."

"What are we going to do about Harris Burton?" Philly asked.

"I'm in denial," Carpenter confessed. "I just don't want to deal with it. I called Harris to ask whether he had a client that accounted for roughly half of his firm's business. For me, dependency on one client would be a negative, and probably a deal breaker. But no such luck. They have one client that roughly accounts for about fifteen percent of the firm's business. They're like us—they're constantly looking for new work."

Philly shared Carpenter's desire to avoid dealing with the whole issue. "There are days when I think Harris' proposal makes sense," she said. "Then the next day I want nothing to do with an association. I can't stand this hanging over our heads."

"You and me both. I spoke to one of our suite mates, the administrative law judge who's never here. He'd be agreeable to giving up his office provided he can keep a desk, receive his mail, and keep his phone. For some reason, he thinks it's important to have a Boston address. He'd be willing to work out an arrangement as to what he'd contribute to rent."

"I wonder if Simon would put up with the guy continuing to have a presence," Philly said. "Upgrading the office is a big deal to him."

Carpenter shrugged.

"I can't face meeting all the partners at Sizemore Klein," Philly blurted out. Thinking of the time commitment of getting to know the partners left her enervated.

"That's odd considering you're such a social animal like I am," Carpenter joked.

"You know, if it weren't for Rachel and Simon, we'd probably be happy working in a cave."

"All kidding aside," Carpenter said, "Rachel and Simon are good for us. Left to our own devices we'd be pathetic with no hope of a decent office, no website, nothing but clutter."

"When do you think we need to get back to Harris?" Philly asked.

"Yesterday," Carpenter said. "But I think we can stay in denial a little longer."

August

From Frank's Playlist

"Wake Me Up"

Avicii

57

On this occasion, the third in Ling's campaign to connect Philly and her mother, Ai Li seemed less reluctant to enter Philly's living room. "My mother needs to get used to you," Ling had told Philly. "She doesn't make friends easily."

"The girls have gone out and should be back any minute," Philly said, playing her role in Ling's strategy. "Can I get you something to drink?"

"A glass of tap water," Li replied, for the first-time accepting liquid refreshment.

Philly hefted Daniel. He'd just come in from the backyard and was sticky with sunscreen. She retreated to the kitchen and returned with a drink in one hand and Daniel balanced on the opposite hip. She sat down on the couch across from Li, who had claimed one of the easy chairs. Then she positioned Daniel so he could stand against the couch and steady himself by placing his hands and arms on a couch cushion. "This is my son's new standing trick," Philly explained as Daniel beat his hands on the couch cushion and bent his knees as be bobbed up and down.

Li didn't comment on Daniel's antics; she appeared distracted. "You look worried," Philly said in an effort to draw her out. "Is everything okay?"

Li took a sip of water. "May I ask you something?" she said.

"Of course."

"This is not to be repeated to anyone, especially Ling. I need to make that clear."

"Of course," Philly repeated.

"I've been thinking about that discrimination case you told me about."

Philly nodded, deciding to let Li proceed at her own pace.

"My law firm has ten partner levels. I am at level five. I was expecting to be promoted to level six, but I was told that I would not advance. That decision came as an unhappy surprise."

"Were you given reasons for the decision?" Philly asked.

"Yes," Li said softly as she clasped her water glass with both hands. "I was told that when the partners considered my promotion it came out in discussion that I was regarded as too aloof and that clients regarded me as too distant and not personally invested in their concerns. I was told I wasn't as aggressive as I needed to be on occasion."

Daniel collapsed on his bum and Philly quickly returned him to a standing position. "Were you ever subject to this kind of criticism before?" she asked.

"No."

"Is there any basis for this criticism?"

"I was told the names of the two clients who said I was aloof."

"Do you believe that the criticism is valid?"

"I tend to be businesslike and methodical. That doesn't mean I don't care about a client's problems. I care very much and do what I can to solve the problems. I believe I am as aggressive as I need to be. We have litigators if we need to go to war on a matter."

Philly considered the subjective element to law firm partnership decisions. Personalities of the decision makers and the individual being evaluated came into play.

"Among the level five partners being considered for promotion along with me, my billable hours were the highest," Li added. "Also, I am responsible for bringing in a major client to the firm. I don't think any of the other level five partners brought in such an important client. Yet three level five partners were promoted to level six and I was not."

"Tell me about the client?" Philly requested.

"It's a software company whose owners are Chinese. I do the corporate work, but the company's business provides a lot of work for our intellectual property department."

Philly worried that her next question would put Li off, but she asked it anyway. "Have you given any thought to leaving your firm and taking your client with you?"

"That is an obvious subject to think about. I think the client would stay with me if I landed at a firm with intellectual property expertise, but I can't be sure. I've put in a lot of time at my current firm. Neither my husband nor I like change. My preference is to stay where I am and be properly rewarded for my work. No client has ever complained about the quality of my work, even the clients who claim I was aloof."

"Do you believe that two of your clients did in fact claim you were aloof?"

"I don't know for sure. I would be very surprised if the more senior partners in the firm made up a story. Periodically, our firm sends out client satisfaction surveys. It's possible that on those surveys two clients said I was aloof. But I don't know for sure."

Daniel started to fuss. Philly pulled him up on the couch where he snuggled against her. "Who were the three level five partners who made the jump to level six?"

"Two white males and one white female."

"Would you know whether any of the three promoted partners has any personality issue with clients?"

"That wouldn't be something I'd know. I can tell you that I find the woman and one of the men totally obnoxious."

"In what way?"

"They are loud and do a lot of phony glad-handing. I once heard the woman tell a joke that was in very poor taste. I dislike those two."

Philly suspected that the feeling was mutual. "Have you gone to any of the more senior partners and complained about not being promoted?"

"Not yet."

"What's holding you back?"

"I don't like to make waves."

Philly tried to be gentle, but there was no way to avoid a hard truth. "You're obviously bothered by the way you were treated. So, unless you're content to live with your resentment, you're going to have to make a wave of some sort. Not all waves have to be tidal waves. I don't see anything inappropriate if you were to approach a very senior partner and say that you're unhappy about not moving up to level six and wish to discuss the matter."

Li lowered her head. Philly wondered if she was in the presence of a woman who would rather be unhappy than give the boat she was in a gentle rock.

Li stood abruptly. "I lost track of time. I need to drive Ling home immediately."

Philly also rose, returning Daniel to her hip. "I'll get your daughter, but you and I are not finished talking. I've learned something that I'm going to share with you. Nursing resentment over being wronged is more destructive than taking action to cure the wrong. I want to finish this discussion when you're not in a rush to go somewhere."

"Please get Ling. We need to go."

58

Rachel finished the drafts of the documents that would be filed opposing Christopher Blaisedell's class action motion. The pleadings included an affidavit from Dean Janet Martin, and an affidavit from Herb McCauley detailing his surveillance of Marshall Hightower and containing a photograph that captured the graduate's face and another man's back. To the draft of a supporting legal memorandum, she had attached excerpts from the depositions of the three named plaintiffs. Before the court would be Regina White's exotic dancer sideline, Noah Branson's answers to questions about the Michigan State economics exam in which cheating was suspected, and Hightower's deposition testimony relating to his concern for money.

Rachel no longer felt conflicted about taking shots at each of the plaintiffs. Somehow, working with Carpenter, Philly, and Simon had hardened her to adopt the hired-gun mentality that Carpenter preached was necessary for a litigator. As she began to attach her work product to an e-mail to her partners, Rachel wondered whether the change in her was for the better. Maybe that was a question best left unanswered.

"Philly Sullivan," Philly said, answering her cell phone and not recognizing the incoming phone number.

"Miranda Hernandez. Carlos Ibanez is also on the line. I wanted to save time and talk to you together."

"Hello everyone," Philly said. "I hope this is a good news call."

"Then you won't be too disappointed," Hernandez said. "The terms you put forward are acceptable with one exception. The defendants will not contribute more than ten thousand dollars to pay for your attorney fees. That figure applies to each of you."

Philly recalled her billings to date. The teacher's union would only be reimbursed approximately half of her fees. Ibanez was in a more difficult situation. He was representing the Hispanic students on a contingency basis with no union or anyone else paying his hourly rate. Assuming that Ibanez had run up around $20,000 in hourly charges as she had done, he would be forced to take money from the amounts due the Hispanic kids if he was to be fully paid for his time. Which meant that each Hispanic kid would not see a net recovery of $10,000 in damages.

"I'll need to discuss this with the teachers' union," Philly said.

"And I will have to discuss this with my clients," Ibanez followed.

"I hope that you will both recommend the modified proposal to your clients," Hernandez pushed.

'I'll bet you would,' Philly thought. "Carlos, please call me," is what she said.

They all rang off, and Carlos Ibanez called back.

"What are your thoughts?" Philly asked.

"I'm disappointed," Ibanez said. "I don't know about you, but I thought my attorney fees were reasonable. I sent Hernandez a figure of just over twenty thousand. That's already a reduced figure because I didn't feel that I could charge for a lot of the time I put in."

"Our situations are pretty much identical," Philly confirmed. "But I have a teachers' union paying me."

"I don't want to take any of my fees out of the students' awards or change the amount each would receive. "There is a psychological significance to the ten thousand dollars we asked for," Ibanez said, and Philly agreed. The round number had a substance to it and, perhaps in a bizarre way, was an easier figure to sell to a client than $11,000.

"I'm pretty sure that the teachers' union would take anything it can get," Philly said. "Do you think Clarke is behind this move to limit attorney fees?" she asked.

"No. My guess is that pointy-headed school bureaucrats are behind it."

"What are you going to do?"

"I'm going to discuss this with Sonia Acevedo and the other parents. I'm not going to recommend that they accept Hernandez's counteroffer."

Philly would probably adopt Ibanez's approach were she in his position, but that didn't diminish her frustration over the fact that a largely reasonable settlement proposal stood a good chance of being derailed over $20,000. The defendants' legal costs in trying the two cases would greatly exceed that figure.

"Let me know how you make out," Philly said.

Ai Li sat in one of the easy chairs in the living room area. This time, Li's visit was of her own volition: Ling was not around to be picked up. Without asking, Philly retreated to her kitchen and returned with a tall glass of juice which she handed to Li.

"I took your advice," Li said, ignoring her drink. "I met with the head of the firm's management committee."

"Man or woman?" Philly asked.

"A woman, Henrietta Coleman. She's a tax lawyer."

"From your manner, I'm guessing that the meeting didn't go well."

Li nodded. "Henrietta heard me out. I'll give her that. But she defended the decision not to promote me to a level six partner. She said it was important for a level six partner to be liked by all clients and that on a client satisfaction survey, two clients who she named had expressed reservations about me being aloof and detached. She said that before I was promoted to level five, one client had made a similar observation. She claimed that I was promoted anyway to level five because the factor of being liked by all firm clients didn't carry as much weight at the lower partnership levels."

Philly found a certain logic to the management committee head's rationale, but privately questioned the validity of the underlying requirement. Over the years, not all of her clients liked her, and she suspected the same was true for Carpenter. Carpenter wasn't concerned whether a client liked him; a lawyer was hired to further a client's interests, not to be a client's friend.

"What else was said?" Philly asked.

"She gave me a pep talk of sorts. She said the management committee was very pleased with my work and my billable hours. She suggested that I try to be more relaxed when meeting with clients, engage in small talk, that kind of thing. She suggested that I might want to explore courses on interpersonal skills."

For a pep talk, Philly found these suggestions degrading and belittling. She couldn't imagine responding civilly to the suggestion that *she* attend a course on interpersonal skills even though she'd be the first to admit that she had some deficits in that area. "When will you next be considered for partnership level six?" she asked.

"In about eighteen months."

A year and half was a long time to nurse the feeling of being unfairly treated, Philly reflected. "Now that you've met with Ms. Coleman, do you have a sense of what you want to do?"

"I want to know whether I have a legal case," Li said.

Philly had thought about that question ever since Li had called her and asked if they could talk late this afternoon. "I'm not sure," she admitted. "It may come down to whether any of the three lawyers who were promoted to level six was given a negative evaluation in any area."

"How am I going to find that out?"

"You may have to file a lawsuit to discover that information."

"My husband won't like filing a lawsuit."

Philly didn't think this was the time to tell Li that what mattered was what she wanted, not what her husband preferred. "Were the two clients who described you as aloof happy with your work?"

"I believe they were. They never complained about my work. For one of the clients, I drafted a very complicated operating agreement for a limited liability company that had various classes of investors. For the other client, I handled a merger agreement in which the client became the surviving corporation."

"Do you mind if I review your situation with my partners? I won't mention your name." Carpenter would probably have a working familiarity with these business arrangements.

"I suppose so," Li said without enthusiasm.

"Did each of the lawyers promoted to level six bring a new client to your firm?" Philly thought to ask.

"I'm not sure," Li said. "But I don't think so."

"I'll get back to you," Philly said. There was someone else who might be useful to call, but she would need Carpenter's blessing to make the contact.

59

Early Saturday morning, Philly made the mistake of checking her e-mail. She and Isabella had done a spinning session at dawn, early enough to avoid the worst of the blistering August heat and, after a shower, she thought what the hell, how much unpleasantness could have been sent her way since she turned off her computer late Friday night?

Enough, it turned out. She had been copied on an e-mail from Carlos Ibanez, the lawyer for the Hispanic students, to Miranda Hernandez. In the terse e-mail, Ibanez rejected Hernandez's proposal on attorney fees, and stated that his original offer would remain on the table through the middle of the following week. If the offer was not accepted by that short deadline, Ibanez's next move was to depose principal Stanley Clarke.

Philly's disappointment was tempered by her admiration for Ibanez taking a hard line. Each of the fifth graders humiliated by Clarke had a chance to recover at least $10,000 at trial. Ibanez probably figured why not roll the dice in front of a jury and try for a big score. Xavier Acevedo didn't appear scarred by having to eat on the floor, but perhaps the boy hid it well. Were any of the other punished Hispanic students traumatized by Clarke's action?

Philly considered her next steps. The teachers' union paying her legal fees had agreed to being repaid only $10,000. If after hearing of Ibanez's gambit the union would still accept the $10,000, then the defendants would be turning down a total settlement of both cases over a little more $10,000. All she could do was forward Ibanez's e-mail to Barton and then deal with her client's disappointment.

Carpenter was working on Saturday morning, too, reading an e-mail from Sophie Teague addressed to him and Lauren Goldman. The e-mail reminded him of one reason he disliked the Internet. Bad news was delivered instantaneously and could suck the joy out of a weekend. Event Planning had reviewed the issues raised at the recent meeting involving the parties and had found no basis for Donald Frazier's claims relating to off-the-books cash payments. In these circumstances, Event Planning was terminating its business relationship with Elite Scripts immediately.

Carpenter thought about Henry Frazier's next moves. Would Frazier continue to pursue his efforts to control a family business that just lost its main source of revenue? If not, then his pending lawsuit against his father had run its course. If Frazier still wanted to take over the business, what role would his father play and how would the business survive?

The ball was in his client's court, and Carpenter hadn't a clue what to advise Frazier. For the moment, his only task was to forward the bad news to Frazier and ruin a client's weekend.

Rachel finished incorporating her partners' and Meredith's comments into her final drafts of the pleadings objecting to the lawsuit against Sloan-Webster being turned into a class action. All the suggested edits had been helpful. She reread the documents and then attached them to an e-mail to Janet Martin and Ralph Cray. "Have a nice weekend," she said, as she touched Send.

Simon completed his list of the questions that he believed Blaisedell would ask at the recently scheduled deposition of Sloan-Webster's dean. He decided not to send the list to Janet Martin. Let the dean enjoy the weekend. Besides, he was anxious to spring the questions on Martin to get a feel for how the dean thought on her feet.

Philly led the way on the Arlington-Lexington bike trail. Daisy was helmeted and belted into the baby carrier attached to Philly's bike, and Daniel was strapped into the front-mounted child seat affixed to Paul's bike. On this warm, sunny Saturday, Philly and Paul were the kind of slowpokes that serious cyclists hoped to avoid. Philip had been one of those serious cyclists, and Philly was struck by an image of him leaning over the handlebars of his bike, his long legs pumping steadily, wisps of long, blonde hair leaking from the margins of his helmet.

"On your left!"

The warning shout preceded six cyclists blowing past them in single file.

"Showoffs!" Paul called out behind her.

Philly kept peddling steadily, but she couldn't get the Barton case out of her head. She had tried to come up with an approach that would provide Clarke with a face-saving way to extricate himself from the litigation, and now she wondered whether her efforts had been off the mark from the start. Maybe she should have adopted a take-no-prisoners approach and pushed for a trial. At the core of the lawsuit she would have a sympathetic plaintiff, a woman who had broken up a playground altercation, and ended a humiliating punishment meted out to Hispanic students.

"Faster, mommy!" Daisy urged.

"Enjoy the ride," Philly called back over her shoulder.

Philly backed off her second-guessing; she had followed her client's lead. Barton had wanted her record cleared and the lawsuit ended; the recently failed settlement efforts would have achieved those ends. Now Barton's objectives were in the distance. A trial in the case would drag matters out and, in all likelihood, wouldn't occur this year.

"Watch the road!" Paul shouted behind her. "You're drifting off to the right!"

'Drifting was the right word,' Philly thought. Sometimes it was hard to stay in a straight line.

"What are you thinking about?" Maxine asked.

Carpenter decided that an unresponsive grunt was called for and produced one. They were seated atop a rocky perch in a Lexington conservation tract that afforded a panoramic view of the Boston skyline, and he could make out the Hancock and Prudential towers. The climb to this resting stop had been steep, and Carpenter realized that he wasn't in as good shape as he thought. Despite the time he was putting in at the gym with spinning and weights, his legs ached and he'd had to breathe deeply during parts of the ascent.

"You haven't answered my question," Maxine persisted.

Maxine's tone convinced Carpenter that evasive action would accomplish nothing. "I've got a client I might not be able to help," he owned up. Henry Frazier's situation had been eating at him before today's hike began.

"That happens," Maxine observed.

"But I don't have to like it."

"No, you don't. But you do have to live with it so we can enjoy our afternoon."

"Stop talking sense to me."

Maxine gestured toward the city skyline. "If your head's going to be in Boston, you should have gone into work. You know I don't bug you when you drift off and start thinking about work. But this is such a nice day I'm going to make an exception and bug the hell out of you."

'So much for the calming effects of meditation and relaxing by getting out in the fresh air,' Carpenter thought, but he knew he'd been beaten. "When you're right, you're right," he said.

Rachel was grateful that Josh had a way of adjusting his pace to make her work hard but not kill herself. They were running along the Charles River on the Boston side in the direction of the Museum of Science, committed to a 10K distance. She spied sailboats far off interweaving in the open water near the museum.

For the first several miles she had been focused on the run, on keeping in step with Josh. But then her thoughts began drifting and had now settled on the Sloan-Webster case. She attributed the change in her concentration to the rhythmic cadence of their running shoes on the blacktopped path along the river. It was as if the steady beat created a vacuum which thoughts of work, more powerful than thoughts of any other daily concern, rapidly rushed to fill.

Simon would be counting on her to make the court argument on Blaisedell's class action motion. She had handled the oral argument on a similar motion Blaisedell had made in the Spenser School of Law case, but the upcoming court hearing would be more demanding because Blaisedell had more ammunition for his position.

Rachel felt the onset of nerves. Was she going to be one of those lawyers who would have to psych herself up for each court appearance no matter how many times she had been in court previously? Probably so.

"Don't slow down," Josh said. "You're doing fine. We're almost there. Just keep going. Concentrate."

'Keep going,' Rachel thought. Sometimes that was all you could do.

Simon had gotten his distance up to five miles. On this beautiful Saturday afternoon, he wished Frank were with him on his run and not at his parents' house. He had started at Davis Square in Somerville, passed the Alewife T Station, and was now headed toward Arlington along a bike path.

Simon had come to like the way he felt after a run: tired in a good way and mentally refreshed. Yet today, the Sloan-Webster case wouldn't release its grip on his mind. The case was at a crossroads with two critical events on the immediate horizon: Dean Martin's deposition, followed by a hearing on Blaisedell's class action motion.

When it came to Martin's deposition, Simon wondered whether he was missing a trick. Blaisedell would try to beat the dean up over the placement office's failure to help with job placement efforts, the low ranking of the law school's faculty, and the law school's lack of information on graduates finding law-related jobs. Was there something else he was missing?

Simon left the bike path and was soon at Massachusetts Avenue in Arlington. He ran in place at a stop light marking a large intersection, and then resumed his run when the blinking WALK figure gave him the all-clear.

Simon didn't like being dependent on others. Yet he had no choice. He would have to rely on Rachel to deal with the class action motion. And he would have to rely on the dean not making any slip at her deposition. His head told him that he couldn't do everything himself; his heart wished that he could.

Meredith accepted the joint that Flash held out and took a deep draw. They had slept in until noon and then, after brunch, returned to bed and hadn't left. There was definitely a positive side to being dependent on another law firm for work. When she did what had been assigned to her, she was done and no longer had to obsess about the completed project. At this moment, if she were a partner in Rachel and Simon's firm, she would probably be fretting about the additional depositions she needed to conduct in the Ship Right case. Instead, she was free to enjoy Flash. She had actually given thought to his question about whether she wanted to have kids. If she were pressed for an answer to that question at this very moment when she was sated and spent, the answer would be yes, with strings attached to ensure that her legal career progressed. Sometimes it seemed there were strings attached to every blessed thing. While being legal help for hire permitted her to veg out on a beautiful day, her lack of a permanent position also meant that she had to worry about when her contract work would end. 'You couldn't win,' she reflected.

60

Philly placed a call to Miranda Hernandez as she glanced down a short list of the points she needed to cover. Earlier this morning she had spent time on the phone with Sasha Barton, trying to calm her distraught client. Barton saw the chances of her lawsuit settling slipping away and was worried by the prospect of going to trial.

"What can I do for you?" Hernandez got on the line.

Philly didn't like her adversary's brusque greeting. "You can listen," she said in a clipped tone. "First, the previous offer I made to settle the lawsuits involved *both* legal actions. Therefore, I need to be clear with you about something. Ms. Barton will not settle *her* suit if the other action isn't also settled. The deadline to settle Ms. Barton's complaint is the same deadline that Ibanez just proposed for his case." Philly paused. "Second, the ten-thousand-dollar ceiling on legal fees you requested is acceptable to the teachers' union notwithstanding that Ibanez rejected it in his case. So, if you don't yield on this issue in his case, your clients are basically blowing up a comprehensive settlement over ten thousand dollars and change." Philly paused again, hoping that a brief delay would permit Hernandez to reflect on the shortsightedness of rejecting a settlement deal over a relatively small sum. Getting Sasha Barton to agree to the position she had just laid out for Hernandez had taken some doing. Since Hernandez had told her that she wouldn't settle with Barton without settling with Ibanez, Philly viewed linking the settlement of the two cases a no-brainer. Barton reluctantly agreed to link settlement of her case to the settlement of Ibanez's case when

Philly explained that even if her case settled, Barton was certain to be called as a witness by Ibanez in his case.

"The last thing I have to say to you is that my present intention is to seek to consolidate Barton's case with Ibanez's case. I've spoken to Ibanez about this and he is prepared to support consolidation of the cases." Ibanez had been excited by this move and had begun berating himself for not thinking of it earlier.

"Anything else?" Hernandez demanded.

"That's it," Philly said, thinking that Ibanez's settlement deadline was two days away. "Tick tock," she added, giving in to the urge to act like an asshole.

"I know what I want to do," Henry Frazier said over the phone, with confidence that Carpenter hoped was real. "In a nutshell, I want to take over the family business, and I want my father out. He can remain a minority stockholder, which was part of our original deal, but his pay checks stop. And before I take over, I want my father to issue the 1099 forms to John Harrison and to pay any late fees to the IRS."

"I'm interested in your thinking," Carpenter said, wishing he was face-to-face with Frazier to get a better read on his newfound certainty. "How'd you arrive at all this?"

"It's not like I was struck by a sudden flash of illumination," Frazier replied. "I just got to thinking and realized that finding something new for myself was probably going to turn into an ordeal. I did some quick math. If my father isn't taking a draw, the hit from losing Event Planning as a client will hurt, but the business will survive. Barely. I'll probably have to take a pay cut at least at the start. My challenge will be to find a new client or clients."

Carpenter couldn't fault Frazier's reasoning. "Is this something you're planning to sort out with your father?"

"No. This time around I'm going to follow your advice before you give it to me. I want you to handle this with my father's attorney. I'm not going to talk to my father about anything, although he's certain to call me."

Carpenter prided himself on not hesitating to ask a hard or unpleasant question. "Are you thinking that your father didn't make payments to this guy Harrison?"

"Let's just say the thought occurred to me. This is my father's mess, and I don't want any involvement in the cleanup."

"And if your father's lawyer says no deal?"

"My lawsuit's still pending. If necessary, I'll pursue it with a different goal. I'm hoping that won't be necessary."

'Hope springs eternal,' Carpenter thought. "I'll call your father's lawyer," is what he said.

"What the hell is Carpenter up to?" Sarah Warren asked. "Is it your turn to harass me? I thought on the Ship Right case Ms. Sweeney was the designated harasser."

Philly laughed. She was holed up in her second-floor office free of kids. The window was open and she could feel the warm air seeping in from outside. "This has nothing to do with Ship Right. Have fun with Meredith on that one. I've got a potential new client and asked Carpenter if it made sense to give you a call."

"I'm sure he said no. Carpenter would never admit that calling me or Brian for advice made sense."

"Then you'd be wrong. Here's the situation. I've been approached by a woman who's a partner in a big law firm. She thinks she was denied a promotion to a higher partner level because of her race and sex. As a woman partner in a large firm, I thought you might have some general insights on the sex discrimination issue. Carpenter agreed I should give you a call."

"Does this mean I have to revise my opinion of Carpenter and entertain the possibility he may have partially come to his senses?"

"I would never ask you to do anything against your nature."

This time it was Warren who laughed. "Fair enough," she said. "In all seriousness, I may not be the right person to ask about discrimination. Brian and I have a unique situation here. I'm not sure how much of the history you know. Years back we both left Dudley, Atkins & Tyng to go out on our own. We did very well. Then the firm wooed us to come back, which we did. Essentially, under the deal we cut, we get to run our own practices and do pretty much what we want. We dictate litigation strategy for the cases that come our way and the other partners leave us alone."

Philly thought of Sizemore Klein and wondered if she and her partners could cut a similar deal with that firm's partners.

"You said this potential client was already a partner in her firm," Warren continued. "Right off the bat, that fact undercuts a discrimination claim in my opinion."

"Why is that?" Philly countered. "If a firm has multiple levels of partners and women aren't moved up to the highest levels, it seems to me that would help with a discrimination claim."

"When you put it that way, you have a point," Warren conceded. "My general impression is that big firms are going out of their way to accommodate and promote women. I can tell you that we do. Today, law schools are turning out more women than men. It would be a mistake for any firm not to treat women with consideration and fairness."

"Am I crossing a line by asking how your firm makes partnership decisions?" Philly asked.

"Probably, but what the hell. We don't have multiple levels of partners. We have partners and associates. I don't think I'm breaching any confidence by telling you that we make partnership decisions by considering billable hours, clients brought to the firm, quality of work, client satisfaction, ability to work with others in the firm—things like that."

"How do you determine client satisfaction?"

"Three years ago, we sent out a client satisfaction survey through a consultant. Clients' names were kept confidential, but we could pretty much figure out which client was making what comment. Most of the partners thought the survey was a waste of time. That was my opinion and Brian's, too. Some clients expressed dissatisfaction with particular lawyers and some of those expressions of dissatisfaction prevented some lawyers from being made partner. These days, we pretty much gauge client satisfaction by looking to whether a client has complained about a lawyer. That doesn't happen very often."

Warren's comments hadn't offered up anything Philly could use to address Ai Li's situation. "This potential client of mine was told that two firm clients she worked for described her as aloof on a client satisfaction survey. She was told these two comments probably influenced the vote that prevented her from being promoted to the next partnership level. Any thoughts?"

"Aloof," Warren repeated. "That might describe me on occasion, although I don't think that word has ever been applied to Brian. My purely subjective opinion is that it's a weak reason to deny a promotion. I don't want to be any client's good buddy; in fact, I think that's a recipe for disaster. There's no excuse for not being cordial to a client. After all, the client is paying you money. But by and large I wouldn't make a partnership decision on whether a lawyer was warm and fuzzy when it came to clients."

"That's helpful," Philly said. She had asked Warren to focus on sex discrimination; she didn't see a need to discuss discrimination based on race. "Thanks for your time."

"Don't mention it," Warren employed Carpenter's standard phrase. "For your information, I thought that your Ms. Sweeney did a nice job on the Ship Right depositions."

"Glad to hear it. I'll share that with Carpenter."

"I'd rather you didn't. I don't want to give the old goat any indication that he's a good judge of legal talent."

"Then I won't tell you that after the court hearing, Murphy asked Meredith to call him when she got tired of working for the old goat."

"Good grief!" Warren exclaimed. "Wasn't that a tactic he tried with you?"

"You've got a good memory. I'm sure Murphy was joking."

"I'm going to have to have a talk with Brian. Another one."

"Do you think it'll do any good?"

"I try to keep an open mind."

61

Today was the day that Carlos Ibanez's offer of settlement expired and that was one of the reasons Philly decided to spend the afternoon in her Boston office. If Miranda Hernandez's response to Ibanez required any immediate action, she wanted to be able to enlist Meredith or Simon or Rachel face-to-face. But the primary reason for heading to the city was an early afternoon meeting with Ai Li. Philly had decided that the informality of her house had served its purpose. Li had a serious decision to make and a law office sit down would drive that point home. Besides, Philly wanted Carpenter to eyeball Li.

Philly entered the office suite to find Carpenter already seated in the conference room. A warm, half-hearted rain had been falling all day, so she shed her raincoat in her old office before joining him. He had a notepad in front of him as well as some sheets of paper on which she recognized his handwriting.

"Anything you want to say about this Li case?" Philly asked.

"I don't think we're really going to know whether she has a case until she gets some discovery," Carpenter answered.

Philly nodded in agreement. Li's situation was problematic. Philly looked up. Li was in the reception area, looking around nervously. "She's here," Philly said.

Li wasn't pleased to have to repeat her story for Carpenter's benefit, but Philly figured, tough shit—Li was exploring legal representation so she could damn well put up with her firm's idiosyncrasies. Li was nervous, and that probably had to do with Carpenter's hard, unrevealing stare as she went through her narrative.

When Li finished her account, there was silence. Philly wasn't sure whether Carpenter expected her to direct this meeting, but he quickly spoke up.

"I understand that Philly has explained to you why we're uncertain whether you have a winnable case against your law firm. If we had more facts, we'd be better able to address that question. For example, it would be helpful to know whether the three lawyers promoted to partner level six received any negative evaluations from the client satisfaction survey. It would also be helpful to know whether anyone promoted to level six had brought a major client to your firm. We'd be interested in knowing how your other partners viewed the quality of your work in relation to the quality of work of those promoted."

Philly noted Li's downcast expression. As a corporate lawyer, Li may not have been used to dealing with the kind of gray areas that frequently arose in litigation.

"You're the only Asian woman partner at the firm," Carpenter continued. "But we haven't heard anything that suggests your race was a reason for you not being promoted to level six. As for a discrimination claim based on sex, the percentage of women partners at your firm is thirty-seven percent. We believe that's pretty high for large Boston firms."

Li slumped in her chair. Carpenter had thrown cold water on her legal claims in much the same way Philly had done.

"That thirty-seven percent figure is misleading," Li said defensively. "Only twenty odd percent of the top five partnership levels are women."

"That's a fair point," Carpenter said. "Explain something to us. What's the difference between being a level ten and a level one partner?"

"There are two main differences. The first has to do with our compensation level and draws. The higher the partnership level the greater the partner's compensation and draws under our formula. The second difference has to do with partner votes. Each partner's vote is weighted by the partner's level."

"Then a level ten partner has ten times the voting power of a level one partner," Carpenter concluded.

"Correct," Li said.

"Do all partners vote on a partner being upgraded to a new partner level?" Philly asked.

"Yes. Obviously, the partners being considered for a promotion to a higher level don't vote."

Carpenter became lost in thought. "I know Philly explained this to you," he broke his silence, "but this may be one of those cases where you're going to have to bring a suit to discover evidence of discrimination."

Li was plainly unhappy with that Carpenter pronouncement. "Wouldn't my case get thrown out before there was any discovery?" she asked.

"That's a possibility," Carpenter said. "We've dealt with this situation before. Your argument would be that your work is excellent, you have higher billable hours than those promoted ahead of you, and you brought a major client to the firm. You'd claim that the firm has the information on those promoted ahead of you and that the information is likely to confirm that your race and sex were the real reasons you were not promoted. You'd ask the Massachusetts Commission Against Discrimination or a court to permit discovery before ruling on any dismissal motion. Obviously, we can't predict what a hearing officer or judge would do in this situation."

Li fell silent and it appeared to Philly that Carpenter had exhausted his comments. "There are some other factors we think you need to consider," Philly said. "Let's say you bring a lawsuit and down the road you win it. Have you given any thought to how difficult it would be working at your firm while your suit is pending or after your lawsuit is resolved?"

Li's blank expression gave no indication whether she had evaluated her working environment.

"I spoke with a woman who's a partner in a large Boston firm. Carpenter and I have litigated against her and we respect her judgment. She told me that large Boston firms are going out of their way to be fair to women when it comes to partnership decisions because women now outnumber men in terms of law school graduates."

"Are you saying that even if I file a lawsuit and win, I will not have a true victory because I will always be resented?"

"We're saying that's a very real factor for you to consider," Philly replied.

"Are you saying I should leave my firm and then sue the firm?" Li followed up.

"Some victims of discrimination decide to do that," Carpenter pointed out. "If they leave their place of employment and sue, the legal action is essentially one for damages. We're not saying you should leave and sue. That's your decision. But it may come down to you going that route."

"This is very discouraging," Li said, her verdict matching her body language: stooped sitting position, head lowered.

Philly couldn't think of a comment to provide Li with a lift.

"Thank you for being so direct," Li said next. "Looking at this logically, I think I should find a new firm to work for if I decide to sue my present firm. That's not an ideal road to follow. I've put in a lot of time at my current firm and have obviously made partner. The idea of starting over again somewhere else is disheartening."

"We don't know the environment at your present firm," Carpenter said. "In my experience, no one likes to be sued and, even if a case settles, there may be residual resentment. That said, you may feel, based on your experience, that you would be treated fairly while any suit you brought is played out and ultimately resolved."

Li shook her head and gestured toward Philly. "I think you're right. The firm would probably resent me for suing."

"Why don't you think about what we've said and get back to me?" Philly suggested.

"I've thought about it," Li said in a tone that could never be described as aloof. "My husband will not like this, but I was not treated fairly and I want to sue. My only decision is when."

Philly was surprised by Li's sudden, emphatic declaration. Li had struck her as someone who would dither over the decision to sue.

"I'm guessing that you would not want to handle this case on a contingency basis," Li said. "I don't believe I'm comfortable with a straight hourly payment arrangement. Maybe there is some kind of modified contingency agreement we could come to."

"We'll discuss it and I'll call you tomorrow," Philly said. She glanced at Carpenter. He had drifted into jaw grinding mode. She hoped that meant he was coming up with both a viable legal claim for Li and a payment arrangement that would work for all. At the moment, she wasn't sure either problem had a good solution.

Philly returned to her office to find Rachel in her desk chair and Simon busy at the workstation that had been added to the room. "Don't get up," Philly said as she advanced to her desk where Rachel was waving several message slips in her direction. Two calls from Carlos Ibanez sandwiched around a call from Sasha Barton. Good news or bad news, she wondered.

Philly returned to the conference room where she called Ibanez on her cell phone.

"We have a deal," Ibanez announced when he picked up his phone.

"That's excellent!" Philly exclaimed, relieved. "Did Hernandez give you any indication what caused her side to cave?"

"I'm reading between the lines here," Ibanez said. "I think it was the call you made to her."

"I don't follow," Philly said.

"She said you had called her and made some very persuasive points. She mentioned that the legal fees would be high if the cases were tried and you correctly pointed out that it made no sense to scuttle a deal over a little more than ten thousand dollars."

"Yeah, I did say that," Philly confirmed.

"She said you sounded pissed off when you spoke to her," Ibanez added. "It sounded to me like you scared her somehow."

"She started off the call unfriendly and it did piss me off," Philly said. "At the end of the call I said something I shouldn't have, something stupid, because I was still pissed off by her tone."

"I might have had something to do with giving her the impression that she *should* be scared of you," Ibanez said.

"I'm listening."

"I called her. I believe I spoke with her immediately after you did. I told her I was excited by the prospect of consolidating our cases. I told her to go to your firm's website, and I said I was looking forward to being on the same side as an attorney who had landed two seven figure jury verdicts a couple of months apart."

Philly and her partners had hoped that displaying the 2011 achievement on the firm's website would lead to bringing in more clients. So far that hadn't happened. Never in her wildest dreams did Philly think it would contribute to settling a case.

"I'm glad there's a deal," Philly reaffirmed. "Between you and me, I don't care how we got there."

"Me either," Ibanez said. "But after talking you up to Hernandez, I began to wonder whether we were settling too cheaply."

"No second-guessing," Philly responded.

"Hernandez had one other condition," Ibanez said. "Clarke wants to meet with Xavier Acevedo and Stanley Brown and their parents. The parents are okay with this."

"What do you think that's about?" Philly asked.

"Maybe the litigation and its settlement caused Clarke to change his spots. I think Clarke wants to apologize to Xavier. I think Clarke's going to take this stereotyping program those girls came up with very seriously. Best of all," Ibanez concluded, "Hernandez is taking the first cut at a settlement agreement."

"She's just trying to keep your legal fees under control."

62

Carpenter had finished explaining Henry Frazier's position to Lauren Goldman. The young attorney had heard him out without interrupting. Maybe Donald Frazier chose Goldman as his lawyer because she hadn't been in practice long and had a low hourly billing rate, but if so, he had lucked out. Goldman had the calm, reflective style of a veteran.

"What do you see happening if my client doesn't go along with this?" Goldman asked after a long pause.

"I'm not totally sure," Carpenter acknowledged. "If you were to press me, my guess is that my client may change the focus of his pending lawsuit to accomplish what I just laid out for you. That's purely a guess."

"Donald Frazier is not going to like his pay checks stopping," Goldman observed.

"With the loss of Event Planning as a client, his pay checks would probably have taken a hit in any event."

"How does your client plan to make a go of the family business?" Goldman asked.

"He's going to try to get new clients."

"That's not a plan," Goldman countered. "That's the wishful thinking any business indulges in. If that were a plan, then I'd have a business plan."

Carpenter laughed aloud. "You and me both."

"Okay," Goldman said. "I'll deliver the proposal and when I have something to report, I'll get back to you."

Meredith had concluded a second round of ten depositions in the Ship Right case and Carpenter was studying a chart of her results, making margin notes from time to time. When he looked up, he was smiling. "So, for this second group, Blake billed Ship Right close to another hundred thousand dollars from lawyers who made no contributions during phone calls and meetings and never drafted any documents. Do I have that right?"

"Ninety-six thousand seven hundred dollars," Meredith amended.

"Don't you just love that team approach they use over there?"

Meredith returned Carpenter's smile. They were in the office suite's conference room and she couldn't recall ever seeing the firm's senior lawyer in such a good mood. "You're in a good mood," she said.

"I guess I am," Carpenter said. "That Frazier case that's been kicking around all year seems to be heading for a resolution. That doesn't mean it will be a happy ending. But I like closing out a case. Always have."

"But then you need to find a replacement," Meredith pointed out, wondering how the closing of a case she hadn't worked on affected the firm work that would come her way. She suspected that *any* loss of firm business reduced the chances of her getting assigned more work.

"Yeah, that's the way it works. It never fucking ends. You just have to keep grinding."

Carpenter's observation drove home for Meredith that she had yet to find a case to replace Noreen Clark's.

"Let me ask you something," Carpenter said. "Philly and I met with a lawyer in a big firm who thinks she got screwed over, discrimination wise. You worked in a big firm for three years. I'm interested in your reaction."

Meredith began to jot down key words as Carpenter filled her in on a Chinese lawyer's belief that she had been denied a partnership promotion because of her sex and race.

"I may not be much help here," Meredith said when Carpenter had finished his account and was regarding her expectantly. "At my former firm, there were senior and junior partners. This is the first time I've heard of a firm having ten partner levels."

Carpenter nodded, but Meredith wondered whether she had disappointed him. She couldn't believe how much she wanted to present him with something he could use. She glanced at the list of key words and phrases she had jotted down while Carpenter had provided her with background information and focused on the notation that had taken her aback: *20+% W Levels 6-10.*

"I was struck by the fact that only twenty plus percent of the highest five partner levels were women. That compares with thirty-seven percent in the overall partnership. I'm sure you focused on this. The difference between these percentages is huge."

"The potential client made the same point," Carpenter said.

"If you believe in conspiracy theories, this firm may have come up with a fiendishly clever way to perpetuate an old boys' network. They get to say thirty-seven percent of partners are women, which has got to be a big selling point to women job applicants. But maybe partnership levels one through five are really glorified associate positions, especially when you consider that a partner's vote is weighted by partnership level."

"Go on," Carpenter requested.

"What you really need is a complete breakdown for each of the ten partnership levels by sex over time. Then you could calculate the actual voting power of men versus women over time."

Carpenter said nothing. Meredith expected him to go into his jaw grinding routine but that didn't happen.

"I wonder if there's a way to get hold of this information before filing a suit and asking for the information in discovery," Carpenter said.

"I bet if you go to this firm's website you would only see the word partner after a partner's name. I bet you wouldn't see the partner level."

"You're probably right about that," Carpenter said sourly, his previous good mood rapidly disappearing.

"Okay," Carpenter said. "Thanks. This has been helpful. Let's go back to the Ship Right case. We may have milked the unproductive lawyer situation for all its worth. We need another angle. Next up for you is to go back through the billings and focus on meetings and conference calls that had at least ten Blake Pennington lawyers. I'm thinking of a chart that lists each lawyer and the lawyer's department and whether the lawyer was a partner or associate. That might give us a different way to look at over-staffing. Let's say there was a firm meeting on Ship Right and there were three real estate department partners sitting in. Is that reasonable even assuming that each of those three partners actually did work on the case?"

"There's still some more money to be found in the unproductive lawyer area," Meredith pointed out. "But I agree that the dollar amount won't be as high as what we've come up with so far."

"All right," Carpenter said. "Try my idea and anything else you can think of."

"Okay," Meredith said, pleased and grateful that work was still coming her way.

63

Simon found it strange for a deposition to be going forward in their office suite's conference room when Jeannie Smith wasn't the stenographer. But that was the case this morning. Simon had offered Christopher Blaisedell the use of the room for the deposition of Dean Janet Martin. He had explained that the conference room was more spacious than any of the offices maintained by Shapiro & Morales and, to his surprise, Blaisedell had accepted the offer and thanked him.

Martin was currently recounting her professional experience, answering Blaisedell's questions in a soft but firm voice, seeming at ease, taking her time before offering a response.

"When you became dean of the law school, did you evaluate the administration of the law school?" Blaisedell asked.

"Objection," Simon interposed. He had explained to Martin that when he objected to a question, the dean should make sure that she understood the question and be aware that she had the option of asking Blaisedell to rephrase his question before she answered. He had stressed that he would object to any question *he* found unclear.

"I'm not sure I understand your question," Martin said. "I took a fresh look at the functions performed by our administrative offices if that's what you were asking."

"What functions did you look at?"

"Pretty much everything. Fund raising. Personnel. Faculty recruitment. I looked at the law school's budget. I reviewed the law school's moot court programs and clinical programs. I looked at tuition and scholarships. I looked at the law school's promotional materials. I reviewed materials relating to the placement office. And I believe that I looked at materials involving the law school's alumni which included some back issues of an alumni magazine that comes out twice a year."

"As a result of your evaluation, did you conclude that any administrative functions needed improvement?"

Martin paused for a long moment before answering, "Yes."

"What functions needed improvement?"

"Again, pretty much everything. Of course, I was the new kid on the block who could probably find something to change about every aspect of the law school."

"Can you provide me with some examples?"

"I considered expanding clinical programs to include internships with Boston firms. I considered whether it was appropriate to launch a capital campaign and what might be a suitable fundraising target for such a campaign. I thought about the possibility of bringing in visiting professors from foreign countries for a semester. I noticed that the alumni magazine was skimpy and wondered if there were ways to expand the magazine and make it a quarterly. Those are some of the improvements I considered."

"Did you consider any improvements for the placement office?"

"Yes. I considered sending out a questionnaire to alumni that would provide a data base for the placement office."

"Was such a questionnaire ever sent out before the filing of this lawsuit?"

"No."

"Why not."

"It was not an initiative that got acted upon. Other needs were addressed sooner."

"What initiatives did get acted upon before this lawsuit?"

Simon now was convinced that Blaisedell would drill down to the bottom of each answer Martin offered.

"The internship program with Boston firms was implemented and approximately twenty students a semester participate. A promotional brochure for a capital campaign is going through what I hope are the last edits. Next semester, the law school will have two guest lecturers from abroad conducting seminars. Next year, we will be bringing in a part time staffer to help expand the alumni magazine."

Simon was pleased with Martin's responses so far. Part of the dean's game plan was to paint a picture of widespread changes that needed to be made to diverse areas of the law school. Not all areas of the school that required change could be addressed immediately.

"What materials did you review in connection with the placement office?"

Martin helped herself to a sip of water and met Blaisedell's gaze. "As best as I can remember, there were file folders containing notes of calls made to the placement office. Placement office files also included promotional materials for the law school and I'm pretty certain I looked through those. There were also file folders containing job opportunities that I believe I glanced through. There may have been other documents. If I'm not mistaken, we've provided you with placement office documents going back five years."

Simon skimmed his notes. Blaisedell had yet to land a damaging blow.

"When you looked at the placement office materials that you just told us about, did you form any opinion as to the effectiveness of the placement office?"

"Yes."

"What opinion did you form?"

"In my opinion, the placement office, as was the case with other administrative offices, could have been more effective."

"In what ways could it have been more effective?"

This was a question that Simon had asked her.

"I think I've already mentioned sending out a questionnaire to alumni to develop a data base for the placement office. Another area where I thought improvement was warranted was in being more proactive about obtaining notices of job openings. And I believe back then I thought about listing job opportunities on the placement office's website."

"Since you became dean and before the law school was sued in this case, did the law school address any of the areas where you thought the placement office could be more effective?"

"No."

"Before the law school was sued in this case, did you evaluate Ms. Snelling, the head of the placement office?"

"Yes."

"What was the result of your evaluation?"

This was another question that Simon had prepped the dean to anticipate. They had spent some time going over her answer.

"Given her other duties, I believed that she was doing an adequate job."

"What were her other duties?"

"She was an administrative assistant to me."

"At her deposition, Ms. Snelling couldn't name a single person that she placed in a law-related job. On what basis did you find her performance before this lawsuit adequate when she can't identify anyone that she placed?"

The dean showed no emotion when confronted with Blaisedell's pointed question. "The placement office at the law school, at the time I became dean and while I have been dean, served the role of trying to answer questions from students and graduates. I believe that this role was set out in the promotional materials that were turned over to your office. Given the role of the placement office, I was of the opinion that Ms. Snelling did her job adequately."

"What's the point of a placement office that doesn't place anybody?" Blaisedell asked, displaying the first sign of irritation during the deposition.

"Objection," Simon immediately responded, hoping to add to Blaisedell's frustration.

Martin paused for what Simon estimated as about ten seconds. "As I've explained, the role of the law school's placement office was to try to answer questions posed by students and graduates."

"What was the office's success rate in answering questions?"

"I'm not able to answer you," Martin replied. "Not all contacts with the placement office were written down and most written notes of contacts don't indicate success or failure on addressing questions."

"Did my firm's lawsuit against the law school prompt the law school to make changes to the placement office?"

Simon tensed in his chair. The dean had been uncomfortable with questions in this area and, although they had gone through some role playing on the subject, neither Simon nor the dean had a comfort level with the post-lawsuit changes made to the placement office.

"To an extent," Martin said. "In my opinion, your lawsuit accelerated changes to the placement office."

"What do you mean by accelerated?"

"I meant that changes to the placement office were under consideration prior to the lawsuit. Therefore, I don't think the lawsuit caused the law school to come up with changes to the placement office, but rather caused the law school to move up the timeline for implementing the changes, while moving back some things we'd been planning to do in other areas."

Simon thought that a jury might find the dean's answer evasive and her distinction self-serving; however, her distinction stuck to their line of defense, and it made the school sound strategic instead of indifferent.

"What changes were accelerated?" Blaisedell asked.

"We've recently brought in a full-time placement office head."

"Excuse me for cutting you off," Blaisedell interrupted. "You never before mentioned bringing in a full-time placement office head. Does that mean that this is a change that was caused by the lawsuit as opposed to one that was previously considered?"

The dean offered Blaisedell an indulgent smile. "You know, the distinction I made before, that you've now asked me about again, is not always clear cut. As I'm thinking about bringing in a full-time person, I'd say it's both. I think that move was both under consideration and accelerated by the lawsuit."

"Did you begin actively recruiting a full-time person before or after the lawsuit was filed?"

"After."

"Before the lawsuit was filed, was bringing in a full-time person ever discussed while you were the dean?"

"I don't believe that was specifically discussed, but I regarded that change as implicit in discussions about providing a general upgrade to the placement office."

Blaisedell rolled his eyes. Simon wasn't concerned by his adversary's theatrics but was concerned with whether a jury would also have engaged in eye-rolling over Martin's refusal to be pinned down.

"I interrupted you before," Blaisedell said. "You had started to list the placement office changes that were accelerated."

"Right. There is now access to job openings on the placement office's website. The new director of the office has introduced himself to many Massachusetts law firms and has requested the law firms to contact him with any job openings. Martin paused. "There may be other changes that were speeded up that I'm not recalling at this moment."

"Did these changes improve the placement office?"

"That's my opinion."

"If made earlier, would the changes have improved the placement office earlier?"

"Yes, in my opinion."

"Since a full-time placement office head has been hired, is the placement office able to identify specific individuals for whom it has found a law-related job?"

"I believe so. The new placement office head would have the details."

Blaisedell placed a Sloan-Webster promotional brochure in front of Martin and had the stenographer mark it as an exhibit. He directed the dean to a paragraph that had been highlighted and asked her to read it aloud.

The dean read from the brochure. "'Sloan-Webster School of Law has a top-notch faculty that is second to none. Students are instructed by a knowledgeable and experienced faculty.'"

"What's the basis for characterizing Sloan-Webster's faculty as top-notch and second to none?"

This time Martin didn't pause before responding. Previously, Simon had highlighted the brochure paragraph and had critiqued her response to a question directed at the paragraph.

"There are approximately fifty applicants for every open faculty position. The law school advertises open faculty positions to ensure a large number of applicants. We make every effort to choose the individual applicant who is most qualified by training and experience. Since I've been dean, we've made approximately a dozen new faculty appointments, and I believe the law school's first choice of applicants has accepted in all but one instance. Given this selection process and our first-choice selection rate, I believe that the law school does possess a top-notch faculty."

Simon noted Blaisedell's irritation. His adversary probably thought that the plaintiffs' claim that the law school had misrepresented the quality of its faculty was a slam dunk.

"Is it true that publications rating law schools rank Sloan-Webster's faculty second lowest in Massachusetts?"

"I've seen at least one publication that gave Sloan-Webster that faculty ranking."

"Do you disagree with the ranking?"

"Generally I do. A lot of factors and opinions can go into a ranking list. It's not entirely clear to me what went into that one. But, as I said, I generally disagree with it."

"How does a second lowest ranking translate into second to none in the law school's brochure?"

"I believe I answered that question previously. By consistently hiring the top applicants, we believe our faculty is second to none."

"Has any outside ranking or rating organization ever ranked Sloan-Webster's faculty in the top ten of law schools being evaluated?"

"Not to my knowledge."

"Are you able to name any member of the Sloan-Webster faculty who is regarded as a national authority in his or her field?"

"It depends what you mean by nationally," Martin replied, and Simon realized he should have objected to Blaisedell's question. "Each of our faculty has published in his or her field. Any publication is available nationally so, from that perspective, any faculty member who has published for any institution can be considered a national authority."

"So you equate publication of an article as conferring national authority status on the author?" Blaisedell asked.

"I don't necessarily. But a case can be made."

"Has any person ever publicly referred to a member of the Sloan-Webster faculty as a national authority in his or her field?"

"Not that I'm aware. However, I don't really keep up with public comments of that nature."

"Outside of publishing articles, has any member of the Sloan-Webster faculty been considered a national authority in his or her field?"

"Again, not that I'm aware," the dean responded evenly. "But as I said, I don't routinely follow who refers to whom as a national authority."

Simon assessed that Blaisedell had bolstered his position on the faculty issue with his latest questions. If any faculty member regarded himself or herself as a national authority on anything, Simon was certain that the faculty member would have brought that to the attention of the dean.

"This might be a good time to take a short break," Blaisedell said.

"There's no need to walk me back to the law school," Dean Martin said as Simon joined her.

"I need to stretch my legs," Simon countered. It was a warm sunny afternoon with occasional wispy clouds overhead and enough of a breeze to keep it comfortable. Simon wanted some exercise. Plus, the walk would give him a chance to share impressions with the dean.

"How do you think it went?" the dean asked, as if reading his thoughts.

"I think you did a good job," Simon said, meaning it. "Blaisdell's questions after the break were weak. Before the break some of his questions were tough, but you didn't concede anything."

"Are you saying that maybe I should have?"

Simon sought for a tactful way to phrase his response. "Perhaps," he said. "I'll have a better idea once I read the transcript. There are some points that simply are what they are to use a current phrase. Fighting them can make you appear unreasonable."

"You mean like digging in my heels when it came to any faculty member being a nationally recognized authority?"

Simon nodded. That was the first example he had thought of.

"Something came over me," the dean said. "I didn't want to give an inch to the guy. I've been told that I have a stubborn streak. I suppose that came out at the deposition."

"As I said, overall I'm pleased."

"What's next?" the dean asked.

"There will be a hearing on the motion to make this case a class action. Rachel will be handling that court hearing. As we've discussed, the judge's ruling will be important. If this becomes a class action, then there's the potential that each member of the class might be entitled to money damages. If the judge denies the class action motion, then only the three plaintiffs would be eligible for monetary damages."

"I keep thinking about whether it makes sense to try to quickly settle the case," the dean said. "But then I remember you saying that if the case settles, the law school is best served if the settlement applies to the entire class."

"Correct. It's complicated. The court papers in the Spenser School of Law case will show that no class was ever certified in the case. Yet the case settled. Spenser is at risk that a student who wasn't one of the three named plaintiffs could sue the law school. Spenser decided to take that risk."

"But you don't think Sloan-Webster should take that risk."

"To be candid, I keep going back and forth on that point. We'll need to see how this plays out."

They walked for a time in silence. Simon wished he could burrow inside Blaisedell's head and gain an insight into what his adversary was thinking.

"Neil Taylor is doing a good job with the placement office," the dean said. "If this case were to drag out for years, I think it would be less likely someone new would bring suit."

Simon had the same thought. "I tend to agree. But I don't think the judicial system will provide us with years. The courts have time standards for disposing of cases. One way or another, I believe this case is going to be sorted out in a year."

64

Carpenter reflected on how little it took to cheer him up. Delaney, one of his fellow Barristers, had delivered his end-of-August prediction on whether the

Red Sox would make the playoffs. His friend's prediction wasn't worth squat; Delaney had often missed the mark including last year and most notably in 2004 when the Sox won the World Series. But Delaney's verdict that the Sox would be playing in the post season was welcome news. The other Barristers who followed the home team—every Barrister except Weiskoff—also appeared buoyed by Delaney's prediction.

This year Delaney appeared perplexed by his prognostication. Last year, in a September swoon, the Sox had blown a big lead and had been shut out of the playoffs on the last day of the season. During last winter, the Sox had made many changes to the team roster, but Delaney was of the view that, on paper, the changes didn't amount to much of an upgrade. Also, the team had been struck by injuries to key players. Yet somehow, the team kept winning. "It's remarkable," Delaney had said. "You look at the team and you can't imagine them having one of the best records in baseball. They have all these guys growing ZZ Top beards and no matter who they put out on the field, someone you least expect comes up with a big hit. It defies logic, but I have to say they're going to make the playoffs. I can't explain my decision, but I don't think I really could come out a different way. I mean how can you vote against a team that has a skinny little Japanese guy that nobody can hit as its closer?"

Carpenter had to agree. This September would be different than last year's. The team was touched by magic. Sometimes logic was useless, and you just had to accept that miracles did happen.

September

From Rachel's Playlist

"Hold On, We're Going Home"

Drake

65

Ai Li was again seated in the office suite's conference room, and Philly was struck by the change in her. She sat straight in her chair and made eye contact, her previous tentativeness and indecisiveness molted. Philly had figured that this meeting would be the money talk meeting, having previously proposed a fee arrangement for taking on Li's discrimination action against her law firm. There would be a $20,000 retainer. If the case settled before billable hours ate up the retainer, the remainder would be returned to Li. If billable hours exceeded $20,000—a near certainty in Philly's and Carpenter's opinion—the retainer would be nonrefundable. Any damage award would be handled on a one-third contingency basis and the retainer would be applied to the contingency fee due. But the look on Li's face suggested that this meeting wouldn't be about financial arrangements.

"I've received a job offer that I wish to accept," Li began.

Philly glanced Carpenter's way and doubted that her own expression mirrored his stony reaction. "What happened?" she asked, surprised by Li's pronouncement.

"It has become clear to me that I cannot remain at my present firm. Particularly if I bring suit against them, which I'm inclined to do. I went to meet with the client I brought to the firm, the one I told you about. I invited the president of the company to lunch. I explained that I was seriously thinking of leaving my current firm and that I wanted to give him a heads up in case I did leave so that the news didn't come to him on short notice. I wanted to ask him what his company would do with its legal work if I ended up at another firm, but I held back from doing so because I was concerned about the partnership agreement I had signed. I implored him not to speak to my firm about this conversation because there was still a chance I wouldn't leave, and he said he would honor that request. He then told me that our lunch had come at a propitious time. He said that his company had been thinking about me and whether it made sense for them to hire someone like me as general corporate counsel. The board of directors didn't want to hire someone *like* me. They preferred to hire *me*. He told me what the starting pay would be and asked if I were interested. I told him I was very interested. The starting pay was more than I'm making now and more than I would have made at partner level six. I mentioned that our firm did other work for his company besides corporate work. I asked what would happen to that work if I was hired by his company. He told me that as general counsel,

I would be free to hire any firm I wished for other work, subject to the approval of the board of directors."

Philly wasn't sure what next to ask, but Carpenter had no such difficulty. "What does your law firm partnership agreement say?" he asked.

Li passed two documents across the table. "I'm hiring you to tell me. As I read the agreement, if I leave the firm, I can't solicit clients of the firm. I don't believe I solicited the company that just made me an offer. That offer came from them. They solicited me."

Philly wondered just how valuable this company was to Li's current firm. Would the firm simply accept Li's assurance that she hadn't solicited the company? Wouldn't the company view Li's lunch with the company's president as a solicitation?

"We'll review the document and get back to you," Carpenter said. "I suppose you want to hear from us before accepting the job and resigning from your firm."

"Yes," Li said emphatically.

"You need to realize that regardless of our opinion, your current law firm and a judge might take a different view of what your firm partnership agreement says."

"I do. I'm also interested in what you think about how my bringing a discrimination suit will affect what my current law firm does."

Carpenter nodded. "Good question. We'll get back to you on that as well."

Philly saw no reason why the money talk shouldn't go forward. "We made a proposal to you about legal fees. If it's acceptable, I propose we also apply it to the contract review you just requested."

Li nodded. "That's fine. You're being very fair."

Philly completed her review of the partnership agreement signed by Ai Li moments before Carpenter finished the task. "You first," Carpenter said when he looked up to see her regarding him.

"There's nothing to prohibit Li from quitting and working for another law firm or any other employer. If she leaves, she can't solicit active firm clients and she can't take with her any trade secrets, firm property, or confidential information."

Carpenter nodded. "That's my read as well. Do you think her taking this company president out to lunch was a solicitation?"

"Not if things played out the way Li described them. God only knows what this company president will say."

"We're on the same page," Carpenter said. "What about Li's last question?" he asked. "If she sues her firm for discrimination, will that deter or encourage her firm to sue her for soliciting a client?"

Philly had no strong opinion one way or the other. "I suppose it comes down to whether the higher ups at her firm are vengeful pricks."

"If Li took the in-house corporate lawyer job, my sense was that she'd take the non-corporate work elsewhere."

"I agree," Philly said. "Which would be added incentive for her current firm to act like vengeful pricks. We need to get a handle on the revenue Li's firm makes from the client she brought in."

"I'm still trying to get a handle on Li's thinking," Carpenter said. "If she goes directly to a job that's paying her more, where are her money damages? Why would she sue?"

"Maybe she truly believes she was discriminated against and wants to put a stop to these guys discriminating against women in the future," Philly offered, not convinced her reasoning had legs.

"The first time we met with her, she didn't strike me as a crusader," Carpenter said. "Anything but. And didn't she go on about her husband not wanting to make waves? If she sues, she's going to make waves."

"She's in a better position than we are to figure out whether her firm will go after her if she sues or doesn't sue," Philly said. "She knows the firm's decision makers."

"If the firm sues her," Carpenter responded, "she could counterclaim for discrimination. But for some reason I think she should make the first move on the discrimination case if she decides to sue for discrimination."

"But if she sues for discrimination," Philly said, "wouldn't her firm throw in a counterclaim against her just for the hell of it and claim she solicited this company she went to work for."

"Fair point," Carpenter acknowledged.

"I think we've covered all the angles," Philly said. "I guess we know what we're going to say to her."

"I'm glad you do," Carpenter retorted. "You can do the talking."

When Lauren Goldman announced herself on the phone, Carpenter couldn't decide whether he was going to end the day on a high or low note.

"Donald Frazier will agree to his son's demands," Goldman got to the bottom line without preliminaries. "He will issue the 1099 forms to John Harrison, settle with the IRS, and then stay on only as a minority stockholder while his son takes over the business. He expects your client's lawsuit to be dismissed with prejudice and a settlement agreement signed in which he doesn't admit liability."

"I find myself in the unusual position of having nothing to bitch and moan about," Carpenter said. "I guess that's what happens when someone agrees with you."

"Who's going to do the paperwork?" Goldman asked.

"I've done a fair number of these," Carpenter said. "How about I draft the settlement agreement, and you draw up the lawsuit dismissal."

"Okay," Goldman said. "I'll await your draft."

Carpenter set down his phone and decided to get his call to Henry Frazier out of the way. Frazier could decide for himself whether the news was good or bad. The man was about to take over a business that had lost its major client.

66

Carpenter figured Spenser School of Law was doing something right. Rachel and Simon were smart, creative, and excelled in court. He still couldn't fathom how neither had landed a job out of law school. And Meredith was further confirmation that Spenser was on to something. She just completed a further analysis that identified a little over $130,000 in Blake Pennington billings that had involved more than two partners in a department participating in a conference call or meeting. In one instance, the firm had billed for four partners within the same department participating on a conference call.

"This is good work," Carpenter said. "I think we have a strong case for knocking out close to three hundred twenty-five thousand in billings for reasons that a jury should have no trouble understanding. Getting more than that figure will depend on whether a jury believes Harris Burton on more general overstaffing by Blake Pennington."

"Are you going to file a Rule 68 motion?" Meredith asked.

Carpenter nodded. "That's the direction I'm heading in. I'm going to review our schedules with Jeremiah Becker. But go ahead and draft the motion. I've done some before and I should be able to dig one out and make you a copy."

"Great," Meredith said.

"I think for the Rule 68 filing we should use the three hundred twenty-five thousand figure we talked about before. Now we can support that number, and if Ship Right recovers at least that, Blake Pennington will end up paying our attorney fees incurred after the law firm rejected the figure."

"Won't Murphy and Warren file a similar motion listing... say three hundred thousand?" Meredith asked.

"They might if they did the same kind of analysis we did. And knowing the two of them, I'm guessing they did do that. Ship Right might accept three hundred thousand dollars since that figure is only twenty-five thousand off the figure Ship Right would use."

"It's like a game of chicken," Meredith observed.

Carpenter liked that analogy. The problem was that Murphy and Warren had nerves of steel.

The conference call feature on the Boston office phones was supposed to be idiot proof, but Carpenter figured his technophobia could screw up even a simple three-way connection. But he did have Philly on the line now and he said a silent prayer as he heard a ring tone on what he hoped was Ai Li's cell phone.

"Ai Li speaking."

'Amazing,' Carpenter thought as Philly took over the call.

"We've reviewed the partnership agreement you signed. We believe that the agreement permits you to accept a job with another law firm or with another employer. If you leave your firm, you've agreed not to do certain things, one of which is soliciting the firm's active clients."

"That's what I thought," Li said.

"From what you said about your luncheon with the president of the company that is now a client of the firm," Philly continued, "it didn't seem to us that you had solicited him or the company. Hiring you appeared to be something the company was thinking about before your lunch."

"I think the president will back me up on that," Li said.

"It's harder to predict whether your filing of a discrimination claim against your firm will cause it to claim you're violating the non-solicitation provision of the partnership agreement," Philly addressed Li's second request for advice. "I'll go into more detail in a minute, but we want to point out that you aren't likely to win money damages in a discrimination case because you'll be making more money than you are now if you go to work for the new company. Your best shot at money damages would be for any emotional distress you suffered from the discrimination against you. Damages for emotional distress are much harder to quantify than are damages for loss of income."

"I'm aware of that," Li said, and from the tone of her voice—clipped, forceful—Carpenter wondered whether he had misjudged her. Perhaps she was a crusader after all.

"Let's go through the permutations," Philly proposed. "First, you could leave your current firm and opt not to sue for discrimination. If that's your choice, your current firm could either decide to do nothing, or decide to sue you by claiming you solicited the company which was an active client of the firm even though you're the one who brought this client to the firm. If that happens, then you could bring a counterclaim alleging discrimination. If you don't raise discrimination in a counterclaim, you'll be precluded from raising discrimination later on. If someone is sued, the rules of procedure require the person to raise in a counterclaim any claim the person has against the party that sued her."

"I remember that from law school," Li said. "Compulsory counterclaims."

"Right," Philly confirmed. "Another option is to leave your current employer and file a claim for discrimination before the Massachusetts Commission Against Discrimination. If the matter ends up in court, your current law firm is in the same position: it will have to bring any counterclaim it has against you and, because you brought suit, your firm may go looking for a counterclaim and come up with the client solicitation claim against you."

"They'd probably claim I solicited the company just to put pressure on me," Li said.

"We think *you* are in the best position to judge whether your law firm would be motivated to seek revenge against you," Philly continued.

"They won't like to lose this client," Li responded.

"We don't have any idea what kind of billings this client generates. Also, although you haven't said this expressly, we're assuming that if you become the company's in-house counsel, you will transfer the company's non-corporate work to another law firm."

"Last year, my law firm's billings to the company were close to a million dollars," Li clarified. "And yes, I would move all non-corporate business to another firm if I became corporate counsel to the company."

Carpenter asked the question that had been bugging him._"If you're aware that money damages won't be significant in a discrimination suit you might bring, what's your motivation to sue for discrimination?"

Carpenter heard Li's deep sigh. "I've never taken a stand to right a wrong," Li said. "My husband and I have always been cautious. Maybe it's a Chinese thing. We both had very strict Chinese upbringings. My parents were very deferential to authority, and they expected the same from me. When my firm told me that I probably didn't receive a promotion because two clients described me as aloof, I was hurt and angry. I've made more of a contribution to the firm than the three who got promotions. I deserved to be made a level six partner. I think that my firm keeps women from reaching the top partnership levels. Changing that is important to me, even if there is little or no money, and even if it means not doing things the way my parents did."

'I'm angry, and I'm not going to take it anymore,' Carpenter thought.

"Carpenter and I were discussing your situation," Philly resumed, "and one of the points he made—which I've come around to—is that if you're going to sue for discrimination, you should do it directly; if you raise discrimination as a counterclaim, it risks coming across as an afterthought, as something that was made up in retaliation for being sued, and not something that's important for its own sake."

Li digested Philly's observation in silence. "I see what you mean," she finally said.

"As we're talking this through," Philly said, "I think you should have the mindset that you will be sued for solicitation of a firm client if you bring a discrimination claim against your firm."

"You're probably right," Li said. "I need to discuss this further with my husband and get back to you."

67

Simon turned to study the seating area in the back of the Suffolk Superior Court courtroom. Janet Martin and Ralph Cray were present as was Neil Taylor, Jane Snelling's successor. Rachel sat next to him composed, reviewing her one-page oral argument outline. To their right, at the plaintiffs' counsel table, Christopher Blaisedell, with an expression as impenetrable as a block of granite, stared at the vacant bench. None of Blaisedell's plaintiffs had come.

For this hearing on the class action motion, they had drawn Judge Charlene Hayes, a recent appointee to the superior court bench. Rachel had researched the judge's background: Harvard Law School, a federal court clerkship, a three-year stint with the US Attorney's Office, and a partnership at a mid-sized Boston law firm where she specialized in government relations and white-collar criminal defense work.

"Court!" announced the court officer.

Judge Hayes surveyed the courtroom as she took her seat. Fiery red hair cascaded over her shoulders. She was almost as pale-complexioned as Philly and, except for lipstick a shade less vibrantly red than her hair, she appeared to wear no makeup. Simon had long ago given up trying to find meaning in a judge's facial expression. Still, he would have preferred a more welcoming look from Judge Hayes.

"I've read the written submissions," the judge announced. "The defendant has challenged the suitability of the three named plaintiffs to represent a class. Do you agree, Mr. Blaisedell, that if I conclude the defendant is correct in its assertion, I need not address any other requirement for class action certification?"

Blaisedell appeared caught off guard by this opening judicial salvo. He rose slowly and spent a moment looking at notes arrayed before him on his counsel table.

"No, Your Honor, I don't agree," Blaisedell said. "The plaintiffs request that the court make findings and rulings on all the requirements for class action certification. I suspect whatever ruling Your Honor ultimately makes will generate a request to appeal your order."

"You didn't respond to my question," the judge said in a tone that fit her unsmiling expression. Simon hoped Rachel had picked up on the judge's attitude.

"If Your Honor concluded that the plaintiffs were not suitable to represent the class they seek to represent, that finding alone would warrant the court's denial of the plaintiffs' motion."

"Does one of the plaintiffs gamble and have gambling debts?" the judge asked.

"At the present time no."

"Does that mean that the answer would have been yes if the question had been asked on the date of... I've got that name somewhere... Mr. McCauley's affidavit?"

"That's correct," Blaisedell answered.

"Given this admitted activity by Mr. Hightower, I will tell you that you need to provide me with a compelling reason why I should overlook the activity in connection with your motion."

Blaisedell studied the judge before responding. "The activity has nothing to do with the ability of Mr. Hightower to represent other graduates of Sloan-Webster who received no placement help whatsoever and were promised a top-notch faculty that no rating agency has ever found to be top-notch."

"The activity goes to Mr. Hightower's character," the judge came back. "My suspicion is that Mr. Hightower's character comes through during interviews with prospective employers and probably accounts for his inability to find a law-related job."

"Respectfully, Your Honor, there is no evidence of that."

"Inferences may be made from Mr. Hightower's admitted activity," the judge replied sharply.

Blaisedell didn't respond to the judge's comment; Simon would have done the same.

"The defendant claims that more discovery is needed with respect to Mr. Branson's involvement with a suspicion of cheating on a college test and that I should hold a hearing on that matter," the judge resumed. "Do you agree?"

"No," Blaisedell replied forcefully. "This matter was fully investigated by the college and the investigation turned up nothing."

"Mr. Blaisedell has a point, doesn't he, Ms. Boyle?"

Rachel stood. "But not a dispositive point. While Mr. Branson denied cheating at his deposition, his manner, which doesn't come across in the transcript, was one of worry and concern, as if he had something to hide. In the college's investigation, no sworn testimony was taken. The defendant, subject to court approval, will seek to remedy this by deposing under oath the teaching assistant who was suspected by the college of being responsible for the cheating."

"My impression is that you are reaching here, Ms. Boyle," the judge said. "You're seeking to open up an event over five years old without any real evidence to do so."

"The defendant respectfully disagrees, Your Honor," Rachel persevered. "We're all familiar with the phrase 'guilty look.' That's what Mr. Branson displayed when deposition questions focused on the cheating episode."

"Maybe you should have videotaped the deposition so this guilty look would have been preserved, because there is no evidence of a guilty look before me."

Simon passed Rachel a note: *LET IT GO!*

Rachel took her seat as the judge consulted the papers before her.

"Exotic dancer isn't likely to enhance the resumé of a person seeking a legal job, is it Mr. Blaisedell?" the judge next asked.

"I submit that would depend on the person or company or agency looking to fill the legal position," Blaisedell replied smartly. "Ms. White's sideline is certainly no impediment to obtaining a legal position."

"I don't know what circles you travel in, Mr. Blaisedell, but prospective legal employers in my experience would not regard exotic dancing—which includes lap dancing—as a plus."

"This activity has no bearing on Ms. White's ability to represent the class," Blaisedell persisted.

"I would disagree. Your complaint claims that the plaintiffs were denied law-related jobs because of failings by the defendant. Yet here we have one of the named plaintiffs engaging in an activity that prospective legal employers are likely to find highly objectionable."

"This has not been an issue in Ms. White's attempts to secure a legal position."

"That's because she's concealed the activity," the judge came back. "The defendant has discovered the sideline of this plaintiff and makes the point that it is not a sideline likely to help in obtaining a legal position. I think the defendant has made a fair point."

Simon wondered whether it was his imagination that so far, the hearing was going as well as could be expected.

The judge took a few moments to study the papers in front of her. When she looked up, she addressed Rachel. "Ms. Boyle. The plaintiffs claim that the law school misrepresented it had a placement office. They claim that an office that has never placed anybody before they filed suit isn't a placement office. What do you say to that?"

"The defendant disputes that allegation. Sloan-Webster did maintain a placement office with functions that were set forth in promotional materials that are before the court. Specifically, the placement office posted job opportunities that came to its attention and tried to answer questions posed by students and graduates. The placement office never promised that any student would be placed."

"A promise the office has lived up to apparently," the judge quipped.

"With all due respect, Your Honor," Rachel said, "the plaintiffs' complaint is not that the placement office didn't do what it said it would do. Rather, the plaintiffs' complaint is that the placement office should have been something different from what it held itself out to be. The latter isn't a viable legal claim."

"I'll decide what's a viable legal claim," the judge said.

"I wasn't suggesting otherwise," Rachel replied, and Simon was pleased that Rachel was keeping her cool.

"Why is any named plaintiff's outside activities relevant to the plaintiff being able to raise the claim that the law school misrepresented it had a placement office when no such office in fact existed?" the judge asked.

"Because," Rachel responded, "a representative of a class is required by the rules of procedure to be a *suitable* representative of the class. That requirement applies to each of the plaintiffs' legal claims."

"You claim in your memorandum, Ms. Boyle, that there can be no class because each student's and graduate's experience is unique. Does that mean that there can never be a class action in cases of this kind?"

"Yes," Rachel said, and Simon was relieved that she gave the answer she needed to provide.

"Mr. Blaisedell has been very active in this area," the judge noted. "In other jurisdictions, he's obtained class certification in similar cases against law schools. Were the decisions wrong in all those other cases?"

"That's certainly a possibility," Rachel replied. "One would have to view the legal claims and analyze the arguments made against class certification. I would simply note that in a similar case handled by me and Mr. Jeffries here in Massachusetts, class certification was denied."

"You are correct," the judge said. "I looked at the written materials in the Spenser School of Law case that involved class action certification. From the papers in that case, it is my impression that Spenser School of Law maintained a placement department that actually placed people."

"I would simply note that the placement offices of the two law schools held themselves out as performing substantially different functions."

The judge flashed a disapproving look. Rachel and Blaisedell had each been respectful while trying to avoid conceding important points, so Simon wondered whether they were dealing with a jurist who resented any lawyer who refused to yield an inch under questioning.

"I also have difficulty understanding why the background of any named plaintiff is crucial to the plaintiff's advancing the claim that the law school misrepresented itself as having a top-notch, second-to-none faculty when no outside rating agency has rated the faculty top-notch or second-to-none."

"My answer to your previous question applies here," Rachel said. "The nature of a legal claim in a class action lawsuit doesn't eliminate the requirement that a plaintiff representing the class be suitable and responsible. With respect to Sloan-Webster's faculty being top-notch, the faculty is. We've recently supplemented our filings by providing an excerpt from the dean's deposition where she pointed out that the law school receives numerous applications for any open position and has been successful in hiring the most qualified applicant on all but one occasion."

"I will tell you, Ms. Boyle, that I have a generally negative reaction to the notion that there can never be a class action in a case of this kind." The judge paused and looked at her papers. "I don't need to hear further oral argument; your written submissions are detailed. However, if either of you wishes to make any final comments, now is the time."

Simon placed a hand on Rachel's knee. "It's his motion," he whispered. "Let Blaisedell go first. If he says nothing, I'd do the same."

Blaisedell, Simon noticed, was considering the judge's invitation with a pained expression. "Nothing further," he finally declared.

For a brief moment Simon thought Rachel was going to make a final point. In the end she followed Blaisedell's lead. "Nothing further," she said.

"The court will be in recess," the judge announced. "I'll take the plaintiffs' motion under advisement."

"Are all judges this surly?" Ralph Cray asked once the Sloan-Webster contingent claimed a quiet spot in the corridor outside the judge's courtroom.

"No," Rachel answered simply.

Simon purposely stayed in the background. This was Rachel's moment. She had done a good job, providing an answer to each of the judge's questions. While the judge didn't appear enamored by certain of her responses, Rachel had made the best case she could.

"I thought you had the better of it," Cray directed to Rachel.

"Court arguments are not particularly reliable in predicting how a judge will rule," Rachel responded.

"How do you think it went?" Cray asked next.

"One of my partners likes to ask who would you rather be, you or the lawyer on the other side? All in all, I'd rather be me."

"When do you think the judge will rule?" Dean Martin asked.

"My guess is two to four weeks," Rachel replied.

"This is nerve-wracking," the dean remarked.

"Welcome to our world," Rachel said.

One of the things Rachel loved about Josh was that he let her vent without jumping in to tell her what to do or offering his own opinion. Over dinner, she had been castigating Judge Charlene Hayes for being a miserable human being and Josh was listening—really listening—not interrupting, nodding from time to time in support of her grievances. Rachel realized that she was running out of steam. "I mean I don't mind a judge telling me I'm all wet so long as it's done nicely."

"It sounds like the guy on the other side took an equal ration of shit," Josh observed.

"Maybe more," Rachel had to admit. Were there moments when she had actually felt sorry for Blaisedell during the oral argument? Carpenter would have reveled in Blaisedell's suffering.

"There are nasty people running loose, and I'm sure they include judges," Josh said.

"It just makes me so mad!"

"You look less mad than when you started unloading."

"A lot you know!"

Rachel had been so busy with her tirade that she hadn't made much progress on her dinner, a vegetarian burrito that Josh had obviously spent time putting together. As she made up for lost time, she noticed that Josh also had barely touched his food, not a common occurrence.

"This is good," Rachel said, thinking this comment would remind Josh to eat.

"Thanks. You mind if I ask you something?"

"Sure," Rachel responded, feeling a pang of guilt because when she got worked up, she often lost sight of the fact that Josh had his own problems.

"It's about this fourteen-year-old girl I'm giving private tennis lessons to. Her parents sent us a video of a recent match which I reviewed, and I got back to them with comments. Basically, the girl's concentration was missing. It was as if her heart wasn't in it. That's pretty much what I reported to her parents. They want to continue with private lessons."

Josh's sports consulting company was taking off. He had been forced to cut down on his tennis and golf lessons and had hired a recent college graduate to help him out in those areas. Rachel was proud of him and his partners; their business plan was bearing fruit.

"The first few times I met with the girl, we just talked," Josh continued. "The talking helped, and she opened up to me. I think I know what went wrong. She went to one of those month-long, intensive tennis camps early this summer. Her parents kind of pushed her to go; they have an inflated view of her talent. It was the girl's first time living away from home. Before this experience, she had only received positive reinforcement. She had taken private lessons with a tennis pro at a club and did well in school matches. But this place she went to over the summer has a reputation as a boot camp. The criticism is harsh. If you screw up, this place is heavily into punishment drills. The girl I'm talking about had to run laps in hundred-degree heat and she threw up."

"That sounds barbaric!" Rachel exclaimed. "What were these people thinking?"

Josh picked at his burrito, washed down a few swallows with a slug of beer. "They think this kind of treatment toughens a kid up," he explained. "For some kids it works. For Noelle, it was a disaster. Tennis stopped being fun for her."

"Did you go through anything like that as a kid?" Rachel asked. Josh seldom volunteered stories from when he was a kid but whenever Rachel asked about his childhood, he answered.

"I spent a couple of summers at a camp specializing in tennis. The instructors worked all of us hard, but there was a lot of counseling and sessions about strategy which provided a respite from the drills."

"What's your plan for Noelle?" Rachel wondered what you could do for a teenage girl who had been... was *traumatized* the right word?

"So far I'm doing two things. I'm hitting with her and talking to her. We've yet to play a set. I'm trying to be low key. I've sort of gone back to basics to try to get her to focus on what she likes about the game. It seems to be working, but it's slow going."

"What's the name of this camp she went to?" Rachel asked.

"Northampton Intensive Tennis Academy. It's got a website."

"Do you mind if I take a look at the website?"

"Why would I mind? Be my guest."

They ate for a time in silence. Josh had recovered his appetite. Rachel then remembered how they got started talking about Josh's teenage client. "You said you wanted to ask me something," Rachel reminded him.

"Right. I got distracted. Can Noelle sue the assholes who put her through hell?"

"Anybody can sue anybody else," Rachel responded. "The real question is whether you'll win."

68

"I just called to thank you," Sasha Barton said.

"Why don't you and Frankie do that in person," Philly replied. "We're cooking outside tonight. Join us."

"Rain check," Barton said. "We've got plans. But here's some news. The Board of Education has approved our program. We've got our first scheduled presentation coming up soon."

"Good for you."

"Did I tell you that Clarke met with Xavier and Stanley and their mothers? He actually apologized to Xavier and thanked the boys for easing tensions at the end of the school year."

"Does that mean there's hope for everybody?" Philly replied.

"We can only hope," Barton said. "And the ten thousand dollars came in handy. So really, thanks for everything."

"Don't mention it," Philly said. "How are you and Clarke doing?"

"We're still a little leery of each other. But we're able to talk more easily."

"Progress," Philly said.

"Progress," Barton echoed.

After ending the call, Philly walked out the backdoor and paused on the blacktop. Daisy and Rosalind were giggling and kicking a soccer ball around on the grass, enjoying the activity that without warning had replaced croquet. Sarah was in attendance encouraging them to give Daniel a turn. Daniel was staggering around, constantly plopping down on his bum as he tried to keep track of the ball. Philly couldn't picture the three kids at Xavier's and Stanley's age. She couldn't imagine them bigger with more defined personalities, with more vocal likes and dislikes. Was this moment the happiest they would ever be?

"You look lost," Sarah called out. "Want to play?"

Philly thought of work she could be doing. The thought was fleeting. "Sure, why not?"

In Carpenter's opinion, once a case had settled, hearing from a client was seldom good news. So when Henry Frazier announced himself on the phone, Carpenter expected doom and gloom.

"I've got some good news and some interesting news," Frazier announced.

"Let's start with the good news," Carpenter said, making an effort to put aside his skepticism.

"Okay. I'm a few days into the job, trying to settle in, when I get a call from the president of this outfit called Events Are Us. My father had tried to land them as a client, but the president wouldn't even talk to him. This outfit is a competitor of Event Planning. The president tells me that news travels fast in his business and he heard that Event Planning had given us the boot. When I confirmed that Event Planning wasn't a client of ours anymore, the guy says he's familiar with our work, likes our work, and asks if we would be interested in working on the printed materials for a charity fundraiser he's got coming up. He didn't have to twist my arm. So Elite Scripts has its first new contract."

"Congratulations," Carpenter said, meaning it.

"Turns out the president of Events Are Us can't stand Warren Anderson. He hates Anderson so much that he wouldn't do business with anyone Anderson did business with. Which explains why my father had struck out with the guy."

Carpenter thought of the expression that when a door closes a window opens. Sappy, feel-good sayings seldom panned out, but maybe this time they did. "Good for you. What about the interesting news?"

"You're going to love this. As you know, my father sent out the 1099 forms to John Harrison. My father had a very good relationship with Harrison's secretary. The secretary calls him, tells my father she has some news he might find interesting. She says she went into Harrison's office to give him some papers he needed to look at and Harrison was on the phone, loud and angry, facing away from her. She heard him say something like, 'That rat bastard Frazier has got the IRS on my case, but I'll be damned if I'm going down alone. Anderson got half and if I have to, I'll rat him out.' The secretary puts the papers on Harrison's desk and Harrison becomes aware of her. But the secretary is a cool customer, and she walks out of his office as if she didn't hear a thing."

Carpenter smiled. "You're right," he said. "I do love this." He thought of Sophie Teague, Anderson's lawyer who had played hardball at their meeting. Let her try playing hardball with the IRS and see how far she'll get. "What are you going to do about your dad?" he asked.

"Nothing for the moment," Frazier said. "I need to settle in, and I also think he really does need a vacation from the business."

Doing nothing was a strategy Carpenter could identify with. "I really appreciate your bringing me up to date."

"This all has a chance of working out for the best," Frazier said. "Thanks again for everything."

"Don't mention it."

Philly was startled by her office phone ringing. "Philly Sullivan."

"This is Ai Li."

Li sounded stressed. "I'm guessing you have some news to report," Philly said, deciding not to say anything that would acknowledge Li's anxiety.

"I do. I accepted the in-house counsel job. I signed a letter agreement and I start in a month."

"Congratulations." Philly wished that she'd been given a chance to look at Li's new employment agreement. True, Li was an experienced corporate attorney. But changing jobs was a big deal for Li emotionally, and Philly believed she would have benefitted by having another, perhaps calmer, set of eyes review her new arrangement.

"I gave notice of leaving to my law firm," Li said, and Philly speculated that this announcement had not progressed smoothly. "I told them where I was going. The head of the management committee, Henrietta Coleman, asked to meet with me. When I went to her office, she asked me why I was leaving. I told her I was not happy with the decision not to promote me to partner level six, and that I believed I had been discriminated against. She denied that I had been discriminated against, and she reminded me that she had given me the likely reasons why I wasn't promoted. Then she asked me what I was going to do about my feeling that I had been discriminated against. I didn't answer her. I had already decided to bring suit. But I kept that decision to myself."

Philly marveled at the blind spots of smart people. Li was obviously smart and experienced. Yet she had not sought legal advice about either her new employment agreement or the best way to sever ties with her current law firm.

"This meeting was in the morning," Li went on. "In the afternoon, Henrietta Coleman came to my office and told me she had met with the rest of the management committee. The committee thought it best that under the circumstances I leave immediately. Henrietta told me to clean out my desk and hand over my office keys. It was okay to pack things up and come get them later. One of the firm's partners escorted me out of the building. It was humiliating."

"When did all this happen?" Philly asked.

"Yesterday."

Philly finished her note taking. "From here on out, do not say anything to anyone at your former law firm. Is that clear?"

"Okay."

"And I mean nothing. If someone calls you to wish you well, you can thank the person but that's it. Are you getting paid by the law firm for the next thirty days?"

"Yes. You may recall that our partnership agreement requires a partner leaving the firm to give thirty days' advance notice. The agreement provides that the leaving partner gets paid for the thirty days even if the firm lets the partner go before the thirty days are up."

"Are you thinking of starting with the new company before the thirty days are up."

"No. I decided I could use a little break."

"That's probably a wise move," Philly said.

"Did I handle things correctly?" Li asked.

Li was probably feeling vulnerable, second-guessing everything she had done and hoping for some support. Philly decided to level with her. Since they were going to represent her in a lawsuit, Li needed to change her way of thinking and acting.

"I'm going to be frank with you," Philly said. "We're going to be meeting and talking together intensely for the near future, so I think it might be helpful if, as your lawyer, I shared some thoughts and expectations I have. First, I think it would have been wise to have a second set of eyes look at the employment letter with your new company."

"I pretty much wrote it," Li interrupted.

"That doesn't matter. You've been doing a lot of soul-searching during an emotional period in your life, and I think it would have been helpful to get a second viewpoint. A second opinion didn't necessarily have to come from us."

Philly paused and Li said nothing, so Philly pressed ahead. "If the head of the management committee or any other partner asks to talk to you about your discrimination concerns or about working out your concerns, don't say anything. You can give anyone who approaches you my name and I'll do the talking for you. Are we clear?"

"But what if I can work things out?" Li complained.

"If things can be worked out, I'll work them out. You've told your firm's management committee head that you believe you have a legal claim against the firm. These people are no longer your friends. Are we clear?"

"I guess so."

"Good. Don't be surprised if one of your partners contacts you and gives you a soft sell by saying he or she is aware you feel like you were discriminated against, and the firm would like to resolve your concerns as soon as possible. Don't say a word. Give the person my name."

"Okay," Li said without any enthusiasm.

"You probably know that we have to start by filing a complaint with a state agency, the Massachusetts Commission Against Discrimination. We'll be preparing a draft for your review. This kind of case has to start with the appropriate administrative agency, but after a set period of time it can become a court action, instead. Generally, Carpenter and I prefer to move a case to court. We'll discuss that strategy when the time comes, but I wanted to tell you up front the way we usually approach these kinds of cases."

"I would think the MCAD would be sympathetic to plaintiffs," Li said.

"I'd agree with that," Philly replied. "But we think a jury is more likely to return a big verdict if it finds in your favor."

Li fell silent and Philly, not for the first time, wondered whether she had overloaded a client's circuits. "Let's focus on the positive," she said. "Congratulations on your new job."

"Thanks. This is all nerve-wracking. My husband is a wreck."

"What's the name of the company you're going to work for?"

"As I told you before, it's a software company. It's known as SSS—Systematic Safe Solutions, LLC."

"Does SSS know you may be filing a discrimination case?"

"I decided not to tell the president, Clarence Chou. I did tell him that I would transfer all non-corporate work to different law firms."

"Carpenter and I will talk about whether you should tell Mr. Chou about the discrimination case. I'll get back to you on that."

"It seems like every move I make presents a new set of problems," Li said in a soft voice.

Philly opted for a morale boost. "But look at it this way: you've solved two major problems. You separated yourself from a firm that treated you shabbily, and you've landed a job with people you like."

"You're saying I should think positively."

"In your case, you've done more than think. You've actually brought about positive results in your life. So, yeah, think positively and give yourself a pat on the back for the positive things you've accomplished."

"Easier said than done."

"What isn't?"

"Listen to this," Rachel said. She was seated at the small kitchen table while Josh saw to washing up the dinner dishes. She had used her iPhone to find the website for Northampton Intensive Tennis Academy and zeroed in on the academy's sales pitch bullet points. "'Instruction by a top-notch staff designed to make each child a formidable competitor.'" It was ironic that the academy and Sloan-Webster had used the same word to describe their respective staffs. "'Tennis isn't our only concern; we care about each child's emotional needs and development, and we recognize that a summer camp is a place to have fun.'"

"Maybe throwing up is supposed to be fun," Josh quipped.

"Here's another one. 'Each child is given a training plan that meets his or her needs. We build confidence and promote sportsmanship in a nurturing environment.'"

"Hence running in hundred-degree heat," Josh commented.

"I've told you about the Sloan-Webster case," Rachel said. "What the plaintiffs in that case are doing is taking the law school's promotional statements and throwing them back in the law school's face. Your student, Noelle, can do the same thing."

Josh placed the last dish in the drying rack. He reached for the ceiling, stretching, and Rachel heard the snap of vertebrae. "The parents might not want to take any legal action," he said, joining Rachel at the kitchen table. "The camp was their idea. Plus, I believe I told you, they think Noelle is a better player than she is. Noelle is an above average player. She has the potential to be a good player. But she'll never be the great player her parents think she already is."

Rachel wondered whether Josh needed to give the parents a facts-of-life talk. That would be an awkward, unpleasant discussion. "Are you going to speak with Noelle's parents?" she asked.

"That's the direction I'm leaning. I'm thinking of sitting down with the parents *and* Noelle. I'm thinking honesty is the best policy here."

"Are you going to say anything about a lawsuit?"

"Yes. I think that goes with the honesty approach."

69

Carpenter had instructed Jeremiah Becker to display no attitude at his deposition, other than a calm and thoughtful confidence. For the most part, under Brian Murphy's initial questioning, Ship Right's president had taken this direction to heart. But now Becker's annoyance was beginning to surface.

"Would you agree, Mr. Becker, that the sale of Ship Right was an important transaction to you and your company?"

Becker glared at Murphy as if the man were an idiot, but Murphy regarded Becker evenly, without attitude, a slight smile on his lips. Carpenter was familiar with how grating Murphy's expression could be on someone excitable such as Becker.

"Yes, it was important."

"If the sale went through, this would be Ship Right owners' only chance to cash out, correct?"

"Right, we were trying to sell the business."

"Why were you trying to sell the business?"

Carpenter realized that he had never asked Becker that question.

"A number of the owners thought it was time. A few of us thought that with terrorist threats all over the place, there could be regulatory changes coming that would change the shipping business for the worse. A few of the owners were getting on in years. We came to a consensus that if we could get the right deal, we would sell."

"What do you mean by the right deal?"

"A good price. A reputable buyer. And some of us wanted a transition period where we would stay on with the company in a meaningful way after the sale."

"Were you one of the owners who wanted to stay on with the company in a meaningful way?"

"Yes."

Murphy wrote on the notepad beside his deposition outline. When he looked up his half smile was still in place.

"Did Ship Right come to an agreement on price with a reputable buyer?"

"Yes."

"Was there an agreement in principle with this reputable buyer that certain owners, including you, would stay on in a transition role?"

"Yes. There was an agreement in principle, but the details hadn't been ironed out."

"These terms that we've been discussing were spelled out in a letter of intent drafted by Blake, Pennington & Dwyer and the buyer's lawyer and signed by Ship Right and the buyer, correct?"

Becker nodded. "Right. But the letter of intent said that a full-blown purchase and sales agreement had to be signed for the deal to happen."

"Did the letter of intent specify that either side could back out of the transaction if the sale wasn't completed within three months from the date on the letter of intent?"

Becker reached for the document, one of various documents marked as exhibits for the record. Becker took his time going over the letter of intent. "Yes, that's what it says."

"So, basically, there was a ninety-day clock running in which the transaction had to be completed, correct?"

"I'd agree with that."

"Is it also correct that given this ninety-day time frame, the parties agreed that they would move forward with *both* the purchase and sale agreement *and* all other matters that had to be addressed at the closing?"

Becker sat silently for a long moment, and Carpenter was relieved that he didn't look like he was in a funk.

"Yes," Becker finally said.

"Are you familiar with transactions involving the sale of a business in which the parties do not proceed with other matters *until* a definitive purchase and sale agreement is signed?"

"Yes."

"Is it correct that for your company's sale, other matters necessary to close the transaction were to be addressed *while* a purchase and sale agreement was being negotiated?"

"I already told you that was the case."

"Would you agree that the method by which Ship Right and its buyer elected to proceed could prove more costly to Ship Right if the parties failed to reach agreement on a purchase and sale agreement?"

"Yes, that's probably right because we would have spent money on other matters."

"Isn't it a fact, Mr. Becker, that you told Mr. Carmichael, the Blake Pennington partner in charge of Ship Right's representation, to do whatever it takes to get the deal done within the ninety-day time period we just discussed?"

Becker glared at Murphy. Carpenter tried to maintain a blank expression. He had asked Becker to recount his discussions with Carmichael. At no time did Becker mention an instruction to Carmichael to do whatever it takes to get the deal done.

"Those weren't my exact words," Becker said.

"What were your exact words?"

"I don't remember exactly, but I did tell him something like do what you have to do to get the deal done on time."

"What did you understand Mr. Carmichael would have to do to meet your directive?"

Becker frowned. "I'm not a lawyer so I didn't really have a complete understanding. I knew we had to transfer our assets which included real estate and patents. I figured that Carmichael would have to draw up bills of sale and things like that."

"Were there corporate formalities that Ship Right would have to address?"

Becker shrugged. "I suppose so. There would have to be corporate votes."

"Did Ship right have contracts with its customers?"

"Yes."

"What was going to happen to those contracts as a result of the sale?"

"Ship Right was going to transfer the contracts to the buyer of the company."

"Did Ship Right have a unilateral right to transfer its contracts?"

"I don't know."

"Isn't it correct that one of the tasks Blake Pennington needed to accomplish in ninety days was a review of each of the contracts Ship Right had with its customers?"

"I suppose so."

"Would it be correct that Ship Right had one hundred thirteen contracts that required the law firm's review?"

"I couldn't tell you the exact number."

"Would you agree that the number of contracts exceeded one hundred?"

"Again, I don't know for sure what the number was, but a hundred sounds about right."

"Would you agree that another Blake Pennington task was to arrange for the contracts to be assigned to the buyer of your business?"

"Again, I suppose so. I wasn't involved in that kind of detail."

"If Ship Right didn't have a right to assign a contract, was Blake Pennington responsible for getting the other party to the contract to agree to the assignment to the buyer?"

"Again, I suppose so. I wasn't really into that level of detail."

Murphy placed Blake Pennington's first bill to Ship Right before Becker. "When this bill came to Ship Right, did you review it?"

"Yes, I went over it."

"Did you contact the Blake firm to object to any item on the bill?"

"No."

"When you reviewed this bill, did you regard any item on the bill as inappropriate for any reason?"

"No."

"Please read to yourself the description of legal services provided on the third day of the month and let me know when you're finished."

Becker read silently and looked up. "I've read it."

"Isn't it correct that the services billed for included review of Ship Right's customer contracts and negotiations with customers to have contracts assigned to Ship Right's buyer?"

"Yes, that's what it says."

Murphy took Becker through fourteen other descriptions of billed work that involved contract review and customer negotiations. To his credit, Becker answered the questions matter-of-factly, without annoyance. But Carpenter knew that his client was inwardly fuming.

Murphy went through a similar series of questions for each of the other bills sent to Ship Right. For each of the bills, Becker acknowledged that he didn't object to any item billed, and identified various charges relating to the review of customer contracts, and to the efforts to obtain customers' consent to the assignment of the contracts to Ship Right's buyer. For the most part, Carpenter was pleased that Becker kept his cool. He could live with Becker looking daggers at Murphy; dirty looks didn't show up on a deposition transcript.

"Did the letter of intent provide for the buyer to have a period for completing its own due diligence?" Murphy asked next.

"Yes. The buyer had forty-five days to review Ship Right's financials and other documents and could back out of the deal if it wasn't satisfied with the results of its review."

"Did Blake Pennington play a role in the buyer's due diligence review?"

"Yes. Ship Right was responsible for most of the due diligence review. We set up a website where documents were posted that the buyer could access through a password. Blake lawyers reviewed documents posted on the site, and I recall they helped Ship Right reply to questions the buyer had with certain documents."

"Is Ship Right complaining about the legal fees charged by the Blake firm in connection with due diligence related matters?"

"Not unless the Blake firm charged for individuals who didn't make any real contribution to the due diligence part of the transaction."

"We've discussed areas where the Blake firm provided services to Ship Right such as contract review, contract negotiation with Ship Right customers, due diligence assistance, and corporate matters such as corporate votes. Did you ever complain about the quality of the firm's work in these or any other areas?"

"No."

"To your knowledge, did anyone else at Ship Right ever complain about the quality of the firm's work?"

"Not to my knowledge."

"Were you satisfied with the quality of the Blake firm's work?"

"I had no cause to complain if that's what you mean."

"No, it's not what I mean. My question was simple. Were you satisfied with the quality of Blake, Pennington & Dwyer's work?"

"I guess so, but I'm not a lawyer so I don't think I'm in any position to critique its work."

"In the last three years, has Ship Right gone to arbitration five times in connection with billing disputes with its customers?"

Becker glared at Murphy. "Yes."

"Did Ship Right prevail in any of those arbitrations?"

Becker took a deep breath. "No."

Murphy consulted his deposition outline. "I don't know about you guys, but I could use a break. Let's take ten minutes. If you want to talk privately, there's a small conference room next door that you can use."

"He's just trying to make me look bad," Becker groused, when they were seated in the conference room.

"Yeah, that's his job," Carpenter acknowledged. "He's trying to bring out that Ship Right comes out on the losing end of billing disputes."

"What if the judge agrees to let this evidence in?" Becker asked.

"If my objection isn't allowed, then the evidence will be before the jury and Murphy will argue that Ship Right continually tries to get out of its contractual obligations and ends up on the losing end."

"So he wants the jury to hate me." Becker said.

"That's the idea."

"Shit! We could lose this case."

Carpenter chose his next words carefully. "I want you to take a deep breath and calm down. When we go back in there, I want you to do what you've been doing. Take your time. Answer Murphy's questions without emotion. So far, Murphy hasn't made a dent in the strongest part of Ship Right's case—the piling-on of billings by lawyers who did nothing. When we go back in there, he's going to go after that part of our case. We've discussed this. He's going to point to the engagement letter where it says the Blake firm would have several of its departments involved in the transaction. You know what your position is."

"Yeah. Ship Right never agreed to pay for a bunch of lawyers who did nothing to sit in on calls and go to meetings."

"Right," Carpenter said. He had to acknowledge that Murphy was doing his job. Their position no longer seemed bulletproof.

"I want you to assume that Ship Right and its buyer did in fact agree to and sign a purchase and sale agreement," Murphy said, about a half hour after Becker's deposition resumed. "Do you understand what I'm asking you to assume?"

Becker nodded glumly. "Yeah."

"If Blake, Pennington & Dwyer had been unable to complete its work in time to permit the sale of Ship Right to take place in ninety days, would Ship Right have held the law firm responsible for the sale not taking place?"

"Objection," Carpenter said. "You may answer," he told Becker.

"I'm pretty sure Ship Right would have considered that option," Becker said. "It's hard for me to answer you without knowing why the ninety-day deadline was missed."

"Are you saying that there could have been any number of occurrences that might have prevented the ninety-day deadline from being met?"

"I suppose that's possible."

"The sale of Ship Right was a large and complicated transaction, wasn't it?"

"Objection," Carpenter said.

"It was a large transaction for us," Becker said. "We were selling the company. As for the transaction being complicated, I can't answer you. I don't believe it was any more complicated than any other sale of a business our size."

"Would you agree that in the sale of any business, something unexpected may come up that can throw a monkey wrench into the plans of the buyer and seller?"

"That's always a possibility."

"When you told Mr. Carmichael to do what he had to do to get the sale done on time, did that include dealing with anything unexpected that might delay the sale?"

"At the time I spoke with Carmichael, I don't recall thinking about unexpected developments. I suppose I assumed that if some unexpected legal matter arose, I would be informed of the matter and briefed as to how the matter was to be addressed."

"Would you agree that an unexpected legal matter might have required the Blake firm to devote substantial manpower to address the problem?"

"It's possible that might have been necessary."

"Would you agree that in devoting manpower to an emergency, it would have been more productive to use lawyers that were familiar with the Ship Right transaction as opposed to lawyers who were unfamiliar with the transaction?"

Becker again paused before answering. "I suppose it would depend on what the emergency was about. For example, there might have been an emergency that could have been explained in a matter of minutes. Or one that could only have been resolved by Ship Right itself, or by some other entity. And I might add that at no time was I ever told by anyone at Blake that an emergency had arisen."

"For the record," Murphy said, "I move to strike the last sentence of the witness' answer."

"Objection," Carpenter said.

Murphy had Becker read aloud a paragraph from the Blake firm's engagement letter with Ship Right.

"That's your signature on this engagement letter, correct, Mr. Becker?"

"Yes."

"When Ship Right was informed in writing in the engagement letter that Blake, Pennington & Dwyer would be using various departments of the firm to handle the Ship Right sale, did you or anybody else at Ship Right object?"

"I didn't object. I'm not aware of anyone else at Ship Right objecting."

"Isn't it true that you were aware that teams of attorneys from various of its departments were being used to handle the sale of Ship Right?"

Becker stared at Murphy and, for the first time during the deposition, smiled. Carpenter couldn't gauge whether the smile was a good or bad sign.

"No," Becker said. "That's not true."

"Why do you say that's not true?"

"Because the bills we received were general bills that were not broken down. It was only after the deal fell through and I demanded backup for the bills that we got the details of what was billed out by attorneys. That was the first time I learned that Blake was loading up on billing for deadwood. Does that answer your question?"

Murphy showed no reaction to Becker's jab; he gazed affably at Becker and returned Becker's smile.

"Why did you wait until the transaction didn't go through to ask for billing backup?"

"I just didn't get around to it," Becker said. "I had my own tasks to complete in connection with the sale and I incorrectly assumed that we weren't getting ripped off."

"How did you come to hire Blake, Pennington & Dwyer for this transaction?"

"Ship Right used a smaller Boston firm for its general work. We didn't think it had the resources to complete the deal, and they pretty much admitted that was the case. They recommended Blake and after we met with Carmichael, we decided to go with them."

"Why didn't Ship Right and the buyer ever sign a purchase and sale agreement?"

"We couldn't agree on the role Ship Right's principals would play in the buyer's organization."

"What exactly was the disagreement?"

"The buyer wanted me and other Ship Right principals to serve in a purely advisory capacity with no ability to vote on business decisions. We wanted a role in decision-making even if that was a minority role."

"Were you the only Ship Right principal who wanted more than an advisory role?"

"No. A majority of the principals wanted more than an advisory role."

Carpenter looked at his deposition outline; he had placed a check mark next to each of the subjects he thought Murphy would cover.

"No further questions," Murphy said.

"No questions," Carpenter echoed.

"This deposition is concluded," Murphy said. "Do you have a minute?" he addressed Carpenter.

"I'll be right back," Carpenter told Becker.

Murphy led Carpenter into the spare conference room. Murphy was totally at ease as he took one of the chairs around the room's small table. Carpenter couldn't help liking his adversary. Murphy oozed charm without coming across as ingratiating. With that barrel chest of his and whitening red hair, Murphy would come across to a jury as both commanding and likeable.

"We meet again, asshole," Murphy led off.

"And you can go fuck yourself," Carpenter played along with their greeting routine.

"Are you having fun yet?" Murphy asked.

"For the most part. How about you?"

"The same," Murphy said. "For the most part. Does it make sense to try to talk about settling this case?"

"I haven't deposed Carmichael yet," Carpenter pointed out.

"So what? We both know what he's going to say."

Murphy was right. Carmichael would justify piling on lawyers for conference calls and meetings on the basis that he wanted a lot of lawyers to be familiar with the transaction so that manpower would be available and knowledgeable in an emergency. Carpenter would drive home the point that no emergency had surfaced and, if an emergency arose, it would have taken minutes to bring lawyers unfamiliar with the transaction up to speed on what needed to be done.

"You're right," Carpenter owned up, wondering if it was fortuitous that Ship Right had not yet filed a Rule 68 motion stating it would accept $325,000. "Do you have anything specific in mind?"

"Sarah and I do. It's nothing we discussed with our client."

"What do you and Sarah have in mind?"

"What do you think we have in mind?"

With most any other lawyer, Carpenter would have remained silent, wanting the other lawyer to be the first to mention a number. With Murphy, he didn't feel the need to show constraint. "Are you thinking about splitting the seven hundred-thousand-dollar baby in half?"

"We are," Murphy admitted. "Sarah and I are trying not to over-think this since thinking isn't our strong suit."

Carpenter laughed. There was a reason he liked Murphy and Warren. Humorous lawyers on the other side were always a plus. Murphy had taken the time to fully investigate Becker. No doubt he and Warren had also reviewed the back up for Blake Pennington's bills, preparing billing charts similar to the ones Meredith had produced. "Splitting the baby makes a kind of sense," Carpenter acknowledged. "So what's the plan?"

"Sarah and I favor the direct approach. We each tell our clients that the lawyers got to talking about settlement and are prepared to recommend to their respective clients dividing the baby in half. Then we duck when our clients direct a serious amount of flak our way."

"You know," Carpenter said, finding he was getting into the spirit of things, "we could try a variation on that approach. I could try to persuade the Blake firm and you could try to persuade Ship Right to take the deal."

This time Murphy laughed. Then he turned serious. "You know, that's not as crazy as it sounds."

"I was kidding around," Carpenter clarified.

"I know. It's weird, but it makes a kind of sick sense."

Carpenter couldn't believe that Murphy was giving serious consideration to what he had thrown out as a joke. "Maybe we need a mediator," he said.

"Fuck mediation," Murphy retorted. "I want to talk this over with Sarah. If we make a recommendation to Blake Pennington, they'll listen with half an ear. I bet the converse is true. Becker has got to be sick of listening to you. Christ, I'm sick of listening to you and we've only been talking for a few minutes. But if I talk to Becker, he'll pay attention. If you talk to Carmichael, he'll pay attention."

"I want to do this the traditional way," Carpenter said. He couldn't tell Murphy that Ship Right was prepared to accept less.

"Pussy," Murphy said.

"Yeah, I am. But I'll discuss this with Philly and my other partners and get back to you. Don't do anything except talk with Sarah until I do."

"What the hell did Murphy want with you?" Becker asked when they were alone in an elevator heading to the ground floor.

"He brought up settlement," Carpenter owned up.

"Does he have a figure in mind?"

"I can't tell you what we discussed."

"Why the hell not?"

"Because there's nothing to discuss at the moment."

"You guys must have said something for Christ's sake!"

Carpenter realized his mistake in mentioning the word settlement. Becker was plainly irritated. He had put up with pointed, unpleasant questions from Murphy and now his own lawyer was giving him a hard time.

"Lawyer talk is often that, just talk. There's no offer on the table. Murphy doesn't have authority to put a number on the table. He mentioned settlement and he's going to discuss the matter with his partner. You need to trust me on this. I have nothing to report."

"A fitting end to a shitty day," Becker muttered.

70

"What's the hurry?" Josh asked.

Rachel had been scurrying around, a little out of control. "Carpenter scheduled a partners' meeting at eight thirty. I don't want to be late."

"It's been a while since the four of you met," Josh said.

"Tell me about it," Rachel said as she downed the last of her green tea and set the mug in the sink. "Carpenter wants to review the few active cases we have. We really could use more business."

"You may get your wish," Josh said. "Remember that girl, Noelle, I mentioned to you?"

Rachel slowed down and gave Josh her full attention. He was seated at the kitchen table wearing only running shorts. His well-muscled, tanned body got her thinking about showing up late to the partners' meeting.

"I met with Mr. and Mrs. Campbell along with Noelle. I went over Noelle's tennis game in detail and gave them a frank assessment of her ability. Noelle didn't seem surprised by my evaluation, but her parents were. You could see the disappointment in their eyes when it became clear that I didn't think Noelle was already a superstar. I told them all that the best thing I could do for Noelle was to help her put the tennis academy summer behind her and help her recapture her love for the game. The thing is, Noelle does love the sport. I went through the areas where I thought I could help Noelle's game improve. I think Noelle was grateful for my honesty. I'm not so sure her parents were. The last thing I said to them was that I had talked to a lawyer friend about what had happened at the academy and the lawyer thought Noelle might have grounds for a lawsuit. When I checked my e-mail this morning, Mr. Campbell had sent me a message saying he and his wife would be interested in talking to the lawyer I mentioned."

"Wow! That sounds great."

Josh frowned. "I have no feel for whether this is something Noelle wants to do, or whether this is something only her parents have in mind. My gut tells me that it would be a mistake to do anything legally unless Noelle was fully on board."

"Didn't you say that you thought a lawsuit might help Noelle deal with what went on at the academy?" Rachel asked.

"I did. But only if Noelle agrees to sue."

Philly thought only the partners were meeting, but Carpenter had apparently asked Meredith to sit in. Philly studied the gathering. They really were a motley crew. The geezer had on his grouchy game face. Simon still slicked his hair back on the sides but for some reason he no longer looked rail thin. The warm smile on Rachel's round face framed by short blond hair always made Philly feel good. Meredith was sitting erect in her chair, serious and somewhat imperious, but maybe that last impression had to do with her height: she towered above everybody at the table.

"I want to go over cases," Carpenter announced without fanfare. "It's been a while since we sat down face-to-face to do that. What prompted me to meet was the possibility of settlement negotiations in the Ship Right case, and I'd like to start with that."

Philly sipped a Dunkin' Donuts iced coffee and took notes while Carpenter talked. He told them he'd mentioned the scenario of each lawyer talking to the other's client as a joke but that Murphy had liked the suggestion.

"What's the point of Murphy talking to Becker?" Philly asked.

"None," Carpenter admitted. "But Murphy doesn't know that."

"I've never heard of anything like this," Philly said. "Have you?"

"No," Carpenter said. "As I said, I was joking when I mentioned this approach."

"Becker would have to playact," Simon pointed out.

"That might not go well," Carpenter conceded. "I can picture Becker smirking while Murphy tried to convince him of something he already was willing to accept. Murphy would know something was off."

"What happens if you tell Murphy you each have to convince your own clients?" Rachel asked.

"We each try to convince our own clients," Carpenter responded.

"Which is the way settlement is usually done," Rachel said.

It wasn't a question, but Carpenter answered, "Yes."

"It seems we've sorted this out," Simon said. "Tell Murphy that he has to deal with this guy Carmichael."

Carpenter nodded perfunctorily as if something was bugging him.

"Do you trust Murphy?" Meredith asked.

"Trust him?" Carpenter snapped, leveling his death ray stare at Meredith, which seemed to Philly to bounce off her. "The guy's a devious litigator and when we're on opposite sides in a courtroom, the man's capable of any and every trick in the book. But yeah, I trust him. I don't think he'd lie to me."

"I should have been more specific," Meredith said. "Do you trust his assessment that you will have a better chance of convincing Carmichael to settle than he would have?"

"Yeah, I guess I do," Carpenter said grudgingly.

"Then you should agree to what he wants; you should talk to Carmichael and tell Becker to act surprised and outraged when Murphy talks to him."

"I'm listening," Carpenter said, and Philly saw he was engaged.

"Becker wants to settle," Meredith began. "So the focus should be on how to get the client what he wants. If Murphy and you agree that the best way to get Blake, Pennington & Dwyer to settle is for you to take a run at Carmichael, then that's the route to follow. I think it really is that simple."

Carpenter didn't say anything.

"There's another factor," Meredith said. "You mentioned Murphy thought it would be fun for each of you to take on the other's client. I think he's right. It would be a blast."

"A blast?" Carpenter echoed.

"If this guy Carmichael is like some of the senior partners who head up departments at a big firm, then you and Carmichael should hit it off famously."

Meredith was grinning broadly, and Philly joined her. "I think Meredith's made some pretty convincing points," Philly said.

Carpenter mumbled something unintelligible.

"If you do meet with Carmichael," Meredith continued, "make sure you meet with him here. You want him to get a good look at where he's going to be deposed if the case doesn't settle."

"All right," Carpenter said. "You've convinced me. Any dissent? No? Okay, that's one matter dealt with. But I'm going to have to deal with Murphy over this unconventional approach. I said it as a joke, but he's now going to take full credit for the idea, especially if it leads to a settlement. What do you want to talk about next?"

"We're waiting for the court's ruling on the class action motion in the Sloan-Webster case," Simon reported. "Depositions are pretty much done unless Blaisedell decides to depose the new placement office head."

"Does that mean you're getting ready for trial?" Philly asked.

Simon glanced Rachel's way before responding. "We haven't gone into trial preparation mode," he said. "Rachel and I have been trying to figure out if there's a way to settle the case. Part of the problem has to do with the class action motion. If we prevent the case going forward as a class action, how do we settle with the three plaintiffs to ensure that some other graduate doesn't come out of the woodwork and sue the law school?"

"We went through this with the Spenser case," Philly pointed out. "You can't protect the law school from a suit by another graduate. The best we could do in the Spenser case was to get Blaisedell to agree that *he* wouldn't bring a new lawsuit against the law school or solicit any person to sue the law school. I think he also agreed not to get involved with any lawsuit brought by somebody else against the law school."

"But Blaisedell didn't get any money for the plaintiffs in the Spenser case," Rachel pointed out. "We don't believe that's going to be the case for Sloan-Webster. We think it's in Sloan-Webster's interests to settle the case, but frankly we don't know when or whether to bring up settlement, and what a fair settlement might be."

"Would Blaisedell be willing to talk about settlement before the judge rules on the class action motion?' Philly asked.

"We don't know," Rachel said.

"And you're not sure which way the judge is going to rule on the class action motion although you think you may have the better side of that motion," Philly added.

"Right," Rachel said.

"Sometimes a judge's ruling on a motion can clarify and narrow a case," Carpenter said. "I don't have any real basis for saying this, but I think you have to wait for the judge to rule on the class action motion before getting involved with settlement. Remember that settlement wasn't broached by Blaisedell in the Spenser case until *after* he lost his class action motion."

Neither Simon nor Rachel seemed happy with waiting for the judge to rule, but Philly believed that Carpenter had made a valid point; sometimes you simply had to let a court narrow or expand the issues in a case.

"We've drafted a discrimination complaint with the MCAD for Ai Li," Philly said, moving on, "and we're waiting to hear back from her." Philly went on to explain that Li had not informed her new employer about suing her former firm for discrimination. "Should she disclose that to her new company?"

Silence greeted her question.

"I think she has to tell her new employer," Meredith spoke up. "Her old law firm is still doing work for this company and will be doing work for the company until Li finds other law firms to take over that work."

"I agree," Carpenter said. "*Before* you file any discrimination complaint, have Li tell her new boss what's up so she can find out whether he's okay with what she wants to do."

There was no other suggestion forthcoming. "I think we're adjourned," Philly said.

Carpenter asked Meredith to leave the conference room; he needed a word with his partners. Philly suspected Meredith was hurt by the exclusion, but the fact was, she wasn't a partner.

"We need to get back to Harris Burton and Ben Klein," Carpenter said. "We owe them a response."

Philly wished they could all just stay in denial. "Why don't we tell him the truth," she suggested. "The truth being that we can't make up our minds. That is, unless some of you have made up your minds."

"If you pressed me at this moment, I would say no," Carpenter said. "The only relationship I would even consider is one where we were independent and only shared overhead. We know that our overhead would more than double if we went to Sizemore Klein and I don't like that."

"I'm for keeping the discussions moving forward," Simon said. "Subject to meeting and liking these guys, I would seriously consider linking up with them."

"I can't make up my mind," Rachel confessed.

"I'm in Rachel's camp," Philly declared.

Carpenter sighed. "Without mentioning names, why don't I tell Harris where the four of us stand," he proposed.

"I'm fine with that," Philly said.

"Okay," Simon and Rachel said together.

"Now we're really adjourned," Philly said.

October

Philly's Untitled Playlist

"Royals"

Lorde

71

A Teenage Tennis Player

The Campbells' colonial in Concord was set well back from the winding, tree-lined, two-lane road that Rachel had been following for the last five minutes. If a mailbox with the house number hadn't been roadside, she probably never would have found the place. As she started up the driveway, Rachel was glad she hadn't mentioned Noelle Campbell's situation at the last partnership meeting. It was too iffy to be a real case. Also, Noelle was a minor and while her parents got to make decisions for her, Noelle was the real client. Until she had talked with the girl alone, Rachel wouldn't feel comfortable representing her no matter what her parents wanted to do.

Rachel parked at the end of a circular loop fronting the house. A fenced-in tennis court was situated a short distance behind the house.

Mr. Campbell greeted her at the door. Rachel shook hands with a man she guessed was in his mid-forties. His grip was weak. He didn't look like an athlete. He was short and thin with no evidence of wiry strength. "Call me Gene," Campbell said without turning around as he led her toward the back of the house.

Rachel followed Campbell into a family room where his wife was seated. "I'm Carrie," the woman said as she rose from a couch. Rachel guessed that Mrs. Campbell was the source of Noelle's athletic genes. The woman was broad-shouldered and fit with a dark tan that called attention to her blue eyes. The Campbells were dressed identically: khaki pants and red collared polo shirts with a logo over the pocket that Rachel couldn't make out.

"I thought we'd chat briefly without Noelle," Mr. Campbell said. "Carrie and I are appalled by what Noelle went through at her camp. When Josh mentioned that he had talked with a lawyer who thought Noelle's rights may have been violated, we wanted to explore the possibility of legal action. How do you know Josh?"

"We're in a relationship," Rachel said.

"I see," Mr. Campbell said, and Rachel couldn't tell whether he was put off by her disclosure. "Why do you think Noelle may have a legal claim?"

"I looked at the tennis academy's website. The academy holds itself out as running a program that will improve a student's game in a nurturing, fun environment. What Josh described as happening to Noelle hardly seemed nurturing or fun. Also, as a matter of common sense, why would anyone make a young girl run around in hundred-degree heat until she threw up?"

The Campbells fell silent.

"We want to be honest with you," Mrs. Campbell finally said. "We chose this tennis camp for a reason. Frankly, we were hoping it would toughen Noelle up. Between us, we've seen pretty much all her matches. She's a solid player, but she lacks a killer instinct that we think is needed to really excel at the sport. We were hoping the academy would provide that killer instinct."

"From what Josh told me, the academy experience left Noelle more tentative than when she started."

Mr. Campbell nodded. "We're worried about her."

Were they concerned that their dreams of tennis stardom for Noelle were no longer realistic, or were they concerned for their daughter's emotional welfare? Rachel didn't ask. "What does Noelle think about getting a lawyer involved?"

"I think it makes her nervous," Mrs. Campbell said.

"That's understandable," Rachel said. "Why don't we hear from your daughter?"

Mrs. Campbell left the family room and during her absence Mr. Campbell remained silent. His wife returned holding the hand of a willowy girl dressed in tennis whites. Noelle had light brown hair, blue eyes that matched her mother's, and a long, thin face. No doubt her ponytail would protrude from the back of a tennis cap.

"Hi, Noelle. I'm Rachel Boyle. I've been looking forward to meeting you. Josh is a friend of mine, and he's told me a little bit about what happened at the tennis camp."

Noelle averted her eyes when she shook hands. Rachel felt for the girl. This had to be more than awkward for her. "What I'd like to do," Rachel continued, "is to say a few things to you and your parents, and then spend a few minutes talking to you alone."

"You're his girlfriend, right?" Noelle interrupted.

"That's right."

Noelle nodded as if that answered a question she'd been pondering.

"Josh basically asked me whether what happened to you at the tennis camp was legal. The camp's website described the camp environment as nurturing and fun. As I just explained to your parents, those website statements about a nurturing and fun environment can be looked at as promises made by the camp. In your case, from what I've heard, the camp didn't keep those promises to you. Therefore, you may have legal claims against the camp."

Rachel couldn't tell whether anything she had said registered with Noelle. "Here are some options that you have. First, you can do nothing. You can continue to take private lessons with Josh and put the tennis camp experience behind you. Second, you could decide to take legal action against the camp because the camp broke its promise that it would provide you with a nurturing and fun environment. Bringing a lawsuit is a big step that should be considered very carefully. Lawsuits can be stressful. Also, there's no guaranty that any lawsuit will be successful. Do you understand these options?"

Noelle nodded. Rachel didn't know whether to trust the gesture. "Noelle, why don't we take a little walk? You can show me around outside."

Once outside, Rachel pointed to the tennis court. "That's got to be neat having your own tennis court," she said, hoping to draw Noelle out.

"It's okay."

"How long have you been playing?"

"Since I was a little kid."

"Has Josh ever hit with you on this court?"

Noelle shook her head. "We hit at the club where he gives lessons."

"Josh has given me lessons," Rachel said. "I'm pretty pathetic. But he's been patient with me, and I have to say I like getting outdoors and rallying with him. I still can't serve."

Noelle didn't say anything but she looked slightly embarrassed, leaving Rachel to wonder whether the girl had a crush on Josh. Well, who wouldn't? "What do you like about tennis?"

"It's fun," Noelle said with feeling that Rachel found genuine. "When I get in a rhythm it's like everything else disappears. It's like I'm in a zone and nobody can touch me. I love that feeling."

Rachel couldn't identify with Noelle's response. She had never felt in a zone even during sustained tennis rallies with Josh. "Why don't you show me the rest of the back yard?"

Noelle led the way across a large, immaculate lawn bordered by trees. Two fenced off gardens were set to the rear of the lawn, one a vegetable garden, the other a flower garden with red and white roses in the center.

"What do you think about what I had to say about a lawsuit?" Rachel asked.

"I don't know," Noelle said in a soft voice.

"Do you have any questions for me?"

Noelle shrugged.

They paused next to the vegetable garden which was dominated by zucchinis with impressive dimensions.

"A lot of the girls threw up," Noelle said out of the blue.

"Why don't you tell me about that?"

"Some of the girls expected to throw up. They knew this camp worked everyone very hard and they thought if they didn't throw up, they weren't working hard enough. For them throwing up wasn't a big deal."

"Was it a big deal for you?"

"I didn't like it. I was embarrassed and I felt sick. Josh would never do anything like that."

"What I heard was that it was very hot, and you were doing some kind of running drills as a punishment."

"I was having trouble hitting my backhand down the line. I kept hitting the ball into the net or long. The instructor was yelling at me that I wasn't concentrating. But I *was* concentrating. Finally, he yelled at me to put my racquet down and do ten laps around the outside of the courts. I finished five laps before I threw up."

"Was there anything about the camp that you liked?"

"I liked some of the girls I bunked with. There were a group of us that hung out together. We weren't in the gung-ho group."

"What do you mean?"

"We weren't in the group that thought it was okay to throw up."

Rachel resumed walking, leading Noelle to the front of the house, which was set so far back from the two-lane road that she could barely make it out from where they stood.

"You don't have to decide today about this lawsuit business," Rachel said. "Take as much time as you need."

"My parents want me to sue them."

"What do you want?" Rachel asked.

"Part of me wants to forget the whole thing," Noelle said with some force.

"What does the rest of you want?"

Noelle chewed her lower lip, and it was all Rachel could do to hold off putting a comforting hand on her shoulder.

"I guess the rest of me wants to get back at them so they don't embarrass anyone else. And there's another thing. Ever since I threw up, my game has sucked big time."

The teenager's last comment tied in with Josh's saying that the teenager might have to take a stand against the tennis camp to regain her game. "I hope Josh is getting your game back to where it should be," Rachel said. "If he's not, let me know and I'll whip him into shape."

Noelle offered a shy smile.

"Take a few days to think about everything," Rachel suggested. "This isn't about what your parents want, although it's important for you to listen to what they have to say. This is about what *you* want. You're the only person who knows what that is."

Noelle seemed overwhelmed and this time Rachel did reach out and gave her a pat on the back. "Whatever you decide is fine. I'm going to take off now, but first I need to say goodbye to your parents. Here's my business card. You should feel free to call me anytime with questions."

Noelle took the card and stared at it. Then she put it in a pocket of her tennis shorts and led the way back inside.

72

"You were right about two things," Ai Li said.

"That's good to hear," Philly said. She was outside, pushing Daniel in his stroller on a tour around the block. Daniel had started out on the ground, pushing the stroller while hanging on to the back of it for balance. But the stroller was too high for him to see where he was going, and he soon ran out of gas. After complaining briefly about being strapped in, he settled down babbling to himself and seemed to find what he had to say interesting. For which Philly was grateful. A fussing Daniel would have meant calling Li back later.

"I told Clarence Chao that I was going to sue my former law firm for discrimination and wanted to make sure he was comfortable with my doing so. It was clear he wasn't comfortable, but he finally said okay."

"Why?" Philly asked.

"Because I played the Chinese card. I told him I was the only Asian partner at the firm, and they had refused to promote me any further even though I was better qualified than the partners who got promoted. Chou understood. Let's just say he had experienced some incidents of discrimination when he was starting to get SSS off the ground."

"Did you tell Chou you wouldn't sue if he objected?"

"I told him I wouldn't sue until all legal work was transferred if he preferred. He said that wasn't necessary."

"That's pretty sporting of him."

"The Chinese card is a powerful card."

"What else did I get right?"

"Henrietta Coleman called me and said that she and the other members of the management committee remained concerned about my mentioning discrimination. She asked me if I wanted to talk about my issues and see if there was a way to resolve my concerns. I gave her your name and number. I think she was shocked that I had an attorney, but she hid it well."

"You did the right thing," Philly said.

"I hope so. She sounded very reasonable and sincere."

"I'm sure she did. Again, you did the right thing."

"Is someone talking in the background?" Li asked.

"That's my son you're hearing. He's talking gibberish to himself."

"Where are you?"

"We're taking a walk. My office is mobile in case you were wondering."

Li didn't say anything. Philly figured that she was again doubting the wisdom of engaging a lawyer who worked from home and was distracted by two little kids.

"You'll call me if you hear from Coleman?"

"Of course. You'll be the second to know."

"Is all of this necessary?" Jeremiah Becker griped.

"Yeah it is," Carpenter said. He was in the conference room, going over Sloan-Webster deposition transcripts, when Becker interrupted by returning a call placed earlier in the day. Carpenter described what he and Murphy proposed to do to settle the Ship Right case and explained why he believed both Murphy and Warren were in favor of the strategy. Becker heard him out and then asked the question Carpenter had anticipated—was he expected to play along?

"Yes, it's necessary. You need to play along, act as if splitting the seven hundred thousand is an outrage. Think of it as a time to have fun and role play."

Fun!" Becker thundered. "It's on my fucking dime!"

"That's the spirit," Carpenter said.

"You think this is funny?" Becker roared.

"To be frank with you, yeah. It's funny in a surreal way. But if it gets you where you want to be, I'm all for it."

"Does this mean I have to listen to more shit about billing disputes Ship Right lost?" Becker asked in a normal tone.

"It does. Murphy is going to insult the hell out of you and do his best to piss you off. He's going to tell you that if you don't take the deal, a jury will award Ship Right nothing because Ship Right has made it a practice to try to weasel out of its contracts with customers. If I was a betting man, I'd bet that Murphy will use the word weasel when he talks to you."

"And I'm just supposed to sit there and take his shit?"

"Yes. You don't have to say a word."

"Like that's going to happen," Becker snarled.

"I've spoken to Murphy. We've agreed that he'll meet with you and I'll meet with Carmichael simultaneously. When I'm finished with Carmichael, the four of us will meet at Murphy's office and we'll see if we have a deal."

Becker fell silent. Carpenter wished Ship Right's president would lighten up, see the bizarre nature of the situation, and find a degree of satisfaction that the case could quickly be over if things went as he and Murphy hoped they would.

"What are you going to say to Carmichael?"

"I haven't worked out the precise details," Carpenter replied. "I need to turn my attention to that after I finish with another matter. But I can tell you how I'm going to start out. After reiterating the split-the-baby-in-half financial deal that Murphy and I are pushing and watching him throw a conniption fit, I'm going to tell him he'd be a fool not to take the deal. I'm going to remind him that he's a goddamn lawyer and the general public regards lawyers as just a shade above child molesters. Anybody on the jury who has ever been billed by a lawyer is going to hate his guts before he opens his mouth. As soon as the jurors hear that his firm billed Ship Right for hundreds of thousands of dollars for people who did nothing, the jury is going to award his firm a big fat fucking zero."

Carpenter expected a reaction from Becker. He had laid it on thick so he'd get a rise out of him. But there was silence on the other end of the phone. The silence then gave way to a noise. For a moment Carpenter couldn't figure out what he was hearing. Then recognition dawned. Becker was laughing.

"I want you to say that to Carmichael just the way you said it to me," Becker said when he calmed down.

"It'll be a pleasure," Carpenter said.

Philly snuggled next to Paul on his side of the bed. The kids were down for the night and the house was quiet. It occurred to Philly that she rarely told Paul when she was happy. "I'm happy," she whispered.

"What brought that on?" Paul whispered back.

"I was just thinking about the big picture," Philly continued to whisper. "The kids are great. You're pretty terrific. I'm sticking with AA and it's working. And we've settled some cases where I think we really helped our clients."

"I still can't get over that case with Frankie Barton's mom... Sasha. That was really creative on your part."

"Thanks. That's the case I'm most proud of. I just loved all the kids we had to deal with."

"Does the fact that you're happy mean you guys have enough business?" Paul kept his voice low.

"No," Philly said laughing. "Leave it to you to burst my bubble."

"What are you going to do about that merger offer?" Paul asked.

"Another bubble burst!" Philly didn't know what to do. She was truly conflicted. "What do you think I should do? Our overhead would more than double if we hooked up with them."

"I'm not in a position to tell you what to do," Paul said. "The only advice I have is not to run scared. I get it that there's a lot of risk if you hook up with Philip's old firm, including financial risk. But we both know there's risk in everything. I would try to look into the future about five years and try to picture the future you want. This guy Burton might not be around and Carpenter might not be around either. What scenario has the best chance of giving you the future you want?"

"What I really want, I can't have," Philly said. "I want to continue to have cases that are interesting, and I don't want to have to agonize over new business coming in. I suppose that's what every lawyer wants. Look at Carpenter. He's been grinding along for decades without any guaranty a new case will come in the door."

Paul didn't say anything. He rubbed her back and then her shoulders.

"We'd really be screwed without Carpenter in the picture," Philly said after a while. "He's got these instincts from being around forever that the rest of us don't have."

"Then maybe you're thinking of hooking up with the wrong firm," Paul said. "Burton's firm doesn't do litigation, which is why they want you, of course. Maybe what you guys need is a firm that does litigation and has a senior person who's younger than Carpenter but has a lot of Carpenter's experience."

"Stop making sense," Philly said, laughing. "Besides, Carpenter would never go for anything like that."

"Have you asked him?"

"I'm not sure I have it in me to do that," Philly admitted.

73

"*You* open it," Rachel said, her hand shaking as she handed Simon the envelope addressed from the superior court.

Simon took the envelope. The decision from Judge Charlotte Hayes was going to determine how they would spend the next months of their lives. And yet, as was the case last year when Christopher Blaisedell's class action motion was decided in the Spenser case, Simon felt calm. As he did last year, he once again reflected that maybe there was something seriously wrong with him because he wasn't experiencing any of the anxiety that gripped Rachel. "Sit," he said, pointing toward Philly's desk chair.

There was something comical about the way Rachel made a beeline for the chair. Simon parked himself in the visitor's chair, opened the envelope, extracted the judge's ruling, and began to read.

"Go to the bottom line," Rachel entreated.

Simon continued to take his time. The decision was nine pages and it was immediately clear that the judge had given considerable thought to her ruling. Like the judge or not, the parties were going to have to address a reasoned opinion.

"Branson is the only plaintiff she found suitable to represent the class," Simon announced after completing the first part of the decision. This news did nothing to settle Rachel's nerves, so he resumed reading.

"This is interesting. The judge says that while the three plaintiffs may have had contacts with the placement office, members of the class the plaintiffs seek to represent may not have contacted the placement office at all. Therefore, the class identified by the plaintiffs is too broad. Students and graduates who never contacted the placement office were not in a position to claim that the placement office prevented them from getting a law-related job. For some of the plaintiffs' claims, the class should be limited to students and graduates who actually contacted the placement office as opposed to all students and graduates who have not been able to find a law-related job."

Rachel had gathered herself. She was writing on her notepad.

Simon resumed reading. "The judge says that it's impossible to generalize as to why each member of the purported class can't find a legal job. She says that when it comes to damages, each of the plaintiffs and each member of the purported class may present a unique situation as to why he or she has been unable to find legal work."

He looked up toward Rachel. "You know, that's pretty much the argument you gave her, and it looks like she agreed. At least about some of it."

Simon returned to the judge's decision. "While the damage part of the case may not present common issues of fact and law, that fact does not mean that class certification is inappropriate generally or for various legal claims made by the plaintiffs."

"That's troubling," Rachel said.

Simon neared the end of the ruling. "There are common issues that are appropriate for a class action. She points to the plaintiffs' claims that the defendants misrepresented the quality of the law school faculty and used the word placement to describe an office that never placed anybody."

"Shit!" Rachel exclaimed.

Simon finished reading. "Bottom line," he said. "The judge is denying the motion to certify a class without prejudice to the plaintiffs renewing their motion after trial. The case will proceed to trial. At the conclusion of the trial, before any findings and rulings on liability, the plaintiffs may request the court to hold a hearing to consider the plaintiffs' class action claims, any issues relating to narrowly defined subclasses, and damages to potential individual class members. In the event the plaintiffs prevail on any of their claims, the court may conclude that a separate evidentiary hearing is necessary to resolve such class action issues, and that a master should be appointed to consider individual damage claims."

Rachel finished her notetaking. Simon handed her the judge's decision which she proceeded to read.

Simon was struck by the speed of Rachel's mood shift. Gone was her high anxiety. She seemed to have totally blocked out everything else as she calmly applied herself to the judge's ruling.

"Aren't the class action aspects of a case usually sorted out before a trial?" Simon asked once Rachel had finished her review.

"Usually. But there's precedent for what the judge did here." Rachel paused, lost in thought. "I'm trying to picture the reaction of Martin and Cray," she said.

"Forget that for a moment," Simon responded. "Let's first address the question Carpenter would ask."

"Which side would you want to be on if you got this decision?" Rachel filled in, waving the judge's ruling in Simon's direction.

"I'd still rather be us than them," Simon said. "Two of the plaintiffs got discredited and, for the moment at least, there's no class."

"All things considered, you're right. I think we did okay. What do we do about Martin and Cray?" Rachel asked.

Simon checked his watch. Eleven o'clock. "First thing is to scan this ruling and send it to Carpenter, Philly, and Meredith. I'll ask for their immediate reactions by one o'clock. At one, I'll be sending the ruling to our client without comment but with a request that we discuss the ruling later in the day."

"Why without comment?"

Simon shrugged. "Instinct. Who knows? Maybe we'll get lucky and they'll think this is a total victory."

"They're going to ask what's next."

"The way I see it, trial or settlement."

In her home office, Philly finished reading the class action ruling in the Sloan-Webster case. She started out her e-mail with *CONGRATULATIONS!* Her general impression was that Rachel and Simon had won the battle, though the outcome of the war remained in doubt. Carpenter and Meredith might have a different view, but she thought Rachel and Simon had earned her praise. She then made the point that Christopher Blaisedell was now in the position of trying a case in which the judge had found two of his three plaintiffs unsuitable to take the lead in a class action. As she touched Send her phone rang.

"Philly Sullivan."

"Ms. Sullivan, this is Henrietta Coleman from Hazelton, Kauffman, Garfield & Smith. I'm informed you represent Ai Li."

Philly took a deep breath. "Give me a minute, please." She opened her working file in the Li case and placed her draft of the complaint to the MCAD in front of her. "How can I help you?"

"Is this a bad time?"

"No," Philly said. "I had just finished something up and needed a moment to find my file."

"No doubt you're aware that your client has left our firm. Before she left, she claimed that she was discriminated against because she wasn't promoted to the next partnership level. We're very concerned about her claim. We treat any allegation of discrimination with the utmost seriousness. When I approached her to discuss addressing her concerns, she referred me to you."

"And here I am," Philly said. "How can I help you?" she repeated.

"Perhaps you can share with me the reasons why your client believes she was subject to discrimination."

Philly decided to be up front with Coleman. Anything she said would shortly be available to Coleman in the MCAD complaint she was about to file.

"Ms. Li believes that she was a superior candidate for the next partnership level compared to the individuals who were promoted. For example, she believes that her billable hours consistently exceeded the billable hours of the three individuals who were promoted. This is information that your firm would know, and perhaps you're in a position to confirm that fact."

Coleman didn't immediately respond. Philly was certain that Coleman had the billable hour information at her fingertips. Coleman had called seeking information; would she balk at providing information?

"I don't have the information in front of me, but I believe that you are correct with respect to billable hours," Coleman said. "But I'm sure you know that billable hours are not the sole factor used in making partner promotion decisions."

Philly ignored Coleman's qualification. Coleman had just confirmed an important fact. "Ms. Li believes that unlike the three individuals who were promoted, she brought to your firm a client that was billed nearly one million dollars as recently as last year. Again, this is something that I'm sure you can verify as head of your firm's management committee."

If Coleman disliked being put on the receiving end of requests for information, she hid her irritation well. "The individuals who were promoted have generated business for the firm, but none of them has produced a client with the volume of business that Ms. Li's client has generated."

Philly had now confirmed two of Li's suspicions. "Ms. Li was told that two firm clients she did work for described her as aloof even though neither of these clients complained about her work. She was told that the aloof comments were likely responsible for her not being promoted. She views that stated reason for denying her a promotion as a pretext for discrimination based on her race and sex."

"I'm just taking a few notes," Coleman said, which Philly viewed as an attempt to buy time. "Obviously, our firm disputes that it discriminates against anybody based on sex or race. The aloof comments were seriously discussed by the partners before they voted on Ai's promotion. An individual advancing up our partnership ladder more and more becomes the face of our firm as she or he climbs higher. People skills are important in our view, and Ms. Li was regarded by two clients as deficient in this area. I don't know if she mentioned this to you, but after she was promoted to the fifth partnership level, she was told by the management committee that she needed to work on people skills such as communication and being able to socialize with firm clients. This was something other senior partners had observed needed work on her part. And obviously, clients picked up on this deficiency."

Now Philly was writing. Li had not previously mentioned this last bit of intelligence. The law firm's defense for not promoting Li had just become more focused and credible.

"Thanks for being forthcoming," Philly said.

"I would point out that I wouldn't be in the position I hold at the firm—the top management position by the way—if the firm practiced sex discrimination."

"Ms. Li told me that the other two members of your management committee were men. She believed that management committee decisions were decided by majority vote."

"What's your point?" Coleman asked sharply.

"One of the things that struck me," Philly said, "was that the top five partnership levels at your firm are dominated by men. Since partner votes are weighted by the partner's partnership level, men actually control your firm."

"With all due respect to you, Ms. Sullivan, that sounds like pretty desperate grasping at straws."

Philly had expected no other reaction from Coleman. "We'll see what the data show," she replied.

"Does this mean you're going forward and filing a complaint with the MCAD?" Coleman asked.

"That's my present intention."

"For obvious reasons, we would like to head that off," Coleman said. "Are you prepared to make any settlement demand at this time?"

"No."

"In that case, I believe we have nothing further to discuss. If you and Ms. Li figure out what you're looking for and come up with a settlement demand *before* filing a complaint, you know where to find me." Coleman abruptly ended the call.

Philly studied her draft complaint. The relief sought in the complaint was general: a finding and ruling that Li had been subject to discrimination and an award of damages that did not identify an amount. In any settlement, Coleman's firm would refuse to admit to any liability. If Li was seeking a public vindication, she was going to have to take her case to trial.

Dean Martin had requested a five o'clock meeting at her office, and Simon had promptly agreed. The comments from his partners and Meredith on Judge Hayes' class action ruling had not been particularly helpful, but Simon was intrigued by Philly's point that Blaisedell now had to go to trial with two plaintiffs whom the judge had determined were not appropriate candidates to represent a class. Blaisedell could, of course, try to swap out the gambler and the exotic dancer with different plaintiffs, but doing so would look bad, and Simon suspected that Blaisedell's desire not to look bad before Judge Hayes was as strong as his own.

For this meeting, the dean had commandeered a conference room that was nearly as cramped as her office. A secretary had shown Simon and Rachel to their seats and promptly at five o'clock, the dean led Ralph Cray and Neil Taylor into the room.

"I don't know how you lawyers deal with this stuff," Cray groused as he took his seat. "I get it that lawyers speak their own language, but I had a hard time understanding what the judge decided. I think we both won and lost."

Simon nodded at Rachel. They'd agreed that she would field questions about the court ruling, and he would deal with questions about what was next.

"That is one way to look at it," Rachel said, "but the fact is that the plaintiffs' motion to certify a class was denied. Therefore, as we speak, we are not dealing with a class action on any claim, including the claim that the placement office prevented students from finding law-related jobs. Before the court is only the claim that the placement office failed these three particular students. That's the good news.

"The less than good news is that the judge will hold a hearing to reconsider the plaintiffs' class action request after the case is tried, and she identified two of the plaintiffs' claims that could be raised for all graduates: misrepresenting the quality of the law school's faculty and using the word placement for an office that never placed anybody."

"So we might have to go through two trials," Cray said irritably.

"That could happen," Rachel said.

"What happens next?" the dean asked.

"I'll address that in a moment," Simon took over, "but first it might be helpful to think about how Blaisedell might view the judge's decision. The judge has given him two options. He can go to trial with the plaintiffs he has, but not as a class action. Or to avoid trial, he can try to settle the case. What would you do in his situation?"

When his question drew no takers, Simon resumed. "One of our partners made an interesting observation. She pointed out that if Blaisedell goes to trial now, two of his three plaintiffs are under a cloud since the judge found that neither Hightower nor White were suitable to represent a class."

Taylor grinned. Martin and Cray remained serious.

"Are you saying that Blaisedell might now consider settlement?" Martin asked.

"That's our thinking. Blaisedell knows that if there is a trial, we will make a strong case that the reason White can't get a legal job is because she engages in lap dancing and that Hightower can't get a legal job because the man has a serious gambling problem. That leaves him with Branson. And if a jury sees Branson squirming when asked about the college cheating incident, like he did at his deposition, the jury may decide he's as bad as the other two."

"Are you going to contact Blaisedell?" Cray asked.

"I don't see a downside. Unless you tell me otherwise, that's what we recommend doing."

Martin and Cray exchanged a glance. "What the hell, go for it," Martin said.

"May I say something," Taylor requested.

Simon had forgotten momentarily that the new placement office head was in the room. "Please do," he invited.

"As you know, I've been contacting graduates and asking them to provide information on their current employment status. The overwhelming majority of responses have come from graduates with legal jobs. This may well be a skewed response because graduates who have law-related jobs arguably are more likely to respond to a survey than graduates who don't. But what's interesting to me is how many respondents have taken the time to provide comments in the space provided. Almost without exception, the comments reflect well on the law school. I've seen comments saying the law school provided excellent preparation for the responder's legal job. Some individuals have expressed gratitude to the law school for admitting them when no other law school would. Overall, it's rather moving what graduates are saying."

Rachel noted the look of surprise on the faces of Martin and Cray. Martin seemed deeply moved. The dean always looked all-business, but Rachel realized that she also took this lawsuit personally and hearing something nice about the school meant a lot to her.

"I'm going to have Meredith Sweeney contact you," Simon said to Taylor. "I'd like you to review your findings with her."

"My pleasure."

"Okay," Simon said. "We have a plan."

74

Morgan Carmichael surveyed Carpenter's conference room with distaste. Carmichael was a tall, thin man with wavy gray hair and washed-out gray eyes. He was wearing a dark blue suit and a blue and white striped shirt and red tie. The shirt collar was solid white, a demerit in Carpenter's eyes: he couldn't stand guys who sported a solid collar on a striped shirt. Talk about affectations! The longer he studied Carmichael, the more Carpenter considered that he may have been hasty. Carmichael's expression may not have reflected distaste. Rather the man's slightly pained look may be the way Carmichael consistently viewed the world. And Meredith thought this would be fun, Carpenter remembered.

"Mr. Murphy and I have discussed resolving the Ship Right case informally and, as Mr. Murphy has undoubtedly told you, we are recommending to our respective clients that the seven hundred thousand dollars in dispute be resolved at a three hundred fifty-thousand-dollar figure."

"If you think we're going to leave three hundred and fifty thousand dollars on the table, you are sadly mistaken. I already said this to Brian. Brian and I are going to have a serious, unpleasant talk once we finish with this nonsense."

'No wonder Murphy didn't want to confront Carmichael directly,' Carpenter thought.

"As a lawyer, you know it's highly unusual for an opposing counsel to pitch a settlement to the other side, but Mr. Murphy and I thought it might be productive to go that route in this case. You don't have to say anything to me. If you do choose to say something to me, that something stays in this room. However, if what you say provides me with information that's helpful to Ship Right, I may choose to try to obtain that information from other sources. Are we clear?"

"This is a waste of time," Carmichael replied.

"Here's why your firm should settle the case for the figure mentioned," Carpenter continued, ignoring Carmichael's pique. "If you go to trial, your firm is likely to recover nothing of what you claim is owed. There are two main reasons for that. The first reason is that you and your partners are lawyers, and jurors will hate your collective guts as soon as they hear what your profession is and what you charge per hour. In terms of people the public hates, only child molesters are despised more than lawyers. Any member of the jury hearing your case who has ever received a bill from a lawyer, is going to want to stick it to you and your firm. Lawyers tend to live in their own insulated world and don't fully appreciate the contempt in which they're held. But that contempt is going to hit you right between the eyes and leave your firm with nothing."

"I don't have to take this crap from you," Carmichael said irately.

"The second reason is that when jurors hear that you billed a client hundreds of thousands of dollars for lawyers who did nothing but listen in on phone calls and sit like potted plants at meetings, your firm will never recover any of those fees."

"We needed lawyers up to speed in case an emergency arose," Carmichael protested. "Your man Becker is just the kind of guy who would sue us if we were caught short responding to an emergency."

"What emergency?" Carpenter fired back. "There was never an emergency. And even if an emergency had arisen, it would have taken five minutes for a partner to tell associates what to do. This was a one-time transaction for your firm and I'm going to argue to the jury that your firm decided to milk it for every penny it could."

Carpenter met Carmichael's hostile stare. Because he couldn't tell if Mr. White-collar-on-a-blue striped shirt was weakening, there was no alternative to continuing to bludgeon the man.

"Harris Burton is one of the most respected transaction attorneys in the state. A jury is going to love him. He's got that avuncular, plainspoken manner that exudes honesty and fairness. You've read his affidavit. He's going to testify that Ship Right was overcharged by your firm in the amount of seven hundred thousand dollars. A jury is going to believe him. And when he gets finished showing the jury the details such as the boatload of lawyers who did nothing, the jurors are going to believe the plaintiff, too.

"But even if you think that how juries feel doesn't matter much, let me tell you what does matter. When Harris Burton gets through testifying, he will have painted a picture of your firm as the quintessential gouger by piling on lawyers to pad your firm's bills. When news of that verdict becomes public, your clients are going to start heading for the exits. And you know it. And there won't be any more clients coming your way, either. No client is ever going to trust a bill from you again."

For the first time, Carmichael appeared concerned. Maybe the broader repercussions had never occurred to him. The possibility of public ignominy was not something he could easily dismiss.

"But getting back to the bills themselves. I don't think I've told you anything you didn't already know," Carpenter continued. "And I think these are things your counsel knows as well. Mr. Murphy's firm has a corporate department and deals with transactions like the Ship Right transaction. No doubt Murphy had his business lawyers review your bills to Ship Right. I'm betting they were as appalled as Harris Burton was by what Blake, Pennington & Dwyer charged Ship Right."

Carmichael took in his last speech with a blank expression. Carpenter was now convinced that Murphy and Warren had already counseled Carmichael that his firm's billings were excessive in certain areas but had decided that Carmichael wasn't capable of hearing that message, at least not from them. Carpenter's joking suggestion presented the perfect way for Murphy to deal with an unreasonable client—hand the client over to Carpenter to do the dirty work.

"Here's another thought," Carpenter said. "I haven't taken your deposition yet, but I'll give you a heads up on one question I'm going to ask you. The question is, 'When your firm prepared the billings to Ship Right, was any lawyer's time written off or written down?'"

Carmichael frowned, and Carpenter wasn't sure what to make of the expression. The Ship Right engagement was complicated, but it was a fact of legal life that a law firm simply couldn't bill for every hour spent on an engagement no matter how difficult and complex the engagement was. "I'm betting that no lawyer's time was written off or written down," he added to see whether the big firm lawyer's expression changed. It did not. "If your firm didn't reduce any lawyer's time, Harris Burton will have a field day with that fact."

Carmichael's frown turned into a scowl. Carpenter believed he had touched a nerve.

"That's all I have," Carpenter said. "How do you think Murphy's making out with Becker?" he asked.

"What the fuck is with you guys?" Becker said without any heat. He and Carpenter were alone in a small conference room at Dudley, Atkins & Tyng while Carmichael was meeting separately with Murphy and Warren.

"What do you mean?" Carpenter asked.

"For starters you were right," Becker said. "Murphy actually called me a weasel and said Ship Right was a nest of weasels. Do weasels even live in a nest? He said I was just the kind of vindictive prick—that's a direct quote—who would have sued the shit out of Carmichael's firm if the deal didn't close and I could find a way to blame the firm. I told him I didn't have to take that shit."

"That's what Carmichael said to me. Only he used crap instead of shit because he's a refined guy, unlike you."

Becker laughed before continuing. "So he abuses me for about thirty minutes, and then he sits back and looks at me and says, 'Let me guess. I'm guessing that Ship Right would have been willing to settle this case for something slightly less than three hundred fifty thousand. I'm guessing three hundred thirty-five thousand.' I look at him and try not to show I'm surprised because, all the while he was shitting all over me, I kept telling him he could shove the three hundred fifty thou up his ass."

Carpenter couldn't help laughing. "Murphy must have put himself in our situation and figured we'd file a Rule 68 motion for slightly less than half the amount in dispute to protect ourselves if the jury decided to simply split the difference."

"Then it's a good thing we didn't file that damn motion you spent hours charging me for."

If Becker hadn't been smiling, Carpenter might have been worried that his firm, also, would have trouble collecting from Ship Right. "That damn motion as you called it helped get us to the place we are today, so I don't think we wasted our time. I believe it's safe to say that the ball is now in Murphy's court."

Twenty minutes later a secretary knocked on the door and led them to a much larger conference room where Brian Murphy, Sarah Warren, and Morgan Carmichael were gathered at one end. The two lawyers looked pleased but their client didn't. Then Carpenter remembered that Carmichael always looked pained. Maybe he was overjoyed. Who could tell?

"Gentlemen," Murphy said, beckoning them to join his group. "We have a deal if you're on board," he ended the suspense.

Becker nodded in his direction. "We're on board," Carpenter said.

"Excellent," Murphy exclaimed. "Please sit down. If anybody wants anything stronger than coffee, tea, juice or soda, speak up. I for one am having a beer."

"Make that two," Carpenter said.

"I'm in," Becker and Sarah Warren said together.

"Morgan," Murphy said, "you are going to join us for a brew. This is legal advice you can't refuse."

"What the hell," Carmichael said resignedly.

Murphy used the conference room phone and in moments the same secretary who led them into the room reappeared with five poured beers in iced beer steins.

Murphy raised his stein. "On the last serious note you're going to hear from me, Sarah and I appreciate the willingness of Mr. Carmichael and Mr. Becker to pursue an unconventional approach to settlement and to come to an agreement. If you're both unhappy, then the conventional wisdom states that it's a good settlement."

Nobody said anything, but everyone drank.

"You realize what this means, Carpenter," Murphy said. "It means you and I have to go into the mediation business. I know what you're going to say. Yes, I despise mediation, but I think we're on to something here. I was thinking of a name for our new venture. How about, If We Don't Abuse, You Lose?"

Sarah Warren rolled her eyes, smiled weakly, and Carpenter wondered about the coping mechanisms she had employed to put up with Murphy over the years.

"You guys are real comedians," Becker said. "I don't know about you," he addressed Carmichael, "but I had no idea I was hiring a lunatic."

"I prefer not to discuss our respective counsel," Carmichael said dryly.

"For God's sake lighten up, Morgan," Murphy said. "The past is past. Leave it there."

Watching Carmichael sip his beer, Carpenter wondered how he would have dealt with the humorless man as a client.

"So you've got these sealed containers," Murphy said to Becker. "Don't the feds demand to open them up every once in a while and inspect them for weapons of mass destruction? And if that happens, how the hell do you reseal them?"

"So far we've been lucky. That hasn't happened." Becker frowned. "But the writing is on the wall. All the experts are predicting that the next real threat will come through containers transported by ship. The experts figure some major port city will be targeted."

"Sounds like a good time to sell your business," Murphy said.

"What the hell do you think we were trying to do?" Becker snapped back. "Do you know anyone who wants to buy our business and give us a meaningful role in the business for a couple of years after the sale?"

Murphy regarded Becker with his business game face on. "Morgan and I will discuss the matter, and we'll let Carpenter know if we come up with anything," Murphy said. "Of course, we'll expect a finder's fee."

"Ship Right might even pay one if the deal was right," Becker said.

Sarah Warren's puzzled look told Carpenter that Murphy was probably winging it. But you could never tell with him. Maybe from the get-go, Murphy had a contingency plan in his head for when the litigation dust had settled.

"Drink up," Murphy urged. "If we're not careful we'll end up drinking that warm piss the British call beer."

75

Simon reviewed his notes for the call he intended to make to Christopher Blaisedell. The other day, Carpenter had regaled them all with the saga of the settlement in the Ship Right case. Simon had racked his brain for a comparable, creative approach to use on Blaisedell but he'd come up empty. The problem was that Blaisedell was not only the lawyer for the plaintiffs; in a real sense, he himself was the plaintiff. Branson, White, and Hightower were not going to participate in any negotiation if Blaisedell had anything to say about it. Blaisedell was handling the case on a contingency basis and from that perspective it was his case. Blaisedell would insist on making all strategic decisions and had probably spelled that out in the fee agreement he had with the three plaintiffs.

Simon was sitting in Philly's desk chair, relieved to be free of his cramped workstation. Rachel was at the Spenser School of Law library doing some research on a matter involving a potential client that she was keeping close to her vest. Hopefully, her efforts would come to something—they needed more business.

If he was successful in resolving the Sloan-Webster case, their workload gauge would register a shade above empty.

Simon thought about Philly's recent e-mail describing her discussion with the chief member of a law firm's management committee. Philly intended to sue the law firm for discrimination, and the management committee head had asked what her client was looking for. Philly couldn't provide the woman with specifics and wanted suggestions. If Blaisedell was asked what he was looking for in the Sloan-Webster case, Simon was certain that his answer would be money damages. True, Blaisedell would probably insist on the reforms that Neil Taylor, the new head of Sloan-Webster's placement office, had already begun to implement. But for Blaisedell, the case would be all about the money. In the Spenser case, Blaisedell had settled for his attorney fees subject to a ceiling. Simon was certain that Blaisedell would insist on damages against Sloan-Webster so that he could make a big financial score through his contingency fee agreement.

Simon made a note of an idea: *graduate student placement advisory committee.* Why not reach out to graduates for placement advice? Branson, White, and Hightower might relish an advisory role as part of a settlement. It would look good on their resumés. A lap dancer, a possible cheater, and a gambler advising on placement matters! That would be a first.

Simon realized that he wasn't ready to speak to Blaisedell about settlement. The dean and Cray would be frustrated by the delay, but those were the breaks. He needed to speak with Carpenter before he did anything else.

Rachel sat in the Spenser School of Law library unable to concentrate on researching cases against sports camps. She couldn't get Philly's e-mail memo about Ai Li out of her head. Philly had been asked what relief Li was looking for if she sued for discrimination, and she hadn't been able to provide specifics. If Noelle Campbell sued the tennis camp she had attended, what relief would she seek?

Noelle had thrown up but had required no medical attention. Therefore, damages resulting from her punishment drill were minimal. She might seek a refund of all or part of the fee she had paid to attend the camp; but that dollar amount couldn't be significant. If she claimed that the camp had ruined her tennis game, how did such a claim, if successful, translate into money damages. By attending the summer camp, hadn't Noelle admitted her game needed improvement? Josh had described Noelle's game as good, not great. If her game had deteriorated in any way, Rachel was confident that in a reasonable time Josh would restore her game to its former level. Maybe this was one of those cases that had merit but was not worth the effort given the legal fees that Noelle's parents would have to bear. Rachel assessed her next step. Legal research could wait. She needed to bring Carpenter up to date on Noelle Campbell's situation and get his input.

Simon was getting ready for bed when his cell phone sounded. Caller ID announced Frank.

"You're calling late,"

"I guess I just wanted to hear your voice."

"You miss your running partner."

"Guilty as charged."

Simon lay down on his bed, turned off the bedroom light, but didn't close his eyes. A long-distance relationship sucked but he thought that he and Frank so far had managed well under the circumstances. "I miss you too," he said.

"I wish the summer hadn't ended."

The summer had thrown them together 24/7 which required adjustments. There had been times when Simon missed his privacy until he thought of what his life would be like with Frank not in it. Now that summer was long gone, he wished it back, lack of privacy and all.

"There's something that's been bugging me," Simon said.

"I don't like the sound of that."

"Earlier in the year, each of us lawyers took a payday of twenty-five thousand dollars."

"No shit!"

"I thought about telling you, but I didn't. Here you were still in college and being supported by your parents and I got it into my head that you'd think I was showing off or putting you down if I spoke about the payday. I was wrong. I made a mistake. I should have shared that good news with you."

"Yeah, you should have. I'm not some jealous little kid."

Simon ignored the rebuke. "What I'm trying to say is it won't happen again. But it means that you get to hear the bad as well as the good."

"I think I can handle that."

"I know you can."

"I'm glad you told me," Frank said. "You didn't have to bring it up and I'd have never known."

"It's taken me awhile but that's not what I want long-term."

"That's good to hear," Frank said.

76

It had been a while since he and Philly had met in the Boston office before nine and Carpenter was looking forward to the alone time with her. Philly had picked the early morning hour to review the Li case and came armed with two large Dunkin' Donut coffees, black, and packets of real and fake sugar for doctoring. 'She looked good,' Carpenter thought. Motherhood seemed to be agreeing with her and it made him realize that it had been a while since he'd seen her kids. He liked her in her current mode: businesslike, determined, loaded for bear.

"This goddamn Li case is driving me up a fucking wall," Philly led off. "When this woman at her old firm asked me what relief Li was looking for, I couldn't answer her. It was embarrassing."

Carpenter hadn't responded to her e-mail seeking advice on what Li should ask for largely because he hadn't come up with a creative idea on what that should be. But maybe the two of them together could do better.

"Li will be paid for the month before she starts her new job, right?" Carpenter said, starting at the top of the half page of notes he had jotted down in advance of this meeting."

"Right."

"And at her new job she'll be making more than she would have made at the partner level she didn't get promoted to."

"Right again," Philly said.

"What the hell's the matter with plaintiffs? Don't they know they're supposed to take a shitty new job that pays squat?"

"Like I said, it's driving me fucking crazy."

Philly was plainly not in the mood for jokes. Carpenter looked at the remainder of his notes which were not much help. "There's something wrong with this picture," he said, hoping that thinking aloud would produce a flash of inspiration. "Here's this woman who gets shafted because she's an Asian woman and the employer that shafted her gets a free pass because she ended up with a better job. That can't be right."

"I told Li that she's out of luck when it comes to clear cut money damages, because she's going to make more money at her new job. If she gets any money, it's going to be for emotional pain and suffering and who the hell can predict a dollar value for that? What she wants is for her firm to be held accountable for discriminating against her."

"Which means her case will end up being tried because her former firm can never agree it discriminated."

"Right," Philly concurred, as she watched Carpenter break into a smile.

"You've answered your question. You tell this woman that what Li wants is an acknowledgement she was discriminated against. Tell her a settlement agreement executed now to that effect will make the case go away without monetary damages or attorney fees."

"Henrietta Coleman will tell me to fuck myself," Philly groused.

"So what? You would have answered her question truthfully."

"I don't know," Philly muttered softly.

"Before you file this complaint, go over things with Li one more time so that this is all spelled out. Tell Li you're going to call Coleman back, as a courtesy, before filing the MCAD complaint, and that you're going to tell Coleman about the relief Li wants as we just discussed. Li needs to be clear that her case isn't going to settle and the best she's going to get on money is damages for emotional pain and suffering."

"This is a woman who keeps her emotions bottled up. She was fired because she was too aloof with clients, too distant. She was criticized for not being sociable with clients. She's not likely to radiate 'pain and suffering' to a jury."

"What are the chances of proving discrimination?" Carpenter asked.

"We need a breakdown of the law firm's partnership levels by sex over time."

That information tied in with Meredith's observation on the law firm's multilevel partnership arrangement. "We'll get it," Carpenter said. "The MCAD is big on allowing broad discovery."

"What do you make of the fact that Henrietta Coleman, the head of the law firm's management committee, is a woman?"

"It doesn't help Li's case," Carpenter said. "Maybe she's okay with what's going on because she's made it at this firm. Maybe she's become one of the boys."

Philly made a note on her notepad.

"You know," Carpenter said, "if there really is a longtime conspiracy to hold women back, Li can't have been the first one to be screwed."

Philly made another note.

"Do you want to talk about merging with Sizemore Klein?" Carpenter asked, changing the subject.

"Not particularly."

"My sentiments exactly."

Carpenter discovered that it was going to be one of those days when he had to make time for his partners. Philly had left. Rachel had made an appointment to meet with him late in the afternoon. And currently Simon sat in his visitor chair explaining his concerns about approaching Christopher Blaisedell to settle the Sloan-Webster case.

Carpenter thought that there was no right answer on how best to approach Blaisedell. "I think you're right about Blaisedell wanting to control the settlement process." Carpenter led off. "But you could always make it a condition of negotiations that he informs the plaintiffs of any settlement proposal the law school makes. I think he has to do that anyway, but you could press him on that. Also, you could tell him that there will be no final settlement agreement unless there's a meeting with the parties. Remember, it doesn't matter what agreements Blaisedell might have made with his clients about negotiating—you're telling him your terms."

Simon hurriedly wrote a few lines on his notepad.

"I think you want Blaisedell to make the first move," Carpenter continued. "In a case like this, you don't want to bid against yourself."

"I'm trying to figure out what he'll ask for," Simon said. "As to money," he added.

"You're right; it's going to come down to money. All the rest of the stuff—revamping the placement office, rewriting the law school's promotional materials—is fixable. And, from what you tell me, a lot of things are already being fixed."

"Blaisedell is going to name a seven-figure number," Simon said.

"That's his prerogative," Carpenter came back. "Who gets the money?"

"I haven't figured that out. There's no certified class to give any money to. The three plaintiffs sure as hell aren't going to walk away with that kind of money in a settlement."

"Maybe the law school should set up a fund that can only be used to help graduates obtain law-related jobs," Carpenter threw out.

"I was thinking about something like that," Simon responded. "I couldn't figure out what amount should be put in the fund or what the money would actually be used for. Outside of upgrading the placement office, I couldn't really come up with any specific use for the funds."

"No problem there," Carpenter said. "This new placement office guy the law school hired will wet himself thinking up job fairs, resumé drafting seminars, and networking strategies."

"What about the amount of the fund?" Simon pursued.

"Hell, I don't know. What about two hundred fifty thousand?"

"How'd you come up with that?"

"I pulled it out of thin air. It's a significant number but not something that's likely to break the law school's bank. At some point, Blaisedell needs to understand that a seven-figure payday isn't going to happen. Remember, the guy could lose at trial. He hasn't won anything yet, and he's got two plaintiffs he probably wishes he could ditch."

"What do you think of mediation?" Simon asked.

"When mediation came up in the Ship Right case, Brian Murphy said fuck mediation. I believe that's a direct quote. I don't have as strong an anti-mediation bias as Murphy, but my instincts tell me to stay away from it in this case. I wouldn't want some bleeding heart telling the law school how it should spend its money. By the way, how much does the law school have to spend to make this case go away?"

"I'm not sure."

"I'd suggest that you get a handle on the answer to that question."

"Should I talk to the dean about money before I call Blaisedell?" Simon asked.

"I'm winging it here, but my instincts are to talk to Blaisedell first. Sometimes it helps not to know what resources your client has. Besides, Blaisedell is going to say what he's going to say regardless of whether the dean has filled you in on the law school's finances. Sloan-Webster is a for-profit law school, right?"

Simon nodded.

"Then the school's finances won't be a matter of public record which would have been the case if the school was nonprofit. Blaisedell will be as much in the dark as you are about what the school is able to pony up."

"Not entirely," Simon said. "The law school turned over some financial information to Blaisedell during discovery and refused to turn over other information. For example, he knows the budget for the placement office."

Simon looked pensive. "What?" Carpenter said.

"I'd almost prefer to try the damn case than get into a settlement discussion with Blaisedell," Simon said.

"Not to worry," Carpenter came back. "If Blaisedell turns out to be a moneygrubbing asshole, you'll get your wish."

Rachel had just finished telling Carpenter the tale of Noelle Campbell and her tennis camp experience, and now she was looking at him expectantly for advice. Carpenter wished they'd had this discussion before Rachel had met with the girl and her parents, but he didn't feel strongly about the timing. Rachel had tried to show initiative; he didn't want to put a damper on that impulse by criticizing her approach. The tennis player's situation reminded Carpenter of the Li case. There was a good chance each defendant could be held liable, but each plaintiff's damages sucked. "If the girl sued the camp and I was defending the camp, I'd think seriously about offering to refund her camp fee to make her go away."

"What about her pain and suffering and the way her game became screwed up?" Rachel said.

"If I was representing the camp, I'd say those damages are speculative. Noelle never needed medical attention and finished out the camp. Moreover, she signed up for the camp which meant she didn't think her tennis game was that great to begin with. I'd take a hard line and offer to return her money."

Rachel's usually cheerful countenance took a gloomy turn. Carpenter knew that he was not telling her what she wanted to hear.

"I guess I have to tell them that Noelle has a legal claim that appears winnable but with legal fees being what they are, it probably doesn't make sense for her to sue. I can't see us taking this case on a straight contingency."

"Neither can I," Carpenter seconded. "You know, every once in a while, there's a story in the newspaper about some kid dropping dead in a late summer football practice conducted in oppressive heat. Noelle was lucky: she wasn't seriously hurt."

"This sucks," Rachel said with feeling. "I was hoping this would be a new case. We could use a new case."

Carpenter didn't want to think about the lack of new business. He refocused on the young tennis player. "This couldn't have been the first time a girl threw up at this camp," he said.

"It wasn't. Noelle said that some girls attending the camp expected to throw up. What are you getting at?"

"I'm just rambling," Carpenter said. "As you know, Simon was in to see me about trying to settle the Sloan-Webster case. I guess I have class actions on the brain."

"Are you thinking Noelle could bring a class action?"

"As I said, I'm just rambling. I'm thinking that there have to be other potential plaintiffs out there."

"How would we find out about them?"

"Beats the hell out of me."

Rachel became lost in thought. "Facebook," she said.

"I don't like the sound of that," Carpenter responded, his distrust of social media kicking in.

"I'm going to have another talk with Noelle and her parents. Thanks. This has been very helpful."

"That's what I'm here for," Carpenter said, unsure what had just happened.

77

Philly had the notes from her recent discussion with Ai Li in front of her as she waited for her call to Henrietta Coleman to be put through. Li had shown resolve. She required a written acknowledgement of discrimination to refrain from filing a complaint with the MCAD. She was also prepared to keep the acknowledgment confidential.

"Henrietta Coleman."

"Philly Sullivan. You asked what it would take to prevent Ai Li from filing a complaint with the MCAD. I now have a specific answer to your question. It would take a written acknowledgement from your firm that Ms. Li was discriminated against when she was denied a promotion to the level six partnership rung. Ms. Li would release the firm from any damage claims or claims for attorney fees that she might have and would expect a release from your firm."

Coleman didn't respond straightaway. If Li had made a monetary damage request, Philly suspected that Coleman had authority to settle the matter up to a certain amount. Perhaps Coleman was unprepared for a settlement demand that didn't include money.

Coleman broke the silence. "Hazelton Kauffman is not going to admit to discriminating against your client when it did nothing of the kind."

"Thank you for your time," Philly said. "I wanted to extend you the courtesy of responding to your question with specifics before an MCAD complaint was filed. I believe I've done that."

"Just out of curiosity, what were you envisioning would happen to this written acknowledgement of discrimination you were looking for?"

"Ms. Li is prepared to be flexible on that. She would agree to keep the written acknowledgement confidential."

"You're saying she wants a written acknowledgement that she would never disclose. Do I have that right?"

"Yes, that is correct," Philly said. Was Coleman actually considering Li's proposal?

"Extend me another courtesy," Coleman said. "I want to report what you've said to my firm's full management committee. I don't see this going anywhere for the reason I stated but give me a few days to confirm that's the case."

"Sure," Philly said. "My pleasure."

Philly set down her phone. She found the business card for Freedman and McCauley and punched in their number.

"Herb McCauley."

"It's Philly Sullivan."

"How's my friend Paul?"

"We're both good. I wonder if you can help me. I need to find the names of women partners who left a large Boston law firm."

"I can do that," McCauley said.

Christopher Blaisedell answered his phone on the second ring. "What can I do for you?"

Simon put Blaisedell on his speaker phone so he could more easily take notes. "You can tell me whether it makes any sense to talk about trying to settle the Sloan-Webster case informally."

"In the Spenser case, I was the one who first brought up settlement," Blaisedell said. "How come you're the one to bring it up in this case? Do I detect a sign of weakness on the law school's part?"

"For a guy who hasn't won a damn thing in this case, you're sounding pretty full of yourself," Simon retorted. "Detect whatever you want. I asked you a question. If your answer is no, we have nothing further to discuss."

"I was kidding around," Blaisedell retreated.

"Well, stop kidding around. Do you want to talk settlement?"

"Sure. What do you have in mind?"

"Nothing. You represent the plaintiffs. Tell me what your clients are looking for in a settlement."

"I'll have to get back to you. I really haven't given settlement any serious consideration."

'What a crock,' Simon thought. "If you think about it and decide you want to talk, you know where to find me."

"Yes, I do."

"And while you're thinking about it, if that's what you choose to do, think about a settlement discussion in which the actual parties participate."

"I much prefer that the lawyers engage in settlement discussions," Blaisedell said.

"We're getting off to a great start," Simon came back. "My client's preference is for the parties to meet directly. But should you get back to me, I'll be sure to listen."

When Blaisedell disconnected, Simon figured he wouldn't hear back from his adversary for a week. Blaisedell would need to save face; he had claimed he hadn't considered settlement and would now pretend to take the time to do so.

Rachel had made the trip to the Campbells' home because her instincts told her a phone call was not the way to go. They were seated at a metal table on a blacktop area abutting the back yard and Mrs. Campbell had provided soft drinks. The gorgeous autumn setting highlighted by maple trees sporting vibrant red and orange leaf clusters was a distraction, but Rachel kept her focus, directing her presentation to Noelle's parents while keeping a close eye on the girl. Noelle had been engaged during her remarks, more so than her parents.

"Here's the bottom line," Rachel summed up. "If Noelle choses to sue the tennis camp, we think there's a good chance that the camp would be held liable for putting her through the punishment drills. But you will need to decide, as a family, whether having the camp held liable is worth spending more money on lawyers than the damages Noelle may recover. I wanted to say this to you personally so that we could address together any questions you may have."

"Basically, you're saying it's probably not worth it to sue," Mr. Campbell said.

"Yes, if money is the objective of the suit."

"Well, I guess that's that," Noelle's father said. "I had my hopes up for a while."

Rachel turned to Noelle. "Do you keep in touch with the kids you met at the camp and you liked?"

"Yeah. We e-mail back and forth and we're on Facebook. It's neat."

"Have you talked about the punishment drills on Facebook?" Rachel followed up.

"No."

"How would you feel about doing that?"

Noelle shrugged. "Okay, I guess."

"I'm interested in trying to find out whether any other kids who went to the camp had a bad experience similar to yours."

"Where are you going with this?" Mrs. Campbell asked.

"I want to know whether there are any other potential plaintiffs out there," Rachel responded.

"I really don't understand anything about Facebook," Mrs. Campbell said.

"Don't worry, mom," Noelle said. "I know what to do."

Philly moved a small bucket of Halloween candy to the farthest corner of her desk, picked up her phone, and pressed the first speed dial number.

"Carpenter."

"It's me," Philly said. "I need to talk to you about this business with Harris Burton and Ben Klein. Paul and I were talking, and he was wondering if we were looking at this the wrong way."

"I'm listening."

"You know by now that I'm not one to think about the future. If things are going okay, I tend to put out of mind what lies ahead. You're different that way."

"Where are you going with this?"

"Paul asked me to think about where I wanted to be in five years, what I wanted my life to be like. I got to thinking that you'd be over seventy and might have decided to pack it in and retire."

"I don't know what the hell I'll be doing in five years," Carpenter said. "With this cancer thing hanging over me, I might not be around in five years."

Carpenter was making this call easier. "So I got to thinking about being hooked up with Klein's firm and you not in the picture, and I didn't like what I saw. I'd have more experience, but what with kids and all, I wouldn't have anywhere near your experience. I'd be senior to Simon and Rachel and to Meredith if she's in the picture. But there'd be nobody to fill your void."

Carpenter sighed. “Nobody’s indispensable.”

Philly ignored the observation. “Paul asked me why we weren’t looking to associate with a litigation firm that had an experienced person older than me but younger than you. I didn’t have an answer for him.”

“Christ,” Carpenter muttered. “To be honest with you, I’ve never envisioned getting involved with other litigators. Maybe I haven’t paid as much attention to the future as you give me credit for.”

Philly stayed silent. She had given Carpenter a lot to think about.

“There’s another way to look at it,” Carpenter finally said. “Young people go out on their own and start litigation and other specialty practices on the fly. You and Simon and Rachel and Meredith have the ability to do that.”

“If you weren’t in the picture these last years, we wouldn’t have been as successful as we were,” Philly pointed out. “That’s a fact, not my opinion. We could go out on our own, but we wouldn’t be as good as we had been with you.”

“Aren’t you kind!”

“You know it’s true,” Philly held firm. “Just think about what I’ve said. To be continued.”

“Fair enough.”

Philly set down her home office phone. Carpenter hadn’t brought up including Simon and Rachel in this discussion. She agreed. She and Carpenter needed to hash this out first.

November

Philly's Attitude Playlist

"Roar"

Katy Perry

78

"Good morning, asshole," Brian Murphy said cheerily after Carpenter picked up his phone.

"You know what I have to say to you," Carpenter continued their routine.

"I do," Murphy owned up. "Sarah and I want to take you and Ms. Sullivan to lunch. I keep wanting to call her Ms. Piper."

"What's the occasion?" Carpenter asked. He was certain that Murphy had an agenda. No way was this a social call.

"We want to run an idea by you. Another senior lawyer in our firm will be joining us—Richard Nye."

"Do I know him?"

"No, probably not. Decades ago, he used to be our managing partner. This goes back to when Sarah and I jumped ship. He's also the guy who was primarily responsible for getting Sarah and me to rejoin Dudley, Atkins & Tyng."

"What's this all about?"

"I'd rather have Richard present it," Murphy said, which surprised Carpenter. Brian Murphy was not the type who deferred to a colleague when a presentation was to be made and he was a party to it.

"Are you going to give me a hint here?" Carpenter pressed.

"Why don't you wait and be surprised? I think you will be."

"I hate surprises," Carpenter vented.

"You may have mentioned that before," Murphy said. "All right. Here's your hint. We're too expensive. It's costing us business. We don't like that."

"What does that have to do with Philly and me?"

"You're not expensive. You're a bargain. We want to run something by you."

"Why us? There are other inexpensive firms out there."

"But how many of them have assholes front and center? Answer me that."

"Good point," Carpenter said. "Philly and I could do lunch."

A pack rat, Herb McCauley kept his notepads in chronological order. Starting with January of 2012, he quickly located an assignment Meredith Sweeney had given him. There was the name he hadn't been able to recall: Jocelyn Weaver, a secretary at the Board of Bar Overseers. Weaver had gone beyond the call of duty and provided useful information about the law firm that had fired Sweeney. He dialed Weaver's direct line.

"Jocelyn Weaver."

"My name is Herb McCauley. I'm a private investigator. You helped me out last year."

"I remember you. I'm glad I was helpful."

"I've got a similar situation. I need to look at the roster of lawyers in a large Boston law firm over a five-year period."

"That's similar to what you were working on last year. I'll need the name of the firm."

"Hazelton, Kauffman, Garfield & Smith."

"Five years, right?"

"Right."

"Call me in two days."

"I think that's what you asked me to do last time."

"Some things never change," Weaver said.

79

Philly was the last to arrive at the trendy fusion restaurant on Newbury Street and everyone stood to greet her. She knew three of the four people seated at the circular table, so the large man who rose when she approached had to be Richard Nye. He towered over the rest of them. Nye struck her as a serious type, yet his smile was warm as he shook her hand. His dark hair was graying along the sides. He seemed fit; a case could be made that he was trimmer than Murphy, despite obviously being slightly older.

"I was telling our hosts that if they were trying to impress us, they've succeeded," Carpenter said resuming his seat. "We're more of a local deli kind of firm."

"Except for me," Philly qualified. "I mostly work from home so I'm more of a leftover kind of person."

"Carpenter's been filling us in on how you're set up," Nye said. "It seems to be working for all of you."

"We're all flexible," Philly responded.

"Brian and Sarah speak very highly of both of you," Nye said. "Why don't we take a moment to look at the menu and once we give our orders, I'll tell you why we wanted to meet with you."

Looking at the prices of the restaurant's offerings, Philly was reminded of Carpenter's dictum that large firms and small firms operated in parallel universes. Over the years, Carpenter had maintained an ingrained prejudice against large law firms. Probably the only reason he agreed to lunch was that he genuinely liked and respected Murphy and Warren.

"Make sure you order something expensive," Murphy suggested. "Sarah and I need to get our expense accounts up to our other partners' level."

"You're not helping," Nye said in a tone that was reproving but resigned. "You're defeating the purpose of this lunch."

"Oops!" Murphy said with a wicked grin that brought a head shake from Nye and an eye roll from Warren.

"Are you ready to order?"

When their waiter departed, Nye took a sip of water and surveyed the table. "Brian gave you a brief idea of why we wanted to talk to you," Nye inclined his head toward Carpenter. "But I'd like to explain what we have in mind in my own way. This is something that I've given considerable thought to in recent years. Decades ago, I was our firm's managing partner. I've stayed a member of the firm's management committee after I gave up that position."

"We won't let him leave firm management," Murphy said.

"Richard can't say this, but Brian and I can," Warren spoke up. "Richard is universally trusted by the partners in our firm."

"What can I say?" Nye responded. "Brian tends to exaggerate, but Sarah doesn't."

"Was that a joke?" Murphy questioned.

"I try," Nye said. "Anyway, in my opinion, our legal system is in a time of crisis. People can't afford lawyers. I'm not saying anything new. Pundits have been making this point for years. I'm going to ask you not to repeat what we talk about this afternoon except to your other two partners. I'm sure it wouldn't surprise you to learn that the hourly rates for each of us exceed seven hundred dollars an hour. Most individuals simply cannot afford our services."

Philly did the simple math. The hourly rates for Simon and Rachel were closer to $200 than $300. Currently they were billing Meredith out at $200 an hour. Her own rate was $250. Carpenter's hourly rate was $350, and he agonized whenever he implemented a small, incremental increase.

"Potential clients have backed off hiring Dudley, Atkins & Tyng because they can't afford to pay our hourly rates. I'm willing to bet that some of our associates who have been out of law school for say five years charge more per hour than either of you."

Carpenter emitted one of his enigmatic grunts.

"The only clients that can truly afford our firm are businesses and extremely wealthy individuals. From a societal standpoint, that's not a good situation; people with a real need for legal services cannot always afford them. True, solo practitioners and small practices such as yours might meet the needs of clients that can't afford our rates. And it's also true that our firm and other large firms do pro bono work. But the way our firm and other large firms are constructed, we're basically locked into high hourly rates."

"But if you're doing well with clients that can pay your rates, why do you care?" Philly asked, thinking she probably should have softened her remark right after she made it.

"Because we do," Nye said without any indication he had been offended. "We actually believe that people who need lawyers shouldn't be priced out of engaging them, and that includes large firms like ours."

"That sounds very noble," Philly said, "but what does that have to do with us?"

"I'm getting to that," Nye said evenly. "Imagine for a moment your firm being merged into ours."

Philly was about to make a joke of Nye's suggestion, but backed off when she noticed that Carpenter was regarding Nye with interest.

"If that were to happen," Nye continued, "we would have to respect your firm's hourly rates for a period of time—there are ethical considerations that come into play—but eventually, the economics of our firm would force us to raise your hourly rates. Over time, you and your other partners would be priced out of the work you are currently doing, work that Dudley, Atkins & Tyng is priced out of now. This result is obviously self-defeating."

Philly saw that Carpenter's jaw muscles were working.

"So let's change that scenario. Let's say that your firm were to merge into ours but remain exactly the way it currently functions."

"You're losing me," Philly said. "I've seen your firm's offices. The overhead has got to be enormous. How could we stay the same?"

"I was coming to that. Your firm name would go away. You would all be Dudley, Atkins & Tyng lawyers. Your office would stay where it is."

"Don't rule out a modest upgrade," Warren interjected. "I've seen their offices, Richard. You haven't."

"Fair enough," Nye said, and Philly was struck by Nye's unruffled air. "Perhaps a modest upgrade when it comes to office space. But we would be linked electronically; our server would become your server. You would be patched into our phone system."

"We have no secretaries or receptionist," Philly pointed out.

"I see," Nye said. "Then you're a true bare bones operation. Frankly, I envision that changing. I envision at least one clerical support person at your location."

"Some of us share an office," Philly said. "You don't know the meaning of bare bones."

"Let's not get bogged down in the details just yet." Nye urged. "I'm trying to get you to picture a scenario."

"What happens with money?" Carpenter made his first contribution to the discussion.

"I told you, Richard, that Carpenter was on the ball when he wasn't acting like an asshole," Murphy said.

"Yes, the money," Nye said. "It always gets back to the money. I envision a budget for your firm's operation. The budget would include guaranteed monthly draws for you and your partners, amounts to be negotiated. I would prefer that the budget include a clerical person, but that can be discussed. We would guaranty paying one hundred percent of that budget during the first year, and a slightly lower percent, say ninety or eighty percent, thereafter. Twenty-five percent of all profit above the budget would go to us. You would deal with the other seventy-five percent anyway you choose."

"Who would manage the work we would do?" Carpenter asked.

"You would. But Sarah would be copied on all letters, pleadings and e-mails involving your cases."

"Would we be partners?" Philly asked.

"Yes," Nye confirmed. "But you would not be part of the partnership agreement we currently have. Your arrangement would be different."

"You must think there's an upside for you," Carpenter said.

"We do," Nye replied. "To put it simply, in an arrangement like this, when you do well, we do well, too. And we think you will do well. Should you not do well, we at least get to feel that we're doing good. Plus, there's something else in it for us," he added. "We think something like what I've outlined would be fun."

"Richard doesn't come across as a fun guy," Murphy said, "but I've been working on him for over twenty-five years and he's started to come around. I think I've rubbed off on him."

"I feel like you're proposing some kind of social experiment where we would be the test subjects," Philly said.

Nye didn't answer straightaway. "I guess there is that sort of aspect to what I've said. There may be no getting around that. The intent is certainly not to treat anyone as a test subject or guinea pig."

Philly couldn't tell from Carpenter's expression whether he shared her concern. "What you said before—about keeping this discussion between ourselves—goes both ways," Philly said.

"Of course," Nye responded.

"So maybe I'm jumping the gun here by sharing a general impression," Philly continued, "but I'm concerned we may be talking about fitting a square peg into a round hole. We operate very informally. We don't have fixed partnership draws. We don't have scheduled partner meetings. We pretty much wing it. When it comes to a court case, all four partners comment on proposed court pleadings. We don't even have billable hour goals because our work is so uneven and some of it is contingency fee work. When I said work was uneven, I meant that we experience down cycles."

Nye nodded but didn't seem put off by her list of perceived obstacles. Philly wanted to believe that Nye, Murphy, and Warren were shrewd businesspeople but, if they saw no problems with Nye's proposal, their business judgment had to be suspect.

"I'm not dismissing anything you've said," Nye came back. "What I would like is for you and your other partners to consider whether there is any interest in the model I sketched out. If this is something that in your gut sounds wrong to you, that's the end of the matter. But if it sounds like a possibility you wish to explore, then we will. Of course, the devil is in the details. But I've found that if there's a consensus on an overall objective, the details get sorted out."

The waiter arrived with their orders. Carpenter seemed to Philly to be off in another world, seemingly unaware that his lunch order was now in front of him.

"Do your other partners approve of this approach?" Carpenter asked when the waiter departed.

"The management committee does," Nye said. "The entire partnership has not been presented with this approach."

"How is Sarah going to find time to manage our operation?" Carpenter followed up.

Nye turned to Warren. "Sarah?"

"I don't see myself being a hands-on, day-to-day manager," Warren said. "But I do see myself reviewing documents and joining in on commenting on them. Brian and I partially head up our litigation department. I say partially because we have control over the cases that come to us but less say on matters that come to other litigation partners in the firm. One of us needs to be in the loop as to what you guys would be up to. I'm probably better suited to doing that than Brian."

"No argument here," Murphy said.

Philly sipped at her ginger ale. She was the only non-beer drinker at the table. Would she have to disclose her AA meetings if she and her partners moved forward with Nye's proposal? Would Carpenter have to reveal his cancer diagnosis?

"I've pretty much said what I had to say," Nye said, "so I believe we can now enjoy lunch. I just want to share two last thoughts with you. The first is, you'd be surprised at how much business doesn't come our way because of our fees. The second is, I don't think what I've described is right for everyone. It may not be right for you and your partners. But from what Brian and Sarah have told me about your firm, I believe that your firm fits the bill for what I have in mind. And now that I'm actually discussing this with a possible candidate, I'd be remiss if I didn't touch on a third factor. You can label this a social experiment or anything else you want to call it, but I'm convinced it would be a lot of fun as well as a success."

"As I just mentioned, fun is not the word you typically associate with Richard," Murphy said. "If Richard thinks this could be fun, then we're in for some real laughs. Besides, Sarah and I are becoming a little bored. We want something new to liven things up for us. Talking to you on a more regular basis, Carpenter, should liven things up for me."

"I'd just like to point out," Warren said, "that we used to be like you guys: small, lean, and mean. True, we always had a secretary or two. And we never shared an office. That would never have worked. Personally, I think we need to get back in touch with how the other half lives. We've become spoiled."

"You don't know the half of how the other half lives," Philly said.

80

"Thank you for giving me a little more time to get back to you," Henrietta Coleman said. "Hazelton Kauffman can't and won't provide the written acknowledgment Ai is looking for. We simply cannot admit to something that isn't true. You may disagree with us as to what's true or not, but I'm sure you understand our position."

Philly had taken Coleman's call in her living room. She sat down on an easy chair and thought about next steps. "Thanks for getting back to me. Ms. Li will be proceeding before the MCAD. Things will play out before the agency."

"I was hoping that Ai had a change of heart," Coleman said. "Very well then."

When Coleman disconnected, Philly wondered why it had taken her more than a few days to deliver the message that there was no agreement on settlement. Had the three firm managers disagreed? Was it possible that Coleman had been outvoted, two to one, by the male members of the management committee? Or had Coleman sided with one of the men?

Herb threw his jacket over the chair next to him and settled himself at his favorite table at the new Cambridge Public Library with the documents he had been given that morning by Jocelyn Weaver of the Board of Bar Overseers spread out in front of him. In return for the documents, he had given Weaver an envelope containing two twenty-five-dollar gift cards—one from Dunkin' Donuts and one from Starbucks. "Not necessary," Weaver had said but Herb had insisted it was, certain that Weaver had saved him countless, fruitless hours of digging.

Weaver had provided him with the name of each male and female partner of Hazelton, Kauffman, Garfield & Smith as of year-end for the four years beginning with 2009. The information for the fifth year, 2013, was on the firm's website. Weaver's list didn't tell him the partnership level attained by any partner and neither did the firm's website. But it was a simple task to compare male and female lists to identify subtractions and additions over the five years. What he found was telling. Male partners outnumbered their female counterparts about two to one. But during that five-year period, six women left, compared to five men. 'Bottom line,' thought Herb, 'more men come in, more women leave.'

Herb didn't see any way around it; he would have to contact the six women who left their partnership positions. He and Philly had kicked around what story to tell the women. In the end, Philly had told him to go with the truth.

81

So far this morning, Herb was batting 0 for 3. Three former women partners of Hazelton, Kauffman, Garfield & Smith had given him the brush off. Two hung up on him when he stated the purpose of his call. The third remained silent for a long moment before telling him that she would not get involved in his case. So the third time hadn't been a charm but there was always the fourth. He was still swinging.

"Hello."

"Good morning. I'm looking for Lynn Chambers." Herb was trying to catch each of the former partners at home before she headed out for work.

"Speaking."

"My name is Herb McCauley. I'm a private investigator. I'm working for an attorney who is representing a former partner of your old firm—Hazelton, Kauffman, Garfield & Smith. The attorney's client was not given a promotion to the level six partner rank and has resigned from the firm. The attorney's client believes that she should have been promoted to the level six partner rank but wasn't because she was a woman. I'm calling you to ask why you left your former firm."

Herb took it as a positive that Chambers hadn't immediately told him to pound sand. He had done some research on the six women who had left partnership positions at Hazelton Kauffman. Chambers was now a litigation associate with a mid-sized Boston law firm.

"I don't see how my personal situation can be of any help to this lawyer's client," Chambers finally said. "Also, I don't believe my situation at Hazelton Kauffman is anybody's business but my own."

"You're right about that last point," Herb said. "Leaving your former firm is your business, but I'm asking you to share with me the reason for your leaving. As to your first point, if you were to tell me why you resigned your partnership position, I'd pass that information on to the lawyer who hired me. I'd leave it up to her to decide whether your situation was of help to her client. You may be right that it won't help, but you also may be wrong."

"I'd prefer not to talk about this," Chambers responded.

"I understand. Would you prefer to talk with the attorney who hired me?"

"I'd prefer not to talk to anyone."

Herb debated whether to make the obvious low-key threat that Chambers had to be aware of. He decided to make that his fallback position. "I've worked with the attorney who hired me before. She's reputable. If you're correct that what you have to say won't help her client, neither she nor I would do anything with the information you provide. If she thought your information could help her client, she'd spell out for you why that would be the case."

"I'm sorry," Chambers said. "I'm just not comfortable talking about this."

"I'm sorry too," Herb said. "I'll report back to the attorney who hired me. Thank you for your time. My suspicion is that sometime down the road, the attorney who hired me will want to take your deposition. Obviously, if she knew you had nothing helpful to say, there would be no need to take your deposition later. So please don't blame me for trying to get a handle on whether you could be helpful or not. I had to try. Again, thanks for your time and for taking my call."

"Are you saying there's a lawsuit filed?" Chambers asked.

"No, not a lawsuit," Herb owned up. "A complaint is about to be filed with the Massachusetts Commission Against Discrimination. Your former firm and the former partner claiming sex discrimination were unable to resolve the matter informally."

"Have you talked to any other woman partner who left Hazelton Kauffman?"

Herb hesitated then thought what the hell. "Yes and no. Yes, in that I called a number of the women who left their partnership position. I have a few more to call after you. But I can't say that I talked to them because like you, they declined to speak with me. So they'll have to be deposed as well."

When Chambers fell silent, Herb resolved to wait her out.

"This is not something I'm prepared to talk about on the phone. I'll meet with you and the attorney who hired you. I may decide to have my own attorney present. Why don't you get back to me with some suggested meeting times?"

"My pleasure," Herb said. "Thank you."

Chambers ended the call. Herb smiled. There was nothing like hitting a nerve.

"The plaintiffs are seeking three million dollars in damages for the class," Christopher Blaisedell said. "That amount is exclusive of attorney fees. You wanted to know what the plaintiffs were looking for. Now you know."

Simon resisted hanging up his phone after telling Blaisedell to fuck off. Instead, he decided to nettle his adversary. "I'm confused. You talked about damages for the class. What class is that? Your motion to certify a class was denied."

"If you want to settle this case, you'll agree to class certification and the three million damages to be divided by the class."

"Now you're really confusing me," Simon replied. "Which class are you talking about? The judge said there were at least two potential classes when it came to the placement office: graduates who contacted the office and graduates who didn't. She didn't certify either group."

"To settle the case, the law school will need to agree to the class identified in the complaint. That's the class I'm talking about."

"That would be a waste of everyone's time. The judge won't certify that class whether the law school agrees to that class or not. The judge has already said the class you identified in your complaint was too broad. Why are you wasting my time?"

"I've responded to you," Blaisedell said heatedly. "Anything else on your mind?"

"Give me some specifics as to any non-damage relief you're seeking," Simon requested.

"I haven't totally decided," Blaisedell said. "Beefing up the placement office is high on my list. Beyond that, I haven't made any hard and fast decisions."

Simon noted the first-person pronoun. "Have the three plaintiffs agreed to what you just proposed?" Simon asked, certain that the three graduates had been kept in the dark about what Blaisedell had advanced.

"I'm not going to get into that as I told you before," Blaisedell said defensively.

"If you want me to take back an offer to the law school, I need to know that your clients authorized you to make the offer. Without that representation, here again, you're wasting my time."

"I think you'll take what I just said back to your client," Blaisedell said.

If Blaisedell hadn't sounded smug, Simon might have reacted differently. Dean Martin might be pissed and rightly so at what he was about to do. Still, Simon decided, there were times when you had to go with your gut. "Think again," he said before terminating the call.

Flash was the most warm-blooded person Meredith knew. He had told her that he liked to keep the heat off from April first through the end of October. During the remaining months, he kept his apartment at sixty-two degrees, yet would wander around in a T-shirt. When Flash's heating season began in November, Meredith dressed in layers, and her hands were constantly cold. She was certain that there would come a day when she'd see her breath in his apartment. If she asked, Meredith knew that Flash would turn up the heat. Back when, he had offered to do so and she had said no. She figured if Flash could stand the cold, so could she. Talk about a miscalculation! She hated feeling cold but couldn't bring herself to tell Flash that she had changed her mind. She viewed bearing the cold as some kind of test that she needed to repeatedly pass.

Meredith shifted position in the easy chair she had appropriated, careful not to disturb Flash's two cats whose heads showed over an edge of the afghan she was huddling under. Flash was at work on a computer he had taken home from a client's office, putting the computer through a series of diagnostic tests, several of which he had come up with on his own. His concentration was total. She loved watching him in this absorbed state, his fingers moving a mile a minute, the remainder of his body at rest.

Still, there was a downside to watching Flash work because it underscored that she had no active legal case bringing in income. If no further legal income came in this year, she still would have made enough to put her in the black for the year. Next year could be a problem, however. Simon and Rachel and her partners also seemed to have run out of work.

"Why the frown?"

Flash rose from his workstation seat and stretched. His T-shirt rose over the buckle of his jeans providing a brief glimpse of his rock-hard stomach.

"I was thinking about the shortage of legal work."

"Anything on the horizon?" Flash asked.

Meredith shook her head. Trying to come up with a way to land a new client left her dispirited and frustrated. She had no brilliant ideas.

"Let's go out to dinner," Flash suggested. "Change of pace."

Meredith nodded absently. There was one subject that she wanted to put behind them. "I have an answer for you," she said.

"I'm blanking on the question."

"You asked me if I ever wanted to have kids."

"I did. I remember."

Flash was looking at her expectantly but not as if anything hinged on her answer. "I'm not going to give you a general answer, just a specific one. If it's you in the picture the answer is yes."

"Excellent," Flash said. He evicted his cats and settled next to Meredith in her chair.

"There's a caveat," Meredith said, having resolved to get everything out in the open.

"What might that be?"

"I'm not prepared to give up women."

Flash was looking at her with his usual calm and Meredith wondered if there would ever be something she said that would throw him off stride.

"Not a problem," Flash said. "I can work with that."

Was that it? Meredith wondered. Was the matter to be laid to rest that simply?

"Let me amend that," Flash said. "That didn't come out right. I'm sure *we* can work with that."

Carpenter, Meredith reflected, would say if something was too good to be true, it probably was. Maybe Flash would be the guy who would prove Carpenter wrong.

82

Rachel couldn't hide her surprise but Simon showed no reaction as Carpenter filled them in on the meeting with Richard Nye, Brian Murphy, and Sarah Warren. If Philly could change anything it would be the conference room seating arrangement. She and Carpenter were sitting across from Simon and Rachel and she didn't want that positioning to suggest that they were two pairs as opposed to a foursome.

"So they sought you out," Simon said when Carpenter finished his account.

Carpenter nodded. "If I had to guess, I think it was the way the Ship Right settlement went that led them to contact us."

"We should have been at that meeting," Simon said. "You knew generally what they were going to bring up."

"Maybe, maybe not," Carpenter replied. "Murphy specifically mentioned me and Philly. I've known him and Warren for a long time. Murphy and Philly have been at each other in court. It was clear that the next step was for the two of us to brief you. If you and Rachel want to meet separately with them, that's fine with me."

"And me," Philly echoed. "As far as I'm concerned, this discussion is no different from the discussion with Harris Burton and Ben Klein. That started out with Harris approaching me. My view is that we have to be unanimous on something like this."

"Is this more attractive to you than what Burton and Klein have in mind?" Rachel asked.

Philly glanced at Carpenter. He didn't appear poised to state a preference so she jumped in. "I keep going back and forth on that, but it might be. I was talking to Paul about Harris' proposition. One of my concerns is that nobody in that firm has any litigation experience. If we hook up with that firm and Carpenter is not in the picture, say in five years, none of us would have his kind of experience, and there wouldn't be anyone to turn to because all they do is business law. When I laid this out for Paul, he asked me why we weren't hooking up with a litigation firm that had someone younger than Carpenter but with his experience. Murphy and Warren fit that bill."

"You mean I won't live forever?" Carpenter asked.

"You just might," Philly said. "Cranky people live longer, I've heard. But I'm simply throwing out a scenario."

"But it's almost as if we'd be an outpost for this firm," Rachel said.

Philly nodded. "I told this guy Nye that what he was proposing sounded like a social experiment. He didn't disagree."

"What if we try it and don't like it after two years?" Simon asked.

"That's solvable," Carpenter said. "We could insist on an opt out provision. For that matter, they might decide they want an opt out provision."

"You know these people best," Rachel said to Carpenter. "What's your reaction?"

Philly was glad to hear Rachel's pointed question and was interested in Carpenter's answer.

"I'm conflicted," Carpenter said. "I have this prejudice against big firms as you know. Dudley, Atkins & Tyng is a big firm. But I also worry about our lack of steady business. Right now, as we all know, we don't have many active matters. If these guys have to turn down business because of their high fees, we could benefit from that. I like and respect Murphy and Warren. Murphy likes to joke around but he's smart. These guys seem serious: they're willing to put their money where their mouths are."

"Does this proposal seem more promising to you than the other one?" Rachel followed up.

Carpenter didn't answer immediately. "I guess I would say yes, subject to working out the details. The reason goes to Philly's point. If I do decide to pack it in, or if my cancer makes that choice for me, I think you guys would be better situated with Brian and Sarah in the picture."

"What's next?" Simon asked.

"You two need to meet with Murphy and Warren and Nye," Carpenter replied. "I need to put Harris Burton and Ben Klein on hold for the moment unless one of you disagrees."

"Is Dudley, Atkins & Tyng being priced out of any transaction work?" Simon asked.

Philly smiled at Carpenter's look of surprise.

"Are you going where I think you're going?" Carpenter asked.

"I am," Simon said.

"Christ!" Carpenter exclaimed. "I think that would make it too complicated. Dudley, Atkins & Tyng is offering us a way to remain independent. When it comes to transaction work, I don't know whether independence is workable."

"Just a thought," Simon said, and Philly found herself smiling over the something new Carpenter would be forced to think about.

"That's disappointing," Janet Martin said after Simon called her to report on his call with Christopher Blaisedell. "Anyway, it's a moot point as you lawyers like to say. We don't have three million dollars lying around to pay anyone."

"Blaisedell appears to be viewing this case as one in which he stands to make a big financial score," Simon pointed out. "His starting-out figure is so high that I don't believe trading financial proposals will be productive."

"You're right," the dean responded.

Simon decided to preempt the dean's next question as to where to go from here. "I've been thinking of ignoring Blaisedell. I don't mean that literally because there's the litigation to deal with. But what if the law school were to simply keep doing what it's been doing and continue to improve the placement office. For example, what if the law school were to dedicate a two-hundred fifty-thousand-dollar fund for placement office projects and turn Neil Taylor loose with the money?"

"Won't Blaisedell beat us to death with the argument we should have done such things before?"

"Yes," Simon conceded. "That's a given. But continuing to improve the office may help us in defeating any subsequent class action motion which Blaisedell is sure to file if the current plaintiffs prevail at trial. The law school will be able to argue that it has moved forward with improvement efforts and there is no need for class certification because the placement office is now functioning properly. Admittedly, this argument doesn't address the plaintiffs' claims for damages for the placement office being unhelpful in the past."

"I'll talk with Ralph and Neil and get back to you," the dean said.

"Meredith Sweeney met with Mr. Taylor," Simon said. "She was impressed with the answers he's gotten to the questionnaire he sent to law school graduates. A fair number of graduates made the point that they knew Sloan-Webster School of Law was not an upper echelon law school with the vast resources of more established law schools but was a newer law school willing to take a chance on applicants who had been turned down by the more established law schools. I want to turn Meredith loose on reaching out to these graduates as witnesses."

"You have my okay," the dean said, "although I don't particularly like where you're heading. It's like saying anyone applying to Sloan-Webster had to know that it was a marginal institution that wouldn't provide many resources. But maybe that's a card we'll have to play."

"We may," Simon agreed. "And I'm not sure it's a bad hand," he added. "Getting some happy graduates in front of a jury could make the three plaintiffs seem like they're just whining."

"Let's see what Ms. Sweeney comes up with," Martin said.

"Something else just occurred to me," Simon went on. "Is there any way to learn the bar exam success rate of Sloan-Webster graduates?"

"I'll ask Neil Taylor," the dean replied.

"The plaintiffs in this case all passed the bar exam on their first try. The faculty must have been doing something right."

"This is amazing," Noelle Campbell said. "Me and my friends from tennis camp—the ones I told you about—began putting up Facebook posts about the tennis camp. And my post said I threw up after running punishment laps and I put a big UGH!!! after that. Well, I got four hits back from girls who went through the same thing. This one girl, she threw up and the instructor made her keep running."

Noelle sounded breathless over the phone. "Good work," Rachel complimented the teen. "It looks like you're not alone."

"That girl who had to keep running? She said she gave up the game after that."

Think like a lawyer, Rachel reminded herself. "Let's friend each other. I'll read what's up on your wall and get back to you."

"This is bigger than I thought," Noelle gushed.

'That's the idea,' Rachel thought.

83

Philly preceded Simon into the conference room. Herb McCauley had alerted her that Lynn Chambers might be accompanied by a lawyer, so Philly assumed that the man to Chambers' right was her attorney. McCauley had taken the seat at the head of the table and began the introductions.

"Lynn Chambers is the woman I spoke to you about," Herb said. "Donald Berenson is a partner at her current firm and is representing her for this meeting."

"Thanks for coming in. I'm Philly Sullivan and this is Simon Jeffries."

Following handshakes, Philly appraised her visitors. She pegged Chambers at Ai Li's age, perhaps mid-forties. The woman appeared nervous. She was dressed conservatively in a black business suit and white blouse. Chambers wore a wedding ring. She was tall, broad-shouldered, and wore her straight, dark hair long. Berenson was middle-aged and studious looking. His pronounced widow's peak pointed to his black-framed glasses.

"Are you able to tell us who your client is?" Berenson asked, and Philly guessed that Berenson would do most of the initial talking. "Ai Li," she said, having received her client's permission to provide Chambers with any needed information.

"I know who she is, but I don't really know her," Chambers said.

Philly nodded. Li had said the same thing about Chambers.

"What details can you provide us about Ms. Li's situation?" Berenson next asked.

"Our client wasn't given a promotion to the sixth partnership level at Hazelton Kauffman. In a nutshell, she believes that she was more deserving of promotion than the three individuals who did receive promotions to that level. Her billable hours exceeded those of the individuals promoted. Plus, unlike those individuals, she had brought a major client to the firm."

Chambers whispered something to Berenson.

"Was she given a reason for not being promoted?" Berenson inquired.

"Ms. Li was told that two clients had described her as aloof on a client satisfaction survey. The firm's managing partner told her that this point was seriously discussed by the partners before there was a vote on her promotion."

"That figures," Chambers muttered.

"Was Ms. Li aloof?" Berenson followed up.

"Ms. Li is reserved. In my opinion, she's not particularly outgoing. She doesn't believe that she was ever aloof in a negative way."

This time it was Berenson who whispered to Chambers.

"Why does your client believe her sex was the reason for her not getting promoted?" Chambers asked.

"Two reasons," Philly replied. "First, she regards the aloof assessment as a trumped-up reason for not promoting her. Second, she believes that the way partners' votes are weighted, women partners are kept below the sixth partnership level to permit men to control the firm."

"When do you intend to file a complaint before the MCAD?" Berenson asked.

"That depends on what happens at this meeting. If Ms. Chambers can't or won't help us, we'll file in a few days. If Ms. Chambers can and does help us, there's likely going to be a further delay while we consider what she has to offer."

As Chambers and Berenson huddled, Simon leaned toward Philly. "Chambers' 'that figures' comment means something happened with her."

Philly nodded. The question was whether Chambers would share her story.

Chambers and Berenson broke off conferring. "I've instructed Lynn not to say anything to you," Berenson said. "I'm concerned about her sharing any information concerning the partnership arrangement at Hazelton Kauffman. If you've read the partnership agreement that Ms. Li signed, you'll understand my concern."

Philly had read the agreement and didn't understand Berenson's concern. If she'd had any issue with the agreement, she wouldn't have said anything to Berenson and Chambers about the specifics of Li's case. "I don't think that this is the time or place to discuss the firm's partnership agreement," she said.

"Agreed," Berenson responded.

"So, what if anything are you prepared to tell us?" Philly pressed.

Berenson glanced briefly at Chambers whose nervousness hadn't abated. "Let's just say," Berenson answered, "that you might discover that similarities exist between the situations of your Ms. Li and Ms. Chambers. Perhaps you can persuade an MCAD hearing officer to allow you to take Ms. Chambers' deposition. You could justify the need to take her deposition by pointing out that a deposition is needed in order to protect Ms. Chambers under the partnership agreement she signed."

"You're not making this easy," Philly said. Although the MCAD was lenient about discovery, it didn't typically permit depositions in discovery, and Hazelton Kauffman would oppose any deposition of a former partner.

Berenson presented a weak smile in response to her observation. "There's another partner who resigned that you might be interested in. Her name is Candace Church. Ms. Chambers resigned two years ago. Ms. Church resigned one year ago."

Philly glanced at McCauley. The private detective's expression was neutral. Chambers was the only former Hazelton Kauffman partner willing to speak with him. Which meant that Candace Church had refused to talk. "Were you friends with Ms. Church?" she asked Chambers.

"Yes," Chambers said.

"Does she know you're meeting with me?"

"Yes."

"Anything else you wish to share?" Philly requested.

"Not at this time," Berenson replied.

"Then I guess we've concluded," Philly said.

After Berenson and Chambers departed, McCauley turned to Philly. "I remember Candace Church. She didn't blow me off immediately. She hesitated before telling me she wouldn't talk to me." McCauley paused, lost in thought. "What's this business about the law firm's partnership agreement?" he asked.

"He's saying Chambers could get in trouble under the agreement if she talked to me about why she left the firm," Philly responded. "I don't read the agreement that way."

Philly passed a document to Simon. "Take a look at this when you can and tell me whether you agree with me. There's a general confidentiality provision that says firm business is to be kept confidential. I didn't read it as prohibiting a partner from obtaining or providing evidence that Hazelton Kauffman practiced sex discrimination."

"I'll take a look at it," Simon said.

"What's your next move?" McCauley asked.

"I'm going to file that MCAD complaint tomorrow. I may tweak it a bit. Simon, please throw together a motion seeking permission to take the depositions of Chambers and Church."

"Should I use the rationale Berenson gave us?"

"No. Just allege that on information and belief, Chambers and Church may be similarly situated to Li."

"What information are you referring to?" Simon asked. "Berenson didn't have Chambers say a thing."

"When it comes time to argue the motion," Philly said, "I'm going to say that I met with Chambers and Berenson, that Chambers didn't say anything, and that Berenson suggested I proceed by deposition if I were to proceed at all."

"Nothing like the truth," Simon said.

Meredith sat in the visitor's chair of one of the principals of the two-man, downtown Boston law firm of Sampson & Shine. George Sampson had to be close to her age, around thirty. He had wavy blond hair, blue eyes, and a long, rugged face. His law firm specialized in domestic relations. Each partner in the firm had a private office. Meredith had been greeted by a receptionist and had noticed a decent-sized conference room behind the receptionist's desk. The office furnishings were modern: glass-topped tables, chrome framed chairs with plush black cushions, polished, light-colored wood desks. The comparison with the offices where she and Rachel and Simon worked was glaring.

"Thanks for seeing me," Meredith said.

"This is my pleasure," Sampson replied. "If I can do anything for Sloan-Webster, I will. I owe the law school big time."

Over the phone, Meredith had filled Sampson in on the lawsuit filed against his alma mater. His offer to help had been spontaneous and sincere.

"You seem very grateful to your law school. Why is that?"

Sampson smiled wryly. "You're forcing me to dig up some painful memories. Let's just say that I was an indifferent college student who partied more than I should have. I also don't do well on standardized tests so the score on my law boards was less than stellar. No other law school accepted me. Sloan-Webster gave me a chance. Everything I have professionally I owe to them."

Meredith had looked up Sampson's record. "You didn't exactly distinguish yourself in law school."

"No, I didn't. I think I barely made the top half of my class. During law school, I toned down the partying, but I was also holding down a job. There were times I had to blow off classes. But I liked law school. I thought the faculty was pretty good and I learned a lot despite how my record looks. I really thought I could make a go of it with a legal career. My partner and I are doing pretty well. I've got no complaints with how things turned out."

Meredith jotted down a few notes. "I've explained the gist of the lawsuit to you. In a nutshell, the plaintiffs claim that the law school took students' tuition money unfairly because the law school did nothing to find students law-related jobs."

Sampson eased back in his desk chair. "Anybody who went to Sloan-Webster had to know the law school was ranked near the bottom of the pack. That's just a fact of life. The way I remember it, Sloan-Webster mostly admitted students who couldn't get into any other school. That was my situation. The law school was relatively new and basically promised a legal education. The placement office would post job openings but little else. I never relied on the placement office for anything. Everyone knew it basically wasn't going to provide any meaningful help. All the people I hung around with knew we were on our own. That was largely because we were competing with graduates from more prestigious law schools."

"So how did you end up where you are?" Meredith asked, curious.

"Luck and guts," Sampson said. "I met Dave Shine studying for the bar. We hit it off. By the way, like you, he's a Spenser grad. Neither of us had jobs. Firms weren't interested in us. We figured what the hell, let's go out on our own. Some woman Dave knew from high school ran into him. She wanted to divorce her husband and was shopping around for a lawyer. Dave said he'd be glad to help, and we had our first case. We didn't know shit about divorce law, but we learned fast. Next thing happened, I picked up another divorce case by luck and we were off and running."

Meredith contrasted her own situation with Sampson's. If another case of substance came her way, should she run with it and sever ties with Simon and Rachel's firm? At the moment, there appeared to be no future there. She had never envisioned herself in a sole practice, but she was being forced in that direction. The idea of practicing alone was a turnoff.

Meredith studied Sampson. He could be an effective witness. He was down to earth, was genuinely grateful to Sloan-Webster, and had had no illusions about the placement office's role in helping graduates.

"I think you can help the law school," Meredith said. "The law school never held the placement office out as anything but an office that would *try* to answer placement questions. You've just confirmed that."

"I'm in," Sampson said. "Just tell me where and when."

84

"Whatever possessed you to partner up with Carpenter?" Brian Murphy asked.

"Isn't that what you're proposing to do?" Simon countered.

"True," Murphy acknowledged. "But I wouldn't have to deal with him on a daily basis. You two will."

Murphy was joking; still, hearing Carpenter being made fun of took some getting used to. Rachel felt at sea. Maybe it was the size of the conference room which could easily swallow their firm's entire footprint. Maybe it was the size of Nye and Murphy—especially Nye—and the way they dominated the room. Maybe it was the prospect of being subsumed within a hierarchical structure that might put an end to the close relationship she had with her partners. Maybe it was as simple as the prospect of no longer having her name on the office door. They hadn't been Carpenter, Sullivan, Jeffries & Boyle for very long, but it meant something to her.

"Do you have any questions or concerns you wish to discuss with us?" Nye asked. "No doubt Carpenter and Philly filled you in on our meeting. I'm sure you have questions."

Nye was looking at them kindly and Rachel decided to be blunt. "I'm finding this overwhelming," she said. She ignored Simon's sharp look and kept her eyes on Nye.

"That's perfectly understandable," Nye said. "It might be hard at first to imagine how the firms would fit together. But I think they *can* fit. We can't avoid imposing some more bureaucracy than you're used to. But when it comes to the practice of law, we think this only works if we have you operate the way you've been operating."

Simon nodded approvingly. His gesture confirmed for Rachel that Simon wanted to make a change. Of her three partners, he had been the most receptive to Harris Burton's proposal. The Dudley, Atkins & Tyng proposal might be even more to his liking.

"Has Carpenter told you how the four of us got together?" Rachel asked, ignoring a mildly reproving look from Simon.

"No," Nye said.

"Simon and I graduated from Spenser School of Law. We were on the law school's honor code committee and Carpenter was defending a student accused of failing to report cheating. Later, when Philly was pregnant with her first child, he remembered us and called us to see whether we were interested in helping to fill in for her. Neither of us had a lawyer job and we agreed to sign on." Rachel paused to make sure she had their hosts' attention. "We owe Carpenter and Philly a lot. They gave us a chance to prove ourselves. You wouldn't believe how generous they've been to us."

"We appreciate the background," Nye said. "I believe that what you've said reinforces the correctness of our approach in wanting the four of you to retain what you've worked to build. Are you feeling that we may gobble you up and you'll lose what you have?"

"The thought occurred to me," Rachel said, avoiding Simon's gaze.

"If we work things out," Nye responded, "you would no longer have your names on the door. You would be Dudley, Atkins & Tyng lawyers, just as we are. Our objective is to expand your practice. We would also take administrative tasks off your shoulders."

"Carpenter should be all in favor of that," Murphy noted.

"Carpenter refuses to accept the title, but he's our de facto managing partner," Rachel pointed out.

"You seem to have a true democracy working," Warren spoke for the first time. "We'll try to preserve that but, as Richard pointed out, there's no avoiding an upper level of supervision. I'll be your contact person and I'll be reporting to Richard and other members of our firm's management committee. They will need to be informed as to how you're doing and what you're up to. There's no getting around that because, as Richard said, you will be Dudley, Atkins & Tyng lawyers."

"What if you don't get a return on your investment?" Simon asked.

"If for a protracted period you break even or lose money, the partners in the firm are likely to question the arrangement and may even seek to break it off," Nye replied. "Law is, after all, a business. Also, the four of you may wish to sever ties with us if your operation becomes stagnant for an appreciable period."

"In which case, we would have lost whatever name branding we may have accomplished while with you," Simon said.

"Correct," Nye confirmed. "That is a risk for you. But I would be surprised if this failure scenario ever played out. I'll repeat what I said to your other two partners. This only makes sense if your hearts are in it."

Rachel wished she knew more about the business side of operating a large law firm. Their current operation was small. They took a payday whenever they could. They had never had an argument over money. They knew they were in it together.

"I'd like to make another observation," Nye said. "Way back when, I was the managing partner of our firm. This firm has been my life. Brian will tell you that I don't get excited all that often."

"Richard doesn't get excited all that often," Murphy confirmed.

"But I'm excited about this," Nye continued without missing a beat. "I'm dedicated to making this work. Philly called it a social experiment. She's probably correct to a degree. Whatever you want to call it, I want to give it a fair shot."

Rachel suspected that in the end, she was going to have to trust Carpenter's and Philly's judgment. The three Dudley, Atkins & Tyng partners seemed nice enough. But being in business together caused people to do crazy things. Wasn't that something Carpenter was constantly preaching?

"I have a question for *you*," Warren said. "What's the story with Ms. Sweeney? Would she be joining you if we worked something out?"

"Meredith doesn't know about these discussions," Simon said.

"I was impressed by her," Warren said. "She took a series of depositions in the Ship Right case. I don't want to be accused of being subtle so here's a direct plug for getting her to join you. If that's a problem, I would like to have a separate discussion about it."

"Something else to think about," Simon said.

'These people really are serious,' Rachel thought.

85

"Do your partners know you're meeting with me?" Richard Nye asked.

Carpenter nodded. Nye was probably wondering why he had been singled out for a private lunch, but the simple fact was that any ongoing connection between the two firms would ultimately be a business decision, and Nye was the businessman of the bunch, not Murphy or Warren, the litigators.

They were seated in a deli that Carpenter liked. He suspected Nye was used to dining at a place that was a cut above a hole-in-the-wall, cafeteria-style eatery where you brought trays to a table. But Nye seemed at ease and was looking at him inquiringly.

"What's it like working with Murphy?" Carpenter asked, opting for chit-chat before business.

"Mercifully, I don't have to work with him since I'm a probate lawyer. Your question should be directed to Sarah. But I will tell you that Brian's my best friend at the firm."

"Talk about odd couples," Carpenter commented.

"It's a long story. In the past, when we were younger, we both played for the firm's basketball team. That created a bond. We've got two season tickets for the Celtics that we mostly use together. When Brian and Sarah went out on their own, I felt a personal loss. I was the one who came up with a package to bring them back. They have a lot of autonomy, similar in many respects to what you would have under the arrangement we've been discussing."

Carpenter disassembled his club sandwich, removing the middle layer of whole wheat toast. He moved his side of salad around on his plate. "I have a question for you. Is your firm losing business and transaction clients because of your firm's high rates?"

Nye gave no indication that the question was unexpected. "May I assume that if I answer your question, you'll fill me in on why you asked it?"

"You may."

"The answer is yes but it's difficult to quantify."

Carpenter continued to move food around on his plate. "Before you approached us, we were approached by a small business firm that wanted to expand into litigation. This firm was farming out litigation and wanted to bring it in-house. I can't tell you the name of the firm because the discussions are confidential. Would you guys be interested in expanding your idea beyond our litigation practice?"

"Are you still in discussions with this business firm?"

Carpenter nodded. "We've been dragging our feet. We like the people we're talking with and they've been flexible, which is a big plus. But it would be a big step for us, just as what you've put on the table would be a big step for us."

Nye sampled his sandwich. Carpenter liked his deliberateness. Nye struck him as the kind of guy who would keep his mouth shut if he had nothing to say and wouldn't say anything until he had thought it through.

"Personally, *I* would be interested," Nye said, "but I'm not sure the business and transaction lawyers in our firm would be. I think they'd have a tough time agreeing to firm lawyers charging lower rates when it came to a business deal. I could be wrong, but that's my impression. Do you feel some duty to this other firm you're talking with?"

"I wouldn't say duty," Carpenter replied, "but we want to be fair and aboveboard with them. The people we've been talking to have an office that's a lot nicer than ours. They've got clerical support. They've got space for additional lawyers. Simon—who you just met—brought this up. He was thinking that if your firm wanted to establish a low-cost outpost, maybe the outpost could be bigger than the one you first had in mind."

Nye paid attention to his food and Carpenter followed suit.

"This adds a layer of complication to what we proposed to you," Nye finally said.

"That was my initial reaction," Carpenter replied. "But I'm throwing it out to you. One of the people we've been talking to is someone that Philly and I know pretty well. He'd be an asset to any law firm."

"Do you want me to raise this with the rest of our firm's management committee?" Nye asked.

"I guess I do," Carpenter said, "unless there's a compelling reason not to. Is there a way you can keep the discussion within the management committee?"

"If I insist that the matter stay within the committee, I believe the other members of the committee will honor my request. Each of us has had occasion to request that a matter stay within the committee."

"Then I'd say present it to the committee, keep it within the committee, and get back to me with their reaction." Carpenter realized the difficult part of this luncheon discussion was over. "How can you stand the bureaucracy your firm has?" he asked.

"The bureaucracy is necessary," Nye said. "It prevents us from being at each other's throats. And when the bureaucracy is working as it should, it's actually a beautiful thing to behold."

"Jesus!" Carpenter said.

"Brian said you were set in your ways."

"You don't know the half of it." 'But you're about to find out,' Carpenter thought.

When Meredith finished her report on the meeting with George Sampson and on her telephone contacts with other Sloan-Webster graduates, she was a little shocked by the dour expressions around the war room conference table. She regarded her report as positive. The lack of enthusiasm from Dean Martin and Ralph Cray was disappointing. Only Neil Taylor was upbeat.

"Every sword does have two edges," the dean remarked. "Sampson and the other graduates you spoke with want to help and I know we should be appreciative. But in helping, they're putting the law school down. They're painting a picture of the law school as a school of last resort for prospective lawyers. Sampson is almost suggesting that the placement office couldn't be expected to help graduates because the graduates were beyond help."

"We think Sampson's testimony will help in this case," Simon said.

"But at what cost?" the dean countered.

"Sampson is a success story," Rachel pointed out.

"But he's saying that he made it on his own and the law school did very little to help him get to where he is today," the dean responded, shaking her head.

"May I say something?" Meredith requested when neither Simon nor Rachel replied to the dean. "This is litigation," she forged ahead before anyone could tell her not to. "The first question should be whether what Sampson said is true. I believe it is. Nobody at this table has disputed that. The next question then becomes whether what Sampson has to say helps us in this case more than it hurts us in this case. I come out that it helps the law school. If you win the case using Sampson's story, you'll have plenty of time to fix the school's image—or embrace its image—later. But if, without his testimony, you lose the case, you may not have time to fix anything. You have to keep your eye on the case in front of us right now."

Meredith paused. Cray and the dean still looked unhappy, but at least they were listening to her. Neither Simon nor Rachel had signaled her to put a sock in it. "Here's my thinking," she continued. "Sloan-Webster *is* at the bottom of the law school pecking order here in Massachusetts. It's a relatively new institution. Its focus has been to provide a superior legal education to students who largely were rejected by other law schools, didn't fit the usual mold. In setting priorities, the law school focused on its educational efforts, which was a proper focus because providing students with a solid legal education would only help the law school and its graduates long term. I think we should go with Sampson and some of the other graduates I reached out to."

"Sampson is a nice contrast to a gambler and a lap dancer," Simon voiced.

"Plus, if you go along with the idea of setting up a fund to enhance the placement office, we would essentially have a three-pronged attack," Rachel said. "First, we go after each of the plaintiffs. Second, we point to Sloan-Webster graduates who did make it in the law. Third, we drive home the point that the law school is continuing to move forward on its priorities and is in fact now able to focus more on the placement office."

"I told you before that I was very moved by the responses to the questionnaire we sent graduates," Neil Taylor joined the discussion. "Sloan-Webster has always had an uphill battle and that's going to continue. I'm in favor of using Sampson and others like him."

"Ralph and I will discuss this," Dean Martin said. "I don't want to make a decision at this moment."

'Delay, delay, delay,' Meredith thought.

"If we dedicate money to the placement office," Cray said, "will you tell Blaisedell?"

"Tell him?" Simon responded. "I'm going to ask him for specific suggestions on how to spend your money."

Maxine always knew when Carpenter wasn't asleep. He could be breathing deeply, regularly, facing away from her with his eyes closed and yet she knew. Maxine moved next to him and began to gently rub his back before asking the question that was driving him nuts.

"What does your gut tell you?" Maxine asked.

"I wish to hell I knew," Carpenter said.

"Your instincts are usually pretty good," Maxine said. "I would trust them."

"I keep going back and forth," Carpenter admitted. "I feel like I'd be surrendering if I hooked up with Murphy and Warren. They say they'll try to keep things the same for us but it's not going to happen. I just can't picture myself as part of some mega-firm. And Burton and Klein… I don't know. I don't like the idea of getting into bed with a bunch of business lawyers."

Maxine began massaging his shoulder muscles. "Do you have it in you for one more adventure?" she asked.

It was an interesting way of looking at it. Carpenter knew that when there were downsides to all the alternatives, he typically followed the rule of doing nothing. Yet he couldn't escape the feeling that doing nothing was a mistake in this situation. Maxine was right: joining up with another firm would be an adventure. Maybe he needed a change to recharge his batteries. "Probably," he answered Maxine. "But it's one of those things where you don't really know what you're getting into until you're into it. I worry that if I make a move, I may end up hating the choice."

"I don't see that as a problem," Maxine said. "If you dislike where you end up, walk away. Didn't you tell me that you would insist on opt-out provisions? So if you don't like the move, opt out."

Maxine had a point. Nothing was irreversible. "If we do make a move, my gut is leaning toward Murphy's firm," Carpenter said.

"Why?"

Carpenter thought for a minute. "There was something about this guy Richard Nye that I liked. You look at the guy and listen to him and sometimes he comes across as a stuffed shirt. But he's given a lot of thought to this and seems determined to make it work. I guess I trusted him. Which is not to say I don't trust Harris Burton—I do. Plus, working with Murphy and Warren would never be dull."

"Is there a time frame for making a decision?" Maxine asked.

"I want this sorted out this year. It's driving me fucking nuts in case you haven't noticed."

The room was comfortably chilly, and Maxine snuggled closer to Carpenter. "I've noticed."

86

Carpenter called Philly so he could vent. "We're living on fumes," he said when she picked up. "The fumes are called Sloan-Webster."

"I was thinking the same thing. My babysitter has got the kids and I'm holed up in my home office with nothing much to do."

"This is beyond troublesome," Carpenter said. "Here we are talking with two firms that want to swallow us up and our well is dry. I feel like an imposter, like I'm negotiating under false pretenses."

"Where are you going with this? Are you saying we should break off discussions because it wouldn't be fair to these other firms to join them?"

"The thought crossed my mind," Carpenter admitted. He should have mentioned this circumstance to Maxine but had chickened out. "Each firm is going to want to get a read on our active cases, and we don't have any cases worth talking about."

"What do we do?" Philly asked.

Carpenter hoped going through available options would clarify his thinking. "First, we could break off discussions. Second, we could simply level with both firms and see whether they're still interested. Third, we could put our heads in the sand and keep talking to the firms as if everything's fine."

"Shit!" Philly muttered.

"The thing is," Carpenter continued, "I had pretty much come around to thinking that merging with another firm, one way or another, made sense. I was talking to Maxine and realized that I was leaning towards Murphy and Warren."

"I could still go either way," Philly said. "Klein's firm might be able to throw some meaty litigation our way. With Murphy and Warren, they have an incentive to try to bring any client into their own shop at their higher rates."

"That's a fair point," Carpenter acknowledged. "But my thinking is that anything that ends up in their shop might be something we lacked the resources to handle. And then there's the point you made about having their experience if I'm, let's say, otherwise occupied."

Philly sighed. "I'm sick to death of dealing with this crap."

"You and me both."

"Aren't you always saying honesty is the best policy? I'm leaning toward being honest with both firms. We'll find out real fast whether they're still hot to get into bed with us."

"We need to circle back with Simon and Rachel," Carpenter said. "I was trying to think about our approach if we were busy as hell. If that were the case, my thought was that we'd probably be opting for staying by ourselves."

"Stop it!" Philly said. "We're tying ourselves up in knots the more we talk about it. Next stop—Simon and Rachel."

"I'll set it up," Carpenter said. "And who knows, maybe a new client will walk in tomorrow. Somehow, one usually does."

"What do you know about robotics?" Jeremiah Becker asked.

"Squat," Carpenter said. He had no idea where this call was headed. Becker had arranged a conference call on short notice. Clyde Atkins was also on the line.

"The same goes for us," Atkins said.

"Clyde told you we were on the board of trustees of a hospital," Becker picked up. "We're calling you as board members."

"This is Rushmore Hospital, up in the Lawrence and Lowell area," Atkins continued their tag team approach.

"For a community hospital, it has a sophisticated operating room," Becker said.

"The hospital is big on new technology and used a robot to participate in a surgical procedure," Atkins supplied, continuing the tag team.

"The procedure didn't have a successful outcome," Becker said. "The hospital is being sued and its insurer has chosen counsel to represent it."

'What am I doing on this call?' Carpenter wondered.

"The robot screwed up," Atkins explained. "The hospital wants to sue the robot manufacturer. You interested in representing the hospital?"

"Yes, I am," Carpenter said, his pulse quickening.

"Good," Becker said. "We both know your hourly rate. The hourly rate of the hospital's corporate law firm litigator was off the charts. So we thought of you."

"Good thinking."

Philly and Sarah Ferguson were on lunch duty. Daisy, Rosalind, and Daniel had deconstructed their BLTs and were nibbling on bacon strips. 'There was something about bacon,' Philly thought. It really was good. Why not start with the best?

Philly heard her office phone ring and waited for the call to be forwarded to her cell phone.

"Philly Sullivan."

"This is Justin Maynard. I wonder if you remember me."

The blank Philly drew was fleeting. "Seacoast Regional Hospital. Of course I remember you. You were very gracious to me in a difficult situation." Maynard was an older lawyer, several years older than Carpenter, who had represented the hospital in a case where the hospital sought to discharge Isabella's uncle to his home in Guatemala. Philly hadn't been able to stop the discharge—equivalent to a deportation—yet had been grateful to Maynard for being sensitive to Isabella's concern for her uncle. Later, Maynard had helped one of Philly's physician clients.

"I had some trouble tracking you down. I knew you as Ms. Piper."

"It's Sullivan now. I'm married, and I'm now in a law firm with three other partners. How did you find me?"

"I found your firm's website. I've wound down my practice, but I still advise the hospital. The hospital is in a situation where it's being sued for negligence. The claim is that the hospital was negligent in granting a physician clinical privileges. It's a complicated case. The theory of negligent credentialing is gaining recognition and there's a recent Massachusetts case that supports the theory. The hospital and its insurer are following my recommendation that we use an outside counsel of our choosing to handle the negligent credentialing claim. I thought of you."

"I'm flattered."

"The theory of negligent credentialing is extremely sensitive. It affects the hospital as an institution and also the hospital's medical staff. Underlying the case is a surgical procedure that was unsuccessful. The surgeon is being sued. The hospital is also being sued for negligence and for negligently giving the surgeon clinical privileges that permitted him to operate. The surgeon has been subject to a number of malpractice actions and has had run-ins with the physician heading up the Surgery Department. Is this something that interests you?"

Philly took a deep breath to get her emotions under control. She was tempted to shout, 'Count me in!' but opted for restraint. "Yes, it interests me. It sounds like a fascinating case."

"Fascinating is not the exact word I'd use. Troublesome comes to mind. But I'm very pleased you're interested."

"You should know that I typically work from home. I've got two little kids. But babysitting is taken care of and the working from home has never been a problem."

"Then congratulations are in order," Maynard said. "I started practicing law at a time when children and family dynamics were studiously ignored. The pendulum has swung the other way on such matters and I, for one, am pleased. I don't foresee any problems in this area. I suggest that the next step is a meeting between you, me, the president of the hospital, and the president of the medical staff. You can send me your engagement letter before the meeting."

"Excellent. Just tell me where and when."

"You should have called me before setting up this placement office fund," Christopher Blaisedell said when Simon took his call.

Blaisedell sounded pissed. Simon didn't care what attitude his adversary was nursing on this phone call. Janet Martin and Ralph Cray had approved the establishment of a placement office fund and had sent out an e-mail blast to students and alumni announcing the initiative. Simon had forwarded a copy of the dean's e-mail to Blaisedell.

"Why would I do that?" Simon responded. "It's not as if the law school needs your approval on this or any other matter."

"I responded to your request for a settlement proposal," Blaisedell came back. "The establishment of a fund is the kind of thing that we should have discussed in terms of settlement."

"Well then, let's get one formality out of the way. Your settlement offer is rejected. Given your unreasonable monetary proposal, the law school sees no point in discussing settlement."

"Then we're headed for trial," Blaisedell said.

"I agree." Simon paused a beat. "If you or your clients wish to make suggestions as to how the fund's money is spent, please feel free to let us know. The law school welcomes your ideas."

"I'm not sure what kind of game you're playing here, but while the lawsuit is pending, and given your failure to discuss the establishment of a fund, you won't be hearing from us with suggestions."

"That's too bad," Simon said, not meaning it in the least. "One other thing. Since you read the dean's e-mail announcement, you're aware that the law school is setting up an advisory group on placement matters. The group will be comprised of students and alumni. Please tell your clients that if any of them is interested in being named to the group, he or she should inform you so that you can let me know of their interest. I'll repeat this in an e-mail to you which I trust you will share with your clients."

"It's pretty obvious what you're up to," Blaisedell said.

"I'm not up to anything. I have no idea what you're talking about."

"You're trying to anticipate what a judge is going to order the law school to do once my clients prevail at trial. You're trying to head off court orders giving relief to the plaintiffs against the law school."

"That's simply not the case," Simon said smoothly, knowing there was more truth than fiction to Blaisedell's charge. "The dean's announcement made clear that the law school established priorities and is working through them. First and foremost was the hiring of a superior faculty. That's been accomplished regardless of your view of the faculty. The alumni newsletter will be published more frequently and expanded. So that goal has also been reached. Next on the list is the placement office."

"You can't expect me to swallow that load of bullshit!" Blaisedell let his irritation show.

"I have no expectation when it comes to you one way or another. By making an exorbitant settlement demand, you and your lawsuit are no longer relevant to the law school's plans and initiatives going forward. The law school will take its chances defending against the claims of a lap dancer and gambler. And by the way, that advisory group I just mentioned? I was serious when I said you should encourage your plaintiffs to participate. Not only will they get to share their views, they'll also have something that should look good on their resumés."

"You really are a fucking asshole," Blaisedell said before disconnecting.

Simon smiled. Mission accomplished.

87

Philly was tired and hoped it didn't show. She'd known Carpenter would be setting up this partners meeting but hadn't expected it would be at eight in the morning. Fortunately, today was Isabella's turn for breakfast duty.

Philly surveyed her colleagues around the conference room table. Rachel and Simon were annoyingly bright eyed and bushy tailed. Carpenter was his unsmiling self.

"Let's get started," Carpenter announced. "Philly and I were talking about the proposals from the two firms that have approached us. We came to a conclusion."

Rachel's eyes widened. Simon looked shocked.

"We both can't stand thinking about these proposals anymore," Carpenter continued. "We're sick to death of them and I suspect you guys are as well. It seemed to us that the four of us needed to talk. So here we are."

Philly noticed how quickly Simon recovered himself. He had to have been thinking that she and Carpenter had made a decision without consulting him or Rachel.

"I'm not really sick of thinking about the proposals," Simon said. "But I don't like stringing people along, which is what we've been doing, especially with Harris Burton. This meeting is a good idea."

"One of the things that's been bugging me," Carpenter said, "is the lack of active cases we have in the office. I mentioned this to Philly. It makes me feel like we're having these discussions with the two firms under false pretenses. They have to be assuming we've got a lot of work. But outside of the Sloan-Webster case and Ai Li's discrimination case, we've finished what we had on hand, and we've got nothing solid lined up to follow."

Philly noted Rachel's downcast expression. Simon was his inscrutable self.

"If we go any farther down the road with either firm," Carpenter went on, "the firm is going to want to see an inventory of active matters. The pantry is bare. So one of the things I want us to try to sort out this morning is what to do about this situation. Do we let these firms know that our case load is in the crapper? Do we do nothing? Do we simply break off discussions?"

Rachel voiced her opinion. "I think we either stop discussions or own up to what's happening. Doing nothing would be wrong."

"I think if we own up to our situation with either firm," Simon responded, "the firm will terminate discussions. Why would Richard Nye's firm fund an operation that had no cases? I don't want to stop discussions. I think joining up with another firm makes a lot of sense for us. But if we reveal our situation, I can't see discussions going forward."

"Does that mean you're in favor of doing nothing?" Rachel asked.

"Not really," Simon said begrudgingly. "You're right; doing nothing is not fair to these other firms. As we're talking this through, I guess I'd lean toward breaking off discussions until we beef up our caseload."

"Let's come back to this point later," Philly suggested. "Which proposal is best for us?"

"I'm leaning toward Dudley, Atkins & Tyng," Carpenter said. "What tips the scales for me is knowing Murphy and Warren and the fact that these guys do litigation. I'm still a little leery about hooking up with a bunch of business law guys. And Nye seems to get it that it's important for us to have autonomy."

"I think we'd have autonomy with Burton's firm exactly because they don't do litigation," Simon countered, "so I'm leaning in that direction. We really would control litigation because nobody there is a litigator. We'd get to build our own department."

Rachel looked torn so Philly spoke up. "I'm leaning toward Murphy and Warren. Harris Burton's age has a lot to do with that. I think without Harris around, Klein's firm might struggle on its business side. That could lead to difficulties down the road."

Rachel sighed. "I just can't make up my mind. I keep thinking that if we had more work, I'd like things to stay the same. Maybe I'm putting my head in the sand." Rachel regarded Carpenter. "I think about you and your cancer and I know we'd be at a disadvantage if you weren't with us and it was just the three of us alone. But I like what we've built up and I like you guys. Maybe we do need nicer offices, but I'd keep things going the way they are if I could choose."

Philly glanced at Carpenter and wondered whether Rachel's short speech had touched a nerve with him. One thing was clear: the four of them weren't close to making a unanimous decision. Standing pat might end up as their default position.

"Let's return to what to say to the two firms about our case load." Philly said. "I'm opting for disclosure. I'm inclined to tell them our case load is down. That said, you'll be happy to hear that we've got a potential new case."

Philly went through her call with Justin Maynard about the problem Seacoast Regional Hospital was facing. Rachel brightened as her narrative progressed. Carpenter also was engaged. Simon listened impassively, but Philly could tell he wasn't missing a thing.

"That's great!" Rachel said.

"There's actually a second potential new matter that's come in," Carpenter revealed. Philly made a few notes as he described a second hospital-related case. The timing of these new developments was eerie.

"You guys are great!" Rachel gushed. "This is wonderful. These sound like great cases."

"Two cases don't pass for an inventory," Carpenter cautioned.

"But this is all positive," Rachel said. "It doesn't take much to give us a boost. And while we're on new cases, I need to bring you up to date on that teenage tennis player I told you about. So far, there are twelve girls who had miserable experiences at the tennis camp. What I'm thinking of doing is holding a conference call with a dial in number to go over legal options. The girls and their parents would be invited to participate. This might be one of those situations where we get a modest non-refundable retainer and a contingency. What do you think?"

Philly loved Rachel's enthusiasm. She wondered whether it would be dampened in a larger firm environment. "I'd say go for it. Why don't you run the options by Carpenter before you have the call?"

"Okay."

"What's the amount of the retainer you're thinking about?" Simon asked.

"A thousand dollars."

"Okay," Simon said.

Rachel was energized. Philly disliked bringing her off her high. "Rachel. You seem to be the only one who would prefer the status quo to linking up with one of the other firms. I want to make sure that's your position."

"It's what I prefer. But I understand things won't stay the same forever which is why I said I might be putting my head in the sand. If you three think it's best to make a move with another firm, I'll make it unanimous."

"Do you have a preference for which firm we pursue?" Philly followed up.

"Not really. There are good points about each. I wish we could predict what life would be like with these firms, but obviously that's not possible. I came away from the meeting Simon and I had with Nye and his partners impressed with their commitment to making an arrangement work. I also liked Harris Burton and Ben Klein a lot. Their culture is different from ours, but it's closer than that of a big-law firm like Nye's. I really can't choose. I'm prepared to go along with what you guys decide. I know I'm coming across as indecisive, but so be it."

"I think we're making some progress," Philly said, wondering why she and not Carpenter was leading the discussion. "Let's go back to our case load. I'm for telling both firms that our volume of active cases is low. If either firm craps out after receiving this information, then we know where our remaining option lies."

"Seconded," Carpenter finally spoke up. "Let's get these two new matters locked up with engagement letters. If both firms stay interested, then we have some decisions to make. The way I see it, if we can't all agree on which firm to pursue, we stay as we are. If Philly and I come around to Simon's view to pursue Harris' firm, then we go forward on that front. If Simon comes around to pursuing Nye's firm which is where Philly and I presently are, then we move forward on that front. Have I got this right?"

Philly couldn't find holes in Carpenter's reasoning. "I think so," she said.

"So do I," Simon added, and Rachel nodded her agreement.

"I would also like to mention to Harris that we have been approached by another firm and see if he will give me permission to mention his firm's name to Nye."

"As you all know, I'm in favor of that," Simon said.

"Sure," said Philly.

"Okay," Rachel agreed.

"Democracy in action," Carpenter said. "If you want, I'll make the calls about our case load."

"Okay," Simon and Rachel said together.

"Then I think we're adjourned," Carpenter said.

88

It was close to midnight when Paul pulled his car into the driveway in Brighton, and Philly was fighting to keep her eyes open. She wanted to be like Daisy and Daniel, conked out in the back seat. On the plus side, another Thanksgiving safari had come to an end.

"I'll get the kids," Paul said. "You get the door."

She did, and then got the kids' beds ready while Paul made two trips from the car. When the kids were settled, Philly shucked her coat onto the bedroom floor and flopped onto the bed. She stared at the ceiling for a long moment and then closed her eyes.

"You think we're getting too old for this?" Paul asked as he took a seat on his side of the bed.

"I know I am."

She replayed the day's journeys. The visit to her parents' house in Fall River was a replay of recent years' Thanksgiving visits. Daniel and Daisy were doted on by their grandparents. Paul had initiated most of the adult talk. The divide between her and her parents had stayed the same with no narrowing in sight. Then on to Cambridge for a gathering at the house of one of Paul's brothers, where multi-generational chaos ruled and Daniel got so overexcited he forgot he was hungry. Finally, the long drive to North Andover to see Philip's parents, a subdued gathering in which Philip's memory had a seat at the dinner table. On leaving, Philly had given Philip's mother a copy of the letter Tom Grange had written to Daisy; she didn't want to be around when his mother read it.

"This remains something we need to do every year," Paul said.

"I know," Philly said, her eyes still closed. "I know."

89

The MCAD hearing room was slowly filling up when Helena Peck introduced herself to Philly and Simon. Philly couldn't quite place the name, but Simon did so immediately.

"I remember you," Simon said. "You represented the Pinkerton firm in a case we brought on behalf of a fired associate."

"And I remember you, Mr. Jeffries. You and Ms. Boyle almost managed to derail a settlement agreement involving your client, Ms. Sweeney."

Philly studied her adversary. Peck was middle-aged with long, blond hair, blue eyes, and a friendly smile. Perhaps Peck had built up a practice niche representing law firms in employment matters.

"I have to admit that the cases you bring are not run of the mill," Peck said, before taking her seat.

The hearing officer entered the room. Beth Starr was young and athletic looking with a swimmer's broad shoulders and tapered upper body. "Let's come to order," she announced as she took her seat at a table in the front of the room. "We're here on a motion to take the depositions of two former partners of the respondent law firm. The petitioner, Ms. Ai Li, has recently resigned from the firm Hazelton, Kauffman, Garfield & Smith, but claims she was discriminated against when she was employed by that firm by being denied a promotion to a level six partner. I would ask counsel to introduce themselves."

"Philly Sullivan for Ms. Li. Simon Jeffries is with me."

"Helena Peck for Hazelton, Kauffman, Garfield & Smith."

"We typically don't permit depositions in cases before the MCAD unless there's a compelling reason," Starr directed at Philly. "If testimony needs to be preserved because a witness may be moving out of Massachusetts, we've been known to make an exception to the no deposition rule. That narrow ground for exception doesn't appear to be involved in this case. May I hear from you, Ms. Sullivan?"

MCAD motion hearings were informal, and Philly thought about remaining seated. But she followed an instinct that treating this hearing as a court matter would earn her points with Starr. She stood and glanced briefly at her one-page outline.

"The witnesses in question are here in Massachusetts and we have no information that they are planning to leave the state. Nonetheless, the witnesses in question are basically unavailable to us. They decline to talk to us. Mr. Jeffries and I met with Ms. Lynn Chambers, one of the witnesses Ms. Li wishes to depose. She was represented by counsel. She declined to answer any questions on the advice of her counsel who was concerned that cooperation by Ms. Chambers would possibly violate the firm's partnership agreement. Her counsel suggested that if we wanted to obtain information from Ms. Chambers, we should take her deposition. We're here to receive permission to do just that. We are not aware of what Ms. Chambers—or Ms. Church for that matter—will say at a deposition. She may in fact provide testimony that will be beneficial to Hazelton Kauffman. Therefore, a deposition is necessary because it is unfair to Ms. Li to proceed to trial by calling witnesses to the stand whose testimony is unknown to her.

"I can't say this with certainty, but I believe that Ms. Chambers and Ms. Church may have resigned from Hazelton, Kauffman after being denied a partner promotion, as was Ms. Li. I have this belief based on the manner of Ms. Chambers' attorney. Ms. Li alleges that women are routinely denied the higher partnership levels at Hazelton, Kauffman. Ms. Li deserves the opportunity to pursue discovery in support of her claims."

"I'll hear from you, Ms. Peck," Starr said.

"Thank you, Your Honor," Peck said, rising. "The point that Your Honor first made is dispositive of the petitioner's motion. The rules of the MCAD do not permit depositions as a matter of right and this is not a situation where witnesses will not be available at trial. Therefore, there is no basis for allowing the depositions to go forward as a matter of law."

"Excuse me, Ms. Peck, for interrupting you," Starr intervened. "But is it your client's position that the two witnesses are free to talk with Ms. Li's counsel?"

"No, Your Honor," Peck replied without hesitation. "The firm's partnership agreement explicitly states that firm business must be kept confidential. Each potential witness' relationship and dealings with the firm may not be disclosed."

"Maybe that's why Ms. Chambers' counsel suggested that Ms. Chambers be deposed," Starr said.

"I wouldn't know what Ms. Chambers' counsel might be thinking," Peck responded. "I would also note that while counsel for Ms. Li claims that it is unfair for Ms. Li to proceed to trial without knowing what the two lawyers will say, Ms. Li is prepared to go through with depositions not knowing what the witnesses will say. If she takes the witnesses' depositions, their testimony under oath will be known to the parties and the party that benefits from the testimony will proceed to use it at trial."

"Ms. Peck's second point is a valid point, isn't it, Ms. Sullivan?" Starr asked.

"I would respectfully disagree," Philly countered. "If the witnesses' deposition testimony is unfavorable to Ms. Li, Ms. Li would have time to try to counter that testimony at trial. Moreover, the witnesses' deposition testimony might lead to other relevant testimony that Ms. Li could produce at trial."

Starr began writing in her trial notebook. When she concluded her note taking, she turned to Peck. "Were the two witnesses denied a promotion to a six or above partnership level?"

Peck hesitated only a beat. "Yes, in the case of Ms. Chambers," she said. "Ms. Church was not promoted to level five."

Starr took her time thinking, and Simon nudged Philly. "She's going to rule on this now," he whispered.

Philly nodded, taking two deep calming breaths that failed to do their job.

"I am sympathetic to Ms. Peck's point that this situation is not the type of situation where the MCAD permits depositions. But I am also sympathetic to Ms. Sullivan's point that it is important for her client to learn what the witnesses will say in advance of trial notwithstanding what the law firm's partnership agreement states. It seems to me that the fairest way to proceed is to permit the depositions to go forward while noting for the record the respondent's objection to the depositions taking place. So that's what I'm going to order. I expect the depositions to go forward under the rules of civil procedure relating to court proceedings and I'm going to put that in my order. So that the depositions don't get bogged down, my order will state that all objections Ms. Peck might have are preserved and that she is free to make any objection at trial. However, if Ms. Peck objects to the form of a deposition question, I would ask her to make that kind of objection at the deposition. At trial, Ms. Peck is free to argue that the firm's partnership agreement bars testimony."

Peck rose. "May I be heard, Your Honor?"

"I've made my ruling," Starr said. "So I don't want to hear anything further on that ruling. If you wish to discuss the deposition rules, please continue."

Peck resumed her seat.

"This hearing is concluded," Starr announced.

December

From Carpenter's Vinyl Collection

"Satisfaction"

The Rolling Stones

90

Neil Taylor was excited. This was the first time the new placement office head had initiated a call. "The response we've gotten to this placement office advisory group has been phenomenal. We've already gotten fifty plus volunteers. And you'll never guess who one of them is."

"Regina White," Simon threw out.

"That Blaisedell guy must have told you," Taylor said, plainly disappointed that his announcement was not a surprise.

"No, he didn't. I just made a lucky guess. I'm willing to bet Blaisedell doesn't know."

"Then he's probably going to be pissed off when he finds out."

"Count on it," Simon said. "Whatever you do, make sure White is chosen."

"I already figured that out," Taylor said cheerfully.

When the call concluded, Simon sat thinking. If he were Blaisdell, he'd be pushing the court for an immediate trial. The sooner the trial, the less time Sloan-Webster had to beef up its placement office.

There might be ways to delay a trial, but what if, instead of opposing an immediate trial, the law school sought an immediate trial date? Simon couldn't imagine Blaisedell anticipating such a move. Representing the plaintiffs, Blaisedell would have to present his case first when it came time to litigate and might not be ready for trial.

Was the law school ready for trial? Simon knew the school's witnesses: Janet Martin, Jane Snelling, and Neil Taylor, for starters. Other possible witnesses included George Sampson and three or four other successful Sloan-Webster graduates whom Meredith had interviewed and were prepared to extol the law school.

Then there was the matter of strategy. Sloan-Webster could make a case that its faculty was, in fact, top-notch. Meredith had reviewed student evaluations of the faculty. For the most part, Sloan-Webster students gave the faculty high marks. With very few exceptions, faculty members who had gotten repeated, negative student evaluations had been let go.

Neil Taylor had determined the success rate of Sloan-Webster graduates taking the Massachusetts Bar Exam. In the last three years, eighty percent of graduates taking the exam for the first time passed, a rate that compared well with both the state average for all schools, and the eighty-two percent first time pass rate of Spencer School of Law, where Simon and Rachel had gotten their own degrees. This, too, reflected well on the school's faculty, especially given Sloan-Webster's tendency to admit students who hadn't excelled in college.

Simon wished he could go after Noah Branson with something tangible. Maybe it was time for Herb McCauley to revisit the college cheating scandal. And no matter how that turned out, Simon was gratified and surprised to discover that, with some intense witness preparation, Sloan-Webster School of Law could be ready for trial.

Carpenter had concluded the uncomfortable, difficult telephone calls he had resolved to make today and took stock of his firm's position.

Richard Nye had listened without comment to the news of their light litigation caseload. "This doesn't change anything as far as I'm concerned," Nye said after some thought. "But I need to mention this to Brian and Sarah and the rest of our management committee. I'll be back to you shortly."

Neither Ben Klein nor Harris Burton reacted outwardly to the small number of active litigation cases either, but Carpenter sensed both were concerned by the light volume. On the other hand, Harris Burton was definitely bothered by hearing that another firm was wooing Carpenter and his partners. Carpenter made clear that the initiative had been recent and had come out of the blue. But these factors did nothing to assuage Harris' irritation.

"Which way are you leaning?" Harris had asked, and Carpenter answered truthfully: "The four of us are divided on that. Would your firm be interested in associating with a large firm?"

"The whole idea of our firm is to provide an alternative to a large firm," Harris had responded testily.

"The large firm we're talking to would want you to remain an alternative to large firms," Carpenter explained, and he supplied the two men with more details on the proposal his own firm had received.

"I don't see this working with business and transaction work," Harris said.

"Would you like me to mention your firm to this firm we've been talking to?" Carpenter asked.

"Harris and I need to talk privately," Ben said. "One of us will get back to you."

Carpenter concluded that the two necessary, uncomfortable calls left two balls up in the air. Both might hit the ground and burst. But at least he had been upfront with both firms. Except for his cancer and Philly's drinking. Those were bombs to drop another day.

91

Simon couldn't remember the conference room being this crowded. Jeannie Smith and her stenographer equipment took up space. For her deposition, Lynn Chambers was again represented by Donald Berenson. Helena Peck was accompanied by a young associate. And he would assist Philly, who would be conducting the deposition.

Smith administered the oath to Chambers and Philly began with background questions. Chambers was a thirty-nine-year-old mother of two. She had started as a litigation associate with Hazelton, Kauffman, Garfield & Smith and had been made a partner after seven years. She had quickly moved up the partnership ladder to the level five rung but had been denied level six partnership status. She had resigned from the firm three months after that denial. Chambers was an experienced litigator. She had tried approximately a dozen cases on her own, mostly in the areas of business and commercial law.

"Were you given a reason for not being promoted to the sixth partnership level?"

"Yes."

"What was the reason?"

"I was told that several clients didn't regard me as sufficiently aggressive."

"Who told you that?"

"The head of the firm's management committee."

"Would that be Henrietta Coleman?"

"No. It was her predecessor, Damian McKinley. He said that of course he didn't know why each partner voted as he or she did, but he suspected it had to do with the comments about me not being sufficiently aggressive."

"What was your view of the 'not sufficiently aggressive' comments?"

Chambers colored and tightly gripped the arms of her chair. "Frankly, I thought it was bullshit."

"Did you actually see the written client evaluations suggesting that you were not sufficiently aggressive?"

"Yes. One was a written comment by a client I had successfully defended in a contract dispute. The client said I could have been more aggressive. The second comment was a check off comment. There was a question something like 'Please evaluate the attorney's aggressiveness in representing your interests.' There were five or so options that the client could check off ranging from 'Very Aggressive' to 'Not Aggressive.' The client had checked off something like 'Could Have Been More Aggressive.' This was a client that had been sued for breach of contract. I remember the case. We had advised the client that it had breached the contract and should pay what it owed under the contract. This advice was rejected. The client litigated and lost."

Peck's associate was taking notes furiously. Peck, in contrast, made an occasional note but for the most part focused on Chambers.

"Prior to learning of these two comments concerning your aggressiveness, had you ever been told by a firm partner that you weren't sufficiently aggressive?"

"No," Chambers said with feeling.

"Were any individuals promoted to the sixth partnership level at the time you were denied that promotion?"

"Yes."

"Who were they?"

"Ryan Mann and Gerard George."

"These are two men, correct?"

"Yes."

"Were they in the litigation department that you were in?"

"Ryan was. Gerard was in the tax department."

"Do you have any information as to how you compared to Mr. Mann and Mr. George in terms of billable hours, client development, or any other factor that might bear on a partnership promotion?"

"Objection," Peck intervened.

"You may answer the question," Berenson instructed his client.

"Yes. For one thing, my billable hours exceeded Ryan's and Gerard's."

"Excuse me for interrupting," Philly said. "I apologize. But how do you know that?"

"I was told that by Damian McKinley. The billable hours came up when he told me I didn't get the level six promotion."

"Thank you," Philly said. "I interrupted you. You were mentioning how you compared to Mr. Mann and Mr. George."

"Right. I also learned that unlike Ryan and Gerard, I had brought in a major piece of litigation to the firm. This came up in my meeting with McKinley. I told him that I had brought in this major case to the firm and I wasn't aware of Ryan or Gerard bringing in any comparable piece of business. McKinley confirmed that I was right about that, but he said that was only one factor in making partnership decisions."

"What happened after you were told you didn't make partnership level six?"

Chambers took a deep breath and sighed when she exhaled. "I was angry and depressed. I thought that it was wrong to deny me a promotion based on the comments I just mentioned, especially the one from a disgruntled client who failed to follow the advice we provided. I knew it would be a while before I would be reconsidered for level six, and that got me further upset and angry. The incident made me think I might not progress farther as a partner, and I began to look for another job." Chambers glanced at Berenson. "Obviously, I found one."

"Are you an associate at your current firm?"

"Yes."

"So this new position involved a step down when it came to title, correct?"

"As to title, yes. I don't consider I took a step down as to anything else. When it comes to the title of partner, I'm hopeful my abilities will be recognized down the road at my new firm."

Philly consulted her deposition outline. "You and Mr. Berenson came to my office recently. Do you remember?"

"I do."

"Do you remember the name Candace Church being mentioned at that meeting?"

"I do."

"Who is Ms. Church?"

"Candace was a partner at Hazelton Kauffman with whom I became friendly. She worked in the corporate law department. I got to know her when a corporate client she had worked for got involved in a suit I handled for that corporate client."

"Did Ms. Church have occasion to resign from Hazelton Kauffman?"

"She resigned about a year after I resigned."

"Had you talked to her about your resignation?"

"Yes."

"What did you tell her about your resignation?"

"I told her I was leaving—she was a friend—and she asked me why. I told her I didn't receive a promotion to level six, and I disagreed with the reasons given for my not being promoted. I told her that I was upset and angry and that I didn't believe I had a future upside with Hazelton Kauffman."

"Did Ms. Church talk to you about her own resignation from Hazelton Kauffman?"

"Yes."

"How did that discussion come about?"

"Candace called me. I remember the call because the first words out of her mouth were something like, 'Guess what? It's déjà vu all over again.' I asked her what she meant, and she said that she had been denied a promotion to partnership level five probably because two clients had reported on a client satisfaction survey that she didn't pay enough attention to detail. We both had a laugh over that. Candace is the most anal, organized person I know. It's a little scary. She doesn't miss anything, and I mean anything."

"What happened to Ms. Church?"

"She found another job. She's doing well. We go out to lunch whenever we can. It's a little unnerving when she pulls out her calorie charts, but she's a sweetheart and I'm glad we've kept up."

Philly leaned toward Simon and he held up his notepad to shield their discussion. "I think I'm done," she whispered.

Simon reviewed his notes, taking his time. "Does she know how Church stacked up to anyone promoted to level five?"

"Good point," Philly replied.

"You mentioned that Ms. Church was denied a promotion to level five. Did Ms. Church mention to you whether anyone did get promoted to level five at the time she was denied that promotion?"

"Yes. She said that two guys were promoted. I remember her saying that because she said she knew the work of one of the guys and it was horrible. She couldn't believe the guy had made any partnership level."

"Did she mention anything else about the two individuals who were promoted?"

"She might have. I don't remember."

"Does Ms. Church know that you're being deposed today?"

"Yes, I told her. I also told her about the MCAD suit you've filed on behalf of your client."

"Did she have any reaction?"

"Yes. She said that she was probably next when it came to depositions and that she'd better get a lawyer."

"Do you have any reason to believe that your sex played a role in not getting the level six promotion?"

Chambers stared at Philly. Then she started to lean towards Berenson but apparently thought better of consulting with him and drew back. "It's funny," she said. "You go through an experience that leaves you embittered and frustrated because it makes no sense to you. Then you hear of someone else going through a similar experience and claiming that her being a woman was the reason she went through the experience. And it's like a light bulb goes off in your mind. Yes, I have a reason to believe that my sex played a role in my not being promoted, because that's the only reason that makes sense."

"No further questions."

"I'm not going to ask any questions at this time," Peck announced. "I am also not agreeing that this deposition is concluded. Hazelton, Kauffman, Garfield & Smith reserves the right to conduct a separate deposition of Ms. Chambers or to resume this deposition at a later date once it has had time to review Ms. Chambers' testimony."

"I don't agree with that," Philly said, "and note my objection. You could have consulted with your client in advance of this deposition so that you were in a position to ask questions. Since you are not going to ask questions, my client's position is that this deposition is concluded. Also, since you had the opportunity to ask questions here today, my client reserves the right to oppose your scheduling a new deposition of Ms. Chambers."

"And for the record," Berenson said, "I'm objecting to Ms. Chambers being put through a second deposition. She will oppose any second deposition. Enough is enough. I agree with Ms. Sullivan that the time for you to question Ms. Chambers is now."

Peck looked unconcerned that she was being ganged up on. Simon admired her cool.

"The party's positions are stated for the record," Peck said. "I believe we can suspend for the day."

"As far as I'm concerned, we're concluding for the day," Philly countered. "In any event, I believe that the witness may leave."

Chambers, Berenson, and Peck and her associate all rose, collected their papers, found their coats and scarves, and left.

"Any impressions?" Simon asked Jeannie Smith as she stowed her stenographer equipment. Philly turned to Smith expectantly.

"A jury would like Chambers," Smith declared. "That is one angry but believable woman."

"But was she discriminated against?" Simon asked.

"I couldn't tell you," Smith responded. "But one thing struck me. I get it that lawyers take client feedback seriously, and I've heard of these client satisfaction surveys that law firms use. But my impression of lawyers and law firms is that money is what counts. If Chambers had brought in a big, money-making case to this law firm and was billing more hours than anyone else, my impression is that a law firm would reward someone like that."

"Unless partners in the law firm had another agenda," Simon said, addressing his comment to Philly.

"Something else occurred to me," Smith said. "Lawyers in her firm had to have seen Chambers in court. They'd know whether she was aggressive enough. Why would they take the word of a client on that point?"

"Are you getting all this for your closing argument?" Simon asked Philly.

"I'm writing," Philly said, and she was. "When Jeannie Smith speaks, we all listen."

92

"When you were representing me, you were constantly preaching that nothing's easy," Harris Burton said. "Of course, you were right. Back then I was somewhat naïve. And here we are with another situation where nothing's easy."

Carpenter wanted Burton to blurt out his firm's decision. He had been awaiting this call with a mixture of curiosity and dread.

"You may mention our firm to the large firm you're talking to," Burton ended the suspense. "Please request that this firm disclose its identity to us."

"Of course," Carpenter said. "Personally, I'm pleased with your decision."

Burton released a heartfelt sigh. "You know it would be beyond ironic if I ended up at a firm bigger than the one I was forced to retire from. If the firm you're talking to has an age seventy retirement policy, maybe I'll have another forced retirement."

Carpenter hadn't considered whether Dudley, Atkins & Tyng had a retirement age policy although, technically, Burton might not be made a partner and might retain his of counsel role. "Is now the time *I* say nothing's easy?"

Burton laughed. "Save your breath. We're thinking it can't hurt to talk to whoever you're talking to. Talk, as we know, is cheap."

"I'm rubbing off on you," Carpenter said. "You've taken to delivering one-liners."

Rachel finished a lengthy e-mail memo to her partners and opted to review it one more time. The thirteen girls and their parents who had participated in the informational conference call had expressed interest in suing Northampton Intensive Tennis Academy. Noelle and her parents were on board largely because of the modest $1,000 retainer. As she reread her action plan, Rachel was struck by the saying about being careful what you wish for. Now that she had potential plaintiffs lined up, she wasn't sure how to proceed. Should there be one lawsuit, or should thirteen separate cases be filed? Was there any potential for bringing a class action? In what court should a lawsuit be filed?

Rachel was struck again by how much she depended on Carpenter for assistance. If they merged with Richard Nye's firm, Carpenter would have Murphy and Warren's help in addressing the questions that she, Simon, and Philly threw at him. In contrast, Harris Burton's firm would provide no backup help for Carpenter. Maybe Carpenter's preference should control the decision her firm had to make.

Rachel sighed and touched Send.

Maybe it had to do with his taking up running, but Simon had discovered that he worked better when he got outside sometime during the day. So early this afternoon he had taken a chilly but bracing walk to a Chinese take-out place and returned to his office with lunch in hand. Once he was settled in, he reviewed the announcement Dean Martin had prepared for release to the Sloane-Webster community. The placement office advisory group had been chosen by the dean with assistance from Ralph Cray and Neil Taylor. Regina White was one of the group's fifteen members. 'And a lap dancer shall lead them,' he thought, smiling.

The dean had done a nice job of thanking all the students and graduates who had offered to serve on the group. She assured students and alumni that the advisory group would reach out to receive input and would be reporting to the Sloan-Webster community on its approaches.

Simon signed off on the dean's announcement and then considered his most recent discussion with her. She had been plainly troubled by the idea of pressing for a speedy trial. Cray was more receptive to that course of action. Simon understood the dean's concern. Martin probably believed that by pushing for trial, the law school would dash any settlement hopes. Simon had pointed out that pushing for a speedy trial might motivate Blaisedell to come back with a more reasonable offer, but the dean had dismissed that possibility, believing instead that Blaisedell would feel he had no choice but to try his case.

Simon knew that he would be anxious until the dean blessed a course of action. The ball was in her court. As the dean had once put it, wasn't that why she got paid the big bucks?

93

Carpenter turned his attention to Rachel's questions about teenagers suing a girls' tennis camp. He dismissed the idea of a class action as unworkable. The girls would probably feel more comfortable being plaintiffs in one lawsuit, but Carpenter believed that each injured girl should file a separate lawsuit through her parents. Damages would likely be different for each girl. Each girl's willingness to settle her case might be different. Filing a single lawsuit for thirteen girls might prevent a reasonable settlement in one case from being accepted since the tennis camp might refuse to settle with any one girl unless all girls settled.

Carpenter's initial impulse was to file all cases in state district court. If any girl had suffered significant damages, that girl's suit could be brought in superior court. He made a note to remind Rachel to obtain details on any medical or other expenses incurred by each girl before filing a suit for the girl.

Carpenter trusted his instincts in responding to Rachel's questions. Still, he realized that if Brian Murphy and Sarah Warren had been in the picture, talking over the tennis camp case with them might have produced some creative approaches. One thing he had learned from litigating against the duo was they excelled at thinking outside the box.

"That's totally dirty pool," Christopher Blaisedell fulminated. "The law school has no business putting Regina White on that advisory group. She's suing the law school for Christ's sake!"

"What are you talking about," Simon feigned denseness. He was starting to enjoy these phone calls with Blaisedell. "I thought you'd be thrilled that one of your clients would be involved in placement office activities."

"You need to get White off that committee," Blaisedell demanded.

"I don't need to do anything," Simon replied. "She's your client. If you think she's made some kind of mistake, you tell her. I'm certainly not going to speak to her. And by the way, I assumed her seeking to join the advisory group had your approval."

"You assumed wrong. There's no way in hell I would have told her to join that self-serving group you created. This is bullshit. I also believe it's unethical."

"Unethical?" Simon tried to muster shock and disbelief. "What are you talking about?"

"You're trying to undermine her status as a plaintiff. I ought to file a complaint against you."

"I'm not aware of anyone associated with the law school encouraging Ms. White to apply for membership on the advisory group."

"But she did apply. The law school didn't have to put her on this group."

"You're losing me," Simon said, trying not to laugh. "Are you saying we should have held White's plaintiff status against her when it came to the committee?"

"This is wrong and you know it!" Blaisedell yelled.

"If you have a problem with anything your client did, work it out with her. If you believe the law school or its counsel has acted inappropriately, take it up with the judge."

"Since you've left me no choice, I will."

"Be my guest."

Simon ended the call. In Blaisedell's position he'd be pissed. But he wasn't in Blaisedell's position, thank goodness. Now if only the dean would authorize pressing for a speedy trial!

94

"The firm that has approached us is Dudley, Atkins & Tyng," Carpenter said when Harris Burton got on his line. "The partner over there who's on point in our discussions is a probate lawyer named Richard Nye. When I gave Nye the name of your firm, his first words were, 'Isn't that where Harris Burton ended up?' So Nye knows of you."

"I know I should be flattered but I never heard of Mr. Nye."

"He seems to have a favorable impression of you. What about Dudley, Atkins & Tyng? Any reaction to those guys?"

"Not really, and I don't want you to read anything into that. I've been on the opposite side of the table from that firm in a number of transactions, but nothing jumps out at me positive or negative."

"I told Nye that if he wants to follow up with you guys, he should call you directly."

"I'm not going to hold my breath," Burton said, sounding dispirited.

"Why so down?" Carpenter asked.

"I'm trying to figure out if I have it in me to enter into the miserable infighting that goes on in big firms. I've been through that once and I don't know whether I have what it takes to do it again."

"I don't think that's going to be an issue. We're being told that our arrangement will be outside the firm's partnership structure. I suspect that the same would apply to your firm."

"Don't be naïve. That partnership structure you think you'll be outside of is going to call all the shots. Remember, I've been there."

"Fair point," Carpenter conceded. "But here's some news you'll like. Dudley, Atkins & Tyng has no mandatory retirement age. Nye told me that the firm has had occasion to let partners go. But he was clear that that could happen no matter what age the partner was."

"I feel better already," Burton came back, with unaccustomed sarcasm.

Now that Dean Martin had authorized him to move for a speedy trial, Simon decided to give Christopher Blaisedell a call. He would tell his adversary that this was a courtesy call. But, in truth, it was simply another opportunity to poke him in the eye.

"I'm hoping that you're going to tell me that Regina White is no longer on the placement advisory group," Blaisedell said when he picked up his line.

"Are you still going on about that?" Simon retorted. "I was actually calling to give you a courtesy heads up that the law school will be filing a motion for a speedy trial."

"*You're* moving for a speedy trial?"

"Yes, that's what I just said."

"I might want more time to obtain a few experts," Blaisedell said.

"Then I suspect you may be opposing my motion. Oh? I almost forgot. One other thing. We'll be updating our witness list. I forget the exact number, but I think we're adding about twenty names."

"Twenty names! Who are you adding?"

Simon was pleased to hear an element of panic in Blaisedell's tone. "Law school graduates. There are some graduates out there who have a different view of the law school than the plaintiffs you've come up with."

"That means I've got twenty depositions to take. There goes your speedy trial."

"As I said before, you're free to oppose a speedy trial."

"Count on it that I will."

Blaisedell ended the call abruptly. Simon set down his phone and assessed his case strategy. Blaisedell had made a valid point; if the law school was identifying new witnesses at this late date, Blaisedell should be given an opportunity to depose them. But would Blaisedell actually do that? If he did, it would delay the trial. On the other hand, he might find the depositions discouraging enough to consider exploring settlement.

Outside Philly's Boston office window, a light snow was falling, and Simon realized that he needed to focus and not be mesmerized by the winter scene. He owed Meredith big time. She had been working overtime and had obtained statements from twenty successful graduates who would praise Sloan-Webster and the education the law school had provided. Simon would provide Blaisedell with all twenty witness statements tomorrow, but he intended to use, at most, five of the graduates as witnesses, and he'd leave it to Blaisedell to guess which ones. It might be more cost effective for Blaisedell to utilize google searches than to take depositions, but that was his problem.

Simon believed that Blaisedell's reference to experts of his own probably involved a law school job placement expert, someone who would provide an opinion that the placement office at Sloan-Webster had been useless. If Blaisedell sought to delay trial until he found such an expert, perhaps the best Simon could do was ask the court to impose a deadline on Blaisedell's efforts.

Blaisedell now had things to do: take twenty depositions and produce his own expert. If Blaisedell was lukewarm about these undertakings, Dean Martin might get her wish that settlement discussions resume.

95

Herb McCauley sat in his favorite spot in the Cambridge Public Library reviewing his notes on his trip to Michigan where he learned about the exam cheating investigation involving Noah Branson. Simon Jeffries was paying for his time, but Herb wasn't sure he would charge for his review unless he came up with something. Besides, he had nothing better to do and the library was a pleasant place to be on a harsh winter day.

His notes were useful. He had the name and number of the helpful economics department secretary he had met with. But it was a long shot that something new would have come to her attention.

So, what about Corey Addison, the teaching assistant suspected of leaking the answers to the economics test? Addison had denied any wrongdoing, and nothing had surfaced suggesting that he had divulged the test answers.

Herb turned on his laptop and googled Addison. Thousands of hits emerged. It would take a year and a day to go through all of them.

He narrowed his search: Corey Addison + Michigan.

An article in the Lansing Journal dated August of this year caught his attention. Three men had been arrested for hacking into the computer records of several insurance agencies. A Corey Addison was one of those arrested. But was it *the* Corey Addison?

No one was at any of the tables near him, so Herb decided to use his cell phone and risk a librarian reprimand. Patricia Littleton picked up on the first ring. Maybe the secretary could be useful, after all.

"Ms. Littleton. My name is Herb McCauley. We met earlier this year and you were very helpful to me."

"The private investigator. I remember you. I remember most everything which is a curse, let me tell you. You had questions about cheating on an economics test many years back."

Herb was impressed. He was reminded of Jocelyn Weaver at the Board of Bar Overseers. There was no shortage of competent women keeping the organizations they worked for on track. "Your memory is everything you say it is." When that drew a laugh from Littleton, Herb soldiered on. "My question today concerns Corey Addison."

"The teaching assistant."

"Wow! You've got to stop impressing me. I was doing a computer search on a hunch and noticed that a Corey Addison was arrested for hacking into the computer records of several Michigan insurance agencies. Was the person arrested the same Corey Addison I previously asked you about?"

"Yes. He was arraigned and he's out on bail."

"Are you keeping track of his case?"

"Yes. Call it a hobby of mine."

"Interesting hobby." Herb considered how to play this information. An idea began to form, but he couldn't share it with Littleton until he got approval from Jeffries and Boyle.

"I may need your help, Ms. Littleton, but first I need to run something by the lawyers who hired me. I'll get back to you one way or the other."

"You obviously know where to find me."

"About this hobby of yours… "

"I told you when we met. It bugs the hell out of me to leave a mystery unsolved."

'My kind of woman,' Herb thought.

Meredith had braved icy conditions to get to the Spencer School of Law library so she could spread out her papers at an isolated desk. Philly had assigned her the task of analyzing the partner information provided by Hazelton, Kauffman, Garfield & Smith. The hearing officer in Ai Li's MCAD case had permitted the law firm to file its discovery responses under seal so that personnel and business information about the firm wouldn't be public information. The hearing officer also entered an order directing Philly's firm to keep the information protected and confidential.

Meredith first skimmed through the foot-high stack of documents provided by Helena Peck to try to get a handle on what she was dealing with. Peck didn't appear to have held anything back. Partnership information was available for a five-year period and was broken down by partnership level.

Meredith focused on 2008, the first year for which information was provided. For that year, of the 202 lawyers in the firm, 91 were partners. Of the 91 partners, 59 (or 65%) were male and 32 (or 35%) were female. It didn't take long to create a chart that reflected voting power.

Level	Men		Women	
Number	Number	Votes	Number	Votes
1	3	3	2	2
2	4	8	6	12
3	5	15	4	12
4	4	16	3	12
5	5	25	5	25
6	6	36	3	18
7	3	21	2	14
8	7	56	3	24
9	9	81	1	9
10	13	130	2	20
Total Partners	59 (65%)		32 (35%)	
Total Votes		391 (72.5%		148 (27.5%)
			539 (100%)	

It wasn't hard to interpret the results. Under the firm's partnership agreement, some matters were to be decided by majority; on these matters the men had a clear majority. A two-thirds majority was required for certain other matters such as whether to make someone a partner and whether to promote a partner to a higher partnership level. Although by numbers men did not make up quite two thirds of the partners in 2008, they did have a comfortable margin of the weighted votes to control partnership decisions.

Meredith next focused her attention on Hazelton Kauffman's 2009 data. One year down, four to go.

96

In the conference room, Meredith was going over her completed charts with Simon and with Philly, who was participating by Skype. "The bottom line," she concluded, "is that the weighted voting power of men never dipped below seventy-two percent in the five years beginning with 2008. For 2012, the last of the five years, the percentage was seventy-three and a half percent."

"I have a feeling about Helena Peck," Simon said. "I'm willing to bet she's done the same analysis you've done. The question is, what's she going to tell the Hazelton Kauffman higher ups?"

"Do we have the detail on the partner votes on promotions?" Philly asked.

"No," Meredith answered. "Partnership votes are done by ballot. Each partner is given a ballot slip. At the top of the slip there's a blank for partner level of the person who is voting that had been filled in. So, for example, a level ten partner would be given a ballot with the level ten written down. After the votes are weighted and tabulated, the ballots are destroyed. The total vote is recorded in the minutes of the partners' meeting."

"Shit!" Philly muttered. "So there's no direct evidence."

"No, but there is a pattern," Meredith resumed. "Look at the chart for 2008. The number of men and women in the first five levels are nearly equal. But in the last five partner levels, the percentage of women drops significantly. Over time, in the last five levels, the percentage of women didn't vary much. Again using 2008 as an example, there were forty-nine partners in levels six through ten. Eleven were women and thirty-eight were men. As the 2008 chart shows, that translates into roughly 72.5% men and 27.5% women. That 27.5% decreased slightly during 2009 through 2012."

Nobody said anything. On the computer monitor, Philly was frowning in concentration, a determined look on her face.

"If we're dealing with a conspiracy," Simon said, "an awful lot of work went into it. There had to have been secret meetings among the men, things like that. I'm just finding it hard to believe that this kind of effort was made. There would always be a risk that some guy would get pissed off about something and leak what was going on out of spite."

"I was thinking the same thing," Philly said. "The numbers we've been looking at could have simply occurred by partners voting their own preferences on promotions."

"But the numbers help us," Meredith joined in. "Isn't that all that matters? Let the firm try to explain them away. The numbers aren't going to change."

"Meredith's right," Philly said. "We have two women, Ai Li and Lynn Campbell, who believe they were screwed when they were denied promotion to level six. Each felt that she was more deserving of promotion than the males who were actually promoted. Plus, we may have a third woman that fits that bill in Candace Church."

"What's our next step?" Simon asked.

Philly paused. "I'm going to talk with Carpenter. But where I'm leaning is to get Hazelton Kauffman to admit to all these facts that Meredith has come up with. We can prepare a series of admissions that the law firm has to either admit or deny. If they admit the facts, there's less we have to do at trial."

"Sounds like a plan," Simon said.

Herb phoned Patricia Littleton and explained what he wanted her to do. The Michigan State administrative assistant listened to his plan without interrupting. "Aren't you a sneaky devil," she said. "My kind of guy. I have to check with my boss. This is beyond my pay grade. But that shouldn't be a problem. I've got my boss well-trained."

Carpenter recognized Harris Burton's number on his caller ID. "Carpenter."

"I just had a long talk with Richard Nye," Harris said. "Ben Klein and I will be meeting him for lunch tomorrow."

"That didn't take long," Carpenter said.

"I have to say he seems interested. His firm's management committee has given him authority to move forward with discussions."

Carpenter knew he shouldn't pry but couldn't help himself. "Is Nye offering you the same kind of deal he's outlined for us?"

"Generally, yes. There would be a partner in the corporate law department we would report to. But we'd basically be doing what we've been doing all along. If we brought in a matter that we couldn't handle and they could, we'd get a financial benefit."

Carpenter made a note to seek a similar provision in any deal they hammered out with Nye. "Good luck. I think you'll like Nye."

"You know what my reservations are about big firms since you represented me in my retirement suit. But I had a good feeling about Nye. He didn't come out and say this, but it seemed to me he was interested in both our firms joining his. He said the business model he had in mind fit better with litigation but could also work with business and corporate law. He was very frank and didn't try to sell me."

Carpenter couldn't easily picture how a low-cost corporate and business practice would fit with a large firm's high costs in those specialties. That was Nye's problem. If Nye solved the problem and made a proposal to both their firms, it would probably involve moving their own offices to Harris' firm. Simon would embrace that. "Good luck at the lunch. Let me know how it turns out."

97

Simon sat next to Meredith in the conference room, working on Ai Li's case. Meredith had prepared a list of statements for Helena Peck to admit or deny as part of the discovery process. It was work that needed to be done meticulously, and Meredith's initial draft had been excellent. Simon was grateful that he had few suggestions to make. They would get final comments from Carpenter and Philly and put the pleading in final form.

"Is it my imagination, or are things suddenly a lot busier?" Meredith asked. "A little while ago, I didn't see any more work coming my way."

Simon nodded. "Short term, yes. We've picked up the pace in the Sloan-Webster case, as you know. Ai Li's case has provided an opportunity to use you. And Rachel is trying to put together a bunch of lawsuits against a tennis camp. We're also trying to tie down engagement letters in two new hospital cases. But long-term, we still have issues."

"I'm trying to figure out my future with you guys," Meredith said.

"I wish I could give you a better read on that, but I can't." Simon didn't want his firm to lose her, but he and his partners were in no position to guaranty her security when they couldn't guaranty their own.

"I suppose I should be grateful for what I have," Meredith said.

"Don't sound so down. It's been great having you work with us. You've been a terrific asset. We all feel the same way."

"I've got to start thinking of the future. We can't go on forever the way we've been going."

"Of course," Simon said. "I understand. You need to do what's best for yourself."

"That's another thing I have to figure out," Meredith said, without elaborating. The new year was rapidly approaching. Maybe it was time to make some resolutions for herself.

"I thought the lunch with Nye went well," Harris Burton said. "We're going to sign a mutual confidentiality agreement and share additional information. It turns out that Nye's firm is priced out of a fair amount of business and corporate work. His idea isn't as far-fetched as I first thought. His next step is to feel out his current partners who specialize in business and corporate law. So we're moving forward."

Several days had gone by since Burton and Ben Klein had dined with Nye. Carpenter had expected a call from Burton before today.

"Baby steps," Carpenter said.

"Cautious baby steps," Burton clarified.

Simon read over the email he was about to send to Christopher Blaisedell.

> *Please see the attached newspaper article from the Lansing Journal. As you can see, the teaching assistant involved in the cheating investigation in which Noah Branson was questioned has been arrested. Michigan State University officials have asked the district attorney's office to look into the cheating incident given the former teaching assistant's arrest. My suspicion is that the teaching assistant may be offered a plea deal on his criminal case if he provides helpful information on the cheating incident. Given these new developments, I'm giving you a courtesy heads up that Sloan-Webster will be requesting to take the teaching assistant's deposition in Michigan. Please don't hesitate to contact me if you have any questions.*

Simon sent silent thanks to Herb McCauley and his contact in Michigan. Patricia Littleton had gotten her boss to issue a news release announcing the university's request for district attorney assistance in the cheating investigation. The district attorney's office had followed with its own press release stating that an assistant district attorney would be providing the university with assistance in taking a fresh look at the cheating incident. Littleton had explained that the timing and content of the two press releases had been coordinated.

Simon was sure that Blaisedell would share this information with Noah Branson. If Branson had been nervous at his deposition when questioned about the cheating incident, the man might crack when he heard the latest news.

Smiling, Simon touched Send. Was there something the matter with him, he wondered? Some sadistic streak he had kept at bay? He was enjoying driving Christopher Blaisedell nuts.

98

Simon took a call from Helena Peck. He had been hoping it would be Christopher Blaisedell calling to restart settlement talks in the Sloan-Webster case, but a call from Helena Peck was a close second on his wish list.

"I have a question for you," Peck said. "Is your client's previous offer still open?"

Simon and Philly had talked to Ai Li about this. When Li read Lynn Chambers deposition, she was overjoyed that another former Hazelton Kauffman partner had resigned under circumstances similar to her own. Li's initial demand for an admission of discrimination by Hazelton Kauffman without money damages had gone by the boards. Now she was looking for damages and the payment of her attorney fees.

"No. Ms. Li would now also be insisting on damages and attorney fees in any settlement."

"Do you have a demand figure?" Peck asked.

"No."

"I would request that you consult with Ms. Li and come back with a demand figure. If you are not going to present a demand figure, I would appreciate hearing that as well."

"I'll be getting back to you one way or another."

"Also, my client will be looking into whether your client violated her partnership agreement by soliciting a position at her new firm."

Simon had wondered when—not whether—this shoe would drop. "Look away," he said.

Simon sent out an SOS e-mail to his partners requesting help. Li would be asking for a recommendation, and Simon was at a loss as to what to tell her.

"Thank you both for joining me," Richard Nye said.

Carpenter was the last to arrive for the impromptu luncheon. Nye had chosen a noisy deli near Harris Burton's office and had staked out a corner booth where at least they could be heard.

"Tell me what you want," Nye requested, "and I'll get our orders."

When Nye left to join the Order line, Carpenter leaned in towards Burton. "Any idea what this is about?"

Harris shrugged. "If I had to guess, I'd say we're about to hear where Dudley, Atkins & Tyng stands on the overtures to our respective firms. The fact that we're both here suggests that we're about to be presented with a package deal."

Carpenter had been thinking the same thing. Nye must have gotten direction from his firm's management committee. Philly's absence bothered him. Perhaps Harris had similar misgivings about Ben Klein not being present.

Nye rejoined them, distributed the orders, and began to eat, apparently in no special hurry to begin talking business. Carpenter realized that he, too, was hungry and set to. Harris picked at his food, seemingly resigned to the delay.

Nye finished half his sandwich and cleared his throat. "That feels better," he announced. "I thought it would move things along if the three of us met. I basically have the same things to impart to each of you. So, where to begin? As Carpenter knows, our firms' litigators are very eager to enter into an arrangement with his firm. As for our corporate and business lawyers, the level of eagerness to enter into a relationship with Sizemore Klein is not as strong. To be specific, the majority of partners in these areas are on board with exploring a relationship. However, several partners are not. The majority of partners in favor of moving forward with discussions is sufficiently large to obtain approval of an arrangement if an arrangement could be worked out. So that's the first point I want to make."

Burton slowly shook his head. "If there's significant resentment on the part of some members of your firm, I have serious misgivings about going forward. Perhaps we should stop any further discussions."

"That's certainly your prerogative," Nye said. "However, I'd like us to continue to talk for two reasons. First, in a firm our size, there is seldom unanimity on any major decision we make. It's almost a given that someone's nose will be out of joint over anything of substance we decide. But what happens with our firm is that once we make a decision, we live with it and move on. Those partners disgruntled over what was decided accept the vote of the majority. I have no idea whether this occurs at other firms, but I can tell you it occurs at ours."

Nye paused as if awaiting questions. Carpenter suspected that Nye himself smoothed a lot of the ruffled feathers of disgruntled partners.

"Secondly, I envision you and Mr. Klein meeting with our business and corporate partners," Nye said to Burton. "There's the possibility that such a meeting will cause the partners currently not in favor of an arrangement to harden their opposition. But I personally think that a face-to-face meeting is more likely to reduce if not eliminate opposition."

"I trust you're not expecting me to react to these comments today," Burton said. "As you know, I'm not a partner of our firm. I'm merely of counsel."

"You and your colleagues should take as much time as you need," Nye assured. "I'd now like to turn to how we see arrangements with your firms working. I've gone over a lot of this with each of you, but I think repetition is useful.

"First, partners in each of your firms would become partners of Dudley, Atkins & Tyng. However, your partners would not be parties to our current partnership agreement. We'd have separate agreements with each of your firms. Mr. Burton can have the title he currently has—of counsel. If you wish to invent a new title for yourself, we will consider it.

"Second, each of your firms would come up with a budget which Dudley, Atkins & Tyng would fund, if approved. The budget should contain draws for partners that you can live on. We'll fund the monthly draws along with any other expense items in the approved budget. At our firm, partner's monthly draws are modest and are supplemented with two larger draws, at the end of June and the end of December."

Burton was writing and Carpenter decided he'd better follow suit.

"Third, about revenue. If your actual revenues exceed your budget, you'll keep seventy-five percent of the excess, and you can divide that up any way you want. The other twenty-five percent comes back to us.

"Fourth, about referrals. If we send a case to you, you don't pay any referral fee to us. If you send a case to us, five percent of any fees we actually collect go back to you to be counted as revenues toward your budget."

'Negotiating an approved budget should be interesting,' Carpenter thought. "What happens to the budget for year two?" he asked.

"We're considering two approaches. Work off year one's budget subject to a cost-of-living increase. Or hash out a new budget."

Carpenter didn't look forward to a yearly negotiating ordeal but kept that sentiment to himself.

"Fifth, I've identified to each of you the Dudley, Atkins & Tyng partner you will be reporting to. We need to have the partner receive copies of all documents and emails that relate to your cases."

"The partners in my firm will not want to take on any of your firm's liabilities," Burton said.

"We feel the same way about your firms' liabilities. We'll need mutual indemnification agreements and would want your firms to purchase tails on your current malpractice policies that insure against claims arising while you were independent." Nye paused. "If we come to agreements on merging, malpractice is beyond complicated. I haven't sorted everything out. We're taking a hard look at how malpractice insurance would work going forward with more than one partnership agreement in place. I hope to have an answer to that issue shortly. It may be as simple as Dudley, Atkins & Tyng's malpractice policy covers everyone. But our insurer needs time to consider that the partners in your firms will not be partners under our current partnership agreement."

Carpenter wondered whether Nye had thought of everything.

"Our preference is for Carpenter's firm to move into the empty space in Mr. Burton's firm. That will provide an upgrade to the offices Carpenter's firm currently has and we would like to see that happen."

"What about benefits?" Burton asked.

"Your firms' partners, associates, and employees would participate in our health insurance, retirement and disability plans. We would help you develop your budgets for these items."

"What should we be asking you that we're not asking you?" Carpenter said.

Nye smiled. "For the moment nothing. But when a question occurs to you, send me an e-mail. I've been working with one of my partners on putting together an agreement that would be used for each of your firms with changes to reflect your different specialties. I think it will save us a lot of time if you have a written document you can refer to."

Nye returned to his lunch. Carpenter took that as a signal that this meeting was over. He realized that his firm needed a lawyer. He thought of Morton, one of his Barrister buddies. There was no way in hell that he and Philly and Simon and Rachel were going to do this on their own.

99

Simon had been at his desk when Christopher Blaisedell called, had seen the caller ID, and had let the call go to voicemail. He had spent the past hour anticipating the purpose of Blaisedell's call, time he couldn't bill for, but time well spent. After sorting through the possible reasons for Blaisedell's contacting him, he now felt composed enough to return the call.

"Do you remember when we settled the Spenser School of Law case how you specified certain parameters a settlement would have to follow?" Blaisedell asked.

"I do," Simon acknowledged. "But I'll remind you, that followed your making an initial proposal and later on your specifying the reforms you wanted Spenser to make."

"That's true," Blaisedell said. "But this time around I would like you to jump ahead and propose something that your client can live with."

"Does that mean that the three million dollars you demanded previously is off the table?"

"That demand is off the table because you rejected it," Blaisedell came back.

Simon debated whether to give Blaisedell a hard time by insisting that he make the first settlement move. He decided to relent. "Let me talk to my client and get back to you. Thanks for reaching out."

Simon set down his phone. Blaisedell had just done a one-eighty. The timing had to involve Noah Branson. Blaisedell must have reported the reopening of the cheating investigation to Branson and gotten a response he didn't like. And then it came to Simon what Branson's response was. In all likelihood, the first named plaintiff in Blaisedell's lawsuit had asked to be dropped from the case.

Next on Simon's to-do list was a conference call with Philly in Brighton and Ai Li at her new job. "What do you recommend?" Li asked, after Simon went over his telephone discussion with Helena Peck.

Philly would handle this part of the discussion. "Before we start talking specifics, we need to clarify a few things," she said. "At the outset, instead of a monetary settlement, you authorized us to propose a settlement in which Hazelton Kauffman admitted it discriminated against you. That offer was rejected. Is that still something you're looking for?"

"Sure, if I can get it," Li responded immediately.

"After reading Lynn Chambers' deposition, you decided that you wanted to be paid damages and have your attorney fees paid for," Philly reminded her. "You probably know this but, typically, if there's a monetary settlement, the party paying out will refuse to admit to any liability as part of the settlement. So if you insist on an admission of liability *and* damages, they might not settle."

"Shouldn't I ask for everything to start out?" Li said.

"That's certainly one approach," Philly acknowledged. "We can come back to that strategy. Is there a damage figure you're looking for?"

"I'd like it to be as much as possible, obviously," Li replied. "But I don't have any way to assess what I should be thinking about. This is all new to me."

"I understand," Philly said. "Simon and I have reviewed your situation with Carpenter, whom you've met. There is simply no exact science in coming up with a monetary demand. And I ought to mention that you are not required to present a monetary demand to your former firm. You may decide that you want to have them make the first move. In which case, as Simon explained, he'll call the lawyer on the other side and tell her that you are not prepared to make a demand."

"I really don't know what to do." Li sounded both confused and irritated.

"If you do make a monetary demand, we recommend that it be one hundred thousand dollars plus attorney fees."

"Where did you come up with that figure?" Li asked, surprised.

"It's somewhat arbitrary," Philly admitted. "We've factored in that you ended up at a higher paying job and that emotional pain and suffering is hard to assign a dollar value to."

"That's a lot of money," Li noted.

"Would you accept that as a monetary settlement if they agreed to that figure?" Philly asked.

"I would. I wasn't thinking of that high a figure."

"If you were paid one hundred thousand dollars, would you be willing to move off of your demand for an admission of discrimination?" Philly followed up. "And a related question is whether you would take less money if there was an admission of discrimination?"

Simon shared Carpenter's fascination with what price would persuade a client to forsake a principle.

"This is a lot to take in," Li said dispiritedly. "I need to talk to my husband."

"Of course," Philly said. "Simon and I weren't expecting a decision on this call. Talk to your husband and let us know if you have any questions."

"If they settle with me, wouldn't they worry that Lynn Chambers would sue them next?" Li asked.

"They're worried about that now," Philly said. "I wouldn't worry about Ms. Chambers at the moment. Just worry about yourself."

100

Yesterday, Simon, Rachel, and Meredith had met with Dean Martin, Ralph Cray and Neil Taylor for three hours to come up with a settlement game plan. Cray had been in favor of moving forward with the trial, but the dean had overruled him: it wasn't worth the risk to try the case if the law school could resolve the litigation on terms it could live with. Simon had decided not to call Blaisedell immediately. He set aside the term sheet they had drafted for the rest of yesterday and had focused on other things. Now, today, after rereading the terms that had been decided upon with what he hoped were fresh eyes, he felt comfortable talking with Blaisedell. But he wanted a witness and Rachel was with him.

"I have you on a speaker phone," Simon said when Blaisedell got on the line. "Rachel Boyle is with me."

"Good afternoon."

"You asked the law school to propose a settlement and I'm prepared to do that."

"I appreciate it."

Simon paused, glanced at Rachel. Blaisedell was being overly respectful.

"I'll start with money," Simon resumed. "For reasons you're familiar with, the law school is not willing to pay damages to the plaintiffs. That is non-negotiable. The law school has, as you know, established a two hundred fifty-thousand-dollar fund to improve its placement office. The law school is agreeable to providing an additional one hundred thousand dollars to that fund. The law school is prepared to earmark that additional one hundred thousand dollars to purposes the plaintiffs designate provided those purposes are approved by the law school. Any questions so far?"

"I'm writing," Blaisedell said after a long pause. "No questions so far."

"Are you able to inform us as to your legal fees incurred to date?" Simon asked.

"Approximately one hundred fifty thousand dollars."

Simon considered his firm's charges to the law school. To date those charges were more than twice the fees Blaisedell had run up.

"The law school is prepared to reimburse one hundred fifty thousand dollars in legal fees. That is a hard cap and also not negotiable."

Rachel reached over and pressed the mute button. "It's eerie that the amount the dean agreed to matched what Blaisedell's charges are to date."

Simon nodded and un-muted the line. "The payment of legal fees would be contingent on you and your firm agreeing not to bring, solicit, or participate in any other lawsuit against Sloan-Webster. We would use the same language that we used in the Spenser case."

There was a long pause. "Anything else?" Blaisedell asked.

"Yes," Simon responded. "If there are wording changes to the law school's promotional materials that you wish the law school to consider, the law school will review those changes and get back to you on whether the changes are agreeable and may be incorporated into the settlement agreement. Similarly, if you wish to propose any other programmatic changes to the law school, the law school will review what you have in mind and get back to you on whether the changes are agreeable."

This time Simon muted the line. "Did I miss anything?"

Rachel shook her head. "I've ticked off everything on the list."

Simon rejoined Blaisedell to the call. "I think that covers it," he said.

"Okay," Blaisedell said. "Again, thanks. Since settlement is back on the table, are you agreeable to giving me an extension to respond to your motion for a speedy trial?"

"I'm going to put you on hold for a minute," Simon said, again muting the line.

"I'm thinking of a week," Rachel said. "I think we need to keep the pressure on him."

"I agree. A week sounds about right."

"Rachel and I have had a brief discussion," Simon informed Blaisedell. "We're agreeable to a week extension. You may inform the clerk that we've assented to a week. Any more time, and we need to confer with our client."

"A week it is," Blaisedell said. "I'll get back to you."

"Any reaction?" Simon asked.

"As I said, I'll get back to you."

Simon ended the call. "What do you think?" he asked Rachel.

"He wants out," Rachel said. "Maybe Branson has told him that if the Michigan State cheating scandal is reopened, Branson could be in trouble."

If Rachel was right, Blaisedell would be stuck with three lead plaintiffs each of whom had a liability. Simon wouldn't want to go to trial in those circumstances. "I said this to myself and now I'm saying it out loud: God bless Herb McCauley."

101

Carpenter arrived at the front door of Philly's Brighton house simultaneously with the household's three resident children, accompanied by Sarah Ferguson. Once inside, Sarah helped the children get out of their winter jackets, scarves, and hats and hung the outerwear on hooks positioned low on the entryway wall.

"Look mommy!" Daisy raced toward Philly who was coming down the stairs. "I found a bird's nest. It was in the snow."

Philly admired the offering. "That is so cool," she said. "You know Mr. Carpenter. Make sure he gets a look."

"Wow!" Carpenter said, hoping to match Philly's enthusiasm over Daisy's find.

"Snack time," the babysitter announced, and the kids headed for the kitchen.

"Alone at last," Philly joked. She plopped down on the living room couch and Carpenter took an easy chair facing her.

"I've been putting this off, but I think I need to tell Nye and Burton about my cancer," Carpenter got straight to the point of his visit. "I don't feel right about not letting them know."

"And then there's my AA meetings," Philly said.

"Maybe I'm wrong, but I think my cancer trumps your issue. I guess what I'm saying is I don't feel strongly one way or the other whether you bring up AA. I think you need to do what you're most comfortable with."

"If we come clean, it's going to end up common knowledge," Philly said. "I don't like that."

"I don't like it either. I was thinking of asking Nye and Burton to only discuss it with people who had to know. But the more I thought about it, I figured all their partners had to know. It's a lousy situation."

Philly sat slumped in a corner of the couch. "I'm going to bring up my drinking," she declared wearily. "If we're going to marry into another firm, I want to be upfront about anything that could present a problem down the road. I don't want my going to AA to be discovered and someone coming back at us for not mentioning it."

Carpenter nodded. "Then I'll arrange a sit down with Nye and Burton. I think we need to bring Murphy and Warren into the meeting."

"Okay," Philly said. "Add Ben Klein to the list."

"Good point," Carpenter said. "It occurred to me that we're doing our best to torpedo any kind of merger."

"What do you mean?"

"First we tell these guys our litigation volume is in the crapper. That doesn't put them off. Now we're going to tell them I've got a fucking incurable disease and you've got a disease that can impair your ability to practice law if you don't continue to keep it under control. These are not exactly selling points."

Philly sat up straight. "Worse comes to worse, they shoot down the idea of hooking up with us. I can live with that. Then we're back where we were before which, for all we know, is where we should be."

"When did you become so wise, young grasshopper?"

"Put a sock in it," Philly said, smiling. "I think we're doing the right thing by coming clean. That's all that counts."

"Okay," Carpenter said. "That settles that. Did someone say snacks?"

Simon tried to picture Helena Peck's expression as Philly followed Ai Li's direction to ask for the moon.

"Let me repeat what you said to make sure I have it right," Peck said. "Your client is looking for one hundred thousand dollars in damages, an admission of discrimination, and attorney fees which you currently estimate are around fifteen to twenty thousand dollars. The admission of liability would be in a settlement agreement that would be kept confidential. The MCAD complaint brought by your client would be dismissed with prejudice. Did I miss anything?"

"No," Philly confirmed.

Peck didn't say anything. The silence continued for so long that Simon considered asking whether Peck was still on the line.

"I've read your request for admissions," Peck broke the silence. "For your information, my initial reaction is that Hazelton, Kauffman, Garfield & Smith will admit to nearly all the facts you wish them to acknowledge."

'I'll believe it when I see it,' Simon thought. Peck was smart and thoughtful. Why would she acknowledge anything her client might admit to during this call?

"Am I correct that your view of this case is that the male partners in Hazelton Kauffman vote as a bloc to deny women promotion to the top partnership levels?"

"That's what the evidence supports," Philly said. "Why are we having this discussion?"

"Humor me," Peck said. "We can have this discussion off the record if you wish. If you prefer, I will say nothing of this discussion to my client if you will do likewise with your client."

Simon wished that he and Philly were physically together so that they could put Peck on hold and frankly discuss her request.

"Off the record then," Philly said.

"Agreed," Peck confirmed. "Here's something to think about then. Your client was denied a promotion to level six because she didn't receive the two-thirds vote required for a partnership promotion. The vote was taken at a partnership meeting this year. Your client and the other partners being considered for level six were not present when her promotion was discussed and voted on. Since the vote concerned them, their absence was required by the rules governing partnership meetings. Any questions so far?"

"Keep going," Philly said.

"As you know, ballots cast on a vote to promote a partner are tabulated and then destroyed. The actual total vote is recorded in the minutes of the partnership meeting when the vote was taken. There was a total of five hundred and fifty-five votes on your client's promotion. That number reflects the weighting of partner votes by level. This meant that your partner needed three hundred seventy votes to be promoted. Feel free to check my math."

Simon wrote down Peck's figures and checked her math. He found no error.

"Of those five hundred fifty-five votes, four hundred five were cast by men and one hundred fifty were cast by women. Even if the ballots had been preserved, one could not tell from the ballets whether the voter was male or female."

Simon thought he saw where Peck was heading. There was, of course, a way to determine how the male and female partners voted.

"Your client received three hundred sixty-five votes in her favor, five votes short of what she needed to be promoted. I met with each partner who cast a vote on your client's promotion," Peck continued. "I did so with the permission of the firm's management committee. Each partner who voted on your client's promotion told me how he or she had voted. Of the one hundred fifty female votes cast, only fifteen votes were in favor of her promotion. In other words, ninety percent of the female votes cast were against your partner being promoted. Of the four hundred and five votes cast by males, three hundred fifty were in favor of her promotion. That is, over eighty-six percent of the male votes were cast in favor of your client while only thirteen plus percent of the male votes were cast against your client being promoted. Do you need me to repeat any of what I said?"

"Why don't you give us a minute," Simon requested. He had Meredith's various charts in front of him and began to construct a new chart based on the information Peck had provided.

Votes Cast:	*555*
2/3 Needed:	*370*
Male Votes:	*405*
For Li:	*350 (86+%)*
Against Li:	*55 (13+%)*
Female Votes:	*150*
For Li:	*15 (10%)*
Against Li:	*135 (90%)*

"Do Hazelton Kauffman partners have these figures?" Simon asked. He wondered whether Philly had made a chart similar to his own.

"The management committee has the overall statistics," Peck said. "I'm the only person who knows how individual partners voted, and I'm under an obligation not to reveal that information to anyone at the firm. However, if we go to trial, I will subpoena all partners who voted, and they will put on the record what I've summarized for you."

"You're saying that it was the women partners who denied Li a promotion," Philly said.

"I'm not saying it; the figures confirm that's exactly what happened. Although, in theory, the men could have denied the promotion, in fact, they didn't. It was the women."

"How do we know you're not making up what you just told us?" Philly asked.

"You don't. Mr. Jeffries has dealt with me before. I assure you that I'm not making up what I told you. I have written acknowledgements from all the partners confirming how they voted. This is attorney work product and not discoverable."

"Can we see those acknowledgements?" Simon asked.

"My instructions are no. However, I will bring this issue up again with the management committee. I don't expect the committee to change its position."

"Neither we nor our client can simply take your word on this," Simon said.

"That's too bad," Peck said. "It appears we're headed for trial. I'll report your settlement demand, but I intend to recommend it be rejected. I believe my recommendation will be accepted."

"Would you agree to depositions of the women partners who cast votes on our client's promotion?" Philly asked.

"There you go again with bending the MCAD rules on depositions. No, I won't agree to any partner being deposed. But I'll take it up with the management committee."

"What about a series of brief meetings with the women partners?" Philly threw out. "You would be present. They would confirm what you have related as to how they voted. Or not."

"I'll take that up with the management committee as well. But I'd like you to take away at least one thing from this discussion. There is no way in hell that Hazelton Kauffman will admit it discriminated against your client on the basis of sex. Anything else we need to discuss?"

"No," Philly said. "We're done."

"One last thing," Peck said. "You don't have to treat this discussion as off the record. Tell your client whatever you want."

When Peck disconnected, Simon followed suit and then phoned Philly.

"And things started out going so well," Philly opened. "Do you believe her?"

"Unfortunately, I do. I remember her from Meredith's lawsuit. She's smart, practical, and reasonably forthcoming."

"What the hell is it with the women partners at that firm?" Philly vented. "You'd think they'd look after their own."

"Maybe they don't want to share the glory of having made partner," Simon speculated. "Given my sexual orientation, I'm the last person to speak on the subject, but my impression has always been that women are more bitchy and vindictive than men."

"I wouldn't necessarily generalize," Philly said.

"Time for a discussion with Li," Simon said.

"That's something I'm not looking forward to."

After lunch, Simon forwarded Christopher Blaisedell's e-mail to Rachel and began to review it for the third time. Blaisedell was moving forward rapidly. The man was motivated. Simon decided not to dwell on what had lit a fire under him.

Subject to other matters being worked out, Blaisedell agreed to the monetary terms proposed by the law school—an additional $100,000 to be added to the funds designated for placement office upgrade and the reimbursement of $150,000 in attorneys' fees. Blaisedell also agreed to refrain from again suing Sloan-Webster.

Blaisedell had come back with requested changes to the law school's promotional materials. The changes were detailed, and Simon concluded that Blaisedell had been working on them for some time. He found most of the changes acceptable; however, the language changes Blaisedell had proposed for descriptions of the faculty were problematic and he didn't see Dean Martin agreeing to those proposed edits.

Blaisedell had also requested that the additional $100,000 be utilized for job fairs and for workshops on resume drafting and interview techniques. These uses struck Simon as reasonable, but Neil Taylor might have a different view.

Simon forwarded Blaisedell's email to Carpenter, Philly, and Meredith, now convinced that the case that had sustained the firm for most of the year was about to settle, not with the expected bang but with something far closer to a whimper.

102

Ai Li sounded unhappy. As Philly completed her telephone account of the discussion with Helena Peck, she wondered whether Li had been mentally spending money she hadn't yet received. "Were you friends with any of the women partners who voted on your promotion?" she asked.

"I didn't really have any close friends at the firm," Li confessed.

Philly thought of Li's daughter, Ling, nicknamed Ding-a-ling. The kid had personality oozing from every pore. In contrast, her mother was coming across as a retiring loner, the kind of lawyer who would shun offers of going for drinks after a long day and evening of work, the kind of lawyer who would attend firm galas and instead of mingling, keep pretty much to herself. Maybe the clients that had pegged her as aloof had gotten it right. Maybe socialization skills counted when it came to partner promotions. Then again, maybe women were as bitchy as Simon suspected they were.

"We've thought about whether a sex discrimination claim exists if women are the ones who act negatively toward another woman, but the little research we've been able to accomplish isn't definitive. Same-sex sexual harassment is a viable claim. But when it comes to something like promotions within a business, from the quick research we've been able to do, your chances of winning on a claim that other women discriminated against you because of your sex seem uncertain.

Also, you would have to change your initial position to make the argument that women as opposed to men discriminated against you."

"I really don't want to get involved in bringing some kind of novel test case," Li said.

Philly sought to conclude this call. "I recommend we do two things on your behalf. First, we need to obtain some kind of confirmation that the voting occurred the way Peck said it did. Second, I believe I need to tell Peck that you are proceeding with your case and if she is interested in settling, the ball is in her court."

"Sure," Li said resignedly. "Why not?"

From her seat at the end of a large conference room table at Dudley, Atkins & Tyng, Philly had a head on view of the participants. Burton frowned and seemed to be bracing himself for bad news. Klein looked worried. Nye, Murphy, and Warren were reserved. All five regarded Carpenter intently.

"Sorry to be taking up so much of your time," Carpenter apologized. "But there are some things that Philly and I need to tell you. To begin with, about four years ago, I was diagnosed with leukemia."

Burton's jaw dropped. Klein gasped. The expressions on the faces of the three Dudley, Atkins & Tyng principals showed genuine concern and shock. Philly was particularly struck by Murphy's expression. Looking at him now, you would never guess that he liked to kid around.

"The bad news is," Carpenter went on, "it's leukemia. My kind is called chronic lymphocytic leukemia or CLL. The good news is that no treatment is required if you don't have symptoms. I don't have symptoms. I get my blood tested every three months. So far, since the diagnosis, the test results show I'm stable. If the test results change, I may need chemo and God only knows what else. I'm only going to worry about that when I have to. I may die with it instead of from it, but there's no way to tell, and I decided you should know."

"Jesus," Murphy said in a soft voice.

"I'd like to keep this quiet," Carpenter said. "If you have to tell anyone else, my request is that it be on a need-to-know basis coupled with a request that this information be kept confidential. I'll rely on your discretion."

"Brian, Sarah, and I will talk about this," Nye responded. "I don't know if this is something we can keep from our other partners."

"Again, do what you need to do," Carpenter replied. "I felt I needed to tell you about this before we moved farther down the road."

"You said that *Philly* and you needed to tell us some things," Nye said. He turned to Philly. "Do you also have some news for us?"

"I've been going to AA meetings for longer than Carpenter has known about his cancer."

"Have you had a drink since you started the meetings?" Nye followed up.

"Not for over four years."

Nye's gaze was steady, but not unkind. "Brian and Sarah know this, but I would ask that the rest of you keep this to yourselves. My wife has been going to AA meetings longer than we've been married. Keep up the good work," Nye said to Philly. "There's something about you that reminds me of my wife," he added.

"You're a pair," Murphy said, and Philly was relieved to see a twinkle in his eyes. "How the hell did you find each other?"

"Luck," Carpenter and Philly said together.

"If there are no other surprises," Murphy continued, "nothing you've told us changes my mind."

"Nor mine," Warren said.

"I'm a little taken aback," Burton said when all eyes turned to him. "Ben and I need to talk. I appreciate you both being up front about all this. I think we'll probably have to mention this to the other firm partners. I don't see a way around that."

"Remember that draft agreement I promised both of you?" Nye said. "It's on its way."

Carpenter passed Nye a business card. "E-mail a copy to our lawyer to save time."

103

Carpenter took Morton's call fifteen minutes before Morton was scheduled to review the Dudley, Atkins & Tyng agreement with all four partners on a conference call.

"You know what this means if you sign this agreement?" Morton said.

"I'm sure you're about to tell me."

"This is extremely serious," Morton said with considerable foreboding. "If you hook up with this mega-firm, I don't see how the rest of us can consider you a Barrister."

"You mean I'll finally have a bona fide excuse to sleep in on Sunday mornings instead of sitting around at breakfast with a bunch of pathetic old farts?"

"Good point," Morton said. "Now that I think about it, we need to keep you a Barrister so you get to suffer every week like the rest of us."

"Is this pre-call just to give me a hard time?"

"No," Morton said. "The truth is I found the agreement extremely interesting. I think that the agreement faithfully sets out the business deal you described to me. I have a few tweaks to suggest, but by and large whoever prepared the draft did an evenhanded job. I'll get into my specific comments when the rest of your partners are on the line."

"Thanks for the overview."

"Don't mention it. This is not a direction I saw your career taking, but if it's what you want, good for you. I just wanted to say that to you personally."

Carpenter reflected that he had never disclosed his cancer to the Barristers. Letting Nye, Murphy, Warren, Burton, and Klein know of his disease had proved surprisingly liberating. The Barristers didn't have a need to know about his CLL, but Carpenter realized that he now wanted to tell them.

"Okay," Carpenter said. "Let's pick this up on the group call."

Simon had placed her in charge and Rachel was actually enjoying working out settlement language with Christopher Blaisedell. She'd expected that Blaisedell would want to control the document and make all the edits, but he had ceded that role to her, and was proving reasonable when it came to sorting through sticking points. They had taken an approach that Rachel was familiar with: the lawyers would reach agreement on settlement language before presenting the agreement to their clients. She had finished the latest edits and paused before sending the revised settlement agreement on to Blaisedell.

During their last round of negotiations, she had decided to ask Blaisedell why he had done an about face on settlement. This was not a question Simon would pose. But she wasn't Simon and she was curious. They seemed to be working well together and perhaps she had earned his trust.

"I really can't speak about it," Blaisedell had responded.

"I realize it's not an appropriate question," she had come back. "But frankly I've been curious and I thought I'd ask you."

"I'm serious," Blaisedell had insisted. "I really can't talk about it."

As she pressed Send to launch her e-mail, Rachel reflected that lawyers were supposed to have all the answers, but her experience was that many lawyer questions remained unanswered. 'So be it,' she thought. Simon was copied on the e-mail and Carpenter, Philly, and Meredith were blind copied. The committee approach was time consuming, but it seemed to be working.

Philly wanted Simon to hear what Helena Peck had to say. She set up a conference call so Simon could listen in.

"I have a settlement proposal in Ms. Li's case," Peck said. "Ten thousand dollars to your client. Attorney fees up to eighteen thousand. The MCAD case gets dismissed with prejudice. The settlement agreement is kept confidential. No admission of liability."

"What about our seeing some evidence that the partnership vote on Li's promotion was what you said it was?"

"I'm authorized to send you a list of the women who voted on Li's promotion. You may choose five names on the list and I will have the women you select confirm their vote in a face-to-face meeting with you. You don't get to question these women."

Philly didn't have it in her to go back and forth with Peck. "Thank you," she said. "We'll review it with our client and get back to you."

"Fair enough," Peck said. "I'll await your call."

Simon stayed on his line after Peck dropped off the call. "What do you think?" Philly asked him.

"I think Li is not going to be happy, but she'll take the deal."

Philly was silent for a moment. "You and Rachel tried to get more money for Meredith and that almost backfired. Do you think we'd be making a mistake trying to get something more for Li?"

"No," Simon replied. "Peck didn't say this was her final offer the way she intimated in Meredith's case. I'd say go for it."

104

"What's your reaction to the agreement?" Harris Burton asked over the phone.

Carpenter wasn't sure what the etiquette was in this three-way negotiation, but he decided to talk freely. "We all think the agreement is evenhanded. Our lawyer has the same view. So if we can come up with a budget that works for us, we're inclined to forge ahead."

"Our reaction is similar," Burton said. "We're also leaning toward coming on board."

"How do we deal with coming up with a budget?" Carpenter asked, repeating a question that had been raised by Morton.

"I spoke to Nye about this and he asked me to fill you in on what we talked about. A major piece of the budget will be partner draws. Nye said that he would like to see our financials for 2012 and for the first three quarters of 2013. He pledged to keep the information confidential. If we provide that information, he's willing to take the first stab at coming up with budgets."

"Frankly, I'm relieved," Carpenter said. "I wouldn't know where to start in coming up with a budget and I think my partners are in the same boat."

"I have some ideas, but I'd just as soon let Nye take first crack at it. Maybe the draws he'll propose will be more favorable than what we'd suggest."

"Do you guys take regular draws?" Carpenter asked.

"We try to. But the draws are very low. When we're flush, we distribute more money. In lean times, we've been known to skip a draw."

"Skipping a draw is not something I believe occurs at Dudley, Atkins & Tyng."

Burton laughed. "Let's hope that's the case if and when we get into bed with each other."

Rachel, Simon, and Meredith had chosen to walk to Sloane-Webster. During the walk, Rachel didn't say it out loud, but she thought there was something magical about Boston in the dark afternoons of late December. Even the office buildings had twinkly lights in their lobbies, and even in 2013 many men still wore tailored woolen topcoats. Once the group had shed their own winterwear, Rachel wondered if this was the last time she would be in the Sloane-Webster war room. She and Christopher Blaisedell had finally signed off on a settlement agreement, and the dean had wanted everyone present for a review.

"Do you have a problem with any of the placement office activities you would be responsible for?" the dean asked Neil Taylor.

"No," Taylor responded. "Truthfully, some of the programs the plaintiffs have asked for would be beneficial. Workshops on interview techniques should help our students and graduates. I'm okay with all this," Taylor pointed toward the agreement.

"Anything of concern to you, Ralph?"

Cray shook his head. "I keep thinking we'd win if we went to trial. I hadn't always thought that, but these plaintiffs seem to be in retreat." Cray nodded in the dean's direction. "But I know you prefer to settle so I don't think we're agreeing to anything too onerous if we sign on."

"That's where I come out," the dean said. "Between us, I'd be more comfortable spending less on placement and more in some other areas. But placement is where we're being sued. Are we all okay with the new brochure language on our faculty?"

This had been the most contentious issue. In the end, Rachel had agreed not to use the terms "top-notch" and "second to none" and Blaisedell agreed to describing the law school's faculty hiring process with emphasis on the number of applicants for each position and the law school's success in hiring its first, qualified choice to fill a vacant position.

"It's accurate," Cray noted. "I was okay with it."

"I don't think the new language will hurt us in attracting applicants," Taylor said.

"Okay," the dean said. "Does our legal team have any advice for us?"

Simon nodded in her direction and Rachel took the floor. "I simply want to review with you how this draft document came together. Blaisedell and I went back and forth on language changes. Simon and our other partners provided me with feedback and suggestions. The settlement agreement is a compromise document. We believe that the law school hasn't given up very much. You may have preferred different language than what the attorneys came up with in various areas, but we do not view any of the compromises as detrimental to the law school. And, of course, the law school is not admitting any liability."

"I need to go over a point that we've discussed before," Simon took over. "The only parties who are bound by this agreement are the three plaintiffs. Because this case never became an approved class action, Sloan-Webster could still be sued by another student or graduate."

"We consider ourselves warned," the dean said. "It's a risk we're prepared to take." Martin paused. "This all feels anticlimactic," she noted. "I'm trying to figure out how I'm going to occupy my time once this case goes away. I'm not complaining by the way. I'm very pleased that Blaisedell backed down off his three-million-dollar high horse."

"I think we know the reason for his change of heart," Simon said. "The private investigator we hired just received an e-mail from the administrative assistant he's been dealing with at Michigan State. It seems that the teaching assistant is trying to cut a plea deal on an unrelated charge by acknowledging a role in the cheating matter that involved Noah Branson."

"That would explain quite a lot," Dean Martin said. "If Blaisedell had vetted his plaintiffs as well as we vet potential faculty hires, we might have been in trouble. Tell Blaisedell I'm prepared to sign the agreement if his clients will."

Rachel and Meredith followed Simon's lead and began to stow their papers.

"I hope this isn't premature, but I want to thank the three of you," Dean Martin said. "You've been creative and direct with us. I think I speak for Ralph and Neil in saying that we've been very pleased."

"That's very kind," Simon said. "And most appreciated."

"Do you do contract work?" the dean asked. "There's an employment agreement and a vendor contract that I would like to have reviewed."

"Yes, we do," Simon said. "Our rates would be the same."

"I was counting on that," the dean said.

Philly phoned Helena Peck. Li had given her further negotiating instructions. She had no confidence the new terms would be acceptable.

"Do we have a deal?" Peck asked when she got on the line.

"At twenty-five thousand dollars we do."

"Will your firm agree not to solicit or represent any female partner of Hazelton, Kauffman, Garfield & Smith in a discrimination suit against the firm?" Peck asked without missing a beat.

Peck was seeking to impose a settlement term that Simon and Rachel insisted Christopher Blaisedell agree to in the Sloan-Webster case. Philly didn't like Peck's new condition and suspected that Carpenter would like it even less.

"Will Hazelton Kauffman agree that Ms. Li may testify at a deposition or trial brought by another former or current female partner alleging discrimination?"

"Yes," Peck said. "The firm will agree that the confidentiality provision in the settlement agreement will not apply if Li is subpoenaed to provide testimony at a deposition or trial or administrative proceeding."

"And the releases would be mutual, correct?" Philly said.

"Correct."

Philly couldn't shake the feeling that Peck was one step ahead of her. It was as if Peck had thought through each potential comeback Philly might come up with.

"I'll have to call you back," Philly said.

"I expected nothing less," Peck replied.

105

Meredith had tried to sound out Rachel and Simon about why she was being asked to this partnership meeting, but her two former law school classmates had refused to answer her question. "Let's just say you're going to be surprised," Simon had said. Simon was smiling when he made his cryptic remark, so Meredith didn't think she was being let go. Still, she was nervous as Carpenter called the meeting to order in the conference room.

"Thanks for joining us, Meredith," Carpenter began. "You're not a member of our firm but the more you hang around the more you might as well be. You've been incredibly valuable to all of us this year and we're all appreciative."

Meredith couldn't shake the feeling that these compliments were a prelude to unpleasant news.

"You may have noticed that the other partners and I have frequently been out of the office recently. We've been having discussions with two law firms. You'll recall Sarah Warren, the lawyer from Dudley, Atkins & Tyng who defended the depositions you conducted in the Ship Right case. Her firm approached us with a proposal. They wanted us to join their firm but continue to operate as we have been at our current hourly rates. Since you've worked for a large firm, you know our hourly rates are much less than a big firm's. In addition, Dudley, Atkins & Tyng has approached Harris Burton's firm with a similar proposal. Previous to all that, Harris' firm had approached us with a merger proposal so that his firm could acquire some litigation expertise."

Meredith felt her heart pounding. Carpenter would shortly be discussing her future.

"I'm not going to bore you with the details, but the bottom line is that both our firm and Harris' firm are going to be merged into Dudley, Atkins & Tyng.

We're going to move out of these offices and move into offices in Harris' firm that are currently vacant. We're going to end up with clerical and IT support. The financial terms are complicated. But Dudley, Atkins & Tyng has approved budgets for our firm and Harris' firm and those budgets include yearly base salaries."

Meredith was struggling to keep up and keep her expression steady. As closely as she had worked with all these people, not one of them had mentioned that they, along with her source of income, were going to disappear.

"We are unanimous in wanting you to join us. And when I say 'we', I mean not just the rest of us in this room, but both of the other firms as well. The merger discussions had to be kept just within the official partners, and I hope you can understand that. But you've been one of us, and we want you to stay. The budget that was approved includes base salaries for the five of us. Your base salary is budgeted at one hundred and eight thousand. Ours are slightly higher than that but not a lot. If our revenue exceeds our budgeted costs, we get to split a major portion of the excess. If you join us, we are prepared to split that excess five ways. We envision you starting out as an associate and if things continue to go well, we will make you a partner in a year."

"This is a lot to take in," Meredith said, feeling overwhelmed.

"No pressure," Philly said. "We're going to keep the office space we're in for January so that our move isn't rushed. But by the end of January, we want to be relocated in the new office suite. You'd have your own office, unless you've become so attached to Carpenter that you want to work something out with him to stay in his space."

"I'm trying to take this all in," Meredith exclaimed. "This is a shock."

"If you elect not to join the four of us in this new format," Carpenter resumed, "you may wish to seek an associate position at Dudley, Atkins & Tyng in their Boston office. Sarah Warren was impressed with the way you handled the Ship Right depositions, and she specifically requested that we make you a part of this new venture. But in fairness to you, if you join her firm's Boston office, I can tell you with certainly that your starting salary will exceed the base draw for the four of us."

"I don't understand what Dudley, Atkins & Tyng is up to," Meredith said.

"The concept," Carpenter replied, "is that the firm's rates are so high, it's priced out of certain business. So they wish to create within their firm what amounts to a separate division, so to speak, that will handle the business that their own economic structure forces them to pass on, or cases that don't even approach them now because of their prices."

Meredith was starting to get her bearings. "Are they expecting to make money off this, somehow?" she asked. "What happens if they don't? Is there some kind of breakeven point where this falls apart if your revenue doesn't exceed your budgeted costs?"

"During the first year, that is an economic risk that Dudley, Atkins & Tyng is willing to take. There's a budget for our base salaries and expenses. If the venture doesn't thrive, the economic formula for year two might have to change."

"I've never heard of anything like this," Meredith said.

"It's unique," Carpenter said. "Let me give you an example. Rachel is about to file three suits against the tennis camp that made life miserable for some girl attendees. More suits are on the way. Some of the girls had to see therapists because of how they were treated. The potential damages are low, and it's not going to be a class action suit. These are cases that the currently structured Dudley, Atkins & Tyng wouldn't touch. But they are cases that our Dudley, Atkins & Tyng division can and will handle."

"I hope you come with us," Rachel said. "I know this is a lot to take in, but we really want you to join us."

"Ditto," Simon said.

"Please take your time to think about all this," Philly said, "provided you give us an answer in the next five minutes."

"Philly's joking," Rachel said, concerned.

"I got that," Meredith said. "But I'll give you my answer now." She paused, considered whether she wanted to talk this over with Flash and whether going with her gut was an impulsive mistake. 'What the hell,' she thought. "I'm in with you guys. I did the big firm thing for three years. I'd just as soon not do it again. I can't believe they'll let you do what you want, but you seem confident that they will."

"We'll be reporting to Sarah Warren on everything," Philly explained. "Sarah gets copied on pleadings, e-mails, everything."

"You did say my own office, right?" Meredith asked.

"Right," Philly said with a grin. "It's nicer than mine I can assure you. Sarah Warren and some of the other Dudley, Atkins & Tyng lawyers will want to meet with you, and we'll set that up."

"Okay," Meredith said. "Wow!" The lingering doubt that she had acted hastily disappeared. She enjoyed working with the four people sitting around the conference room table. Had she gone through an agonizing, lengthy internal debate, she might have talked herself out of the very thing she had wanted. Hasty as her decision had been, it was the right one.

"Is there anything else we need to discuss now that we've overloaded Meredith's circuits?" Carpenter asked.

"The Sloan-Webster settlement agreement has been signed," Simon announced. "Shortly, the law school will be sending out a check for the attorney fees and will be providing the additional funding for the placement office fund. Once Blaisedell acknowledges receipt of his fees, the dismissal of the case will be filed."

"Great work," Philly said. "Only good things happen when you keep Carpenter and me out of the loop."

"Very funny," Rachel said. "Both of you had settlement agreement comments that made it into the final document."

"Then there's Ai Li's case," Philly said. "Helena Peck doesn't want us to represent any other Hazelton Kauffman partner in a discrimination suit against that firm. It's the same notion that Blaisedell signed off on. I had a brief discussion with Carpenter about this. Any thoughts?"

"Is it limited to sex discrimination?" Meredith asked, pleased she was being included in this discussion.

"Yes," Philly said.

"We know two other female partners who resigned because they were denied a promotion," Simon noted. "Would we take their cases knowing what we learned in Li's case, that it was the women partners who largely didn't want to see Li promoted?"

"Those two possible cases don't excite me," Carpenter said.

"Me neither," Simon said.

"That's the direction I'm leaning," Philly said. "I'll talk to Li and if she's on board with everything, I'll meet with five female partners at Hazelton Kauffman and confirm how they voted on Li's promotion. If the five confirm what Peck has told us, then we'll draw up the settlement papers and get rid of the case."

"Two more cases bite the dust," Carpenter said.

"If anybody needs work, there's a tennis camp that needs suing," Rachel reminded the gathering.

"Throw a couple my way," Meredith requested.

106

Philly surveyed what would be her new office. It was an interior office, small, no windows. Two low file cabinets were set against the wall furthest from her desk. The office had two visitor chairs, but she doubted that she'd meet with clients in the cramped space. Whatever personal items she introduced to the room were never going to make this room feel like home. But for the few times she came into Boston, the office would do. She'd seen no point in insisting on an office with a window; better for the other four to have that perk.

"How are you doing?"

Ben Klein stood at her office door and then entered the room, taking his time to look around. He paused at her desk and picked up the framed photograph of Philly, Paul, Daisy, and Daniel. "Your daughter's eyes," he said. "They get me every time."

Philly didn't respond. She'd never been able to bring herself to have a photograph of Philip in her office.

"How about a brief walk?" Klein suggested.

"It's freezing out!"

"So maybe we'll pop into a coffee place. Come on, stretch your legs."

It was one of those mornings when the wind blew steadily, cold and raw from the ocean, and no matter which way you turned, it was blowing in your face. Philly pulled up the hood of her parka and snapped it under her chin. Klein was bareheaded, and she didn't know how he could stand the cold.

"Are you okay with this move?" Klein asked, as they walked.

"I guess so. It makes me nervous. But what the hell. What about you?"

"It's complicated," Klein said. "This joining up with a much bigger firm is not what Philip and the rest of us envisioned. There's a part of me that feels I'm betraying him."

"So you don't think he would have approved?"

Klein shrugged, a movement barely noticeable under his long, heavy, dark overcoat. "I don't know. We tried to position ourselves as an alternative to big firms. Now we're going to be part of one. In my gloomier moments, I think we've sold out in some way."

"What about in your less gloomy moments?" Philly asked.

"From a practical point of view, we probably did the right thing. Philip was our rainmaker. Then Harris became our rainmaker. But Harris is getting on in years and slowing down, which he's certainly entitled to do. Without Harris in the picture the rest of us could see ourselves struggling when it came to new business. So here we are. I don't think we've made a deal with the devil, but time will tell."

Philly figured that Klein had needed to talk about Philip so he could bring some sort of closure to Philip's role in founding their firm. If he was looking for absolution, Philly decided to give it to him. "Don't for a moment think that you're betraying Philip or his memory or his vision. Philip was practical. I can picture him viewing this change as necessary and as a challenge. He would embrace a change of that kind. You're being too hard on yourself."

"That's very kind of you to say."

"Maybe a little. I think I'm also being practical and realistic. I'm trying to think positively, and I guess I'm urging you to do the same. We're all placing a lot of trust in Richard Nye. There's a guy I want to be around for a while."

"Agreed," Klein said. "Sometimes I think that if anyone else was on point, we wouldn't be doing this. Nye has been honest with us and fair. I hope it stays that way."

"Okay, I'm freezing my ass off," Philly complained. "Where's that coffee you were promising?"

"Follow me."

"I haven't been to a Celtics game in a century," Carpenter remarked, as he and Brian Murphy made their way down a row of numbered folding seats. "I never got into basketball the way I did baseball.

"You have Richard to thank for this," Murphy responded. "He gave up his seat for tonight."

They were seated in the TD Bank Garden, almost on a line with midcourt, their seats about fifty feet from courtside. The teams were warming up and Carpenter didn't recognize a fair number of Celtics and most of the Sixers. The Red Sox had had a lot of new players this year, too, but he was confident he could recognize and name each one.

"I think I told you that Richard and I have had these seats forever. It's a chance for us to kick back. For Richard to kick back takes some work. He won't admit it, but I think he enjoys hanging out with me and coming as close as he's ever going to come to letting his hair down."

"Then thank you, Richard," Carpenter said. "I wasn't complaining before. This is a rare treat."

"How about a beer?" Murphy suggested.

"Let's wait a few minutes."

"Fair enough," Murphy said. "Let's squander those few minutes on a serious moment."

Carpenter had wondered whether Murphy had an agenda for this outing.

"Are you okay with all this?" Murphy asked. "I mean really okay? This can't have been easy for you coming aboard with us after all those years of being on your own. And as I recall, you've given me a fair amount of shit about being in a big firm."

Murphy's concern appeared genuine, so Carpenter answered him frankly. "I'm not going to bullshit you and say I'm totally comfortable with everything. I'm nervous. The lady I live with asked me if I had one more adventure in me. I told her I did. This arrangement we've come up with is my one more adventure. I hope it works out."

"I think it will," Murphy said. "Of course, there are no guaranties. With Richard committed to and invested in this project's success, I'd say the odds are good we'll make a go of it."

"Are you trying to cheer me up?"

Murphy laughed. "I'm not an idiot. You love being a grouch."

"I don't need cheering up," Carpenter said. "I'm in this."

"Good. I'm glad. I guess I wanted to hear that directly."

"Those few minutes must be up," Carpenter said. "Didn't you mention beer?"

Murphy stayed seated. "One last thing. I'm still trying to wrap my mind around your cancer. So I'm just going to say this. If anything occurs on that front, you need to make sure that Sarah and I know. I hope you'll let us be here for you instead of being your irascible, stubborn, loner self."

"Okay, *now* I need cheering up. A beer would help."

"I'm serious," Murphy said.

"I know you are, Brian. I'll keep you and Sarah informed. And thanks for your concern. I don't always show it, but I am grateful."

Murphy still made no move to rise. "I have one more last thing," he said. "Morgan Carmichael and I have found a buyer for Ship Right."

"No shit!"

"No shit. We told the potential buyer that we guessed Ship Right was going to seek a purchase price in excess of two hundred eighty million. I want to make sure a finder's fee comes out of this especially if the purchase price exceeds two hundred seventy-five million. I'll be looking for at least three hundred fifty thousand of any finder's fee going to Morgan's firm. We'll work out how part of the finder's fee counts as revenue to your group. I want you to think about whether Burton and Klein can do the deal for Ship Right. Remember, Burton and Klein will be Dudley, Atkins & Tyng lawyers when a deal is explored. Hopefully, their lower rates should ensure a finder's fee."

"Sounds promising," Carpenter said. "Let me think about it."

"I was counting on that." Murphy rose. "Two beers coming up!"

107

Carpenter glanced at his watch—an hour before midnight and a new year. The Boston hotel ballroom rented by Dudley, Atkins & Tyng was packed. An elegant, late dinner had been served and the tables had been cleared of main course and dessert dishes. Now there was dancing to a five-piece band whose repertoire had a little something for every generation. The bar remained open and was serving a steady stream of guests. Carpenter contrasted the scene with the more intimate year-end dinners he and Philly, and eventually Simon and Rachel and Meredith, had shared. Well, those days were gone for good.

He surveyed the dance floor. Frank Stevens was doing a fox trot with Maxine; Simon's significant other knew how to dance. Simon was off to the side of the bar grinning at them while he nursed a drink. Rachel and Josh, Meredith and Flash, Philly and Paul were also dancing, the couples plainly enjoying themselves. The trio of Dudley, Atkins and Tyng lawyers that had entered his life were also on the dance floor: Richard Nye gazed adoringly at a compactly built woman with a spiky haircut that Carpenter believed most middle-aged women wouldn't be caught dead with; Brian Murphy was moving gracefully as he held a long-legged beauty in his arms; and Sarah Warren seemed to be leading her partner, a guy who had the look of an absentminded academic. Introductions to spouses and to partners had been made at the beginning of the evening, and now everyone seemed relaxed and happy.

Carpenter returned his gaze to Philly. She had stopped dancing and stood on tiptoe to whisper to Paul. Paul nodded and moved past dancers toward the bar where Simon was standing. Philly headed in his direction.

Philly sat down next to Carpenter at the table that had been reserved for their group of ten. Carpenter was always thrown off by seeing Philly in a dress and this evening was no exception. She looked good.

"Stop playing at being a geezer and cut in on Maxine," Philly urged.

"Trust me. Maxine is in hands more capable than mine."

"Do you believe this?" Philly said making a sweeping arm gesture that took in the entire ballroom.

"I'm suspending disbelief," Carpenter replied.

"You know, it seems like yesterday when I lucked out and ended up in your office suite. I didn't have a pot to piss in, had no clients, and didn't know my ass from a hole in the ground." Philly again made a sweeping arm movement. "This is an improvement and progress, right?"

"That's what I'm telling myself," Carpenter answered.

"Yeah, me too. And I'm starting to believe it. We've got those new hospital cases. Brian and Sarah have unloaded two cases on us that I'm guessing they were saving for us. Rachel's running around filing suits against that tennis academy. And Simon has landed some contract work from Sloan-Webster. Not a bad start to the new year."

Philly reached for her water glass and raised it. "To us. It's been a great fucking run and it could get even better. I'm actually psyched."

Carpenter touched his water glass to Philly's. "To us. And by the way, just to set the record straight, I'm the one who lucked out when you landed in my suite."

"Aren't you sweet!"

"During chapter one of my legal life, I was a sole practitioner. When you and I started collaborating on just about everything, that was chapter two. When we joined with Rachel and Simon, that was chapter three. You'll note that each chapter was shorter than its predecessor." Carpenter again clinked water glasses. "But so long as we're toasting, here's to a long chapter four."

Philly grinned. "To chapter four," she said. "Even you have to admit that next year is starting out okay."

Carpenter gave her a broad smile and nodded. "Yeah, not too shabby!"

Author's Note

I am indebted to Meredith Larson for her edits, comments, and suggestions. This book benefitted from her frank assessments and proposed changes.

I want to thank Jon Behar for proofreading the novel and offering suggestions on big picture issues that made their way into the novel.

Any and all errors are mine.

Lastly, I want to thank Carpenter and Philly for keeping me company, surprising me, inspiring me, and enriching my life.

Made in the USA
Monee, IL
04 November 2026

67384041R00266